BEYOND CORPORATION

THE AMAZING SPIDER-MAN

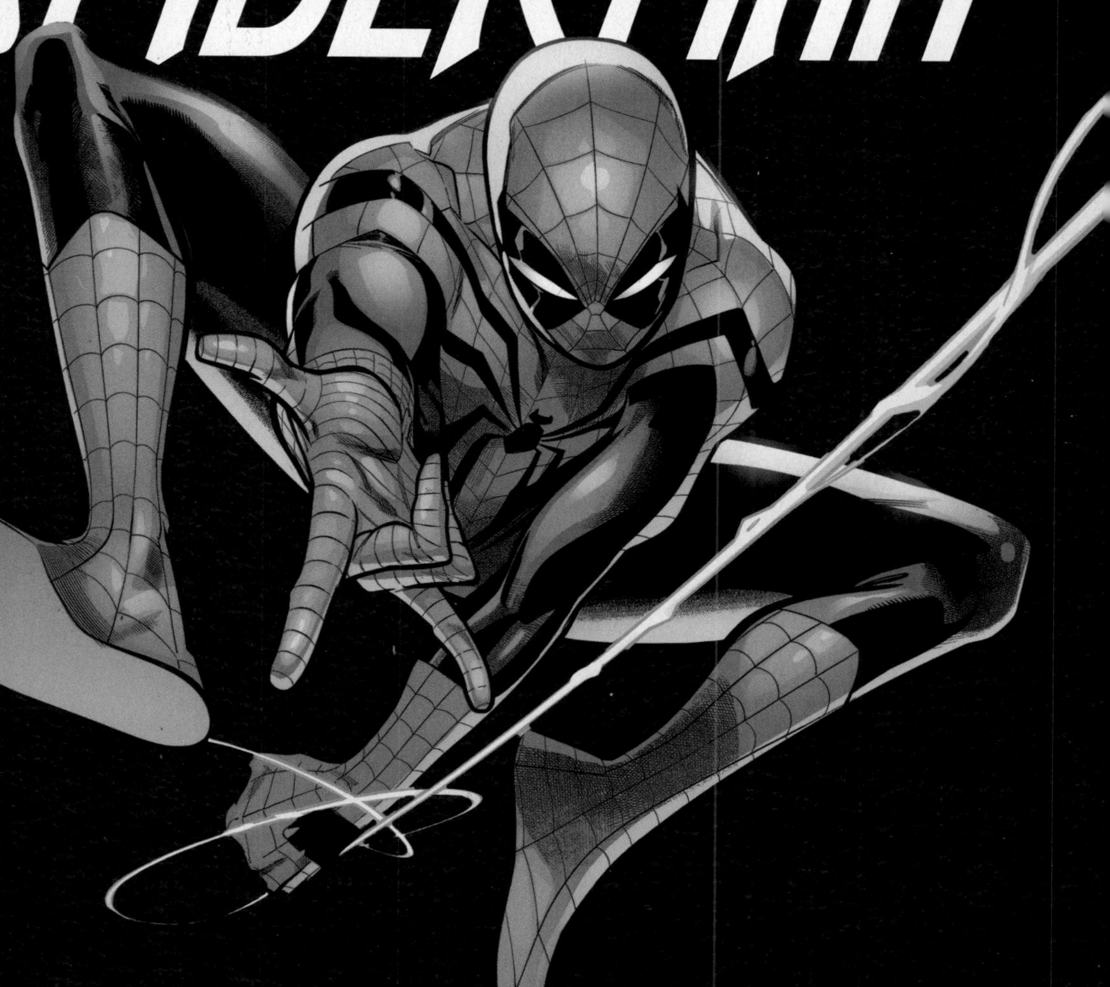

PETER PARKER was bitten by a radioactive spider and gained the proportional speed, strength and agility of a SPIDER, adhesive fingertips and toes, and the unique precognitive awareness of danger called "SPIDER-SENSE"! After the tragic death of his UNCLE BEN, Peter understood that with great power there must also come great responsibility. He became the crimefighting super hero called...

THE AMAZING SPID

AMAZING SPIDER-MAN #80.BEY

CODY ZIGLAR/WRITER
IVAN FIORELLI WITH
CARLOS GÓMEZ &
PACO MEDINA/ARTISTS
RACHELLE ROSENBERG
/COLOR ARTIST

AMAZING SPIDER-MAN #81

SALADIN AHMED/WRITER
CARLOS GÓMEZ/ARTIST
BRYAN VALENZA/COLOR ARTIST

AMAZING SPIDER-MAN #82

SALADIN AHMED/WRITER
JORGE FORNÉS/ARTIST
DAN BROWN/COLOR ARTIST

AMAZING SPIDER-MAN #83

PATRICK GLEASON/WRITER/ARTIST
MORRY HOLLOWELL &
NATHAN FAIRBAIRN/COLOR ARTISTS

AMAZING SPIDER-MAN #84-85

CODY ZIGLAR/WRITER
PACO MEDINA/PENCILER
PACO MEDINA (#84-85),
WALDEN WONG (#85),
WAYNE FAUCHER (#85),
ANDREW HENNESSY (#85),
VICTOR OLAZABA (#85) &
ROBERTO POGGI (#85)
/INKERS
ESPEN GRUNDETJERN/COLOR ARTIST

Peter Parker is in a coma after a disastrous fight with the U-FOES, during which he got hit with a deadly dose of poisonous gas and radiation. Luckily for New York, BEN REILLY has taken on the mantle of Spider-Man with the support of the BEYOND CORPORATION, who bought the rights to the Spider-Man name and likeness as part of their Super Hero Development Program.

While Ben safeguards the streets, Peter is fighting for his life against the poison inside him, but his doctors are at a loss. Good thing Peter has someone in his corner who won't take "no" for an answer — the pluckiest and most tenacious woman in his life: AUNT MAY.

ER-MAN

VC's **JOE CARAMAGNA**/LETTERER

**KELLY THOMPSON,
CODY ZIGLAR,
SALADIN AHMED,
PATRICK GLEASON** &
ZEB WELLS/BEYOND BOARD

**MARK BAGLEY,
JOHN DELL** & **BRIAN REBER** (#80.BEY),
ARTHUR ADAMS &
ROMULO FAJARDO JR. (#81-83)
AND **ARTHUR ADAMS** &
ALEJANDRO SÁNCHEZ (#84-85)
/COVER ART

LINDSEY COHICK &
KAEDEN McGAHEY/ASSISTANT EDITORS

NICK LOWE/EDITOR

SPECIAL THANKS TO
DEVIN LEWIS & **DANNY KHAZEM**

SPIDER-MAN CREATED BY
STAN LEE & **STEVE DITKO**

JENNIFER GRÜNWALD/COLLECTION EDITOR
DANIEL KIRCHHOFFER/ASSISTANT EDITOR
MAIA LOY/ASSISTANT MANAGING EDITOR
LISA MONTALBANO/ASSOCIATE MANAGER, TALENT RELATIONS
JEFF YOUNGQUIST/VP PRODUCTION & SPECIAL PROJECTS
DAVID GABRIEL/SVP PRINT, SALES & MARKETING
JAY BOWEN &
ANTHONY GAMBINO/BOOK DESIGNERS
C.B. CEBULSKI/EDITOR IN CHIEF

AMAZING SPIDER-MAN: BEYOND VOL. 2. Contains material originally published in magazine form as AMAZING SPIDER-MAN (2018) #81-85 and #80.BEY. First printing 2021. ISBN 978-1-302-93257-2. Published by MARVEL WORLDWIDE, INC., a subsidiary of MARVEL ENTERTAINMENT, LLC. OFFICE OF PUBLICATION: 1290 Avenue of the Americas, New York, NY 10104. © 2021 MARVEL No similarity between any of the names, characters, persons, and/or institutions in this book with those of any living or dead person or institution is intended, and any such similarity which may exist is purely coincidental. **Printed in Canada.** KEVIN FEIGE, Chief Creative Officer; DAN BUCKLEY, President, Marvel Entertainment; JOE QUESADA, EVP & Creative Director; DAVID BOGART, Associate Publisher & SVP of Talent Affairs; TOM BREVOORT, VP, Executive Editor; NICK LOWE, Executive Editor, VP of Content, Digital Publishing; DAVID GABRIEL, VP of Print & Digital Publishing; JEFF YOUNGQUIST, VP of Production & Special Projects; ALEX MORALES, Director of Publishing Operations; DAN EDINGTON, Managing Editor; RICKEY PURDIN, Director of Talent Relations; JENNIFER GRUNWALD, Senior Editor, Special Projects; SUSAN CRESPI, Production Manager; STAN LEE, Chairman Emeritus. For information regarding advertising in Marvel Comics or on Marvel.com, please contact Vit DeBellis, Custom Solutions & Integrated Advertising Manager, at vdebellis@marvel.com. For Marvel subscription inquiries, please call 888-511-5480. **Manufactured between 12/17/2021 and 1/25/2022 by SOLISCO PRINTERS, SCOTT, QC, CANADA.**

10 9 8 7 6 5 4 3 2 1

BEYOND CORPORATION #80.BEY

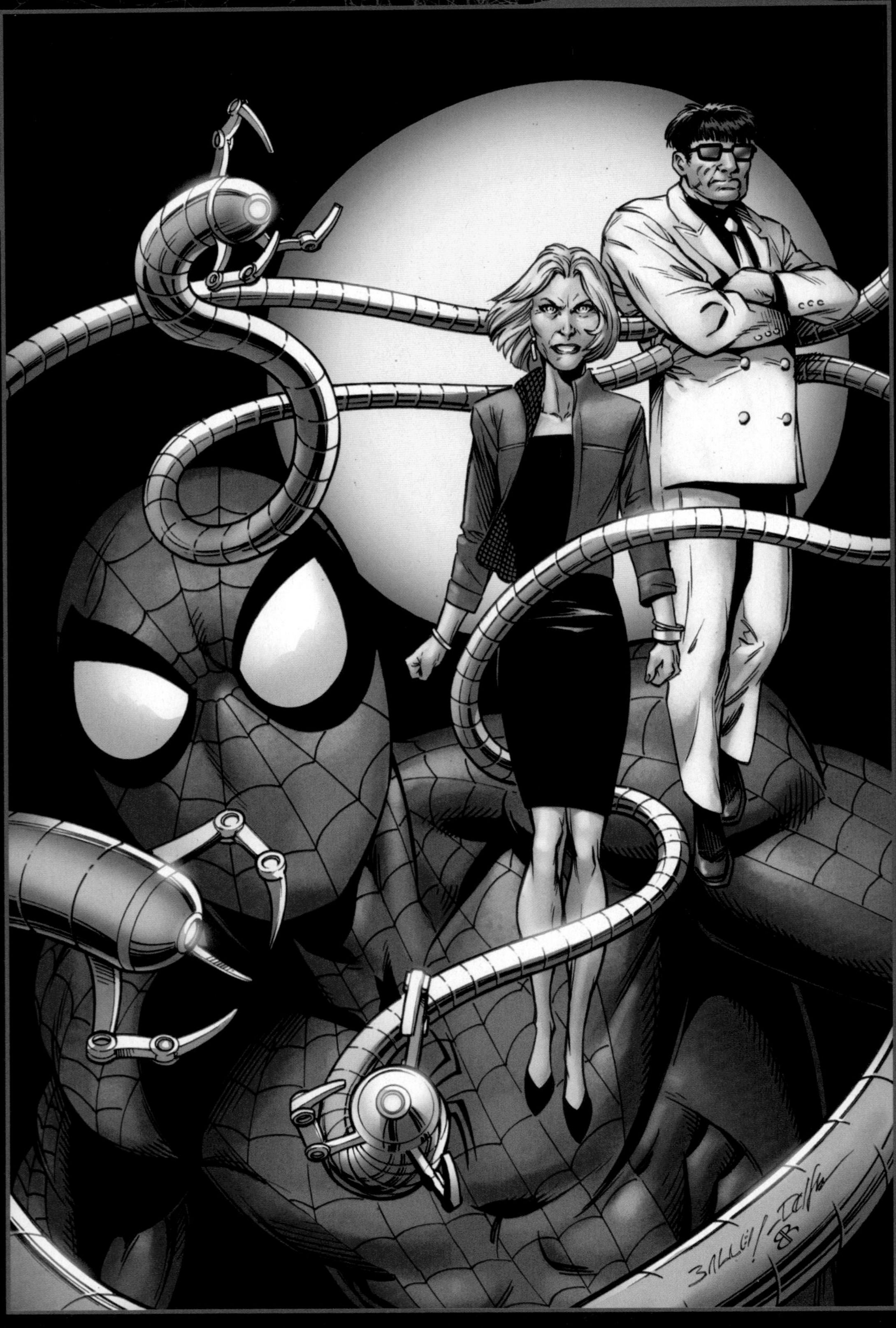

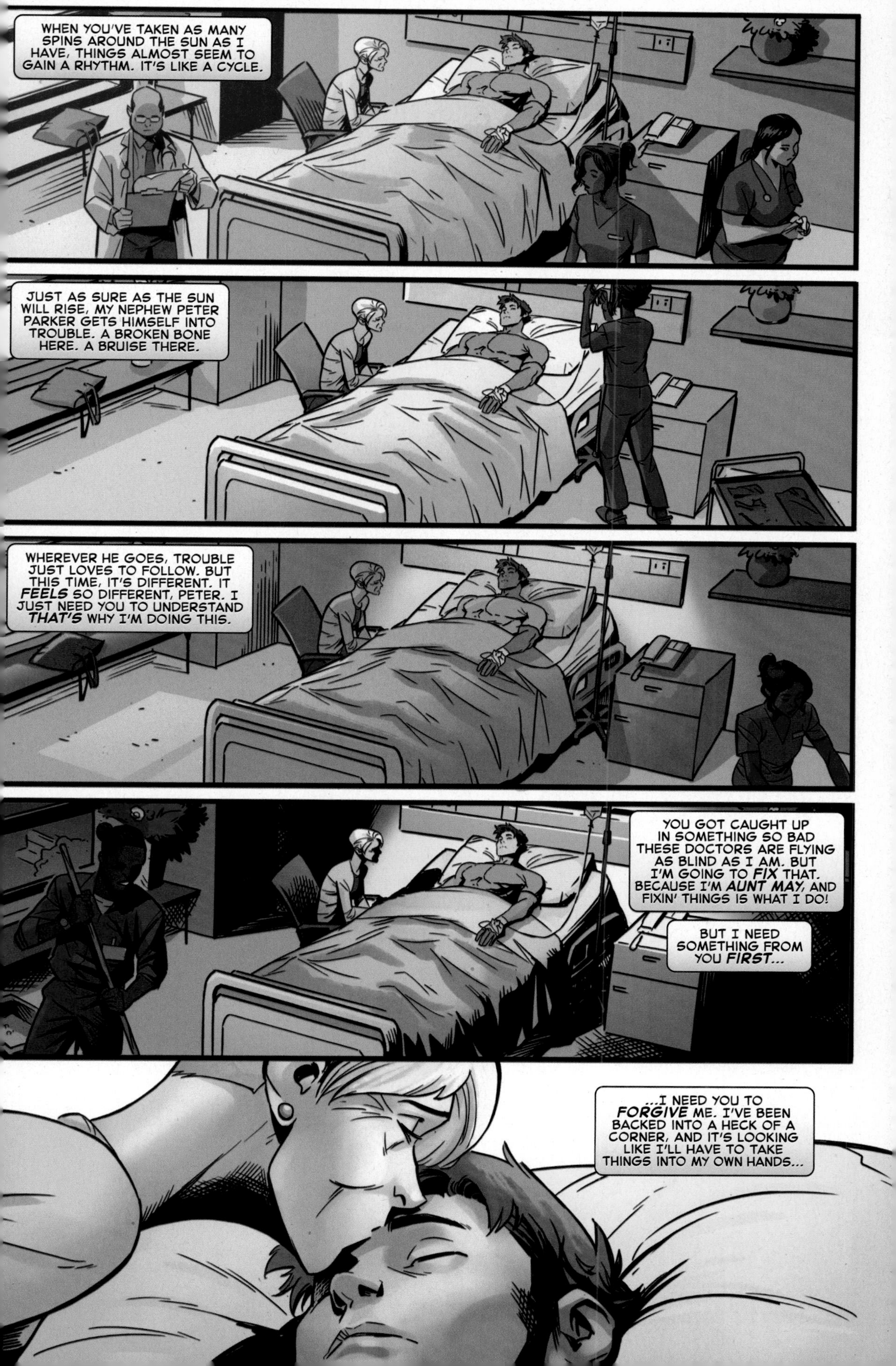
WHEN YOU'VE TAKEN AS MANY SPINS AROUND THE SUN AS I HAVE, THINGS ALMOST SEEM TO GAIN A RHYTHM. IT'S LIKE A CYCLE.
JUST AS SURE AS THE SUN WILL RISE, MY NEPHEW PETER PARKER GETS HIMSELF INTO TROUBLE. A BROKEN BONE HERE. A BRUISE THERE.
WHEREVER HE GOES, TROUBLE JUST LOVES TO FOLLOW. BUT THIS TIME, IT'S DIFFERENT. IT FEELS SO DIFFERENT, PETER. I JUST NEED YOU TO UNDERSTAND THAT'S WHY I'M DOING THIS.
YOU GOT CAUGHT UP IN SOMETHING SO BAD THESE DOCTORS ARE FLYING AS BLIND AS I AM. BUT I'M GOING TO FIX THAT. BECAUSE I'M AUNT MAY, AND FIXIN' THINGS IS WHAT I DO!
BUT I NEED SOMETHING FROM YOU FIRST...
...I NEED YOU TO FORGIVE ME. I'VE BEEN BACKED INTO A HECK OF A CORNER, AND IT'S LOOKING LIKE I'LL HAVE TO TAKE THINGS INTO MY OWN HANDS...

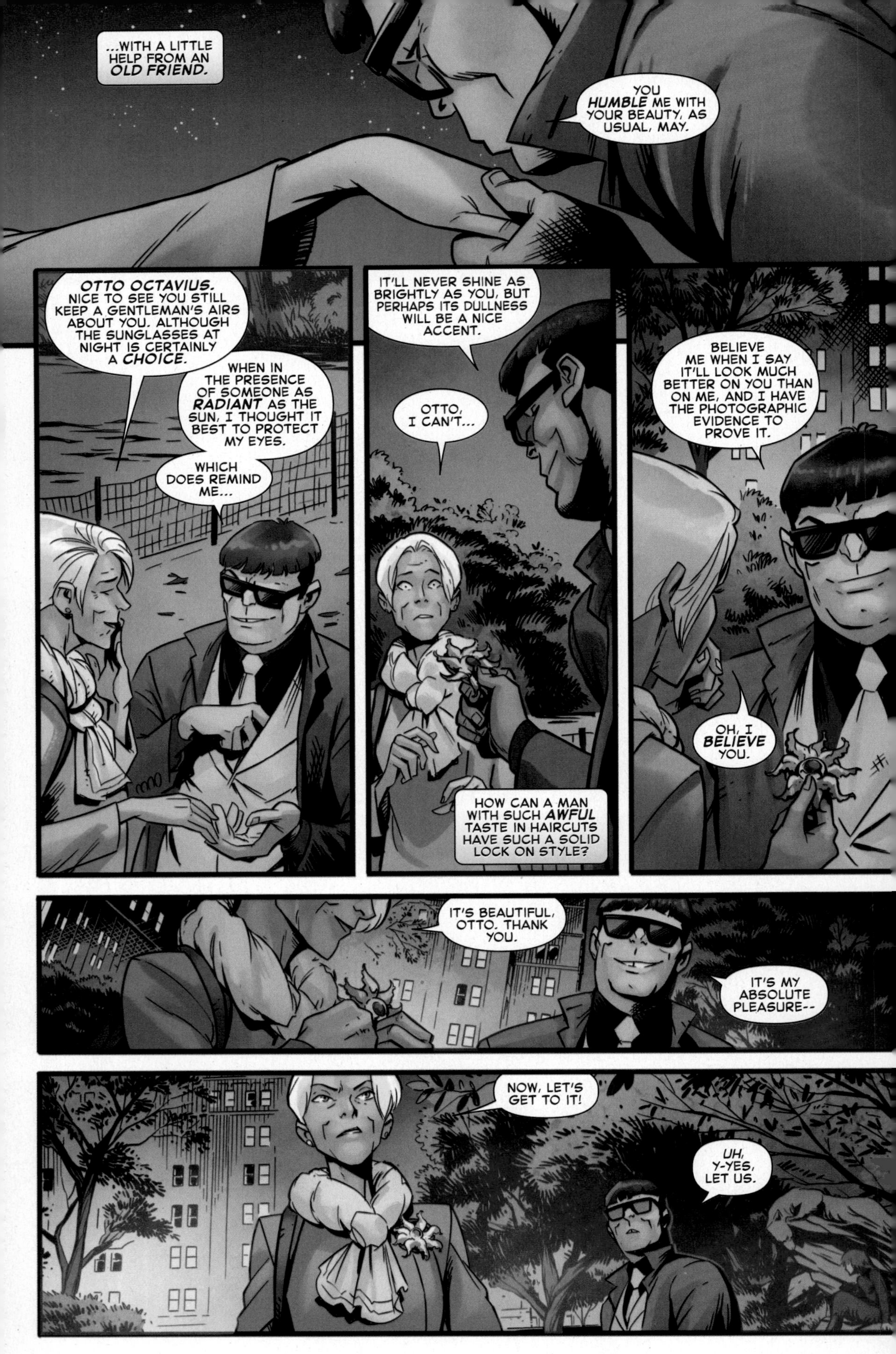
...WITH A LITTLE HELP FROM AN OLD FRIEND.
YOU HUMBLE ME WITH YOUR BEAUTY, AS USUAL, MAY.
OTTO OCTAVIUS. NICE TO SEE YOU STILL KEEP A GENTLEMAN'S AIRS ABOUT YOU. ALTHOUGH THE SUNGLASSES AT NIGHT IS CERTAINLY A CHOICE.
WHEN IN THE PRESENCE OF SOMEONE AS RADIANT AS THE SUN, I THOUGHT IT BEST TO PROTECT MY EYES.
WHICH DOES REMIND ME...
IT'LL NEVER SHINE AS BRIGHTLY AS YOU, BUT PERHAPS ITS DULLNESS WILL BE A NICE ACCENT.
OTTO, I CAN'T...
HOW CAN A MAN WITH SUCH AWFUL TASTE IN HAIRCUTS HAVE SUCH A SOLID LOCK ON STYLE?
BELIEVE ME WHEN I SAY IT'LL LOOK MUCH BETTER ON YOU THAN ON ME, AND I HAVE THE PHOTOGRAPHIC EVIDENCE TO PROVE IT.
OH, I BELIEVE YOU.
IT'S BEAUTIFUL, OTTO. THANK YOU.
IT'S MY ABSOLUTE PLEASURE--
NOW, LET'S GET TO IT!
UH, Y-YES, LET US.

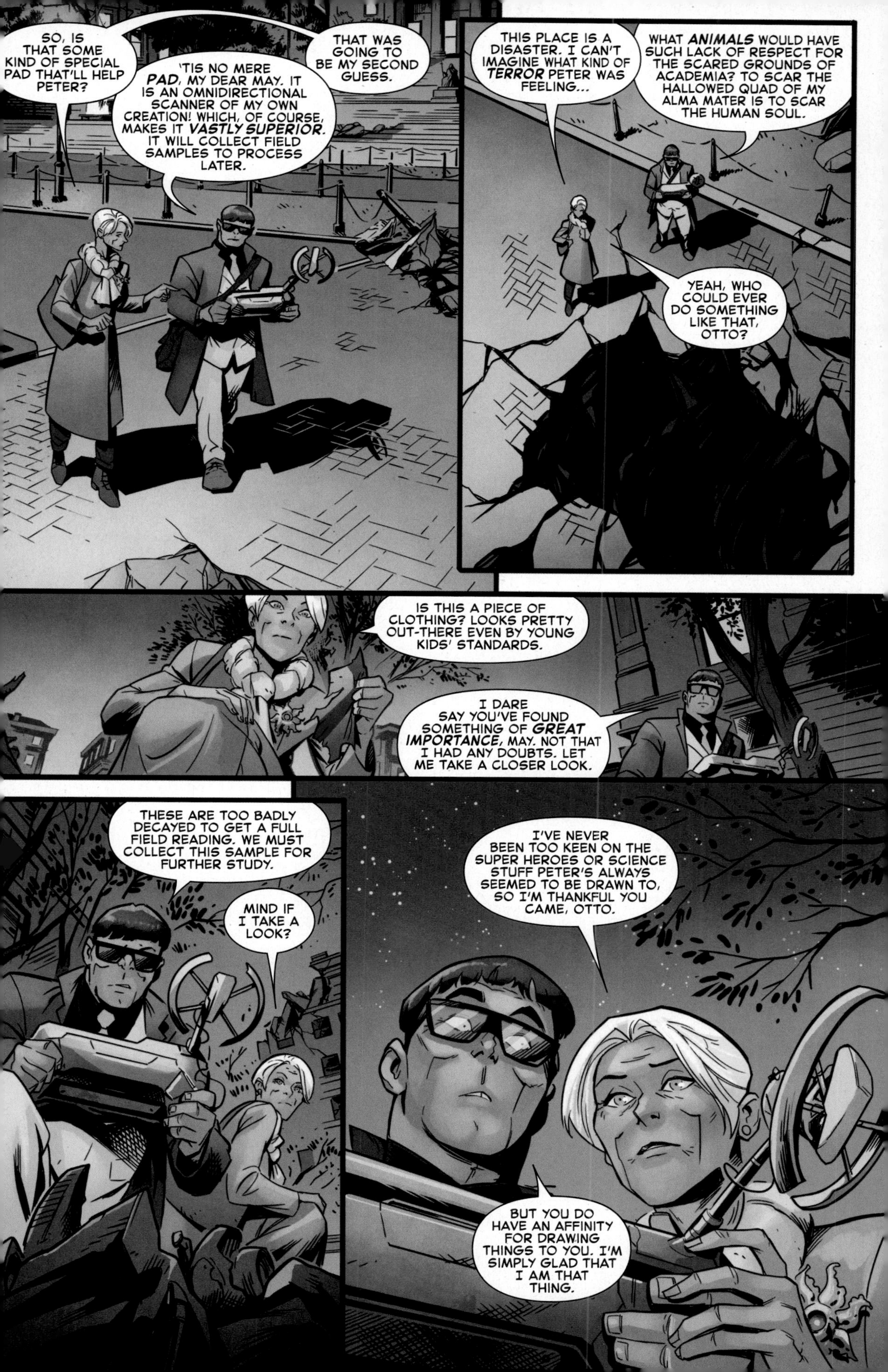
SO, IS THAT SOME KIND OF SPECIAL PAD THAT'LL HELP PETER?
'TIS NO MERE PAD, MY DEAR MAY. IT IS AN OMNIDIRECTIONAL SCANNER OF MY OWN CREATION! WHICH, OF COURSE, MAKES IT VASTLY SUPERIOR. IT WILL COLLECT FIELD SAMPLES TO PROCESS LATER.
THAT WAS GOING TO BE MY SECOND GUESS.
THIS PLACE IS A DISASTER. I CAN'T IMAGINE WHAT KIND OF TERROR PETER WAS FEELING...
WHAT ANIMALS WOULD HAVE SUCH LACK OF RESPECT FOR THE SCARED GROUNDS OF ACADEMIA? TO SCAR THE HALLOWED QUAD OF MY ALMA MATER IS TO SCAR THE HUMAN SOUL.
YEAH, WHO COULD EVER DO SOMETHING LIKE THAT, OTTO?
IS THIS A PIECE OF CLOTHING? LOOKS PRETTY OUT-THERE EVEN BY YOUNG KIDS' STANDARDS.
I DARE SAY YOU'VE FOUND SOMETHING OF GREAT IMPORTANCE, MAY. NOT THAT I HAD ANY DOUBTS. LET ME TAKE A CLOSER LOOK.
THESE ARE TOO BADLY DECAYED TO GET A FULL FIELD READING. WE MUST COLLECT THIS SAMPLE FOR FURTHER STUDY.
MIND IF I TAKE A LOOK?
I'VE NEVER BEEN TOO KEEN ON THE SUPER HEROES OR SCIENCE STUFF PETER'S ALWAYS SEEMED TO BE DRAWN TO, SO I'M THANKFUL YOU CAME, OTTO.
BUT YOU DO HAVE AN AFFINITY FOR DRAWING THINGS TO YOU. I'M SIMPLY GLAD THAT I AM THAT THING.

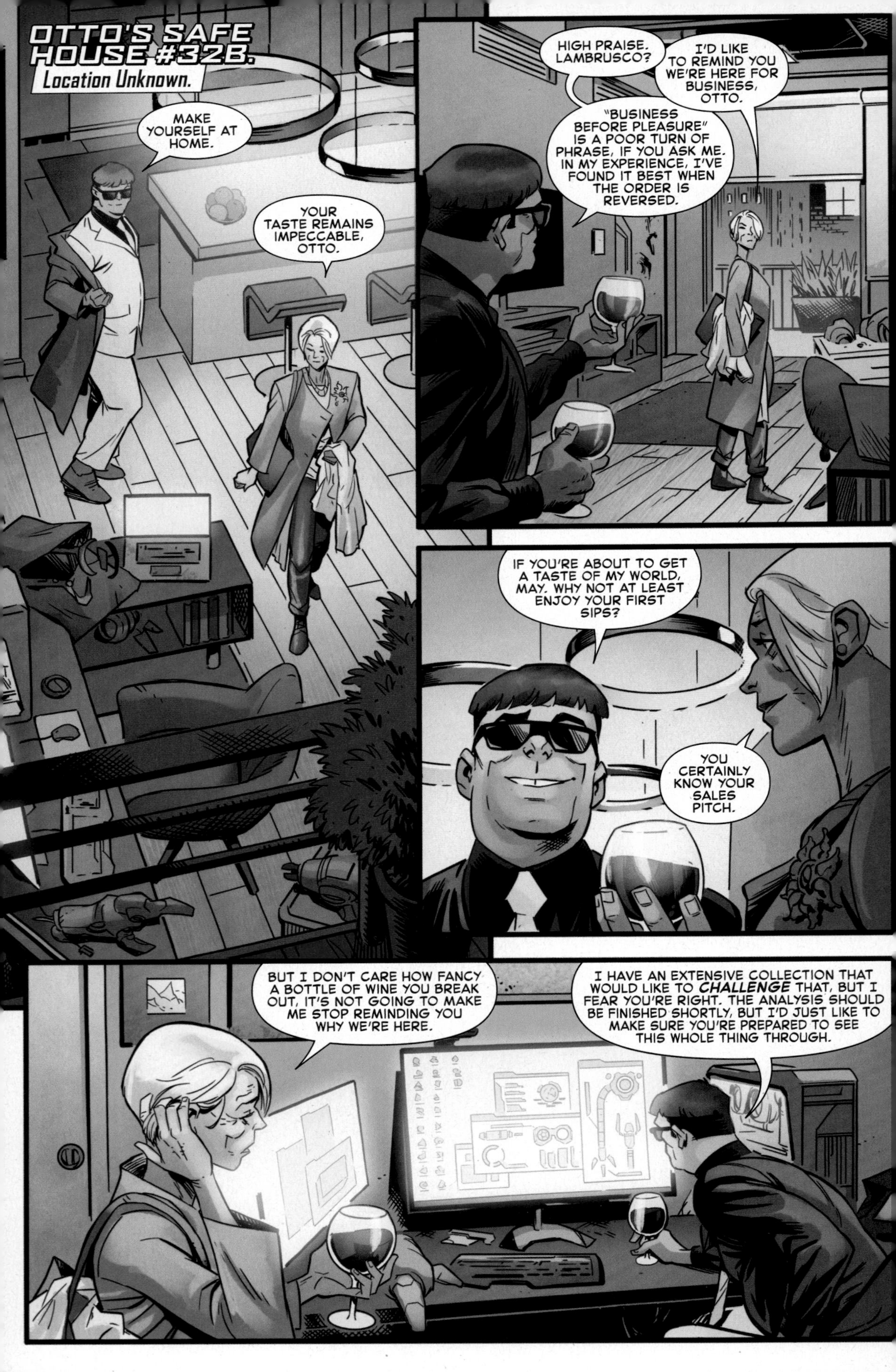
OTTO'S SAFE HOUSE #32B.
Location Unknown.
MAKE YOURSELF AT HOME.
YOUR TASTE REMAINS IMPECCABLE, OTTO.
HIGH PRAISE. LAMBRUSCO?
I'D LIKE TO REMIND YOU WE'RE HERE FOR BUSINESS, OTTO.
"BUSINESS BEFORE PLEASURE" IS A POOR TURN OF PHRASE, IF YOU ASK ME. IN MY EXPERIENCE, I'VE FOUND IT BEST WHEN THE ORDER IS REVERSED.
IF YOU'RE ABOUT TO GET A TASTE OF MY WORLD, MAY. WHY NOT AT LEAST ENJOY YOUR FIRST SIPS?
YOU CERTAINLY KNOW YOUR SALES PITCH.
BUT I DON'T CARE HOW FANCY A BOTTLE OF WINE YOU BREAK OUT, IT'S NOT GOING TO MAKE ME STOP REMINDING YOU WHY WE'RE HERE.
I HAVE AN EXTENSIVE COLLECTION THAT WOULD LIKE TO CHALLENGE THAT, BUT I FEAR YOU'RE RIGHT. THE ANALYSIS SHOULD BE FINISHED SHORTLY, BUT I'D JUST LIKE TO MAKE SURE YOU'RE PREPARED TO SEE THIS WHOLE THING THROUGH.

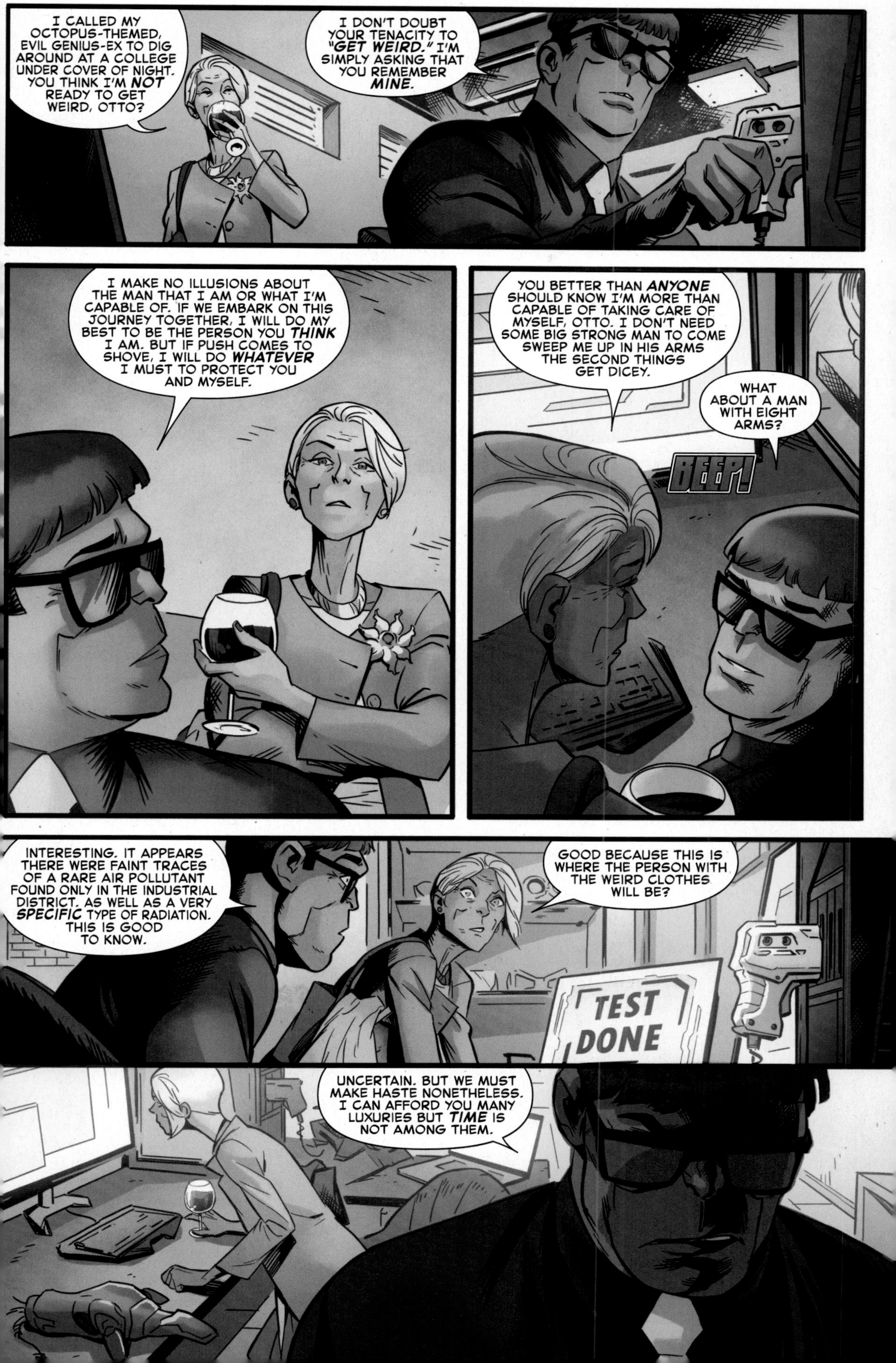
I CALLED MY OCTOPUS-THEMED, EVIL GENIUS-EX TO DIG AROUND AT A COLLEGE UNDER COVER OF NIGHT. YOU THINK I'M NOT READY TO GET WEIRD, OTTO?
I DON'T DOUBT YOUR TENACITY TO "GET WEIRD." I'M SIMPLY ASKING THAT YOU REMEMBER MINE.
I MAKE NO ILLUSIONS ABOUT THE MAN THAT I AM OR WHAT I'M CAPABLE OF. IF WE EMBARK ON THIS JOURNEY TOGETHER, I WILL DO MY BEST TO BE THE PERSON YOU THINK I AM. BUT IF PUSH COMES TO SHOVE, I WILL DO WHATEVER I MUST TO PROTECT YOU AND MYSELF.
YOU BETTER THAN ANYONE SHOULD KNOW I'M MORE THAN CAPABLE OF TAKING CARE OF MYSELF, OTTO. I DON'T NEED SOME BIG STRONG MAN TO COME SWEEP ME UP IN HIS ARMS THE SECOND THINGS GET DICEY.
WHAT ABOUT A MAN WITH EIGHT ARMS?
BEEP!
INTERESTING. IT APPEARS THERE WERE FAINT TRACES OF A RARE AIR POLLUTANT FOUND ONLY IN THE INDUSTRIAL DISTRICT. AS WELL AS A VERY SPECIFIC TYPE OF RADIATION. THIS IS GOOD TO KNOW.
GOOD BECAUSE THIS IS WHERE THE PERSON WITH THE WEIRD CLOTHES WILL BE?
TEST DONE
UNCERTAIN. BUT WE MUST MAKE HASTE NONETHELESS. I CAN AFFORD YOU MANY LUXURIES BUT TIME IS NOT AMONG THEM.

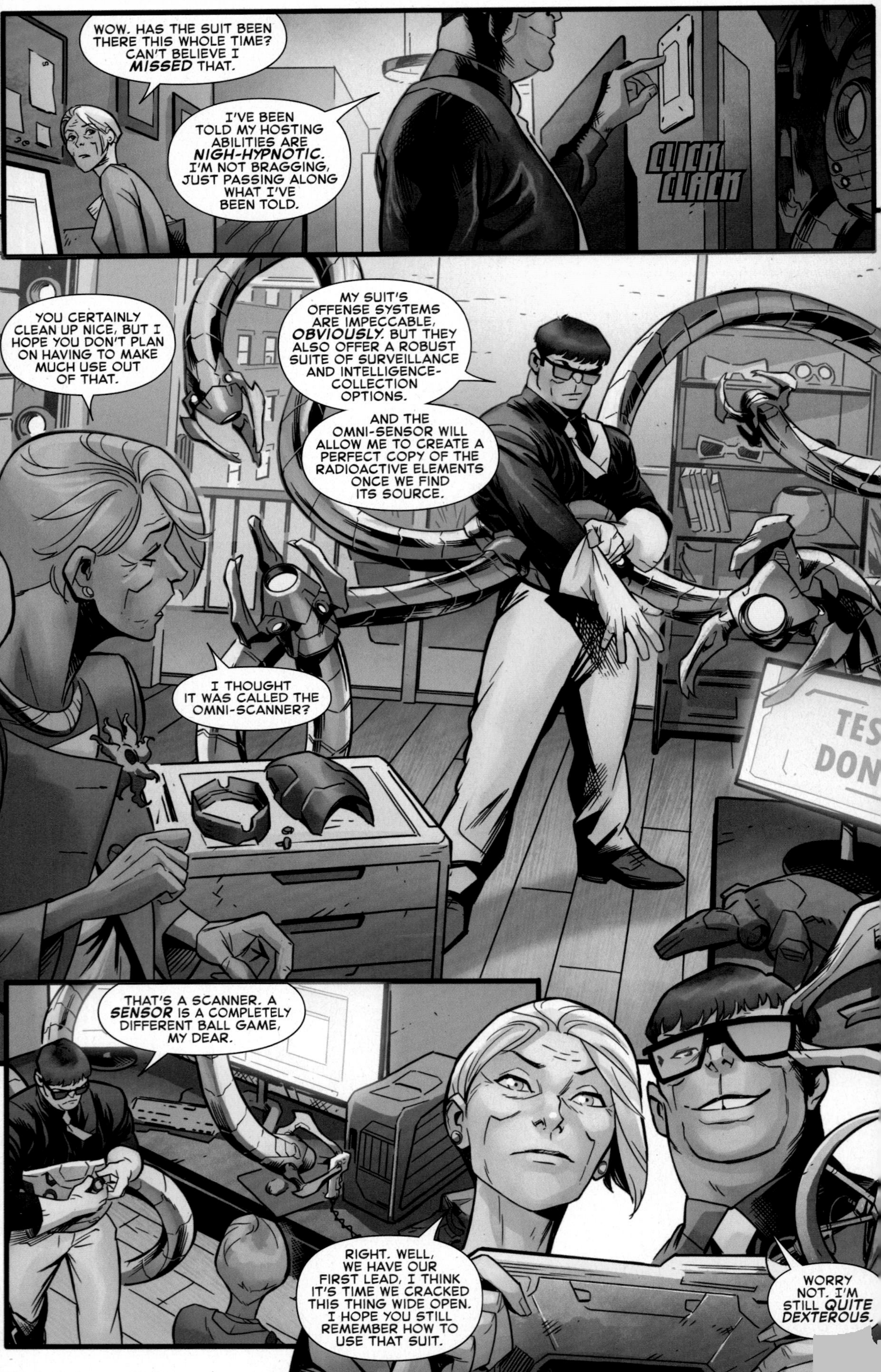
WOW. HAS THE SUIT BEEN THERE THIS WHOLE TIME? CAN'T BELIEVE I MISSED THAT.
I'VE BEEN TOLD MY HOSTING ABILITIES ARE NIGH-HYPNOTIC. I'M NOT BRAGGING, JUST PASSING ALONG WHAT I'VE BEEN TOLD.
CLICK CLACK
YOU CERTAINLY CLEAN UP NICE, BUT I HOPE YOU DON'T PLAN ON HAVING TO MAKE MUCH USE OUT OF THAT.
MY SUIT'S OFFENSE SYSTEMS ARE IMPECCABLE, OBVIOUSLY. BUT THEY ALSO OFFER A ROBUST SUITE OF SURVEILLANCE AND INTELLIGENCE-COLLECTION OPTIONS.
AND THE OMNI-SENSOR WILL ALLOW ME TO CREATE A PERFECT COPY OF THE RADIOACTIVE ELEMENTS ONCE WE FIND ITS SOURCE.
I THOUGHT IT WAS CALLED THE OMNI-SCANNER?
TES
DON
THAT'S A SCANNER. A SENSOR IS A COMPLETELY DIFFERENT BALL GAME, MY DEAR.
RIGHT. WELL, WE HAVE OUR FIRST LEAD, I THINK IT'S TIME WE CRACKED THIS THING WIDE OPEN. I HOPE YOU STILL REMEMBER HOW TO USE THAT SUIT.
WORRY NOT. I'M STILL QUITE DEXTEROUS.

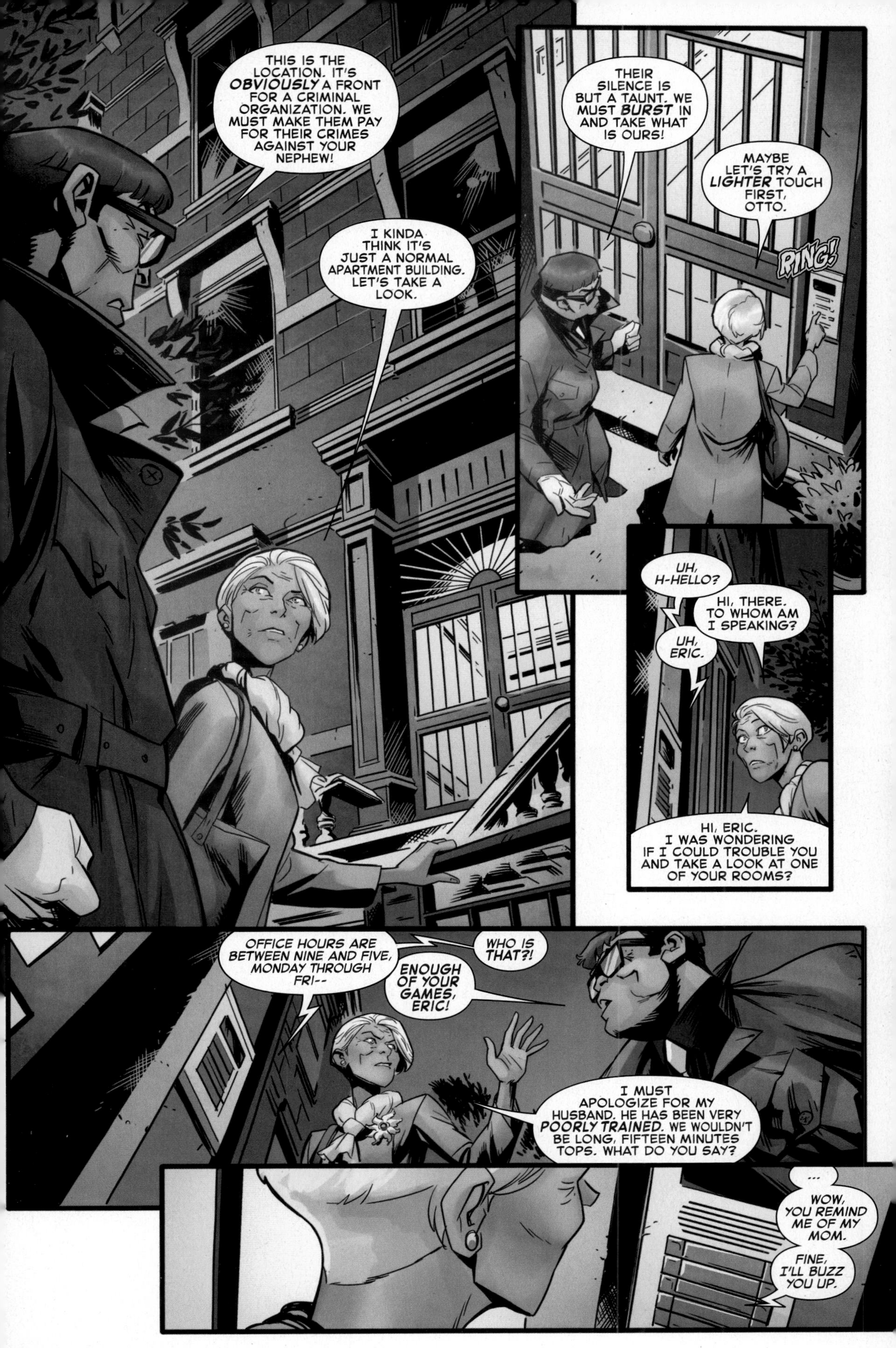

THIS IS THE LOCATION. IT'S OBVIOUSLY A FRONT FOR A CRIMINAL ORGANIZATION. WE MUST MAKE THEM PAY FOR THEIR CRIMES AGAINST YOUR NEPHEW!
I KINDA THINK IT'S JUST A NORMAL APARTMENT BUILDING. LET'S TAKE A LOOK.
THEIR SILENCE IS BUT A TAUNT. WE MUST BURST IN AND TAKE WHAT IS OURS!
MAYBE LET'S TRY A LIGHTER TOUCH FIRST, OTTO.
RING!
UH, H-HELLO?
HI, THERE. TO WHOM AM I SPEAKING?
UH, ERIC.
HI, ERIC. I WAS WONDERING IF I COULD TROUBLE YOU AND TAKE A LOOK AT ONE OF YOUR ROOMS?
OFFICE HOURS ARE BETWEEN NINE AND FIVE, MONDAY THROUGH FRI--
WHO IS THAT?!
ENOUGH OF YOUR GAMES, ERIC!
I MUST APOLOGIZE FOR MY HUSBAND. HE HAS BEEN VERY POORLY TRAINED. WE WOULDN'T BE LONG, FIFTEEN MINUTES TOPS. WHAT DO YOU SAY?
...
WOW, YOU REMIND ME OF MY MOM.
FINE, I'LL BUZZ YOU UP.

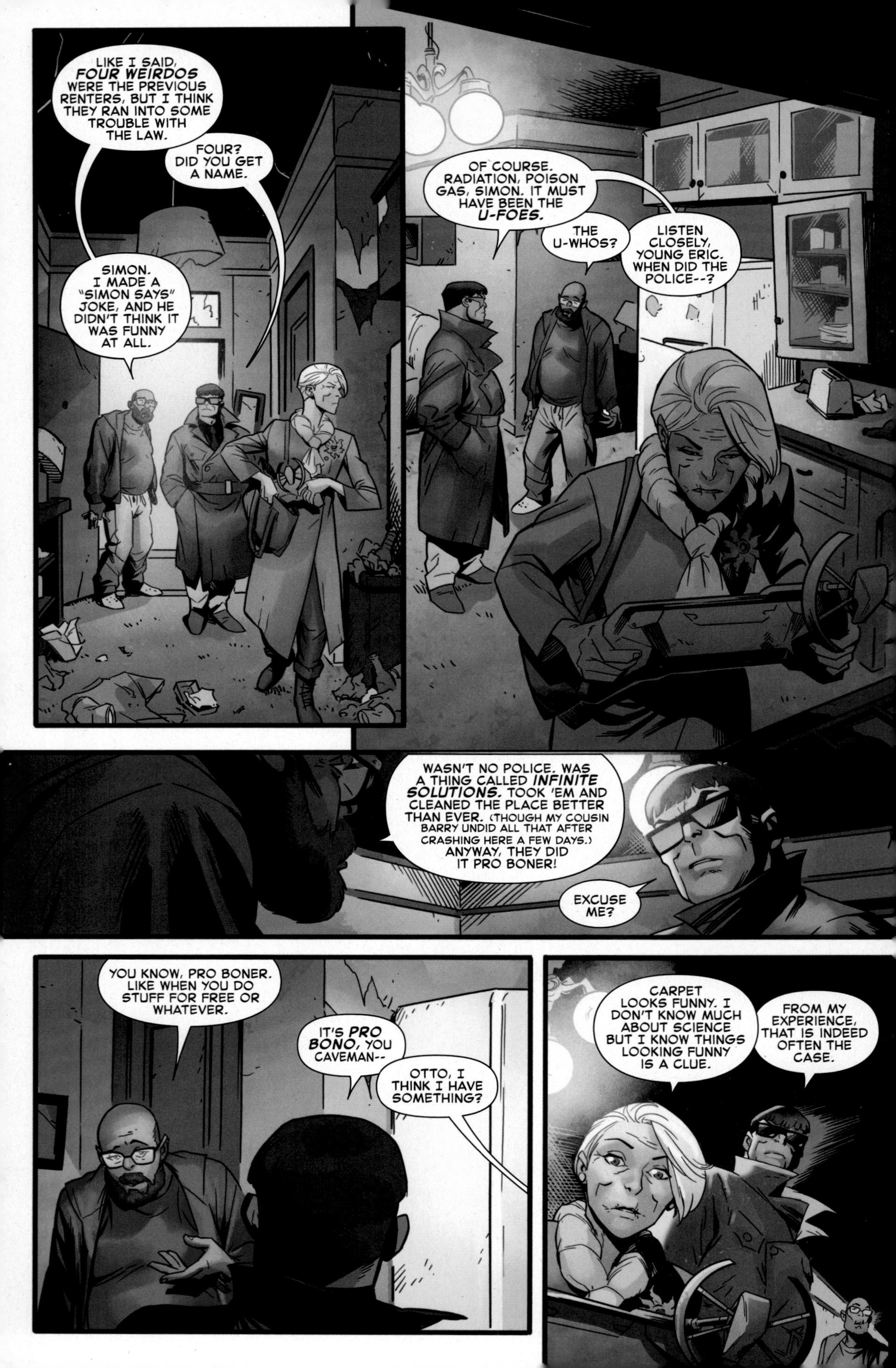
LIKE I SAID, FOUR WEIRDOS WERE THE PREVIOUS RENTERS, BUT I THINK THEY RAN INTO SOME TROUBLE WITH THE LAW.
FOUR? DID YOU GET A NAME.
SIMON. I MADE A "SIMON SAYS" JOKE, AND HE DIDN'T THINK IT WAS FUNNY AT ALL.
OF COURSE. RADIATION, POISON GAS, SIMON. IT MUST HAVE BEEN THE U-FOES.
THE U-WHOS?
LISTEN CLOSELY, YOUNG ERIC. WHEN DID THE POLICE--?
WASN'T NO POLICE. WAS A THING CALLED INFINITE SOLUTIONS. TOOK 'EM AND CLEANED THE PLACE BETTER THAN EVER. (THOUGH MY COUSIN BARRY UNDID ALL THAT AFTER CRASHING HERE A FEW DAYS.) ANYWAY, THEY DID IT PRO BONER!
EXCUSE ME?
YOU KNOW, PRO BONER. LIKE WHEN YOU DO STUFF FOR FREE OR WHATEVER.
IT'S PRO BONO, YOU CAVEMAN--
OTTO, I THINK I HAVE SOMETHING?
CARPET LOOKS FUNNY. I DON'T KNOW MUCH ABOUT SCIENCE BUT I KNOW THINGS LOOKING FUNNY IS A CLUE.
FROM MY EXPERIENCE, THAT IS INDEED OFTEN THE CASE.

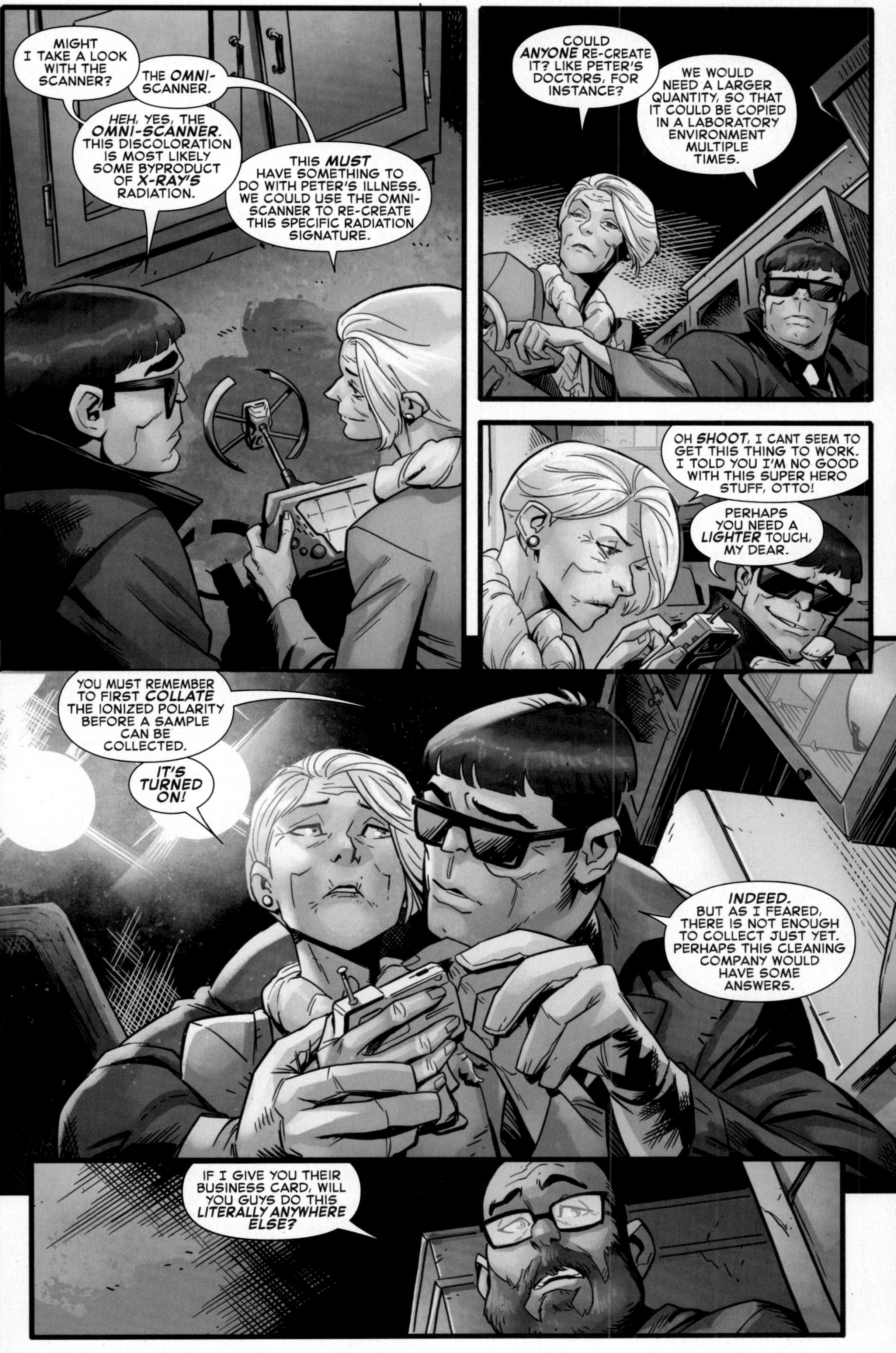
MIGHT I TAKE A LOOK WITH THE SCANNER?
THE OMNI-SCANNER.
HEH, YES, THE OMNI-SCANNER. THIS DISCOLORATION IS MOST LIKELY SOME BYPRODUCT OF X-RAY'S RADIATION.
THIS MUST HAVE SOMETHING TO DO WITH PETER'S ILLNESS. WE COULD USE THE OMNI-SCANNER TO RE-CREATE THIS SPECIFIC RADIATION SIGNATURE.
COULD ANYONE RE-CREATE IT? LIKE PETER'S DOCTORS, FOR INSTANCE?
WE WOULD NEED A LARGER QUANTITY, SO THAT IT COULD BE COPIED IN A LABORATORY ENVIRONMENT MULTIPLE TIMES.
OH SHOOT, I CANT SEEM TO GET THIS THING TO WORK. I TOLD YOU I'M NO GOOD WITH THIS SUPER HERO STUFF, OTTO!
PERHAPS YOU NEED A LIGHTER TOUCH, MY DEAR.
YOU MUST REMEMBER TO FIRST COLLATE THE IONIZED POLARITY BEFORE A SAMPLE CAN BE COLLECTED.
IT'S TURNED ON!
INDEED. BUT AS I FEARED, THERE IS NOT ENOUGH TO COLLECT JUST YET. PERHAPS THIS CLEANING COMPANY WOULD HAVE SOME ANSWERS.
IF I GIVE YOU THEIR BUSINESS CARD, WILL YOU GUYS DO THIS LITERALLY ANYWHERE ELSE?

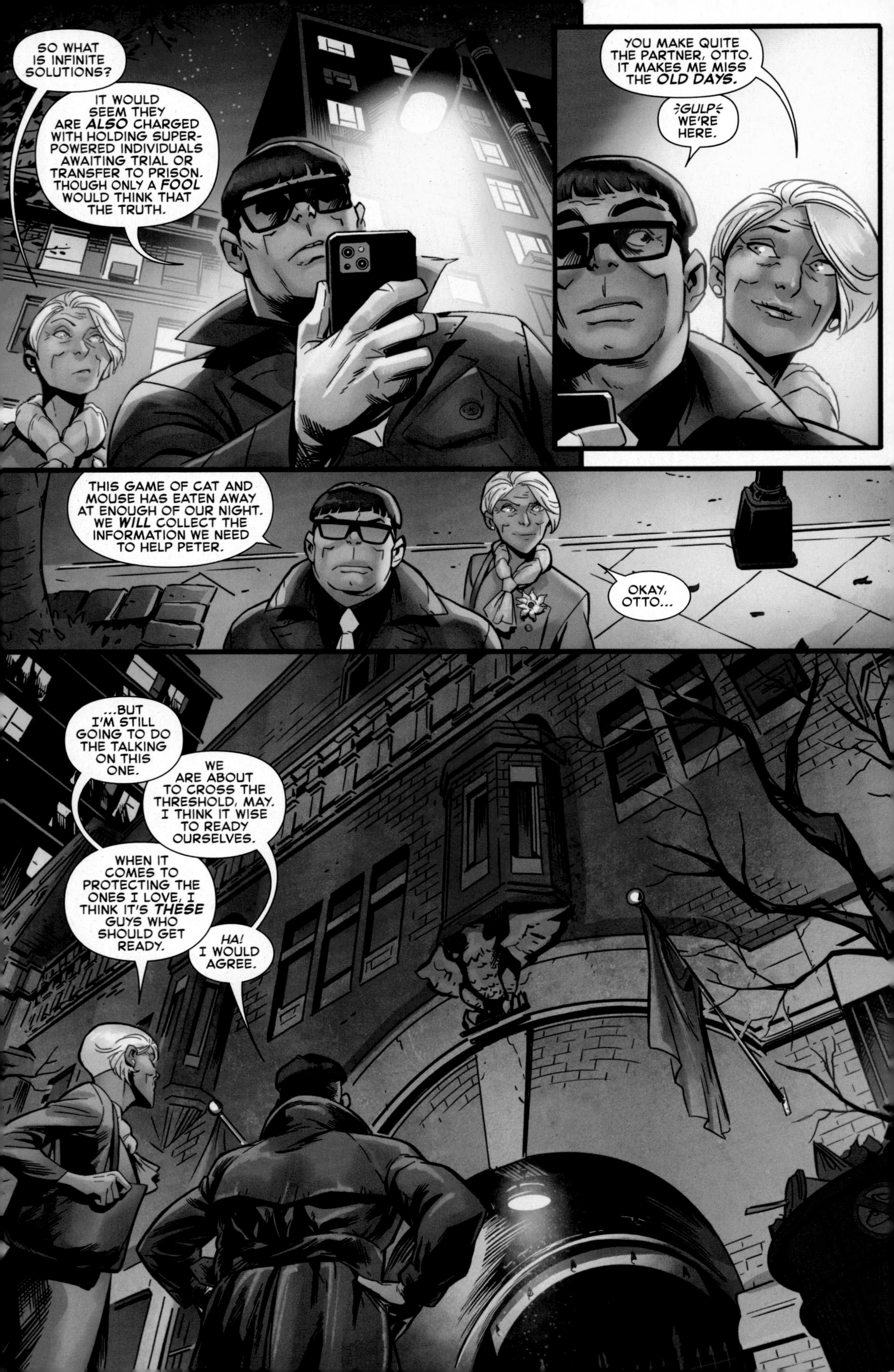
SO WHAT IS INFINITE SOLUTIONS?
IT WOULD SEEM THEY ARE ALSO CHARGED WITH HOLDING SUPER-POWERED INDIVIDUALS AWAITING TRIAL OR TRANSFER TO PRISON. THOUGH ONLY A FOOL WOULD THINK THAT THE TRUTH.
YOU MAKE QUITE THE PARTNER, OTTO. IT MAKES ME MISS THE OLD DAYS.
GULP WE'RE HERE.
THIS GAME OF CAT AND MOUSE HAS EATEN AWAY AT ENOUGH OF OUR NIGHT. WE WILL COLLECT THE INFORMATION WE NEED TO HELP PETER.
OKAY, OTTO...
...BUT I'M STILL GOING TO DO THE TALKING ON THIS ONE.
WE ARE ABOUT TO CROSS THE THRESHOLD, MAY. I THINK IT WISE TO READY OURSELVES.
WHEN IT COMES TO PROTECTING THE ONES I LOVE, I THINK IT'S THESE GUYS WHO SHOULD GET READY.
HA! I WOULD AGREE.

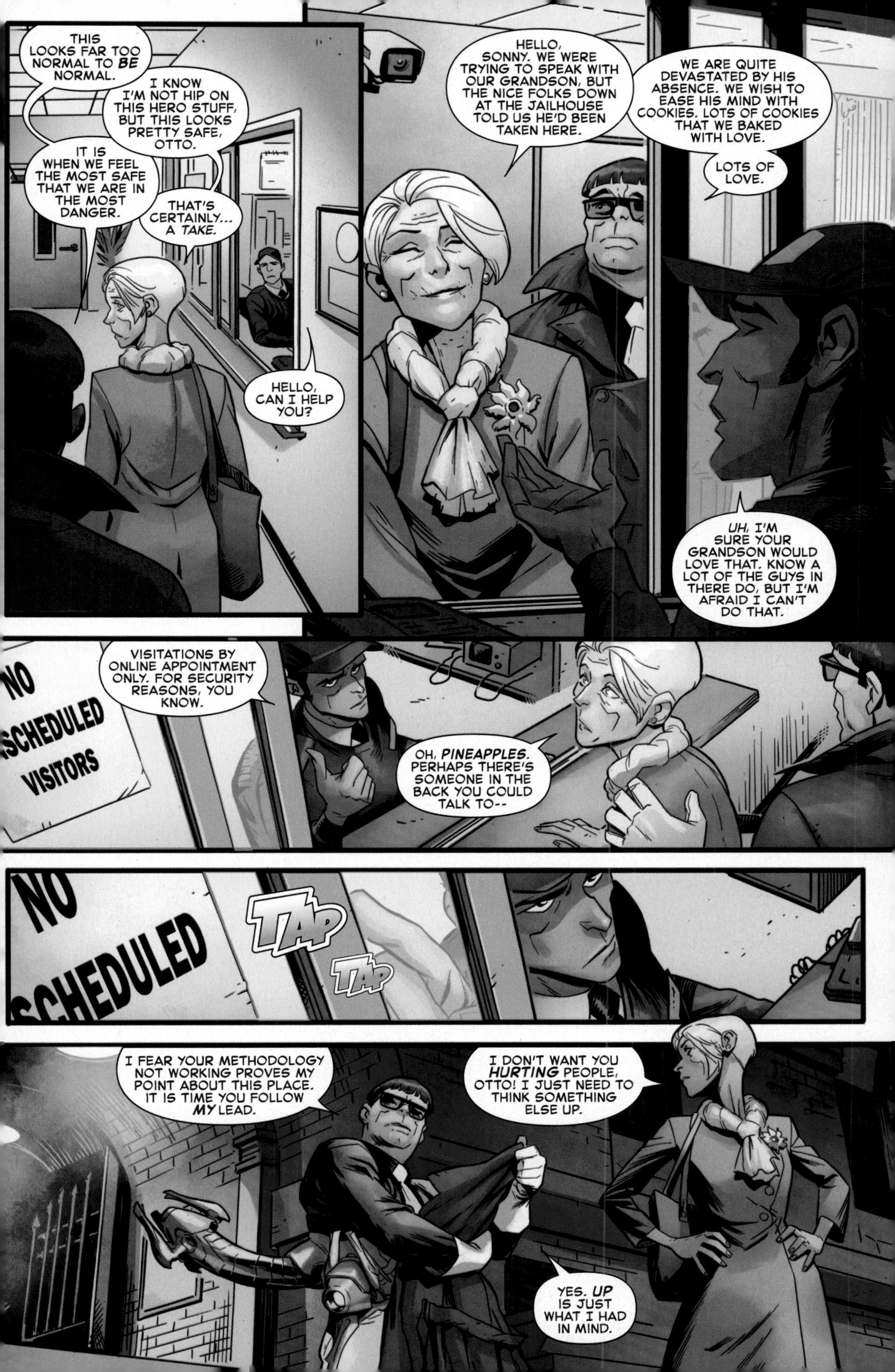
THIS LOOKS FAR TOO NORMAL TO BE NORMAL.
I KNOW I'M NOT HIP ON THIS HERO STUFF, BUT THIS LOOKS PRETTY SAFE, OTTO.
IT IS WHEN WE FEEL THE MOST SAFE THAT WE ARE IN THE MOST DANGER.
THAT'S CERTAINLY... A TAKE.
HELLO, CAN I HELP YOU?
HELLO, SONNY. WE WERE TRYING TO SPEAK WITH OUR GRANDSON, BUT THE NICE FOLKS DOWN AT THE JAILHOUSE TOLD US HE'D BEEN TAKEN HERE.
WE ARE QUITE DEVASTATED BY HIS ABSENCE. WE WISH TO EASE HIS MIND WITH COOKIES. LOTS OF COOKIES THAT WE BAKED WITH LOVE.
LOTS OF LOVE.
UH, I'M SURE YOUR GRANDSON WOULD LOVE THAT. KNOW A LOT OF THE GUYS IN THERE DO, BUT I'M AFRAID I CAN'T DO THAT.
NO SCHEDULED VISITORS
VISITATIONS BY ONLINE APPOINTMENT ONLY. FOR SECURITY REASONS, YOU KNOW.
OH, PINEAPPLES. PERHAPS THERE'S SOMEONE IN THE BACK YOU COULD TALK TO--
NO SCHEDULED
TAP
TAP
I FEAR YOUR METHODOLOGY NOT WORKING PROVES MY POINT ABOUT THIS PLACE. IT IS TIME YOU FOLLOW MY LEAD.
I DON'T WANT YOU HURTING PEOPLE, OTTO! I JUST NEED TO THINK SOMETHING ELSE UP.
YES. UP IS JUST WHAT I HAD IN MIND.

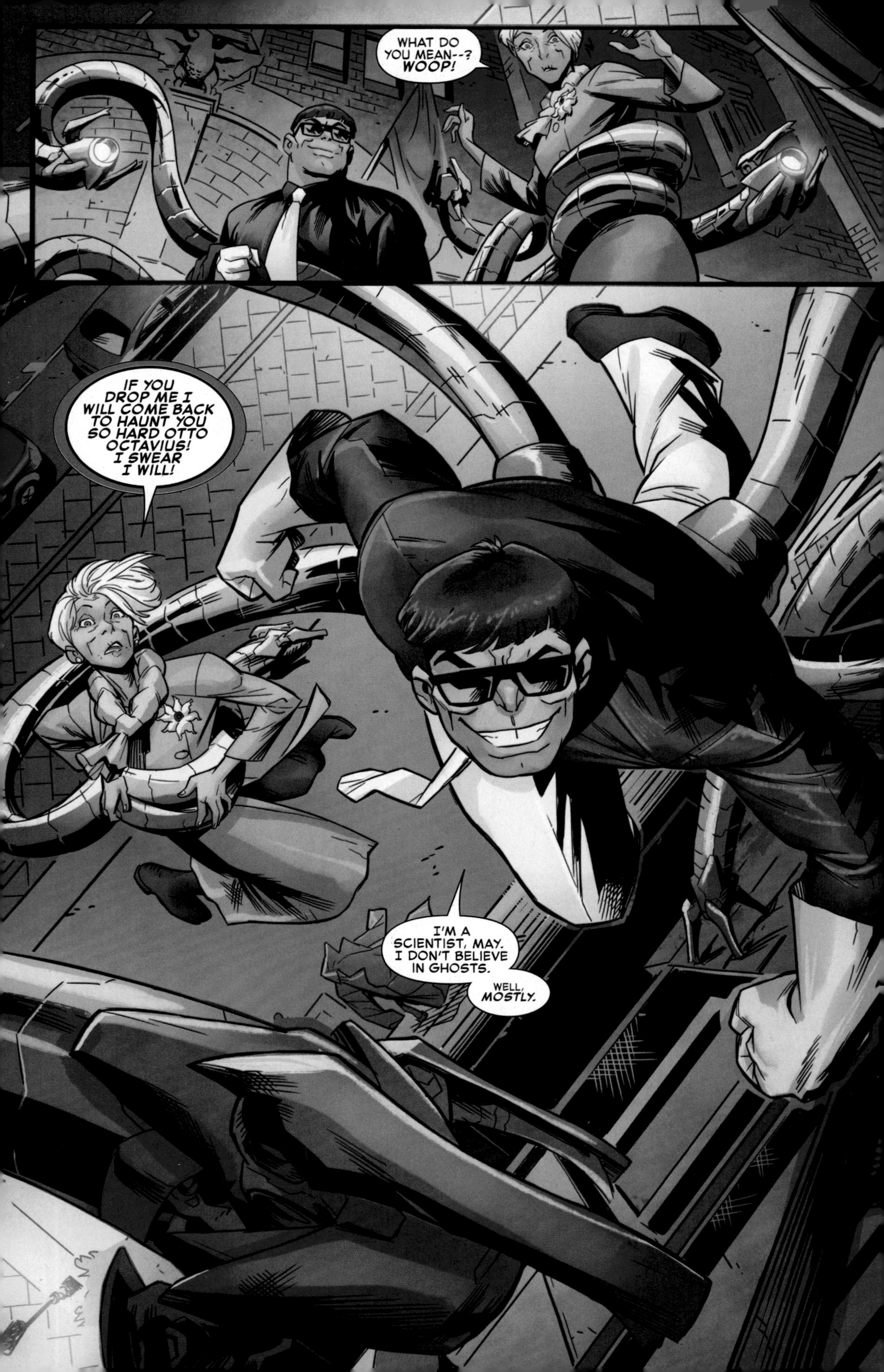
WHAT DO YOU MEAN--? WOOP!
IF YOU DROP ME I WILL COME BACK TO HAUNT YOU SO HARD OTTO OCTAVIUS! I SWEAR I WILL!
I'M A SCIENTIST, MAY. I DON'T BELIEVE IN GHOSTS.
WELL, MOSTLY.

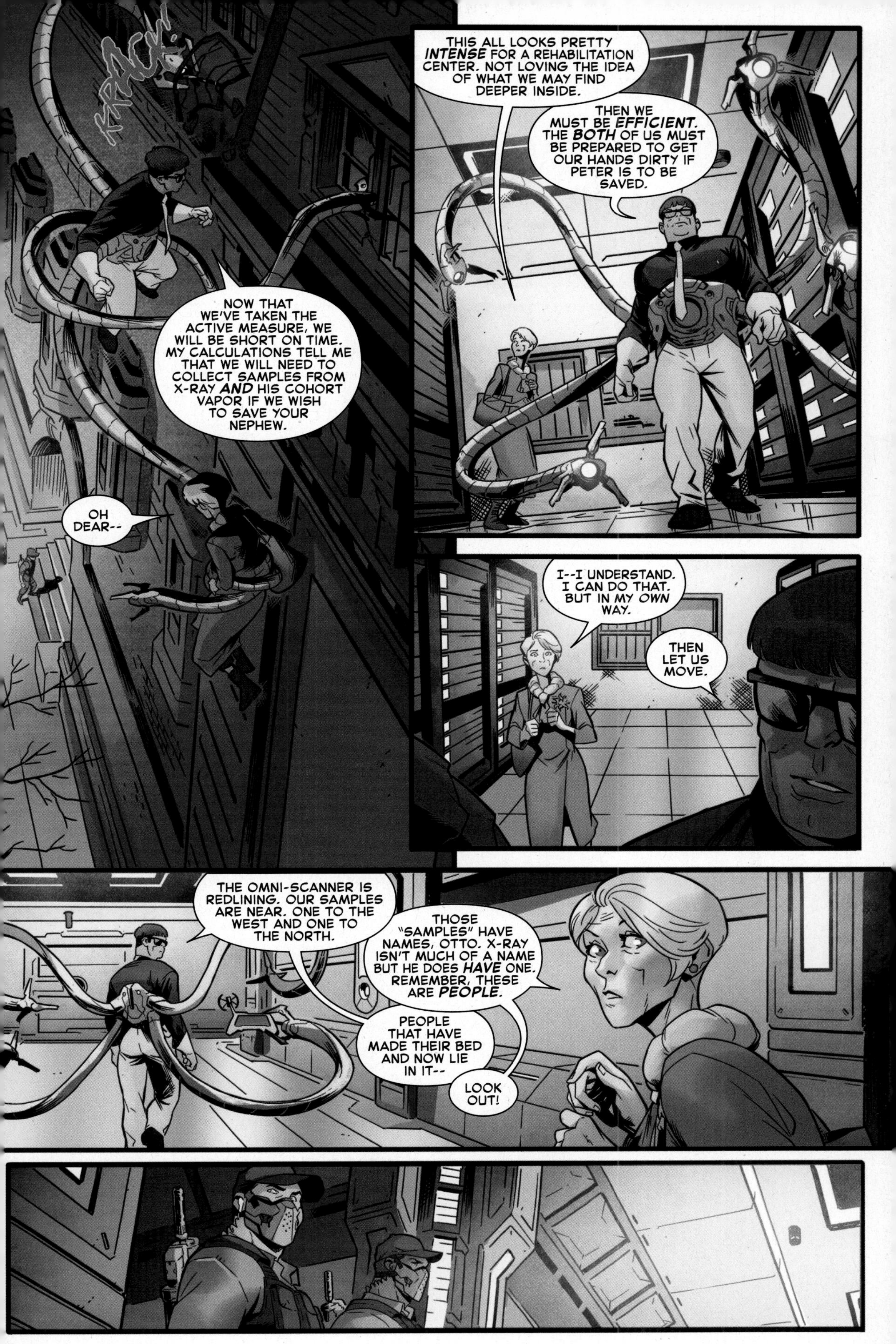
KRACK!
NOW THAT WE'VE TAKEN THE ACTIVE MEASURE, WE WILL BE SHORT ON TIME. MY CALCULATIONS TELL ME THAT WE WILL NEED TO COLLECT SAMPLES FROM X-RAY AND HIS COHORT VAPOR IF WE WISH TO SAVE YOUR NEPHEW.
OH DEAR--
THIS ALL LOOKS PRETTY INTENSE FOR A REHABILITATION CENTER. NOT LOVING THE IDEA OF WHAT WE MAY FIND DEEPER INSIDE.
THEN WE MUST BE EFFICIENT. THE BOTH OF US MUST BE PREPARED TO GET OUR HANDS DIRTY IF PETER IS TO BE SAVED.
I--I UNDERSTAND. I CAN DO THAT. BUT IN MY OWN WAY.
THEN LET US MOVE.
THE OMNI-SCANNER IS REDLINING. OUR SAMPLES ARE NEAR. ONE TO THE WEST AND ONE TO THE NORTH.
THOSE "SAMPLES" HAVE NAMES, OTTO. X-RAY ISN'T MUCH OF A NAME BUT HE DOES HAVE ONE. REMEMBER, THESE ARE PEOPLE.
PEOPLE THAT HAVE MADE THEIR BED AND NOW LIE IN IT--
LOOK OUT!

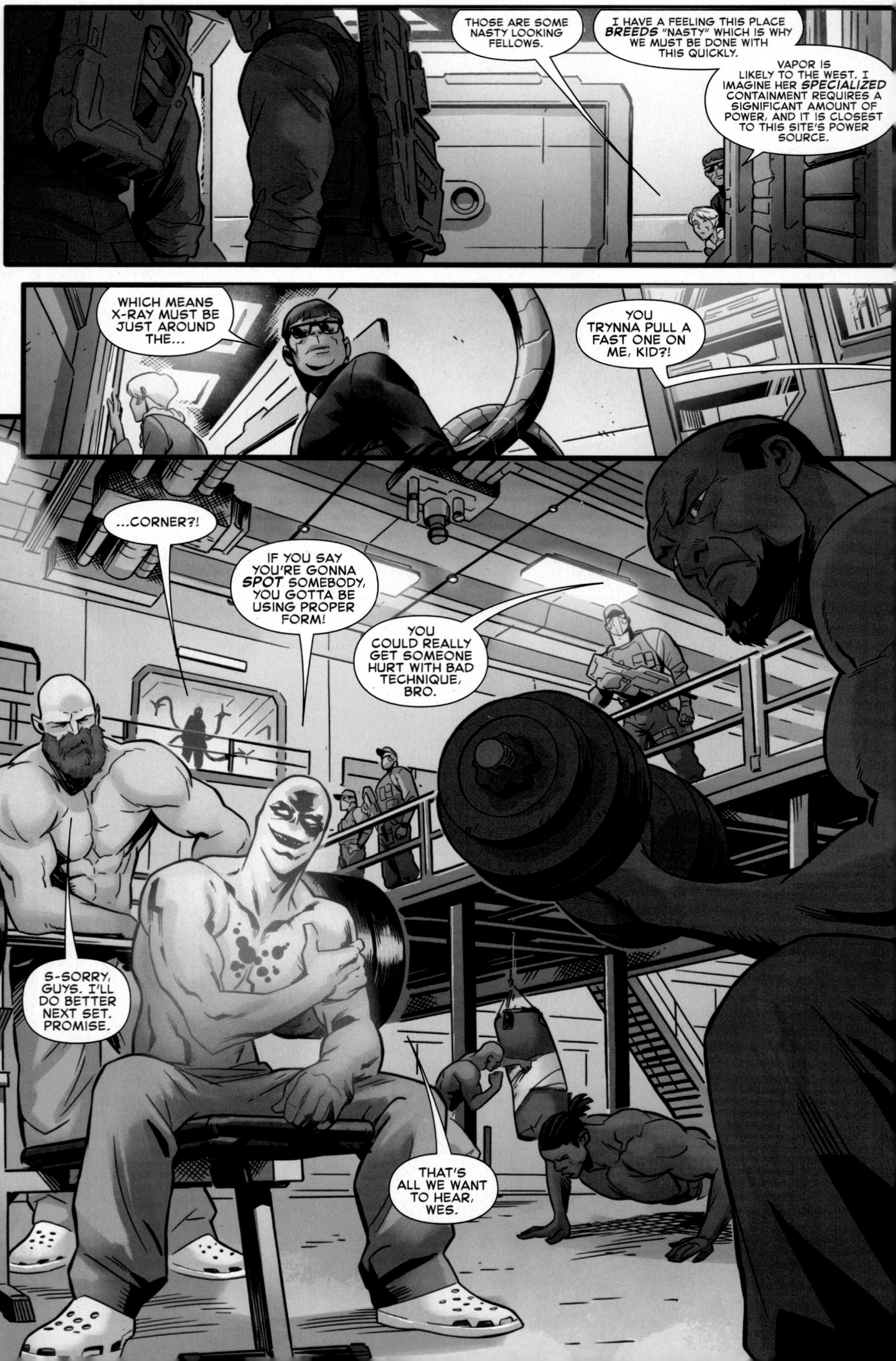
THOSE ARE SOME NASTY LOOKING FELLOWS.
I HAVE A FEELING THIS PLACE BREEDS "NASTY" WHICH IS WHY WE MUST BE DONE WITH THIS QUICKLY.
VAPOR IS LIKELY TO THE WEST. I IMAGINE HER SPECIALIZED CONTAINMENT REQUIRES A SIGNIFICANT AMOUNT OF POWER, AND IT IS CLOSEST TO THIS SITE'S POWER SOURCE.
WHICH MEANS X-RAY MUST BE JUST AROUND THE...
YOU TRYNNA PULL A FAST ONE ON ME, KID?!
...CORNER?!
IF YOU SAY YOU'RE GONNA SPOT SOMEBODY, YOU GOTTA BE USING PROPER FORM!
YOU COULD REALLY GET SOMEONE HURT WITH BAD TECHNIQUE, BRO.
S-SORRY, GUYS. I'LL DO BETTER NEXT SET. PROMISE.
THAT'S ALL WE WANT TO HEAR, WES.

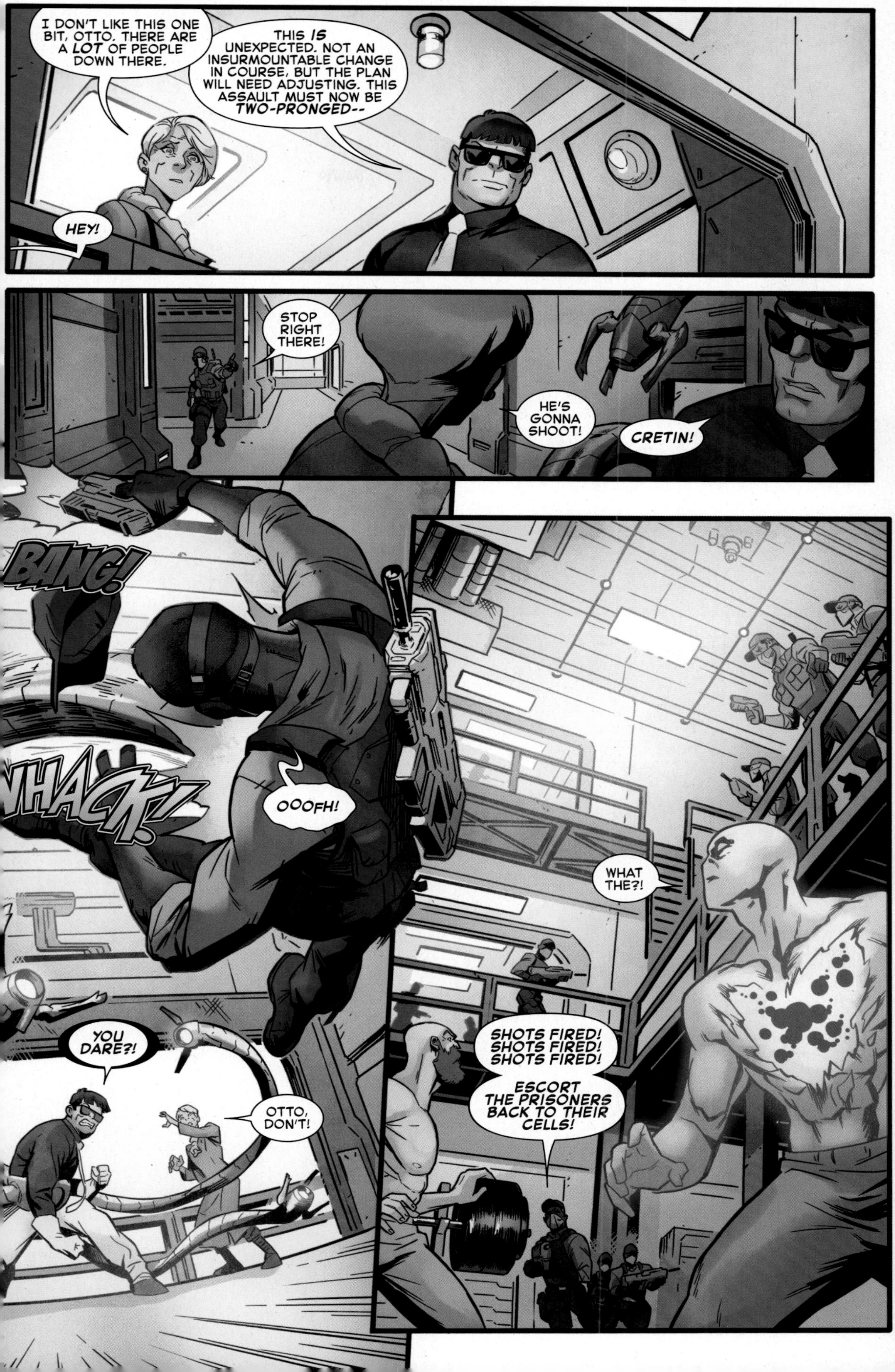
I DON'T LIKE THIS ONE BIT, OTTO. THERE ARE A LOT OF PEOPLE DOWN THERE.
THIS IS UNEXPECTED. NOT AN INSURMOUNTABLE CHANGE IN COURSE, BUT THE PLAN WILL NEED ADJUSTING. THIS ASSAULT MUST NOW BE TWO-PRONGED--
HEY!
STOP RIGHT THERE!
HE'S GONNA SHOOT!
CRETIN!
BANG!
WHACK!
OOOFH!
WHAT THE?!
YOU DARE?!
OTTO, DON'T!
SHOTS FIRED! SHOTS FIRED! SHOTS FIRED!
ESCORT THE PRISONERS BACK TO THEIR CELLS!

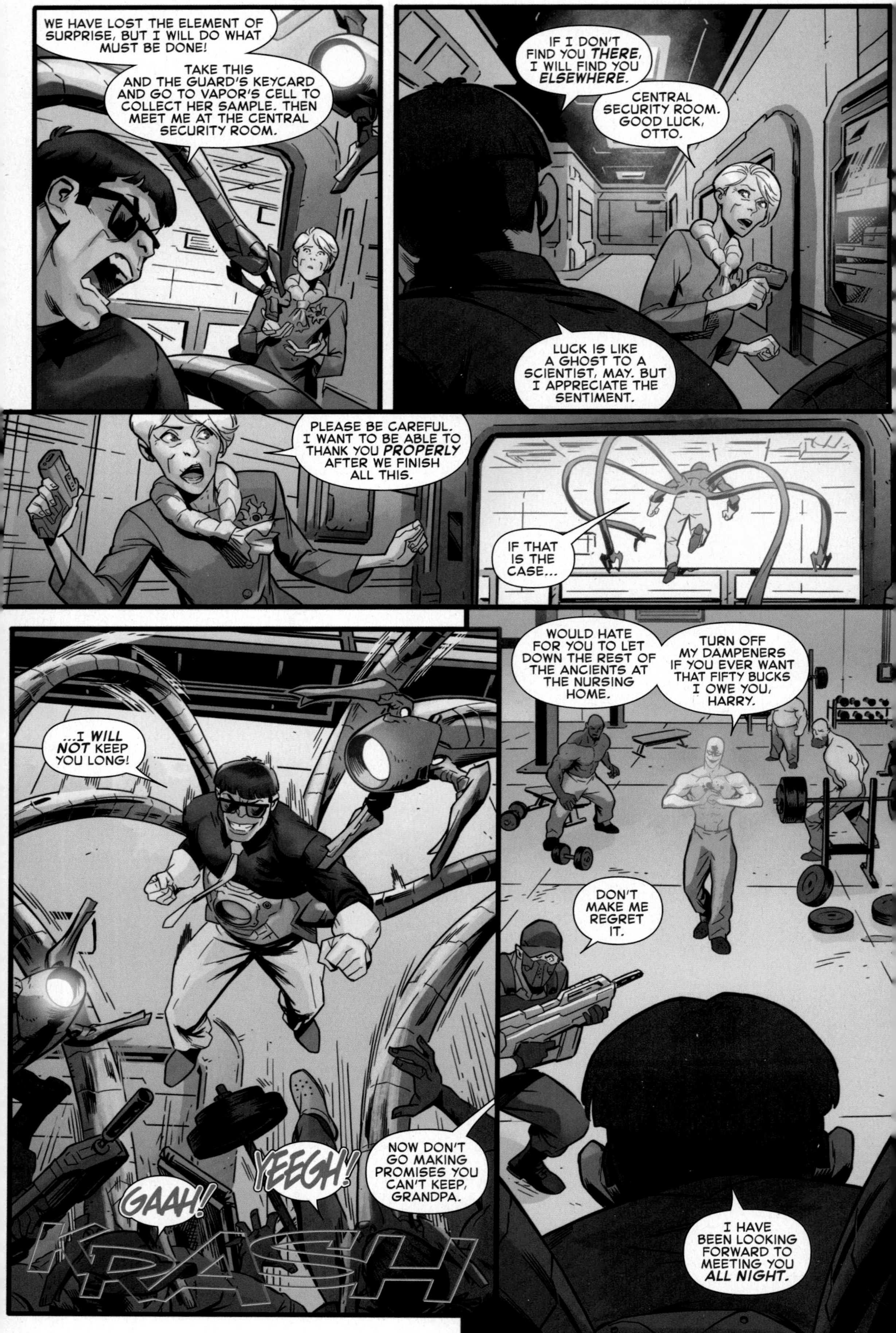
WE HAVE LOST THE ELEMENT OF SURPRISE, BUT I WILL DO WHAT MUST BE DONE!
TAKE THIS AND THE GUARD'S KEYCARD AND GO TO VAPOR'S CELL TO COLLECT HER SAMPLE. THEN MEET ME AT THE CENTRAL SECURITY ROOM.
IF I DON'T FIND YOU *THERE*, I WILL FIND YOU *ELSEWHERE*.
CENTRAL SECURITY ROOM. GOOD LUCK, OTTO.
LUCK IS LIKE A GHOST TO A SCIENTIST, MAY. BUT I APPRECIATE THE SENTIMENT.
PLEASE BE CAREFUL. I WANT TO BE ABLE TO THANK YOU *PROPERLY* AFTER WE FINISH ALL THIS.
IF THAT IS THE CASE...
...I *WILL NOT* KEEP YOU LONG!
YEEGH!
GAAH!
KRASH
NOW DON'T GO MAKING PROMISES YOU CAN'T KEEP, GRANDPA.
WOULD HATE FOR YOU TO LET DOWN THE REST OF THE ANCIENTS AT THE NURSING HOME.
TURN OFF MY DAMPENERS IF YOU EVER WANT THAT FIFTY BUCKS I OWE YOU, HARRY.
DON'T MAKE ME REGRET IT.
I HAVE BEEN LOOKING FORWARD TO MEETING YOU *ALL NIGHT*.

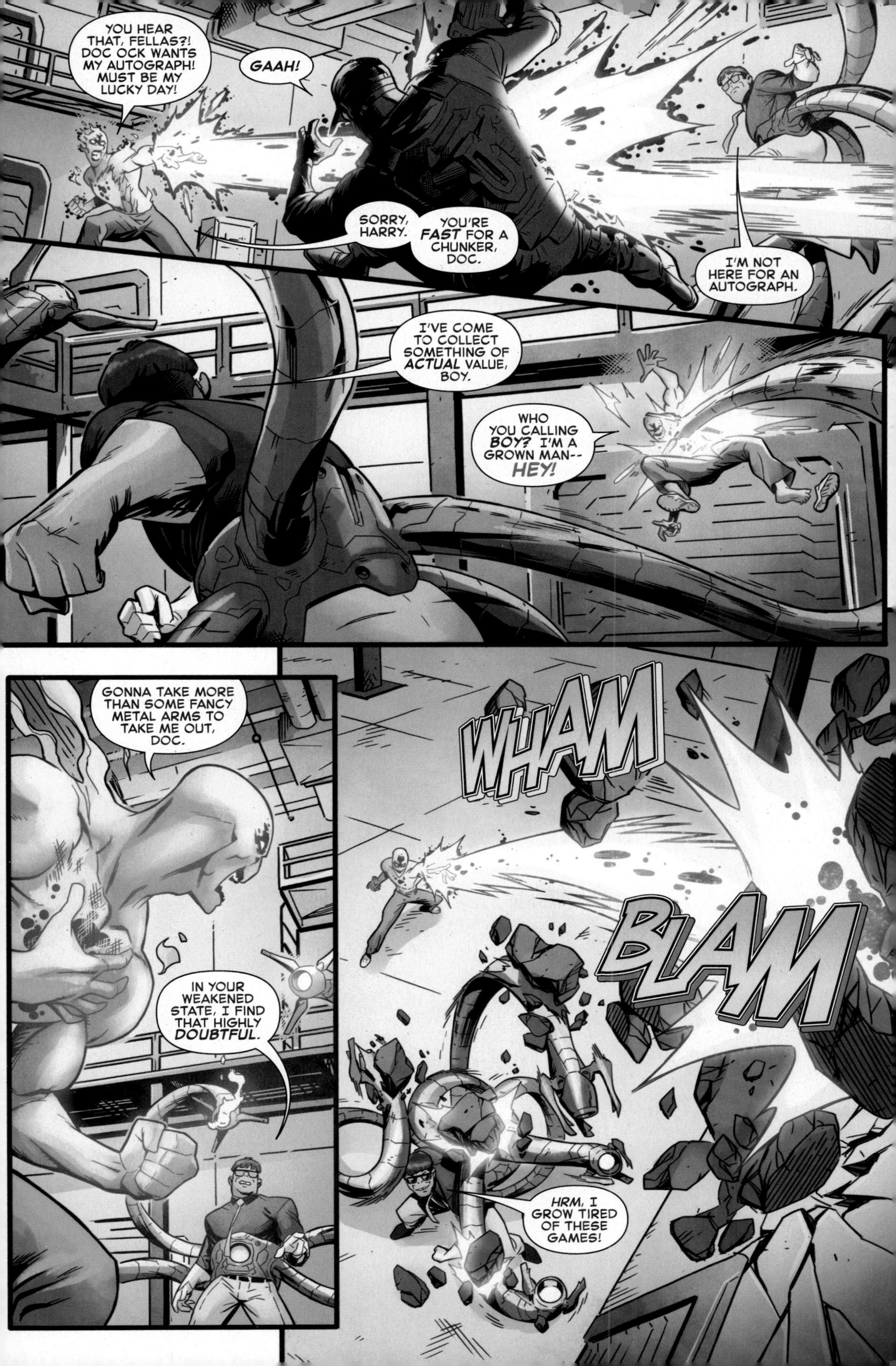
YOU HEAR THAT, FELLAS?! DOC OCK WANTS MY AUTOGRAPH! MUST BE MY LUCKY DAY!
GAAH!
SORRY, HARRY.
YOU'RE FAST FOR A CHUNKER, DOC.
I'M NOT HERE FOR AN AUTOGRAPH.
I'VE COME TO COLLECT SOMETHING OF ACTUAL VALUE, BOY.
WHO YOU CALLING BOY? I'M A GROWN MAN-- HEY!
GONNA TAKE MORE THAN SOME FANCY METAL ARMS TO TAKE ME OUT, DOC.
IN YOUR WEAKENED STATE, I FIND THAT HIGHLY DOUBTFUL.
WHAM
BLAM
HRM, I GROW TIRED OF THESE GAMES!

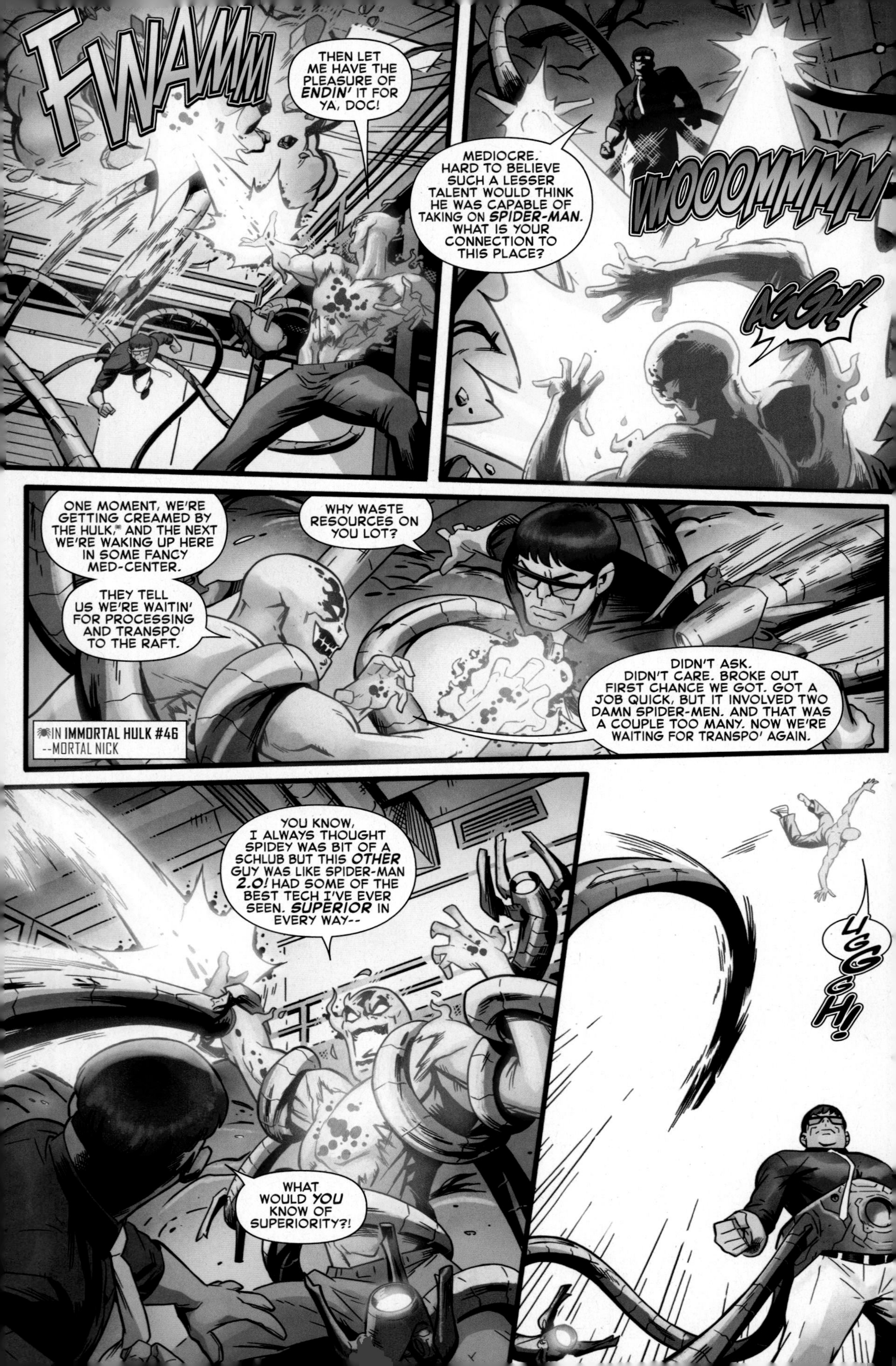
FWAMM
THEN LET ME HAVE THE PLEASURE OF ENDIN' IT FOR YA, DOC!
MEDIOCRE. HARD TO BELIEVE SUCH A LESSER TALENT WOULD THINK HE WAS CAPABLE OF TAKING ON SPIDER-MAN. WHAT IS YOUR CONNECTION TO THIS PLACE?
VWOOOMMMM
AGGH!
ONE MOMENT, WE'RE GETTING CREAMED BY THE HULK,* AND THE NEXT WE'RE WAKING UP HERE IN SOME FANCY MED-CENTER.
THEY TELL US WE'RE WAITIN' FOR PROCESSING AND TRANSPO' TO THE RAFT.
WHY WASTE RESOURCES ON YOU LOT?
DIDN'T ASK. DIDN'T CARE. BROKE OUT FIRST CHANCE WE GOT. GOT A JOB QUICK, BUT IT INVOLVED TWO DAMN SPIDER-MEN. AND THAT WAS A COUPLE TOO MANY. NOW WE'RE WAITING FOR TRANSPO' AGAIN.
*IN IMMORTAL HULK #46 --MORTAL NICK
YOU KNOW, I ALWAYS THOUGHT SPIDEY WAS BIT OF A SCHLUB BUT THIS OTHER GUY WAS LIKE SPIDER-MAN 2.0! HAD SOME OF THE BEST TECH I'VE EVER SEEN. SUPERIOR IN EVERY WAY--
WHAT WOULD YOU KNOW OF SUPERIORITY?!
UGGGH!

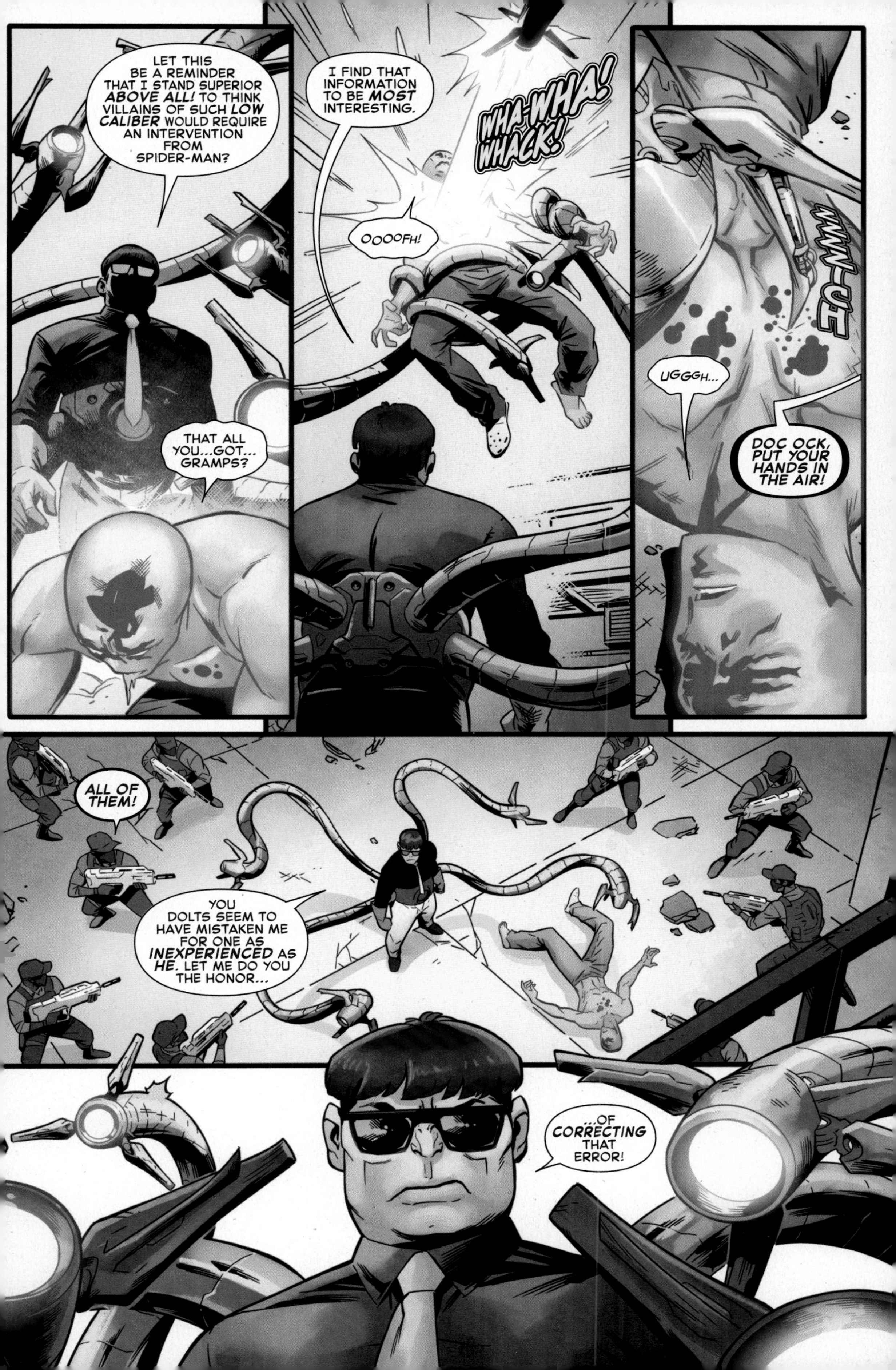
LET THIS BE A REMINDER THAT I STAND SUPERIOR ABOVE ALL! TO THINK VILLAINS OF SUCH LOW CALIBER WOULD REQUIRE AN INTERVENTION FROM SPIDER-MAN?
THAT ALL YOU...GOT... GRAMPS?
I FIND THAT INFORMATION TO BE MOST INTERESTING.
WHA-WHA! WHACK!
OOOOFH!
NNN-CH
UGGGH...
DOC OCK, PUT YOUR HANDS IN THE AIR!
ALL OF THEM!
YOU DOLTS SEEM TO HAVE MISTAKEN ME FOR ONE AS INEXPERIENCED AS HE. LET ME DO YOU THE HONOR...
...OF CORRECTING THAT ERROR!

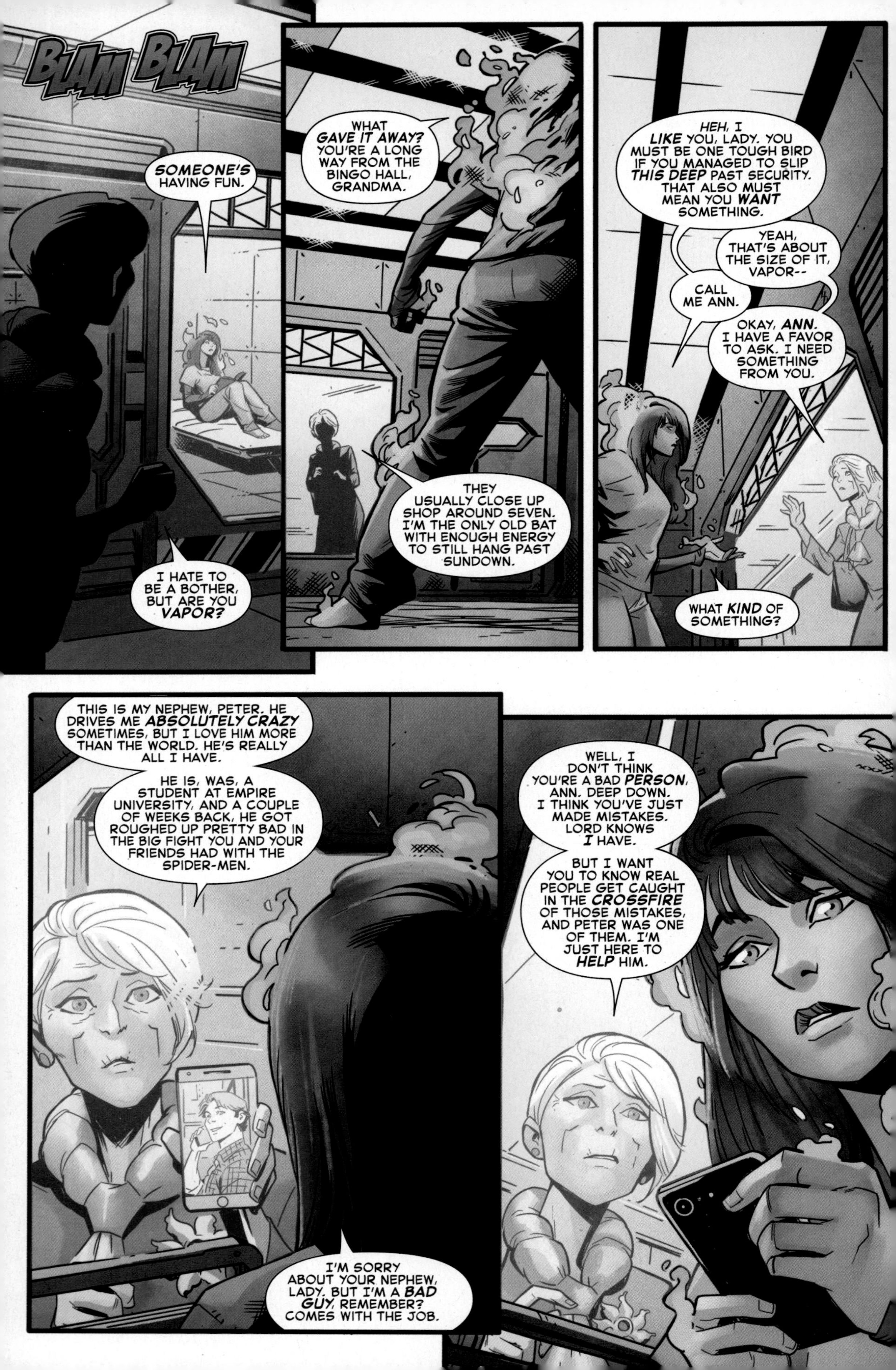
BLAM BLAM
SOMEONE'S HAVING FUN.
I HATE TO BE A BOTHER, BUT ARE YOU VAPOR?
WHAT GAVE IT AWAY? YOU'RE A LONG WAY FROM THE BINGO HALL, GRANDMA.
THEY USUALLY CLOSE UP SHOP AROUND SEVEN. I'M THE ONLY OLD BAT WITH ENOUGH ENERGY TO STILL HANG PAST SUNDOWN.
HEH, I LIKE YOU, LADY. YOU MUST BE ONE TOUGH BIRD IF YOU MANAGED TO SLIP THIS DEEP PAST SECURITY. THAT ALSO MUST MEAN YOU WANT SOMETHING.
YEAH, THAT'S ABOUT THE SIZE OF IT, VAPOR--
CALL ME ANN.
OKAY, ANN. I HAVE A FAVOR TO ASK. I NEED SOMETHING FROM YOU.
WHAT KIND OF SOMETHING?
THIS IS MY NEPHEW, PETER. HE DRIVES ME ABSOLUTELY CRAZY SOMETIMES, BUT I LOVE HIM MORE THAN THE WORLD. HE'S REALLY ALL I HAVE.
HE IS, WAS, A STUDENT AT EMPIRE UNIVERSITY, AND A COUPLE OF WEEKS BACK, HE GOT ROUGHED UP PRETTY BAD IN THE BIG FIGHT YOU AND YOUR FRIENDS HAD WITH THE SPIDER-MEN.
I'M SORRY ABOUT YOUR NEPHEW, LADY. BUT I'M A BAD GUY, REMEMBER? COMES WITH THE JOB.
WELL, I DON'T THINK YOU'RE A BAD PERSON, ANN. DEEP DOWN. I THINK YOU'VE JUST MADE MISTAKES. LORD KNOWS I HAVE.
BUT I WANT YOU TO KNOW REAL PEOPLE GET CAUGHT IN THE CROSSFIRE OF THOSE MISTAKES, AND PETER WAS ONE OF THEM. I'M JUST HERE TO HELP HIM.

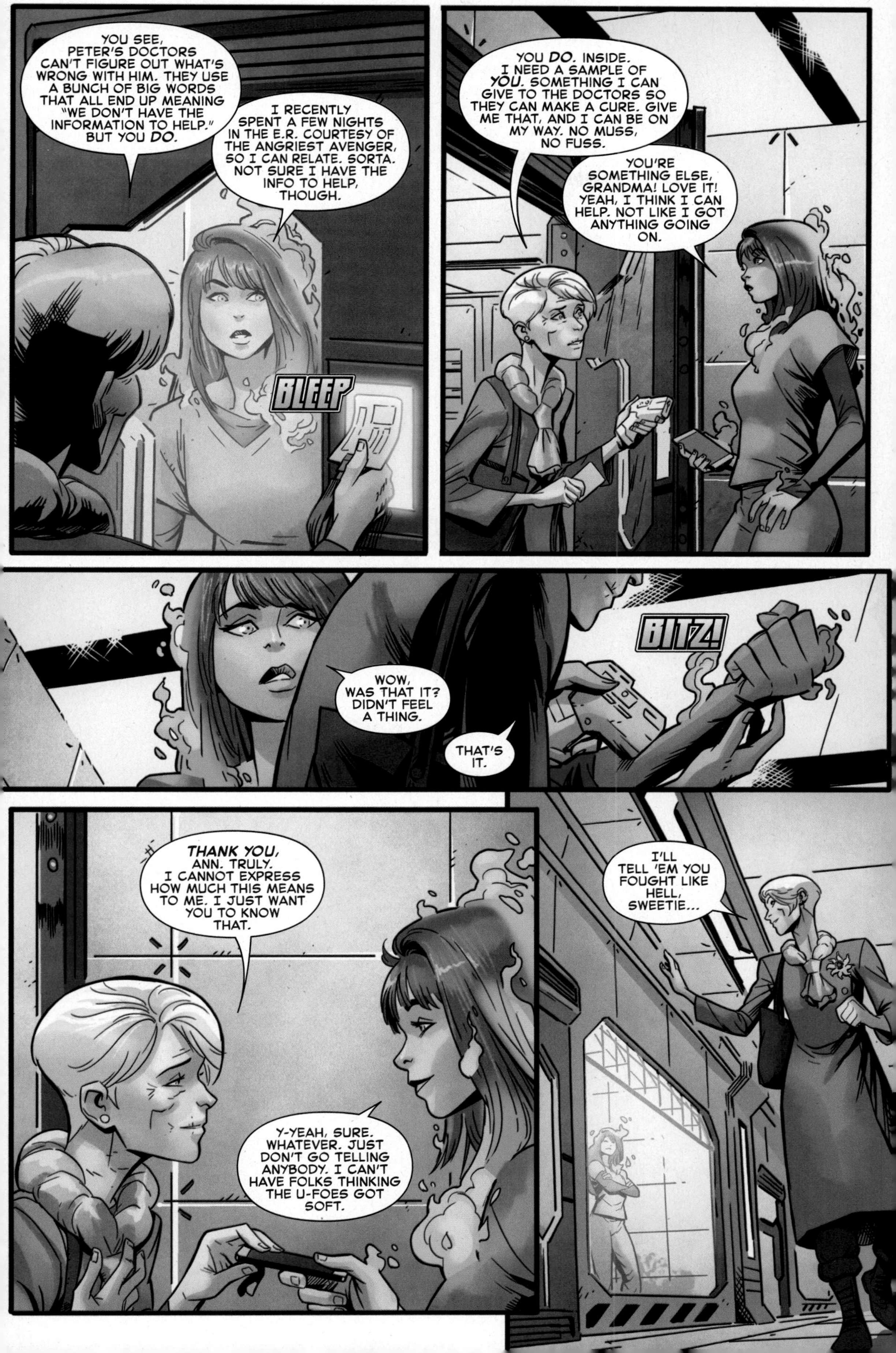
YOU SEE, PETER'S DOCTORS CAN'T FIGURE OUT WHAT'S WRONG WITH HIM. THEY USE A BUNCH OF BIG WORDS THAT ALL END UP MEANING "WE DON'T HAVE THE INFORMATION TO HELP." BUT YOU *DO*.
I RECENTLY SPENT A FEW NIGHTS IN THE E.R. COURTESY OF THE ANGRIEST AVENGER, SO I CAN RELATE. SORTA. NOT SURE I HAVE THE INFO TO HELP, THOUGH.
BLEEP
YOU *DO*. INSIDE. I NEED A SAMPLE OF *YOU*. SOMETHING I CAN GIVE TO THE DOCTORS SO THEY CAN MAKE A CURE. GIVE ME THAT, AND I CAN BE ON MY WAY. NO MUSS, NO FUSS.
YOU'RE SOMETHING ELSE, GRANDMA! LOVE IT! YEAH, I THINK I CAN HELP. NOT LIKE I GOT ANYTHING GOING ON.
BITZ!
WOW, WAS THAT IT? DIDN'T FEEL A THING.
THAT'S IT.
THANK YOU, ANN. TRULY. I CANNOT EXPRESS HOW MUCH THIS MEANS TO ME. I JUST WANT YOU TO KNOW THAT.
Y-YEAH, SURE. WHATEVER. JUST DON'T GO TELLING ANYBODY. I CAN'T HAVE FOLKS THINKING THE U-FOES GOT SOFT.
I'LL TELL 'EM YOU FOUGHT LIKE HELL, SWEETIE...

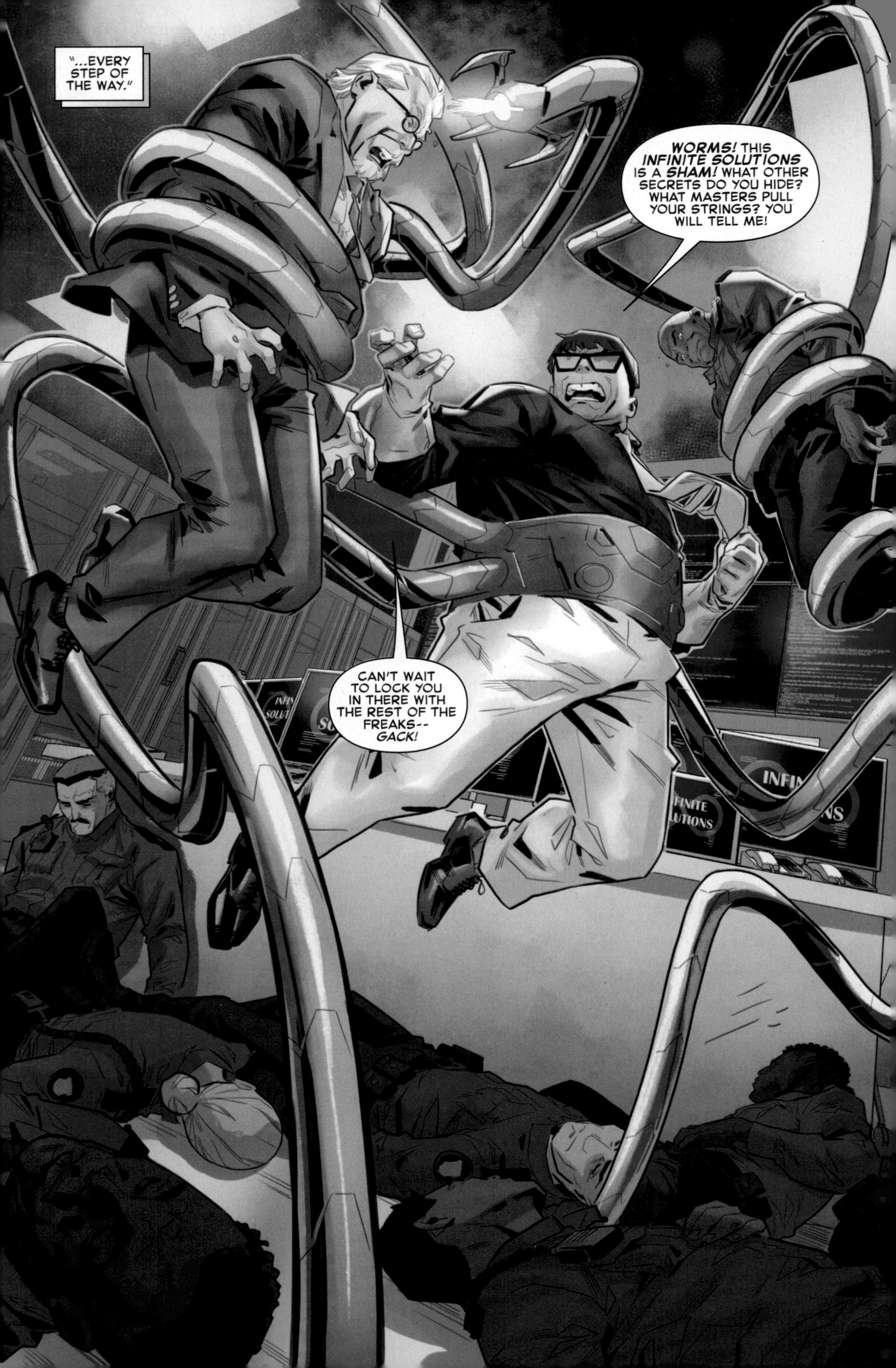
"...EVERY STEP OF THE WAY."
WORMS! THIS INFINITE SOLUTIONS IS A SHAM! WHAT OTHER SECRETS DO YOU HIDE? WHAT MASTERS PULL YOUR STRINGS? YOU WILL TELL ME!
CAN'T WAIT TO LOCK YOU IN THERE WITH THE REST OF THE FREAKS-- GACK!

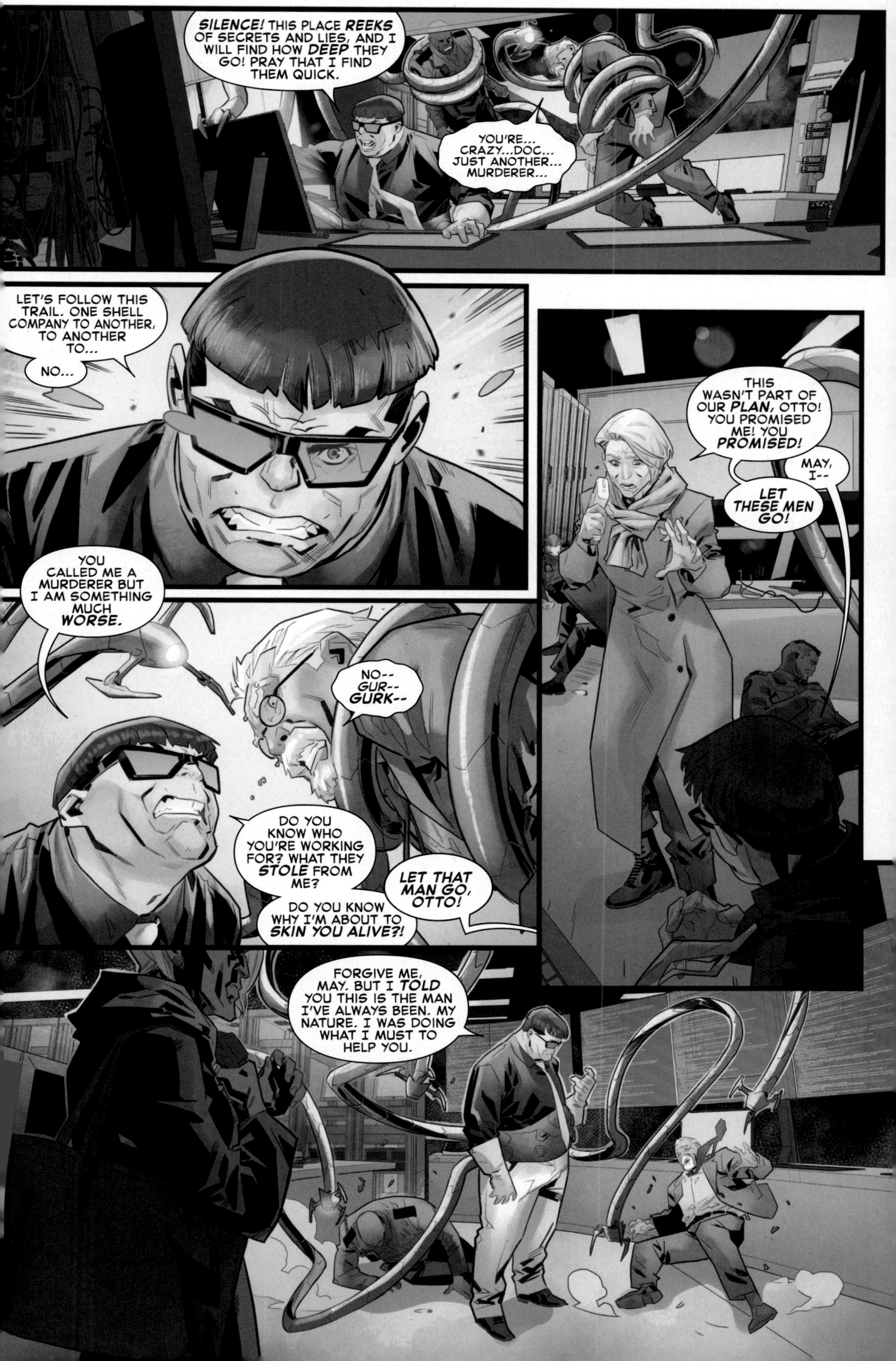
SILENCE! THIS PLACE REEKS OF SECRETS AND LIES, AND I WILL FIND HOW DEEP THEY GO! PRAY THAT I FIND THEM QUICK.
YOU'RE... CRAZY...DOC... JUST ANOTHER... MURDERER...
LET'S FOLLOW THIS TRAIL. ONE SHELL COMPANY TO ANOTHER, TO ANOTHER TO...
NO...
YOU CALLED ME A MURDERER BUT I AM SOMETHING MUCH WORSE.
NO-- GUR-- GURK--
DO YOU KNOW WHO YOU'RE WORKING FOR? WHAT THEY STOLE FROM ME?
DO YOU KNOW WHY I'M ABOUT TO SKIN YOU ALIVE?!
LET THAT MAN GO, OTTO!
THIS WASN'T PART OF OUR PLAN, OTTO! YOU PROMISED ME! YOU PROMISED!
MAY, I--
LET THESE MEN GO!
FORGIVE ME, MAY. BUT I TOLD YOU THIS IS THE MAN I'VE ALWAYS BEEN. MY NATURE. I WAS DOING WHAT I MUST TO HELP YOU.

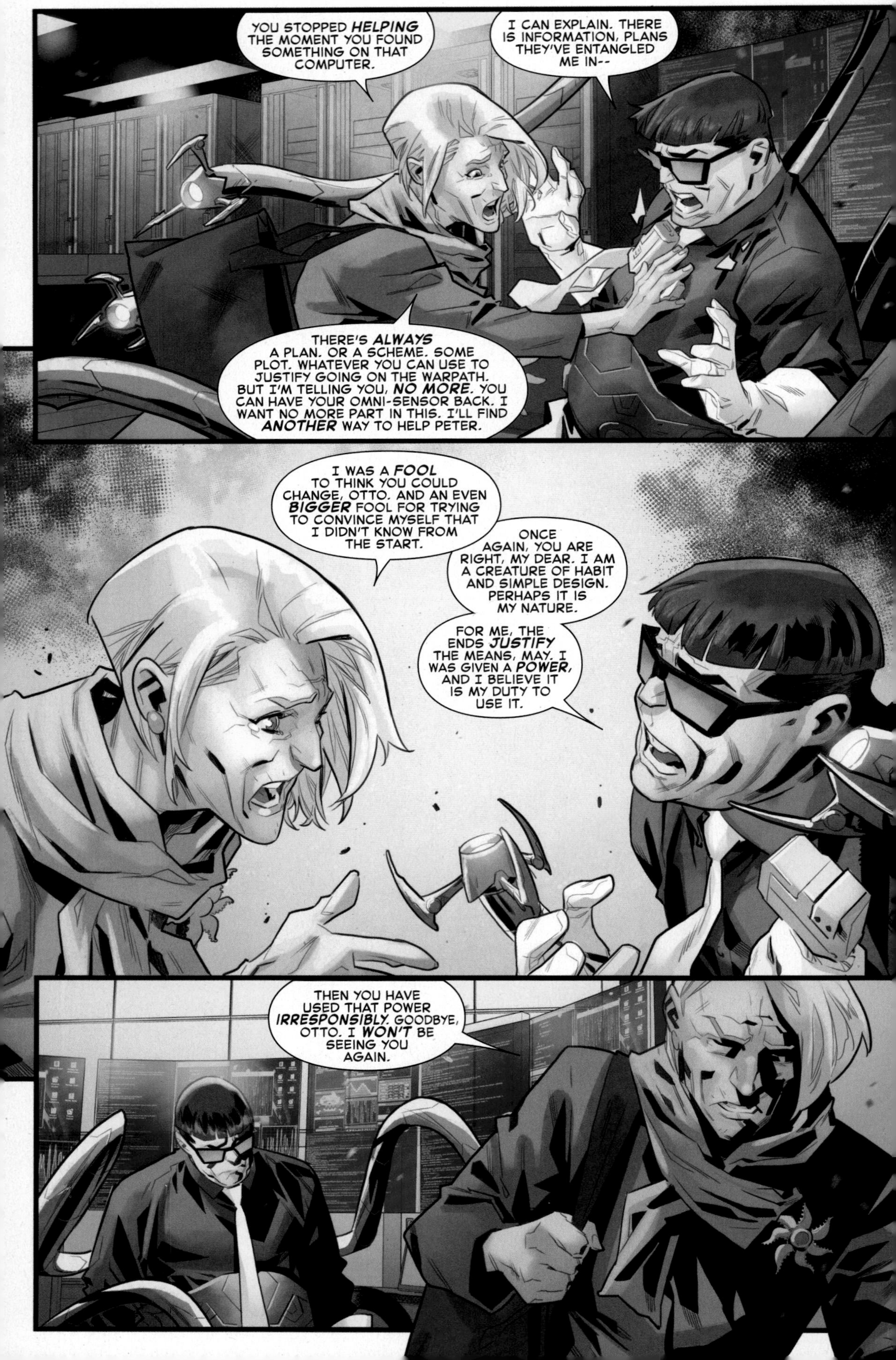
YOU STOPPED HELPING THE MOMENT YOU FOUND SOMETHING ON THAT COMPUTER.
I CAN EXPLAIN. THERE IS INFORMATION, PLANS THEY'VE ENTANGLED ME IN--
THERE'S ALWAYS A PLAN. OR A SCHEME. SOME PLOT. WHATEVER YOU CAN USE TO JUSTIFY GOING ON THE WARPATH. BUT I'M TELLING YOU, NO MORE. YOU CAN HAVE YOUR OMNI-SENSOR BACK. I WANT NO MORE PART IN THIS. I'LL FIND ANOTHER WAY TO HELP PETER.
I WAS A FOOL TO THINK YOU COULD CHANGE, OTTO. AND AN EVEN BIGGER FOOL FOR TRYING TO CONVINCE MYSELF THAT I DIDN'T KNOW FROM THE START.
ONCE AGAIN, YOU ARE RIGHT, MY DEAR. I AM A CREATURE OF HABIT AND SIMPLE DESIGN. PERHAPS IT IS MY NATURE.
FOR ME, THE ENDS JUSTIFY THE MEANS, MAY. I WAS GIVEN A POWER, AND I BELIEVE IT IS MY DUTY TO USE IT.
THEN YOU HAVE USED THAT POWER IRRESPONSIBLY. GOODBYE, OTTO. I WON'T BE SEEING YOU AGAIN.

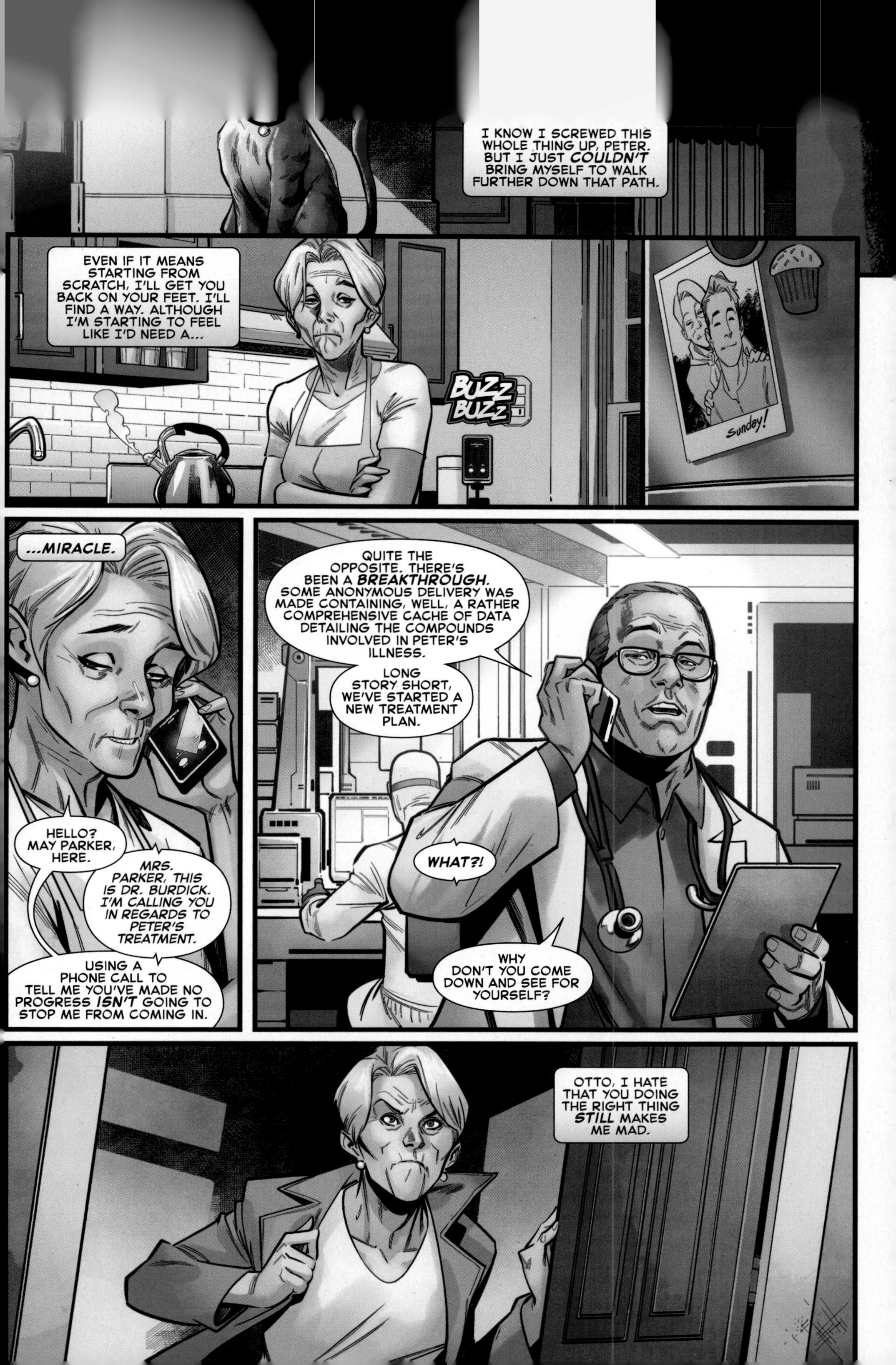
I KNOW I SCREWED THIS WHOLE THING UP, PETER. BUT I JUST COULDN'T BRING MYSELF TO WALK FURTHER DOWN THAT PATH.
EVEN IF IT MEANS STARTING FROM SCRATCH, I'LL GET YOU BACK ON YOUR FEET. I'LL FIND A WAY. ALTHOUGH I'M STARTING TO FEEL LIKE I'D NEED A...
BUZZ BUZZ
Sunday!
...MIRACLE.
HELLO? MAY PARKER, HERE.
MRS. PARKER, THIS IS DR. BURDICK. I'M CALLING YOU IN REGARDS TO PETER'S TREATMENT.
USING A PHONE CALL TO TELL ME YOU'VE MADE NO PROGRESS ISN'T GOING TO STOP ME FROM COMING IN.
QUITE THE OPPOSITE. THERE'S BEEN A BREAKTHROUGH. SOME ANONYMOUS DELIVERY WAS MADE CONTAINING, WELL, A RATHER COMPREHENSIVE CACHE OF DATA DETAILING THE COMPOUNDS INVOLVED IN PETER'S ILLNESS.
LONG STORY SHORT, WE'VE STARTED A NEW TREATMENT PLAN.
WHAT?!
WHY DON'T YOU COME DOWN AND SEE FOR YOURSELF?
OTTO, I HATE THAT YOU DOING THE RIGHT THING STILL MAKES ME MAD.

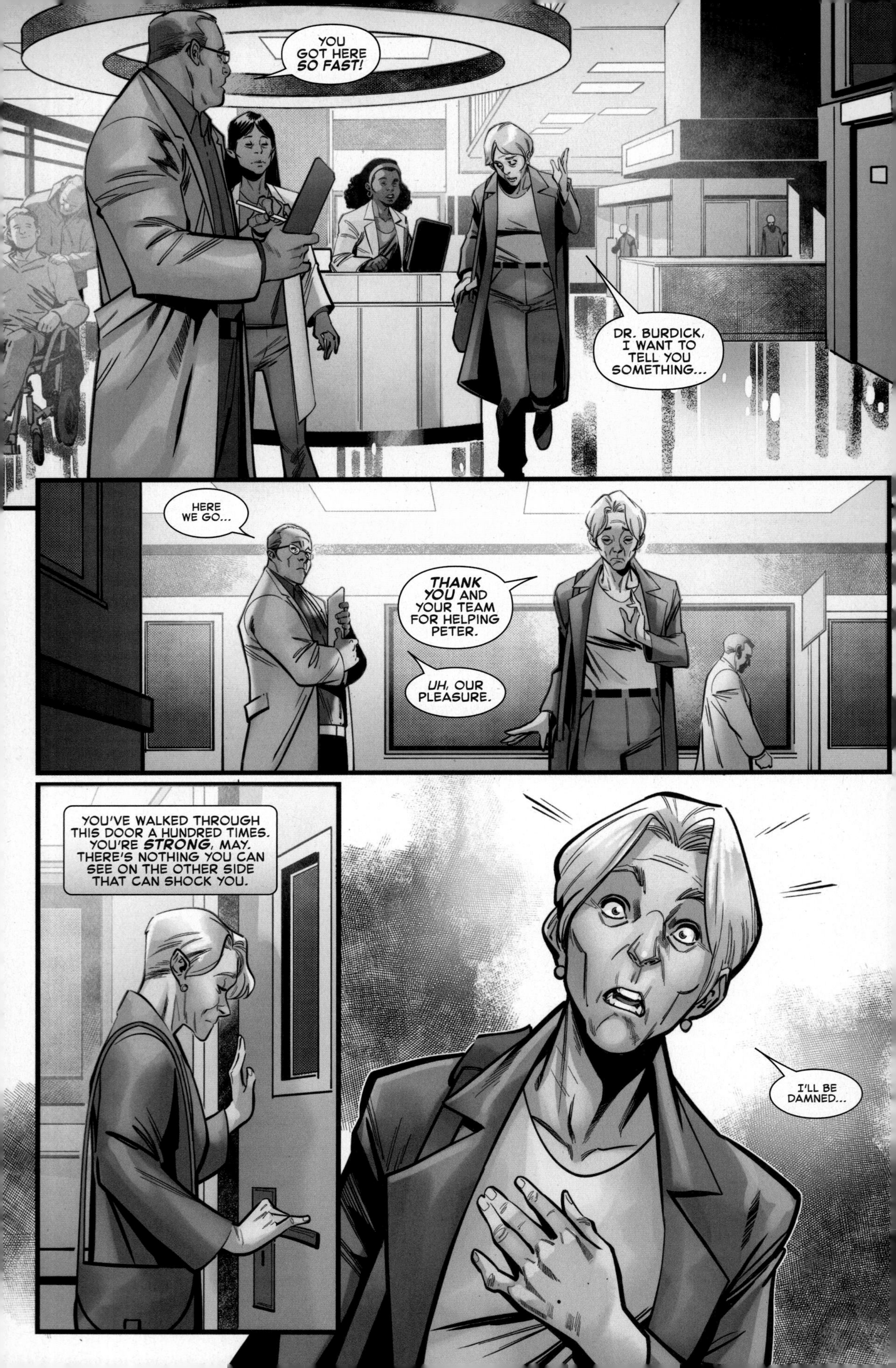
YOU GOT HERE SO FAST!
DR. BURDICK, I WANT TO TELL YOU SOMETHING...
HERE WE GO...
THANK YOU AND YOUR TEAM FOR HELPING PETER.
UH, OUR PLEASURE.
YOU'VE WALKED THROUGH THIS DOOR A HUNDRED TIMES. YOU'RE STRONG, MAY. THERE'S NOTHING YOU CAN SEE ON THE OTHER SIDE THAT CAN SHOCK YOU.
I'LL BE DAMNED...

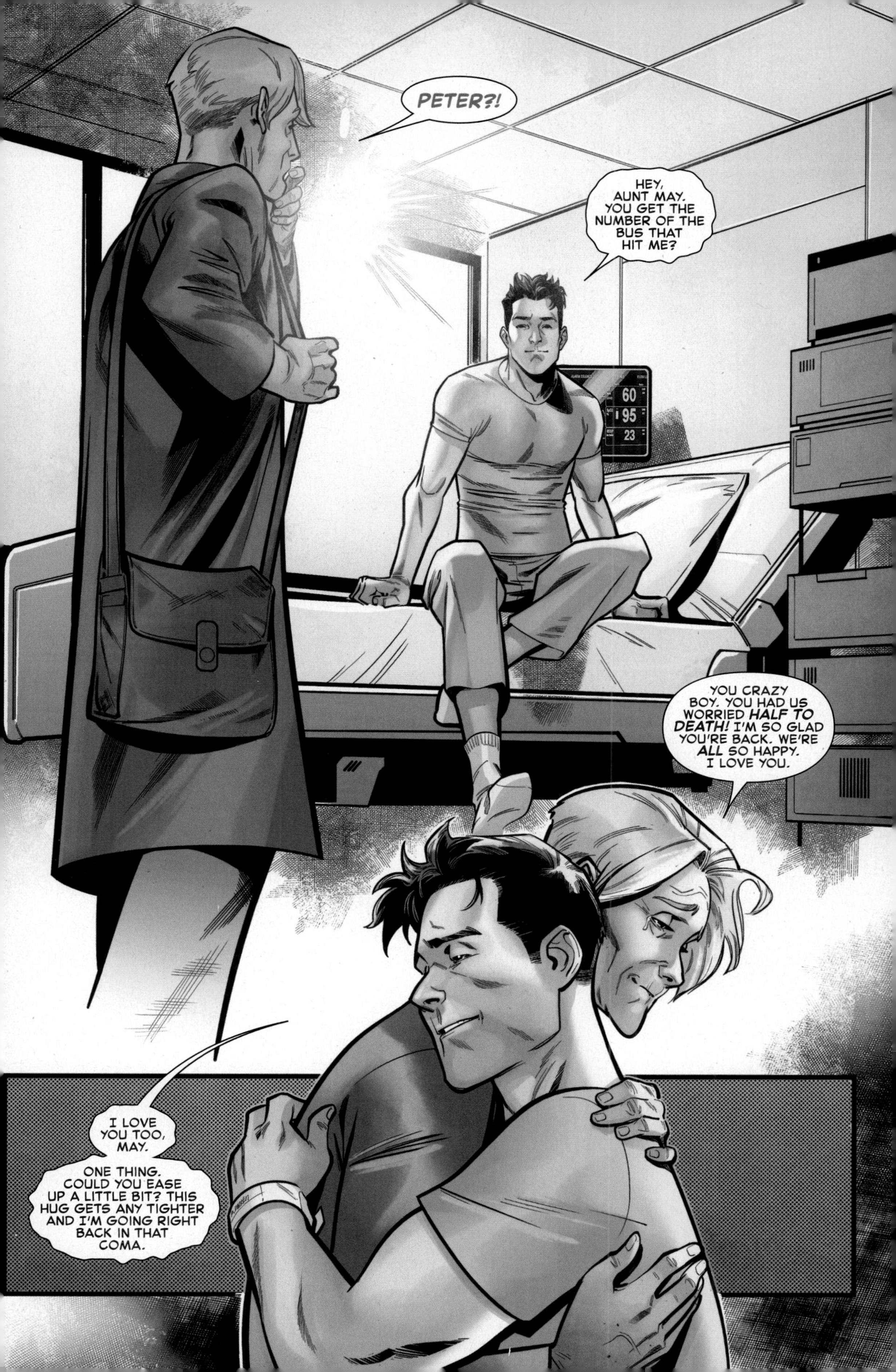
PETER?!
HEY, AUNT MAY. YOU GET THE NUMBER OF THE BUS THAT HIT ME?
YOU CRAZY BOY. YOU HAD US WORRIED HALF TO DEATH! I'M SO GLAD YOU'RE BACK. WE'RE ALL SO HAPPY. I LOVE YOU.
I LOVE YOU TOO, MAY.
ONE THING. COULD YOU EASE UP A LITTLE BIT? THIS HUG GETS ANY TIGHTER AND I'M GOING RIGHT BACK IN THAT COMA.

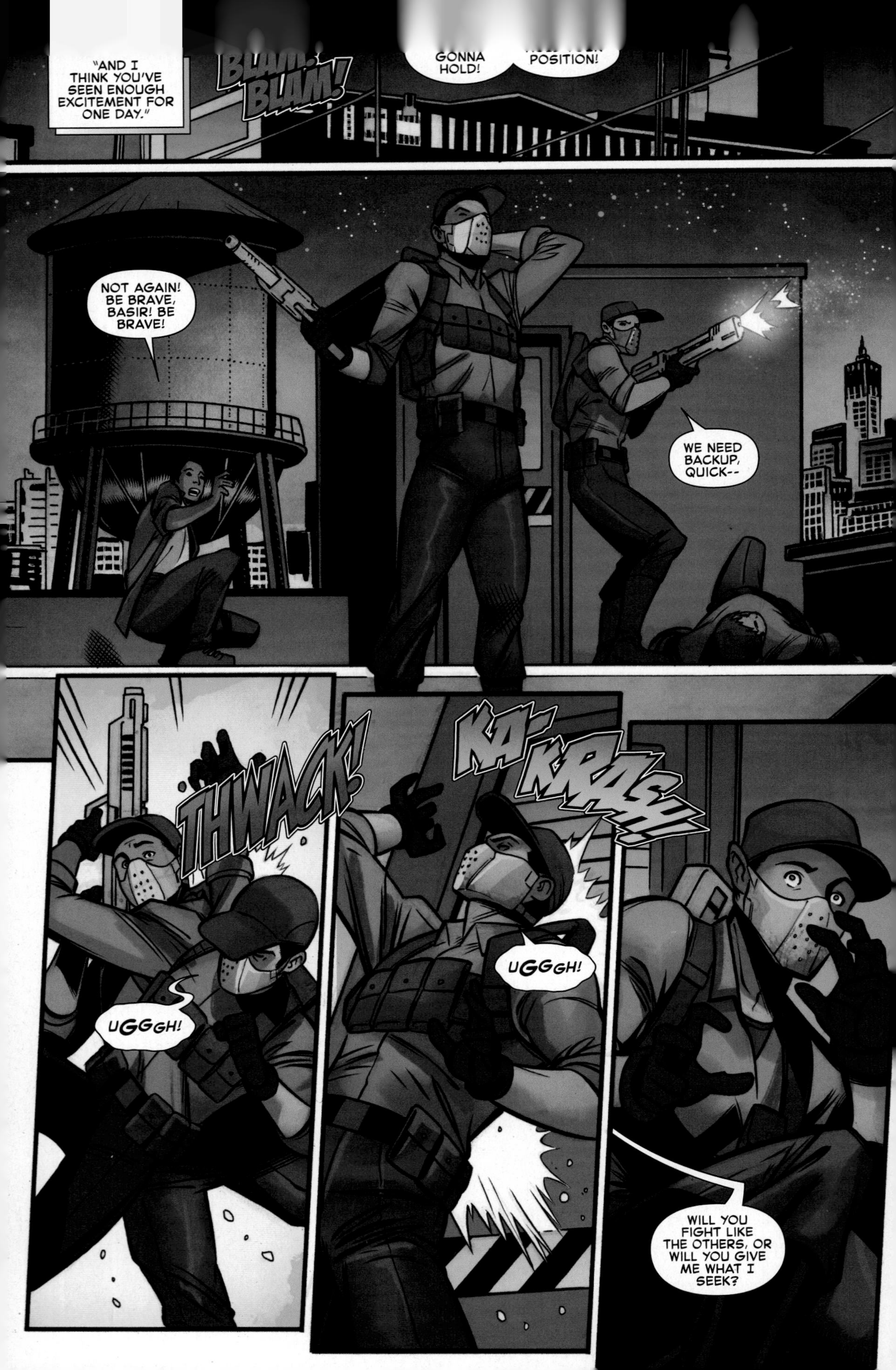
"AND I THINK YOU'VE SEEN ENOUGH EXCITEMENT FOR ONE DAY."
BLAM! BLAM!
GONNA HOLD!
POSITION!
NOT AGAIN! BE BRAVE, BASIR! BE BRAVE!
WE NEED BACKUP, QUICK--
THWACK!
UGGGH!
KA-KRASH!!
UGGGH!
WILL YOU FIGHT LIKE THE OTHERS, OR WILL YOU GIVE ME WHAT I SEEK?

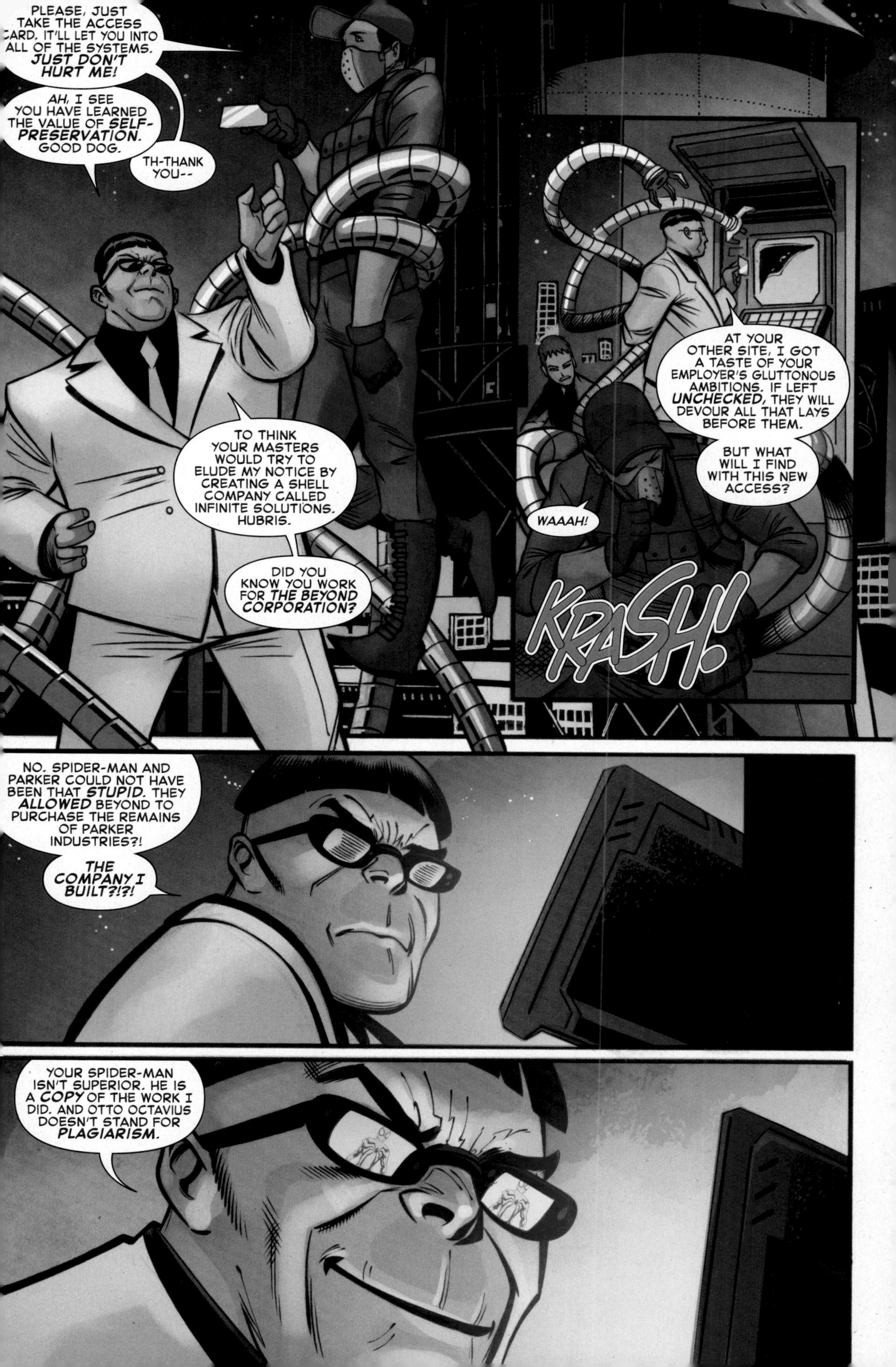
PLEASE, JUST TAKE THE ACCESS CARD. IT'LL LET YOU INTO ALL OF THE SYSTEMS. JUST DON'T HURT ME!
AH, I SEE YOU HAVE LEARNED THE VALUE OF SELF-PRESERVATION. GOOD DOG.
TH-THANK YOU--
TO THINK YOUR MASTERS WOULD TRY TO ELUDE MY NOTICE BY CREATING A SHELL COMPANY CALLED INFINITE SOLUTIONS. HUBRIS.
DID YOU KNOW YOU WORK FOR THE BEYOND CORPORATION?
AT YOUR OTHER SITE, I GOT A TASTE OF YOUR EMPLOYER'S GLUTTONOUS AMBITIONS. IF LEFT UNCHECKED, THEY WILL DEVOUR ALL THAT LAYS BEFORE THEM.
BUT WHAT WILL I FIND WITH THIS NEW ACCESS?
WAAAH!
KRASH!
NO. SPIDER-MAN AND PARKER COULD NOT HAVE BEEN THAT STUPID. THEY ALLOWED BEYOND TO PURCHASE THE REMAINS OF PARKER INDUSTRIES?!
THE COMPANY I BUILT?!?!
YOUR SPIDER-MAN ISN'T SUPERIOR. HE IS A COPY OF THE WORK I DID. AND OTTO OCTAVIUS DOESN'T STAND FOR PLAGIARISM.

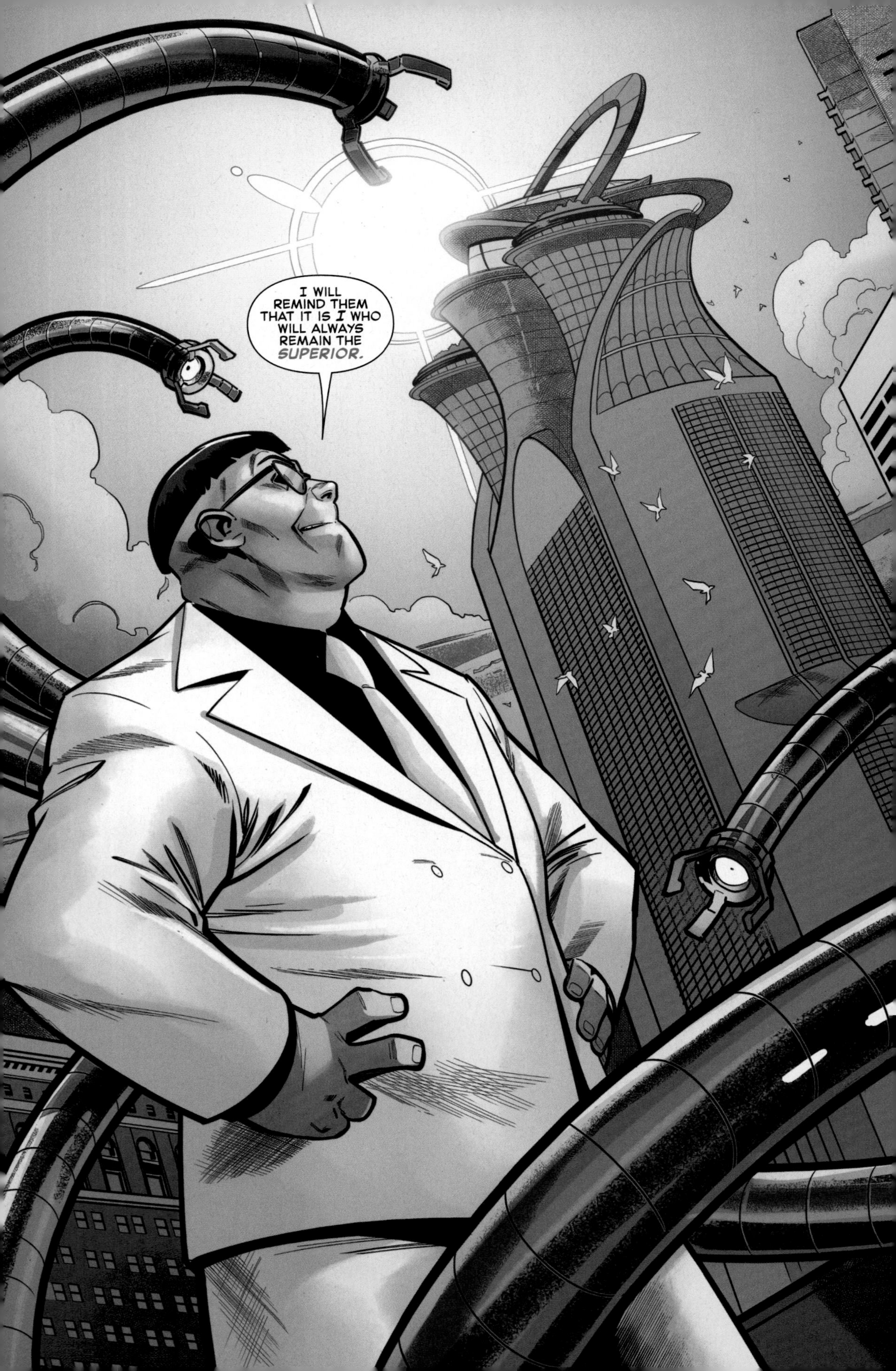
I WILL REMIND THEM THAT IT IS *I* WHO WILL ALWAYS REMAIN THE *SUPERIOR.*

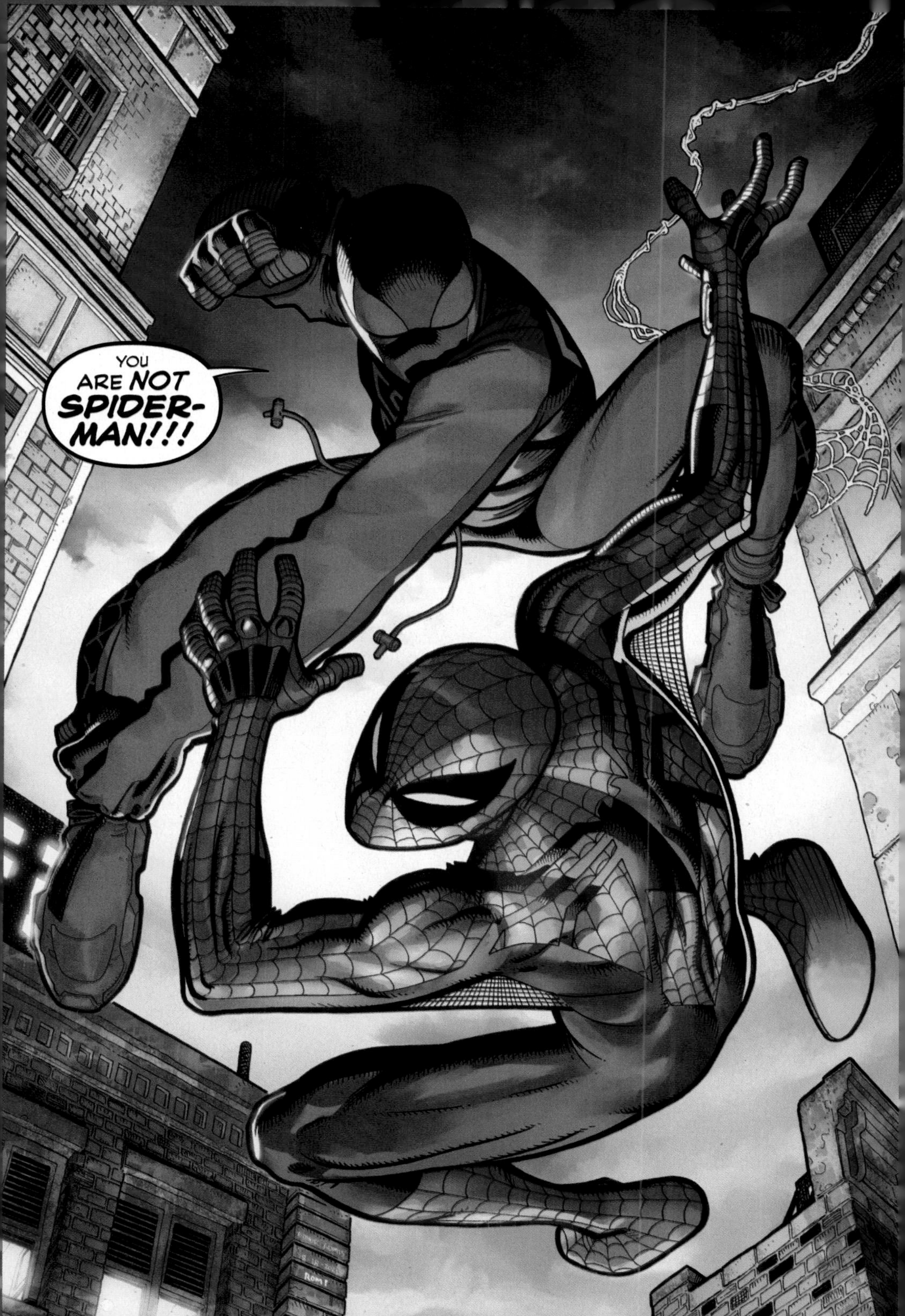
YOU ARE NOT SPIDER-MAN!!!

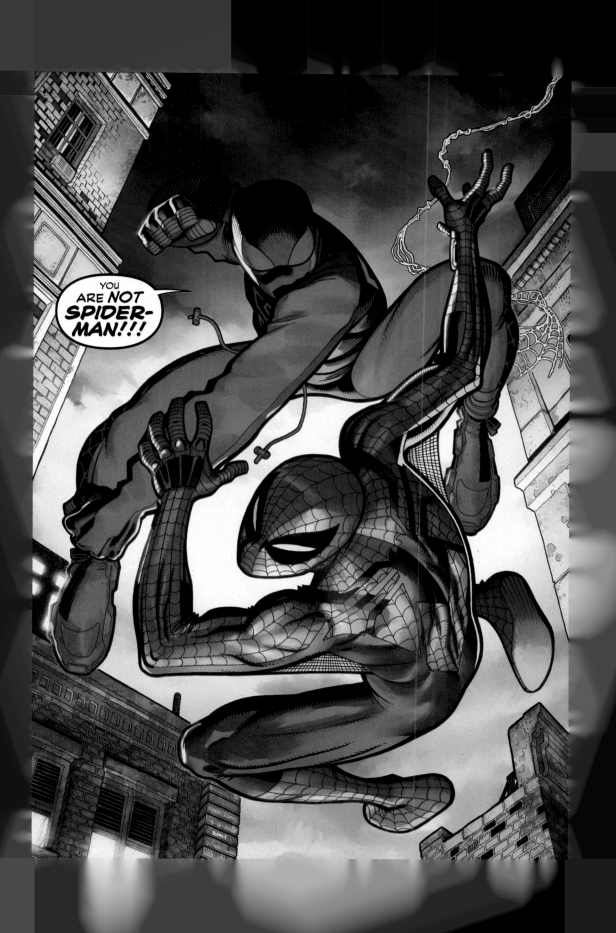

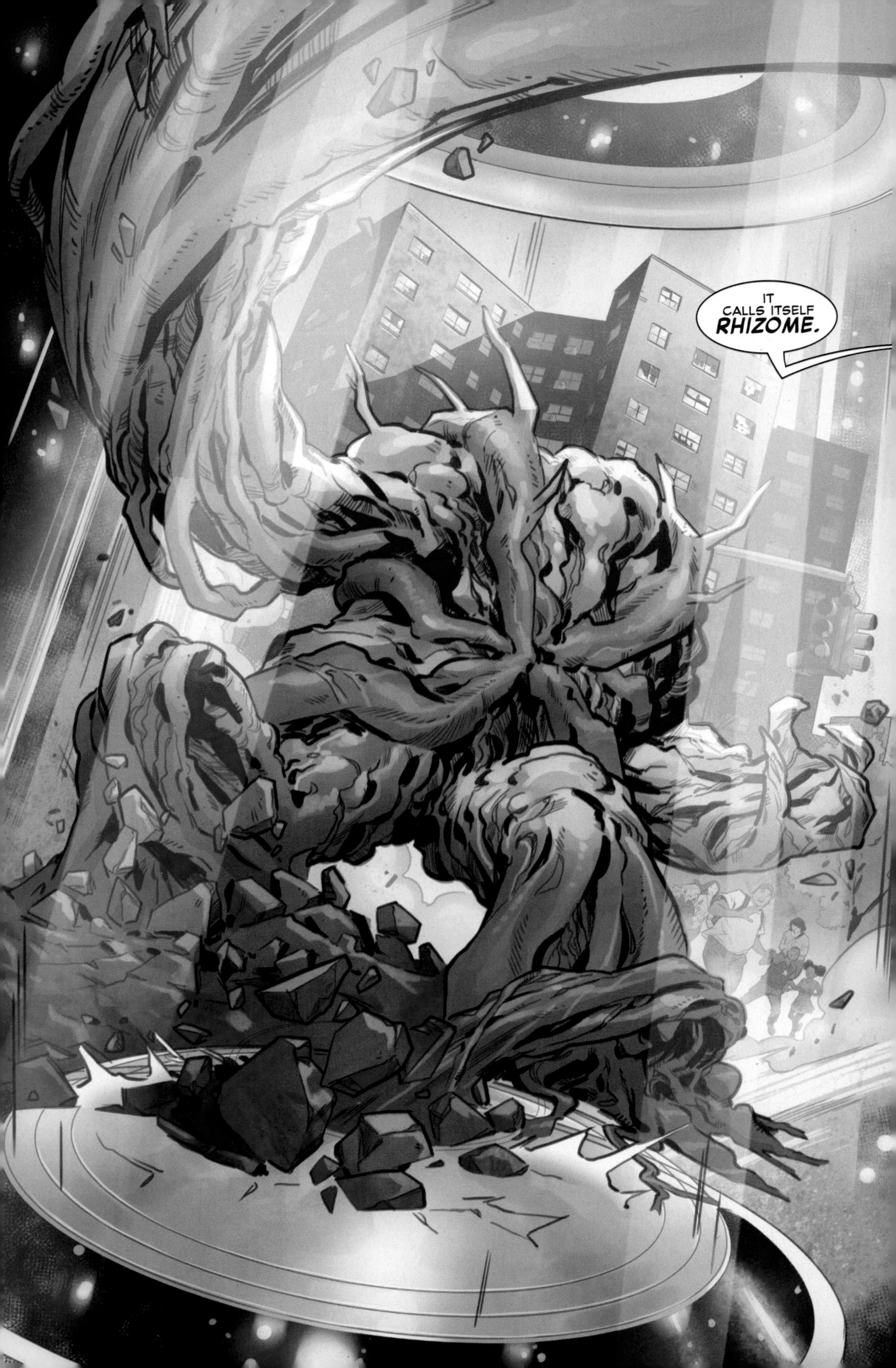
IT CALLS ITSELF RHIZOME.

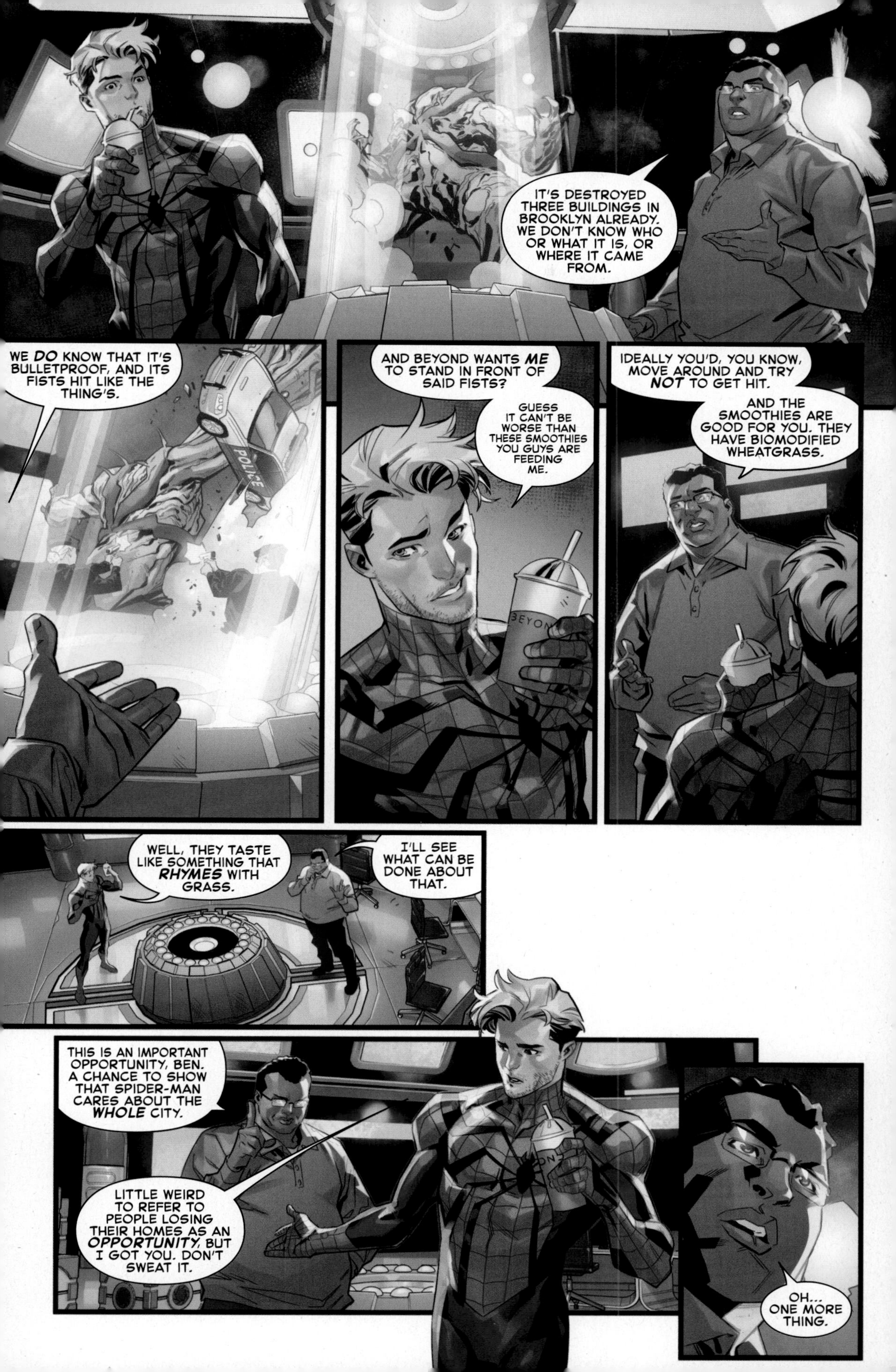

IT'S DESTROYED THREE BUILDINGS IN BROOKLYN ALREADY. WE DON'T KNOW WHO OR WHAT IT IS, OR WHERE IT CAME FROM.
WE DO KNOW THAT IT'S BULLETPROOF, AND ITS FISTS HIT LIKE THE THING'S.
POLICE
AND BEYOND WANTS ME TO STAND IN FRONT OF SAID FISTS?
GUESS IT CAN'T BE WORSE THAN THESE SMOOTHIES YOU GUYS ARE FEEDING ME.
IDEALLY YOU'D, YOU KNOW, MOVE AROUND AND TRY NOT TO GET HIT.
AND THE SMOOTHIES ARE GOOD FOR YOU. THEY HAVE BIOMODIFIED WHEATGRASS.
WELL, THEY TASTE LIKE SOMETHING THAT RHYMES WITH GRASS.
I'LL SEE WHAT CAN BE DONE ABOUT THAT.
THIS IS AN IMPORTANT OPPORTUNITY, BEN. A CHANCE TO SHOW THAT SPIDER-MAN CARES ABOUT THE WHOLE CITY.
LITTLE WEIRD TO REFER TO PEOPLE LOSING THEIR HOMES AS AN OPPORTUNITY, BUT I GOT YOU. DON'T SWEAT IT.
OH... ONE MORE THING.

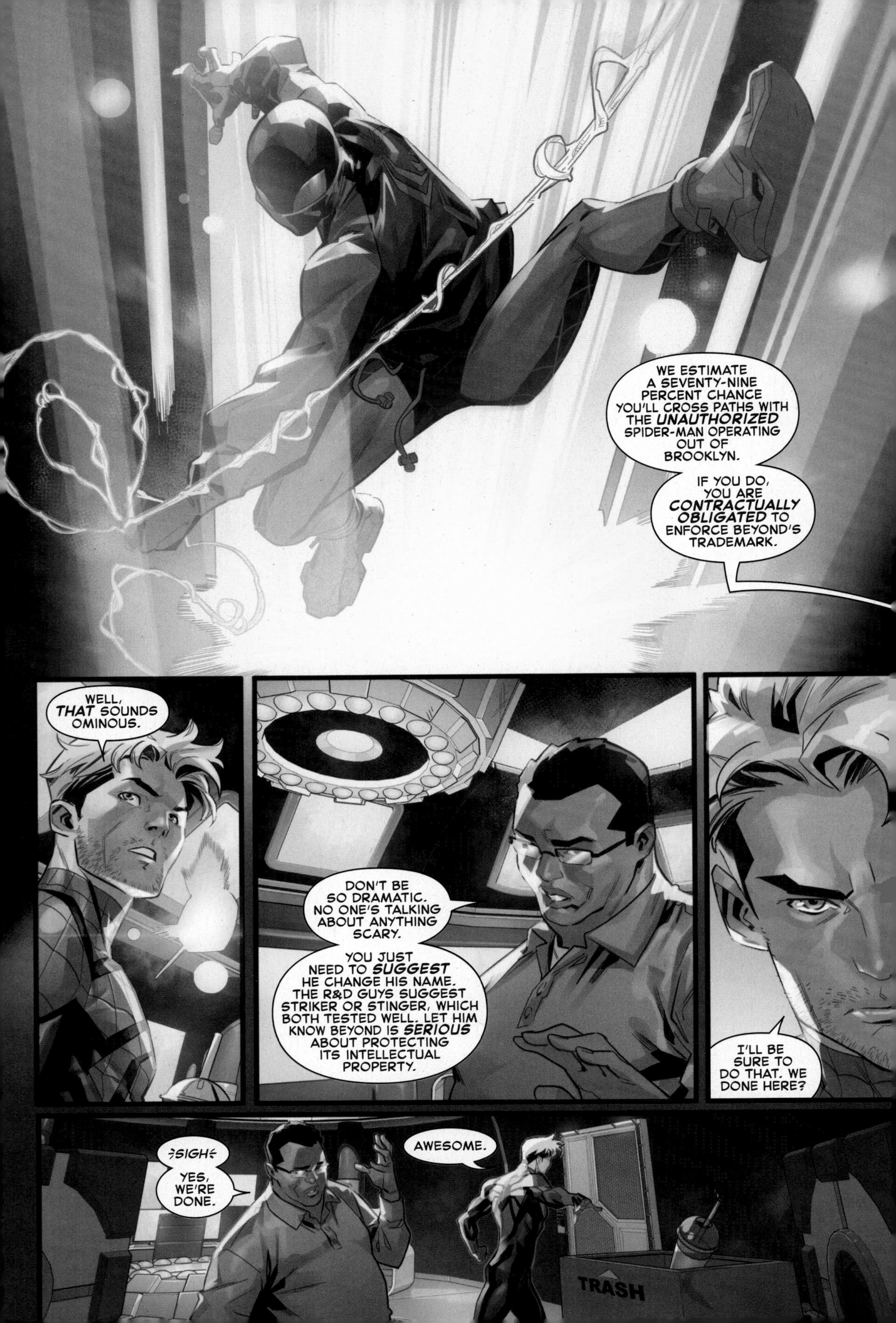
WE ESTIMATE A SEVENTY-NINE PERCENT CHANCE YOU'LL CROSS PATHS WITH THE UNAUTHORIZED SPIDER-MAN OPERATING OUT OF BROOKLYN.
IF YOU DO, YOU ARE CONTRACTUALLY OBLIGATED TO ENFORCE BEYOND'S TRADEMARK.
WELL, THAT SOUNDS OMINOUS.
DON'T BE SO DRAMATIC. NO ONE'S TALKING ABOUT ANYTHING SCARY.
YOU JUST NEED TO SUGGEST HE CHANGE HIS NAME. THE R&D GUYS SUGGEST STRIKER OR STINGER, WHICH BOTH TESTED WELL. LET HIM KNOW BEYOND IS SERIOUS ABOUT PROTECTING ITS INTELLECTUAL PROPERTY.
I'LL BE SURE TO DO THAT. WE DONE HERE?
SIGH
YES, WE'RE DONE.
AWESOME.
TRASH

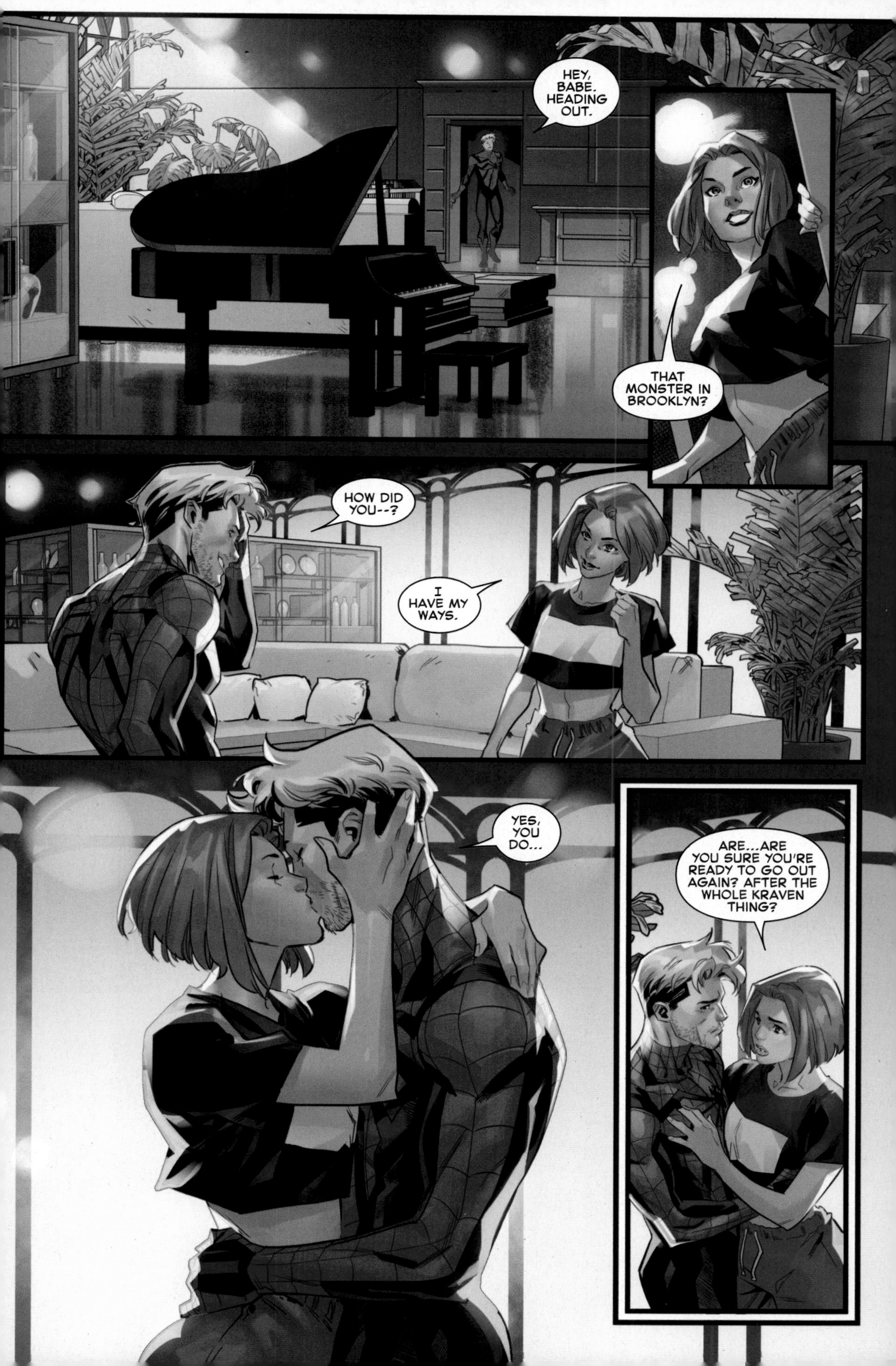
HEY, BABE. HEADING OUT.
THAT MONSTER IN BROOKLYN?
HOW DID YOU--?
I HAVE MY WAYS.
YES, YOU DO...
ARE...ARE YOU SURE YOU'RE READY TO GO OUT AGAIN? AFTER THE WHOLE KRAVEN THING?

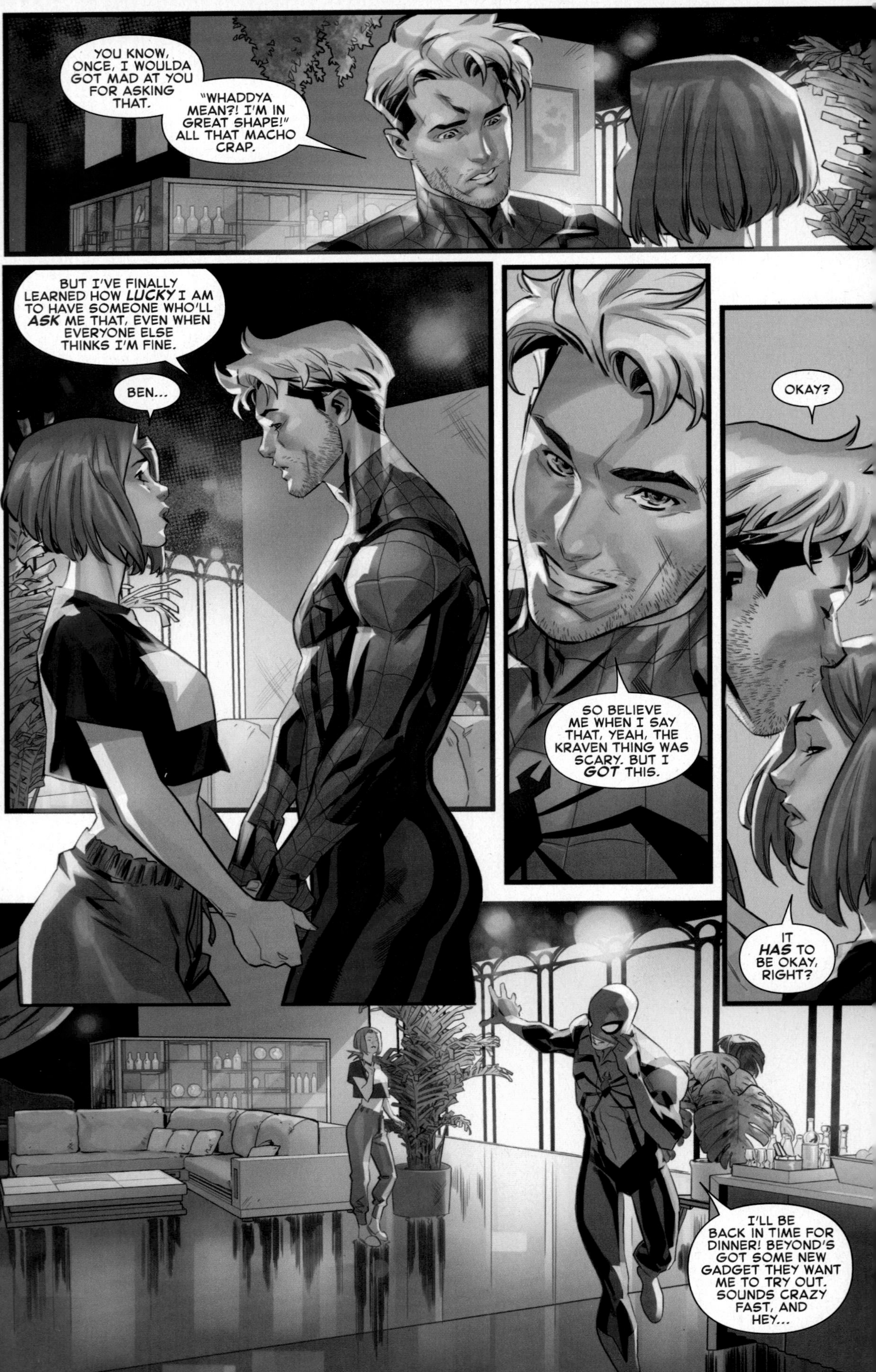
YOU KNOW, ONCE, I WOULDA GOT MAD AT YOU FOR ASKING THAT.
"WHADDYA MEAN?! I'M IN GREAT SHAPE!" ALL THAT MACHO CRAP.
BUT I'VE FINALLY LEARNED HOW LUCKY I AM TO HAVE SOMEONE WHO'LL ASK ME THAT, EVEN WHEN EVERYONE ELSE THINKS I'M FINE.
BEN...
SO BELIEVE ME WHEN I SAY THAT, YEAH, THE KRAVEN THING WAS SCARY. BUT I GOT THIS.
OKAY?
IT HAS TO BE OKAY, RIGHT?
I'LL BE BACK IN TIME FOR DINNER! BEYOND'S GOT SOME NEW GADGET THEY WANT ME TO TRY OUT. SOUNDS CRAZY FAST, AND HEY...

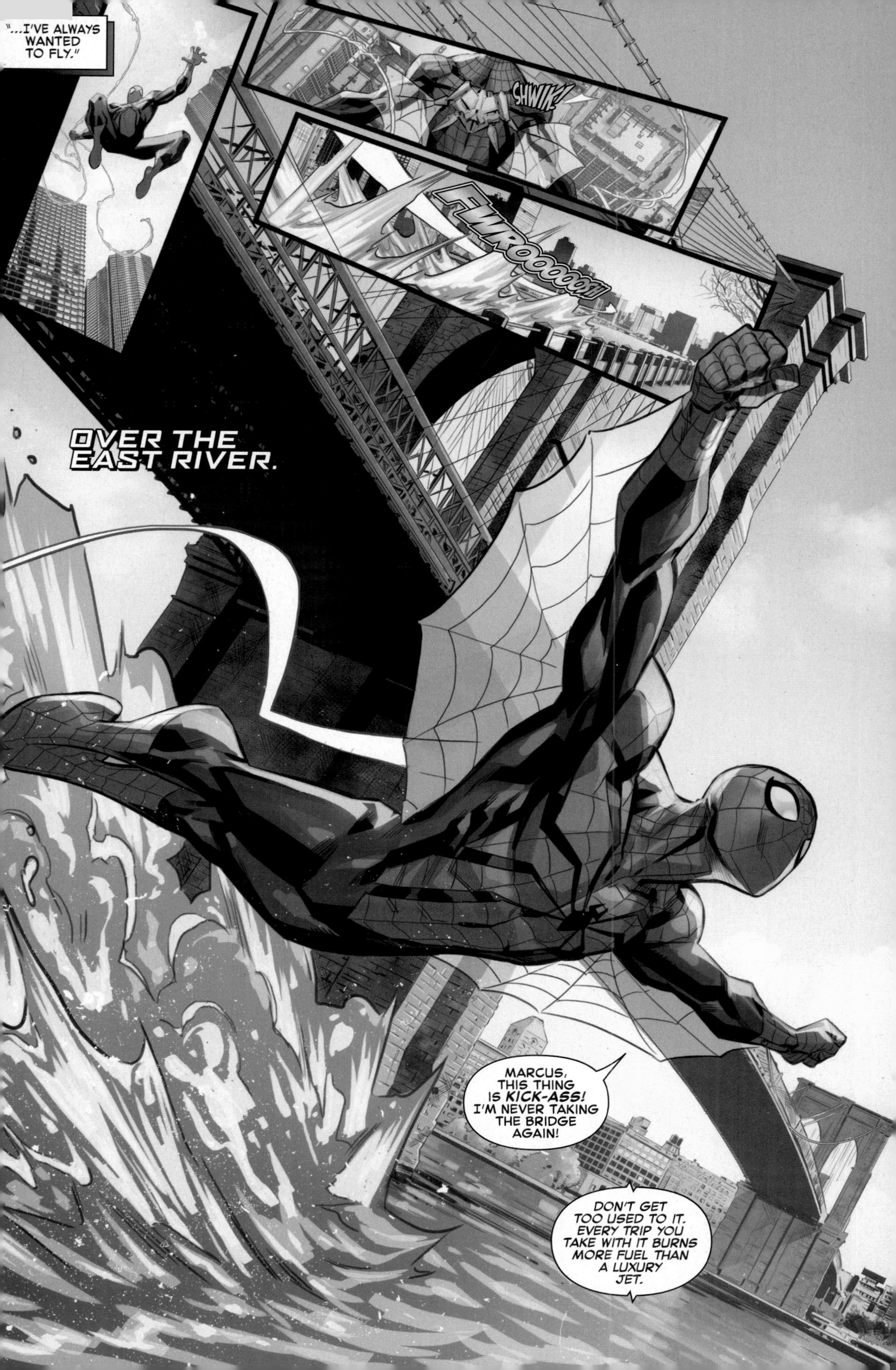
"...I'VE ALWAYS WANTED TO FLY."
SHWIK!
FWROOOOOSH!
OVER THE EAST RIVER.
MARCUS, THIS THING IS KICK-ASS! I'M NEVER TAKING THE BRIDGE AGAIN!
DON'T GET TOO USED TO IT. EVERY TRIP YOU TAKE WITH IT BURNS MORE FUEL THAN A LUXURY JET.

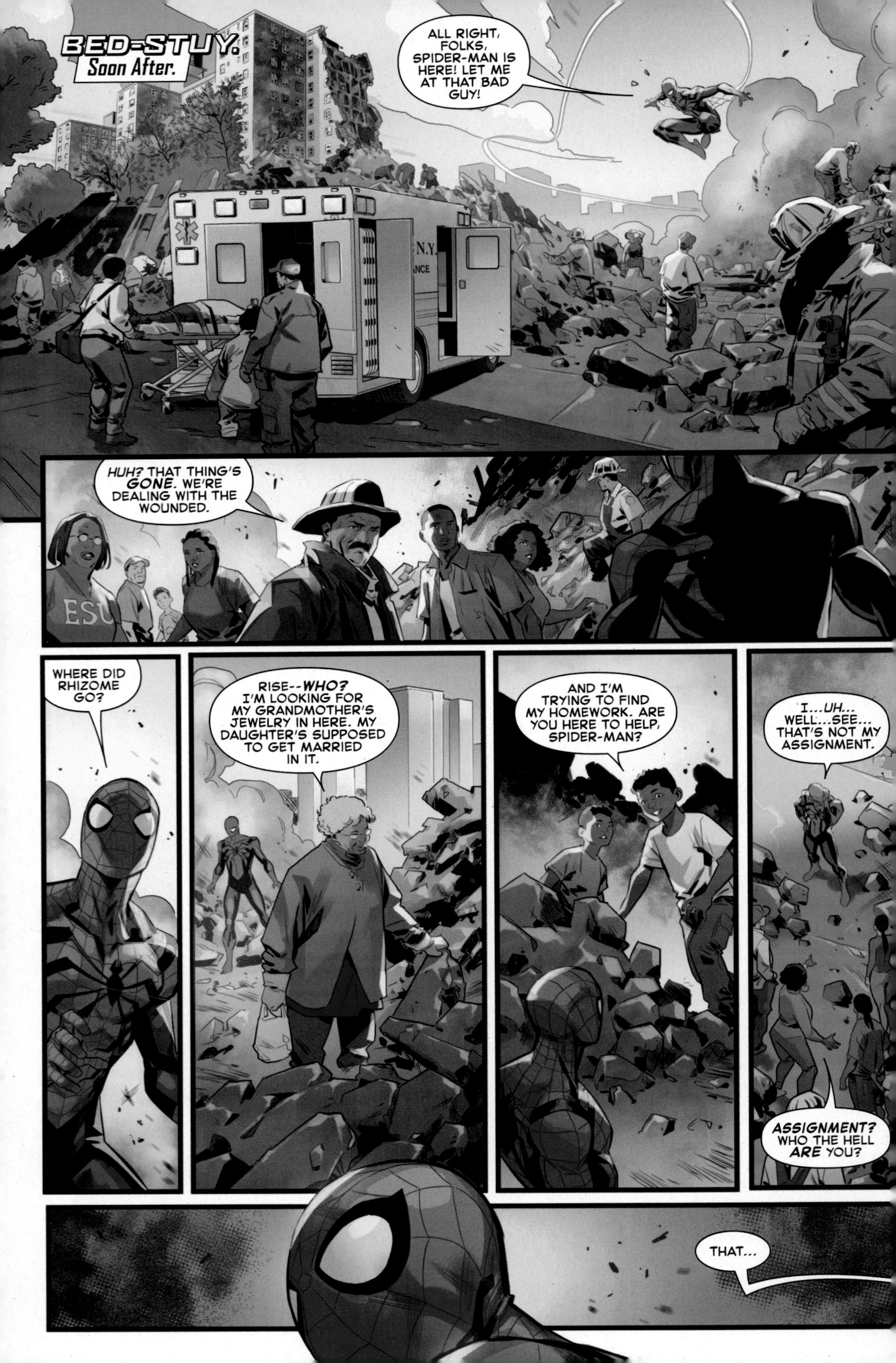
BED-STUY. Soon After.
ALL RIGHT, FOLKS, SPIDER-MAN IS HERE! LET ME AT THAT BAD GUY!
N.Y.
HUH? THAT THING'S GONE. WE'RE DEALING WITH THE WOUNDED.
ESU
WHERE DID RHIZOME GO?
RISE--WHO? I'M LOOKING FOR MY GRANDMOTHER'S JEWELRY IN HERE. MY DAUGHTER'S SUPPOSED TO GET MARRIED IN IT.
AND I'M TRYING TO FIND MY HOMEWORK. ARE YOU HERE TO HELP, SPIDER-MAN?
I...UH... WELL...SEE... THAT'S NOT MY ASSIGNMENT.
ASSIGNMENT? WHO THE HELL ARE YOU?
THAT...

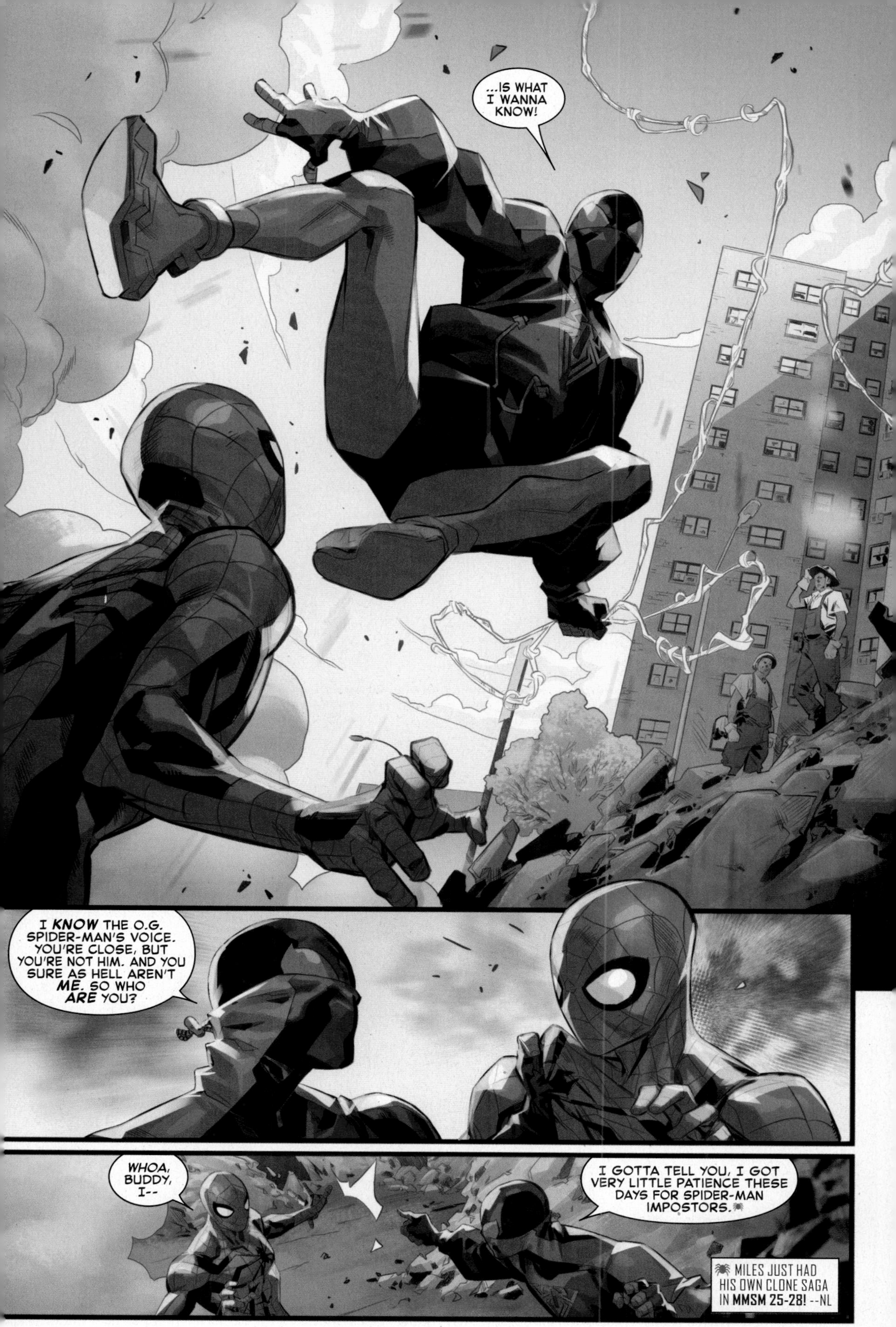
...IS WHAT I WANNA KNOW!
I KNOW THE O.G. SPIDER-MAN'S VOICE. YOU'RE CLOSE, BUT YOU'RE NOT HIM. AND YOU SURE AS HELL AREN'T ME. SO WHO ARE YOU?
WHOA, BUDDY, I--
I GOTTA TELL YOU, I GOT VERY LITTLE PATIENCE THESE DAYS FOR SPIDER-MAN IMPOSTORS.
MILES JUST HAD HIS OWN CLONE SAGA IN MMSM 25-28! --NL

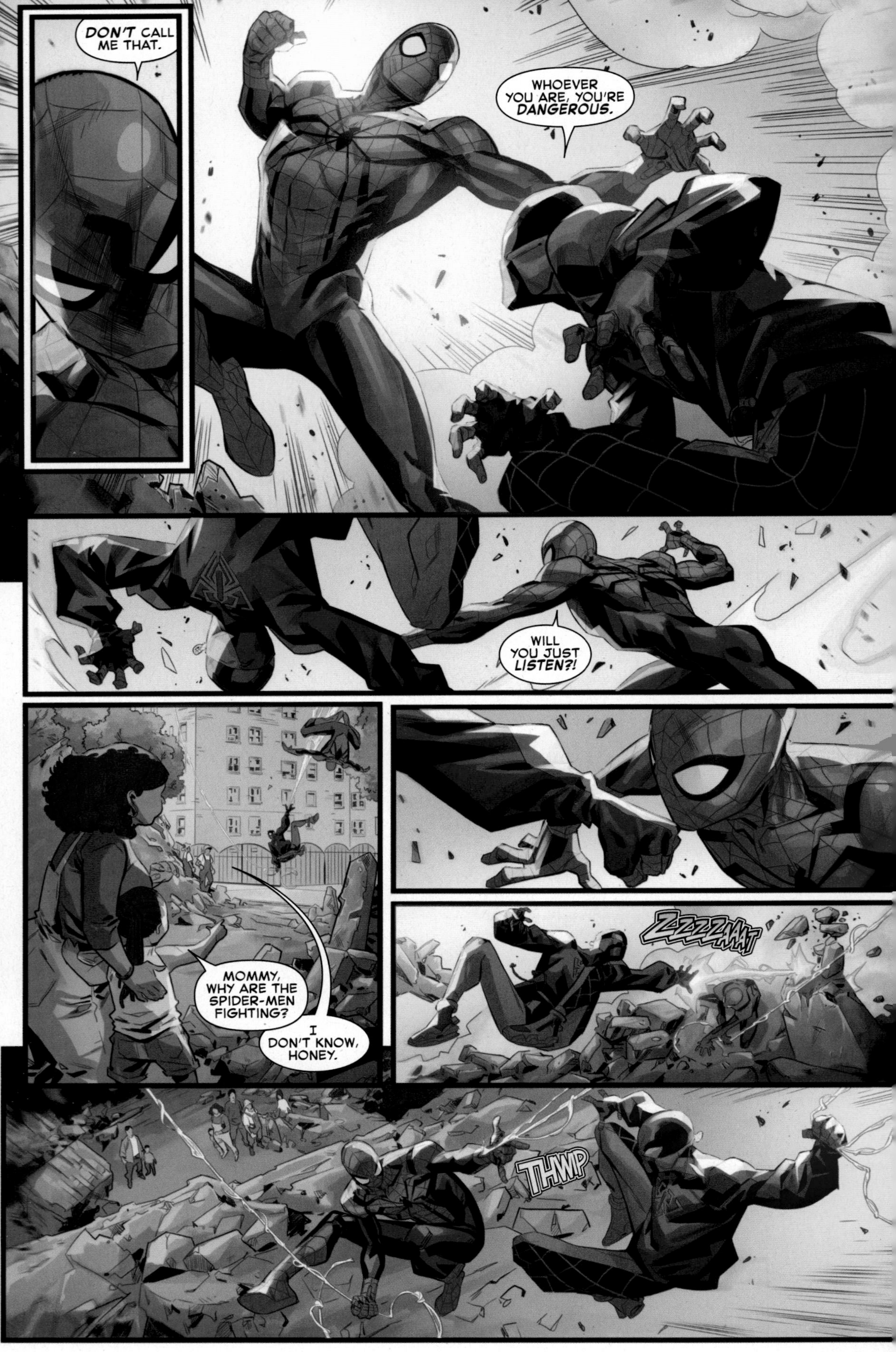
DON'T CALL ME THAT.
WHOEVER YOU ARE, YOU'RE DANGEROUS.
WILL YOU JUST LISTEN?!
MOMMY, WHY ARE THE SPIDER-MEN FIGHTING?
I DON'T KNOW, HONEY.
ZZZZAAAT
THWIP

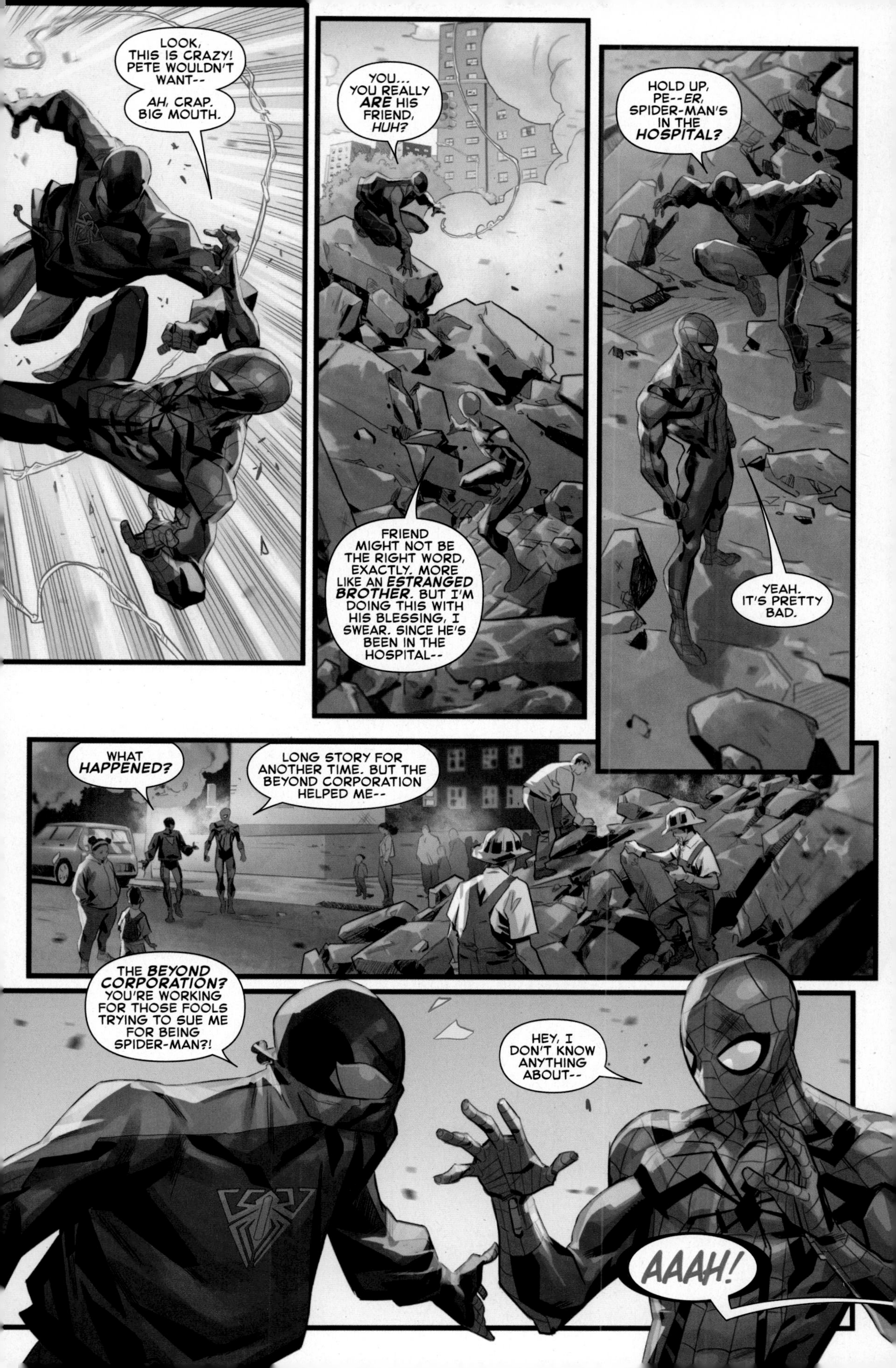
LOOK, THIS IS CRAZY! PETE WOULDN'T WANT--
AH, CRAP. BIG MOUTH.
YOU... YOU REALLY ARE HIS FRIEND, HUH?
FRIEND MIGHT NOT BE THE RIGHT WORD, EXACTLY. MORE LIKE AN ESTRANGED BROTHER. BUT I'M DOING THIS WITH HIS BLESSING, I SWEAR. SINCE HE'S BEEN IN THE HOSPITAL--
HOLD UP, PE--ER, SPIDER-MAN'S IN THE HOSPITAL?
YEAH. IT'S PRETTY BAD.
WHAT HAPPENED?
LONG STORY FOR ANOTHER TIME. BUT THE BEYOND CORPORATION HELPED ME--
THE BEYOND CORPORATION? YOU'RE WORKING FOR THOSE FOOLS TRYING TO SUE ME FOR BEING SPIDER-MAN?!
HEY, I DON'T KNOW ANYTHING ABOUT--
AAAH!

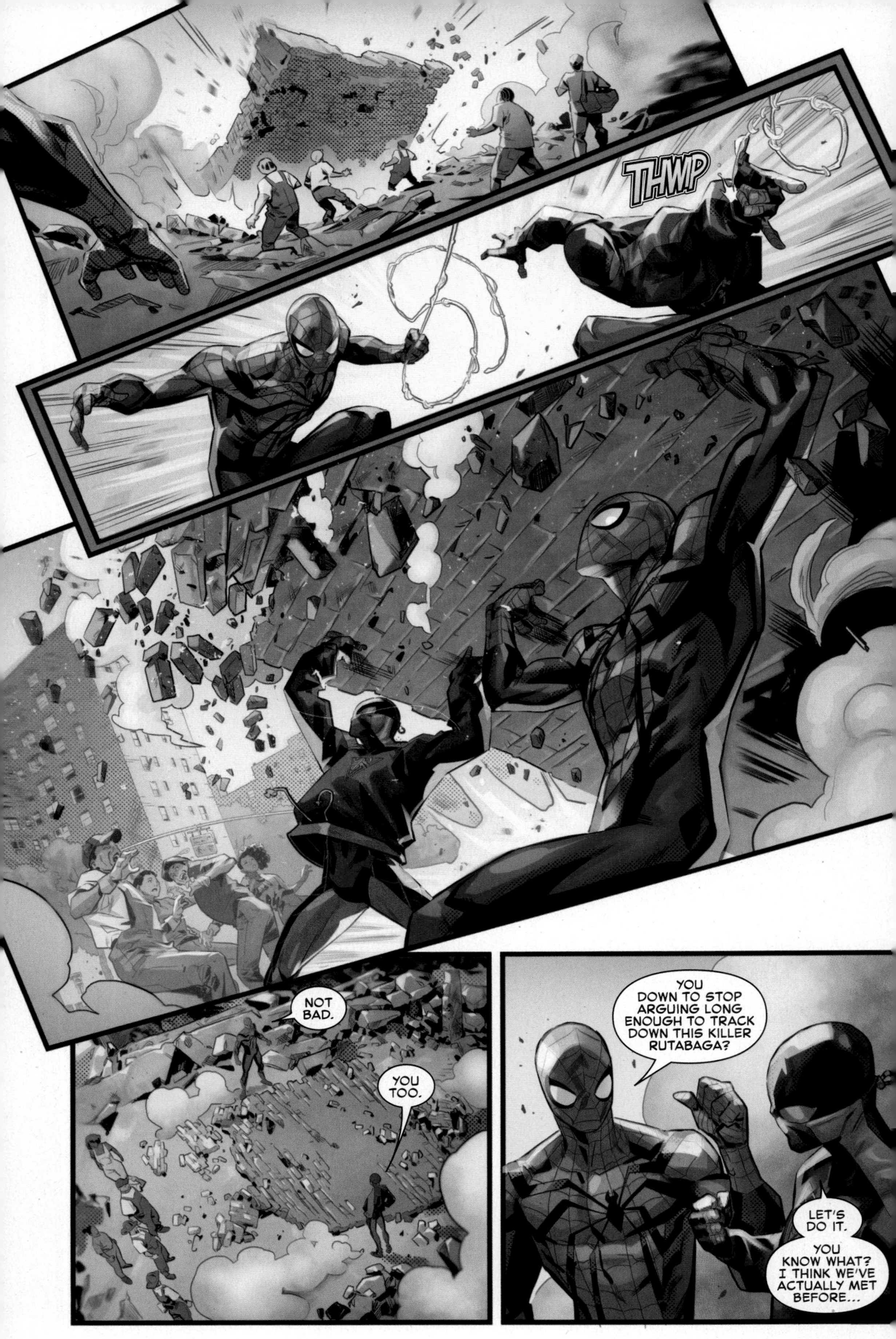
THWIP
NOT BAD.
YOU TOO.
YOU DOWN TO STOP ARGUING LONG ENOUGH TO TRACK DOWN THIS KILLER RUTABAGA?
LET'S DO IT.
YOU KNOW WHAT? I THINK WE'VE ACTUALLY MET BEFORE...

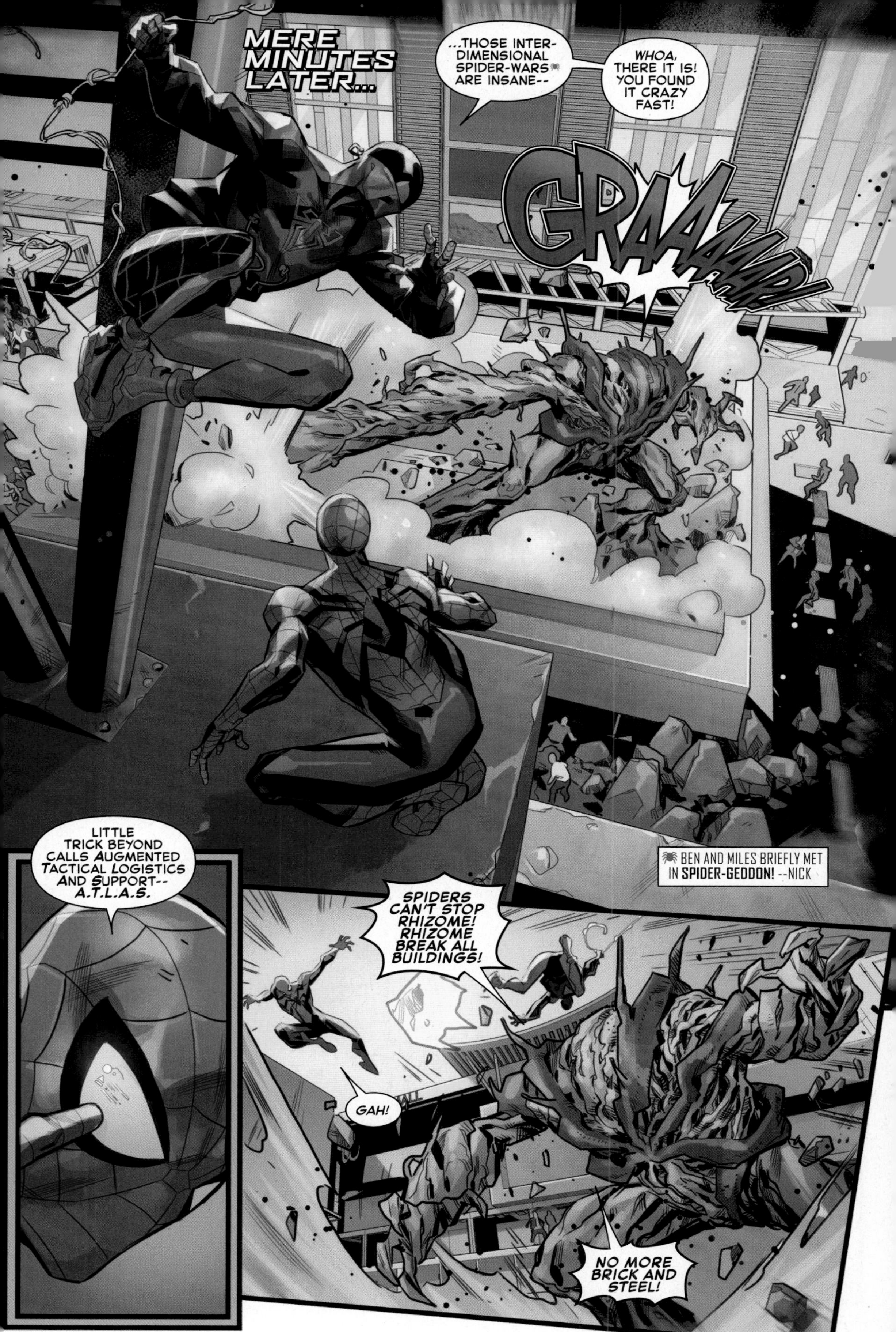
MERE MINUTES LATER...
...THOSE INTER-DIMENSIONAL SPIDER-WARS ARE INSANE--
WHOA, THERE IT IS! YOU FOUND IT CRAZY FAST!
GRAAAAAR!
LITTLE TRICK BEYOND CALLS AUGMENTED TACTICAL LOGISTICS AND SUPPORT-- A.T.L.A.S.
BEN AND MILES BRIEFLY MET IN SPIDER-GEDDON! --NICK
SPIDERS CAN'T STOP RHIZOME! RHIZOME BREAK ALL BUILDINGS!
GAH!
NO MORE BRICK AND STEEL!

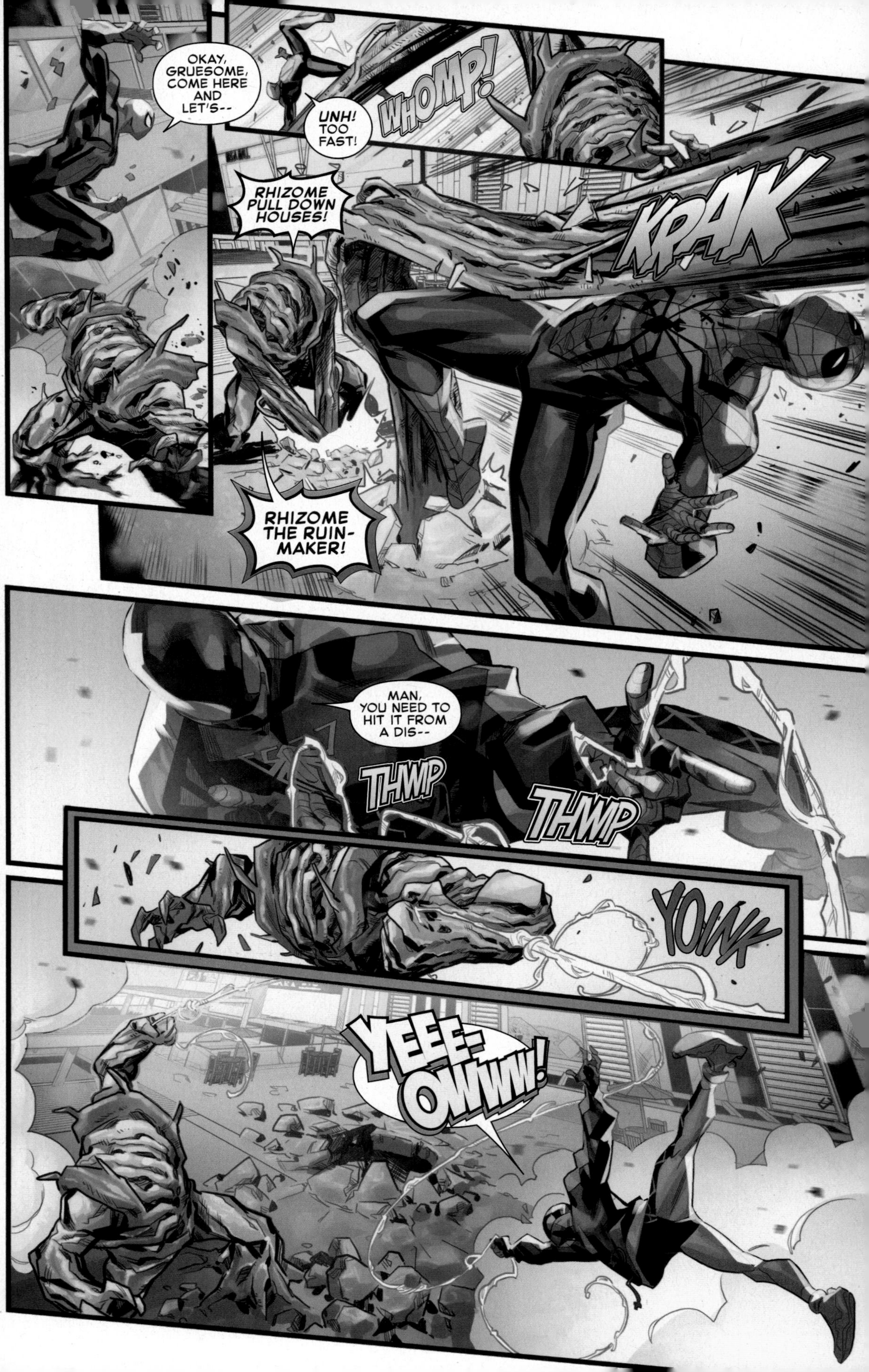
OKAY, GRUESOME, COME HERE AND LET'S--
WHOMP!
UNH! TOO FAST!
RHIZOME PULL DOWN HOUSES!
KRAK
RHIZOME THE RUIN-MAKER!
MAN, YOU NEED TO HIT IT FROM A DIS--
THWIP
THWIP
YOINK
YEEE-OWWW!

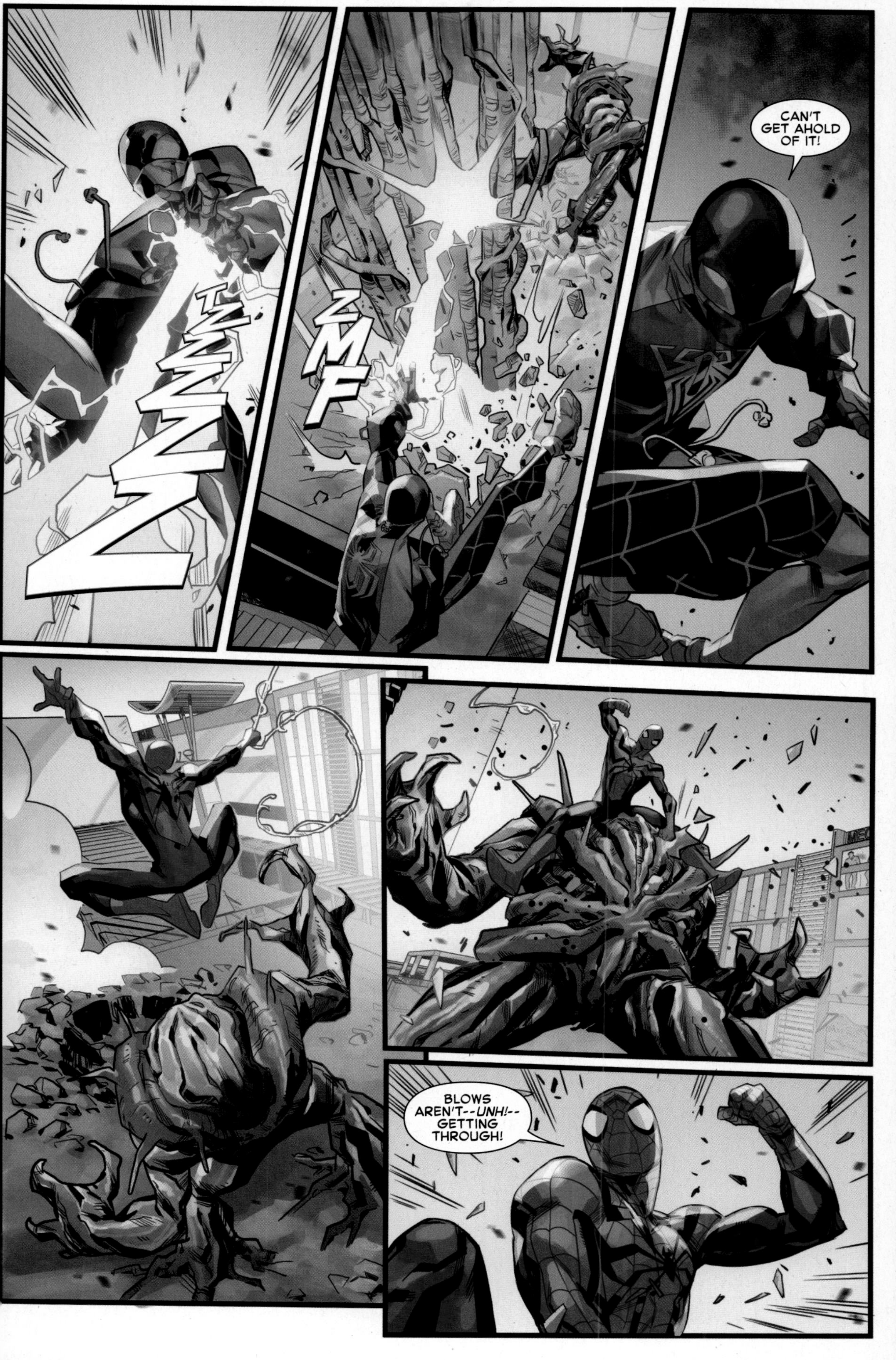
ZZZWWMMM
ZMF
CAN'T GET AHOLD OF IT!
BLOWS AREN'T--UNH!--GETTING THROUGH!

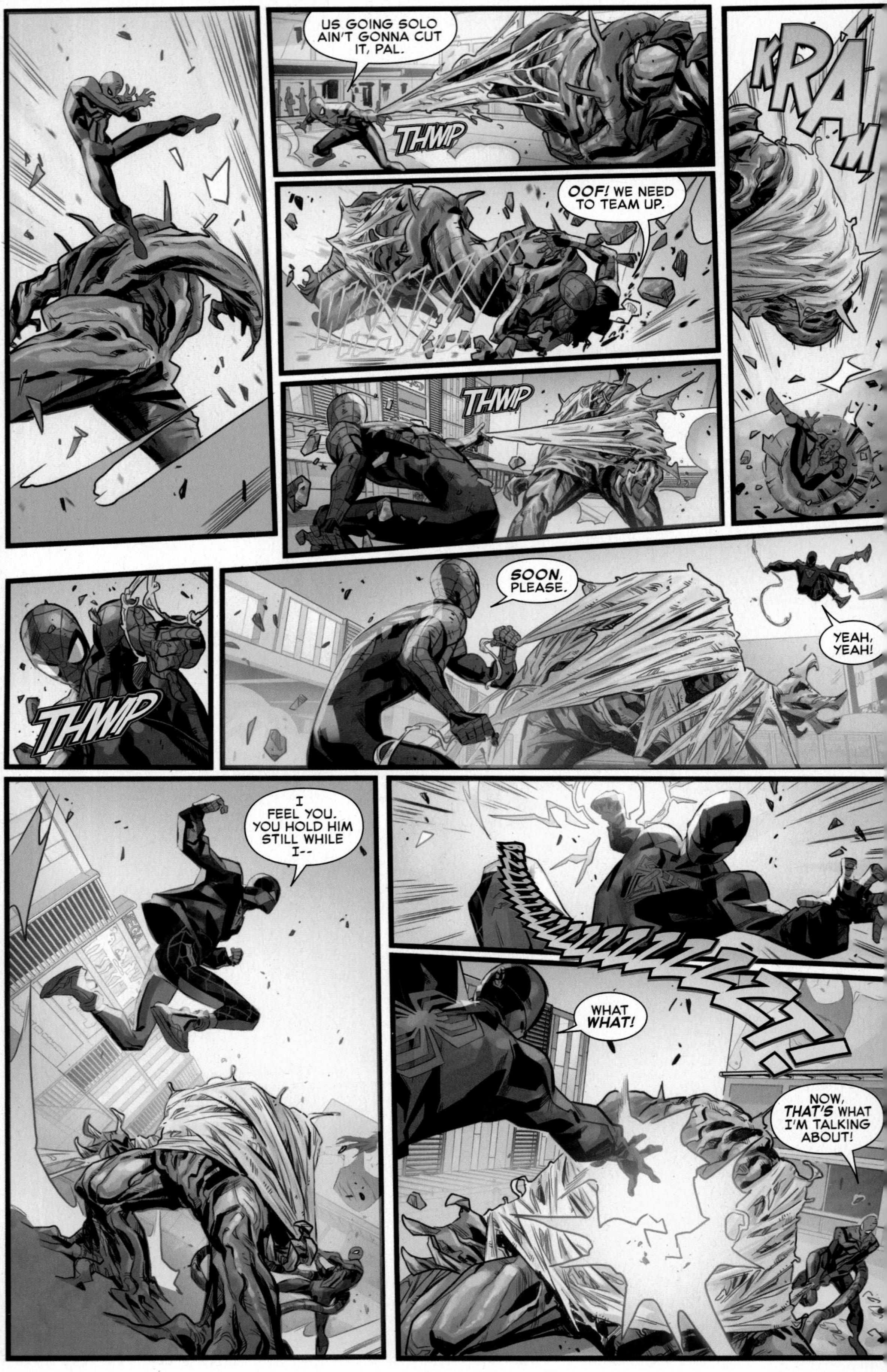

US GOING SOLO AIN'T GONNA CUT IT, PAL.
THWIP
OOF! WE NEED TO TEAM UP.
THWIP
KRAM
THWIP
SOON, PLEASE.
YEAH, YEAH!
I FEEL YOU. YOU HOLD HIM STILL WHILE I--
WHAT WHAT!
NOW, THAT'S WHAT I'M TALKING ABOUT!

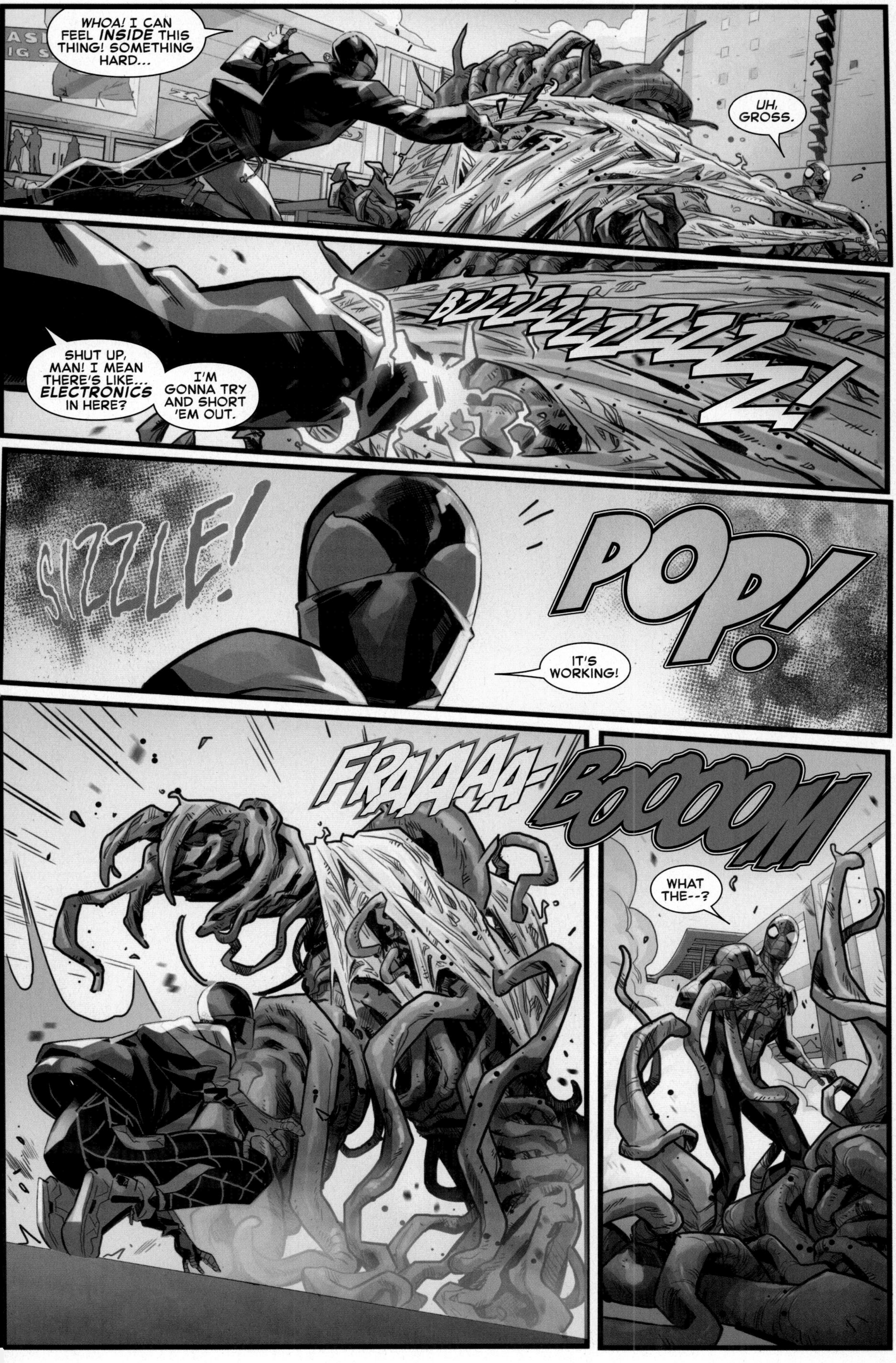

WHOA! I CAN FEEL INSIDE THIS THING! SOMETHING HARD...
UH, GROSS.
SHUT UP, MAN! I MEAN THERE'S LIKE... ELECTRONICS IN HERE?
I'M GONNA TRY AND SHORT 'EM OUT.
BZZZZZZZZZZZZZ!
SIZZLE!
POP!
IT'S WORKING!
FRAAAA-BOOOOM
WHAT THE--?

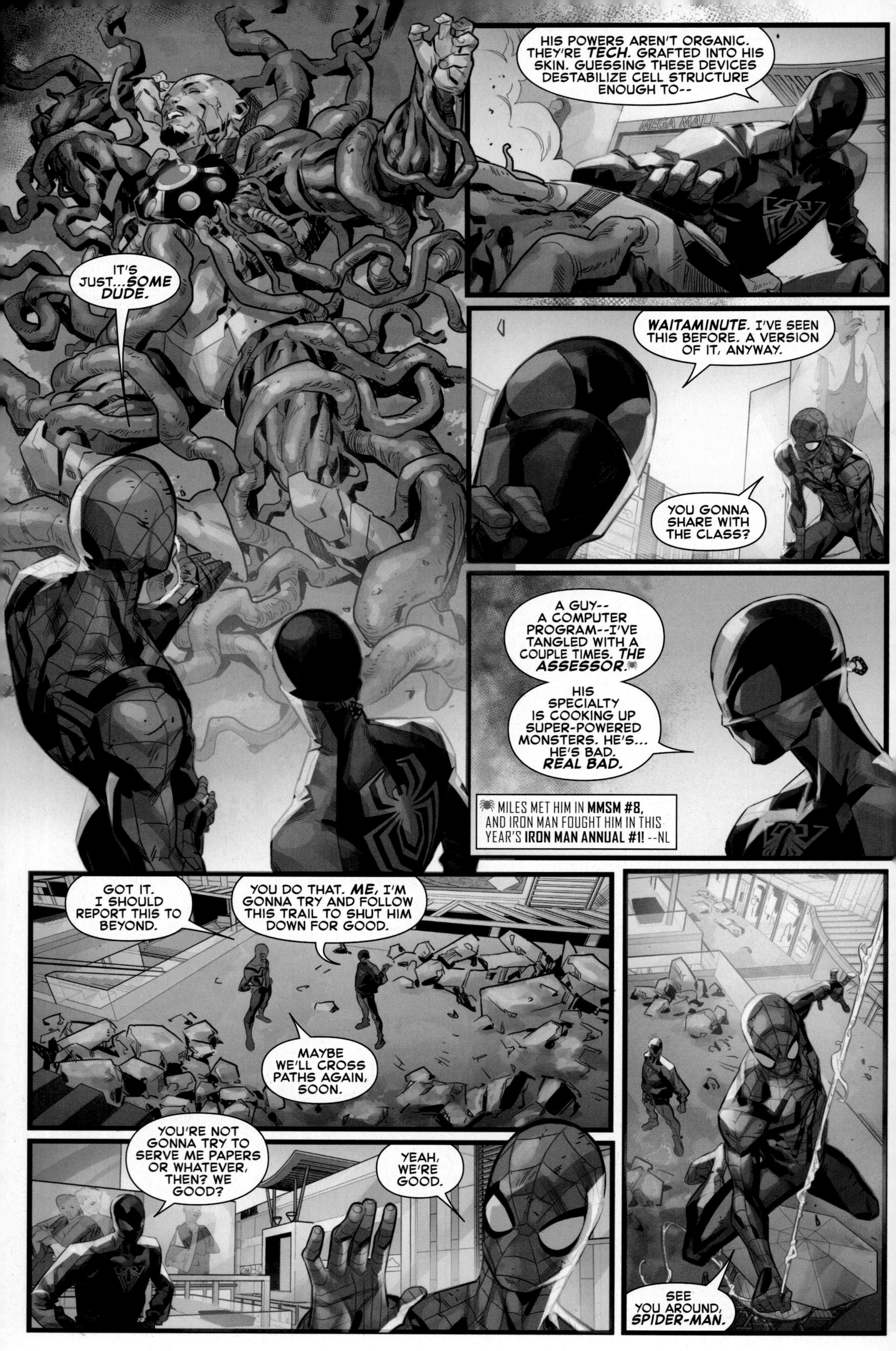
IT'S JUST...SOME DUDE.
HIS POWERS AREN'T ORGANIC. THEY'RE TECH. GRAFTED INTO HIS SKIN. GUESSING THESE DEVICES DESTABILIZE CELL STRUCTURE ENOUGH TO--
MEGA MALL
WAITAMINUTE. I'VE SEEN THIS BEFORE. A VERSION OF IT, ANYWAY.
YOU GONNA SHARE WITH THE CLASS?
A GUY-- A COMPUTER PROGRAM--I'VE TANGLED WITH A COUPLE TIMES. THE ASSESSOR.
HIS SPECIALTY IS COOKING UP SUPER-POWERED MONSTERS. HE'S... HE'S BAD. REAL BAD.
MILES MET HIM IN MMSM #8, AND IRON MAN FOUGHT HIM IN THIS YEAR'S IRON MAN ANNUAL #1! --NL
GOT IT. I SHOULD REPORT THIS TO BEYOND.
YOU DO THAT. ME, I'M GONNA TRY AND FOLLOW THIS TRAIL TO SHUT HIM DOWN FOR GOOD.
MAYBE WE'LL CROSS PATHS AGAIN, SOON.
YOU'RE NOT GONNA TRY TO SERVE ME PAPERS OR WHATEVER, THEN? WE GOOD?
YEAH, WE'RE GOOD.
SEE YOU AROUND, SPIDER-MAN.

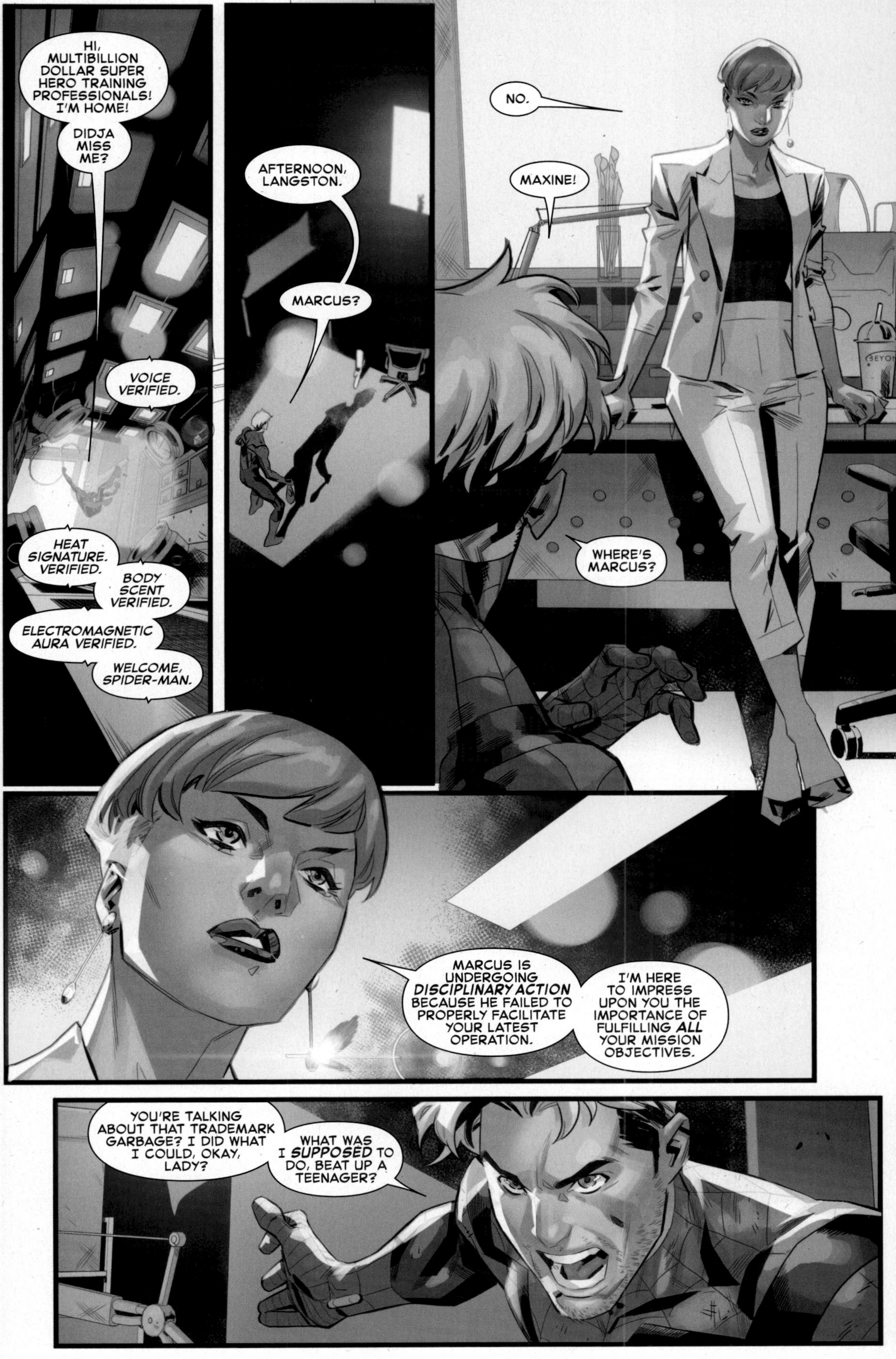
HI, MULTIBILLION DOLLAR SUPER HERO TRAINING PROFESSIONALS! I'M HOME!
DIDJA MISS ME?
VOICE VERIFIED.
HEAT SIGNATURE. VERIFIED.
BODY SCENT VERIFIED.
ELECTROMAGNETIC AURA VERIFIED.
WELCOME, SPIDER-MAN.
AFTERNOON, LANGSTON.
MARCUS?
NO.
MAXINE!
WHERE'S MARCUS?
MARCUS IS UNDERGOING *DISCIPLINARY ACTION* BECAUSE HE FAILED TO PROPERLY FACILITATE YOUR LATEST OPERATION.
I'M HERE TO IMPRESS UPON YOU THE IMPORTANCE OF FULFILLING *ALL* YOUR MISSION OBJECTIVES.
YOU'RE TALKING ABOUT THAT TRADEMARK GARBAGE? I DID WHAT I COULD, OKAY, LADY?
WHAT WAS I *SUPPOSED* TO DO, BEAT UP A TEENAGER?

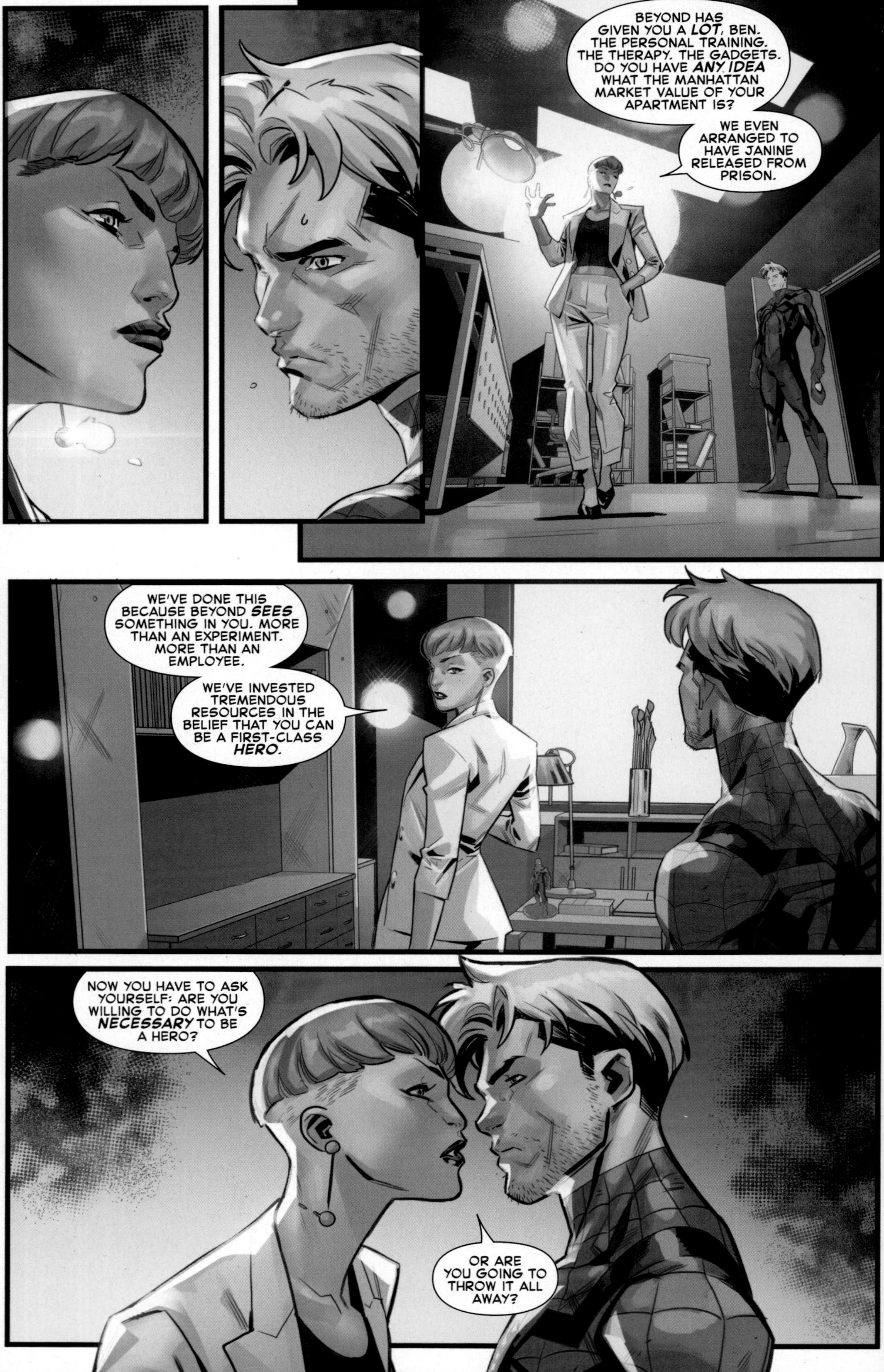

BEYOND HAS GIVEN YOU A LOT, BEN. THE PERSONAL TRAINING. THE THERAPY. THE GADGETS. DO YOU HAVE ANY IDEA WHAT THE MANHATTAN MARKET VALUE OF YOUR APARTMENT IS?
WE EVEN ARRANGED TO HAVE JANINE RELEASED FROM PRISON.
WE'VE DONE THIS BECAUSE BEYOND SEES SOMETHING IN YOU. MORE THAN AN EXPERIMENT. MORE THAN AN EMPLOYEE.
WE'VE INVESTED TREMENDOUS RESOURCES IN THE BELIEF THAT YOU CAN BE A FIRST-CLASS HERO.
NOW YOU HAVE TO ASK YOURSELF: ARE YOU WILLING TO DO WHAT'S NECESSARY TO BE A HERO?
OR ARE YOU GOING TO THROW IT ALL AWAY?

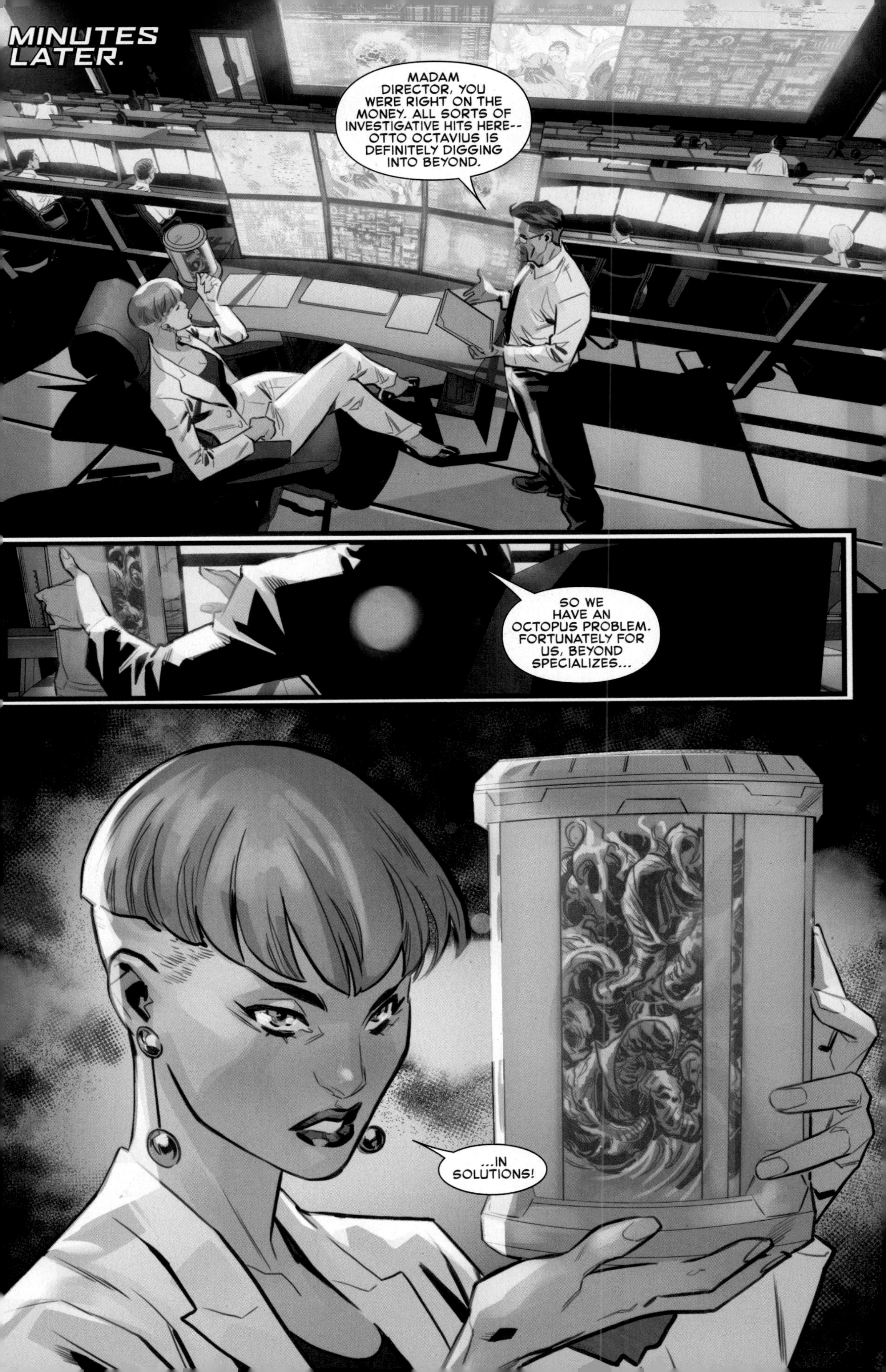
MINUTES LATER.
MADAM DIRECTOR, YOU WERE RIGHT ON THE MONEY. ALL SORTS OF INVESTIGATIVE HITS HERE--OTTO OCTAVIUS IS DEFINITELY DIGGING INTO BEYOND.
SO WE HAVE AN OCTOPUS PROBLEM. FORTUNATELY FOR US, BEYOND SPECIALIZES...
...IN SOLUTIONS!

BEYOND CORPORATION #82

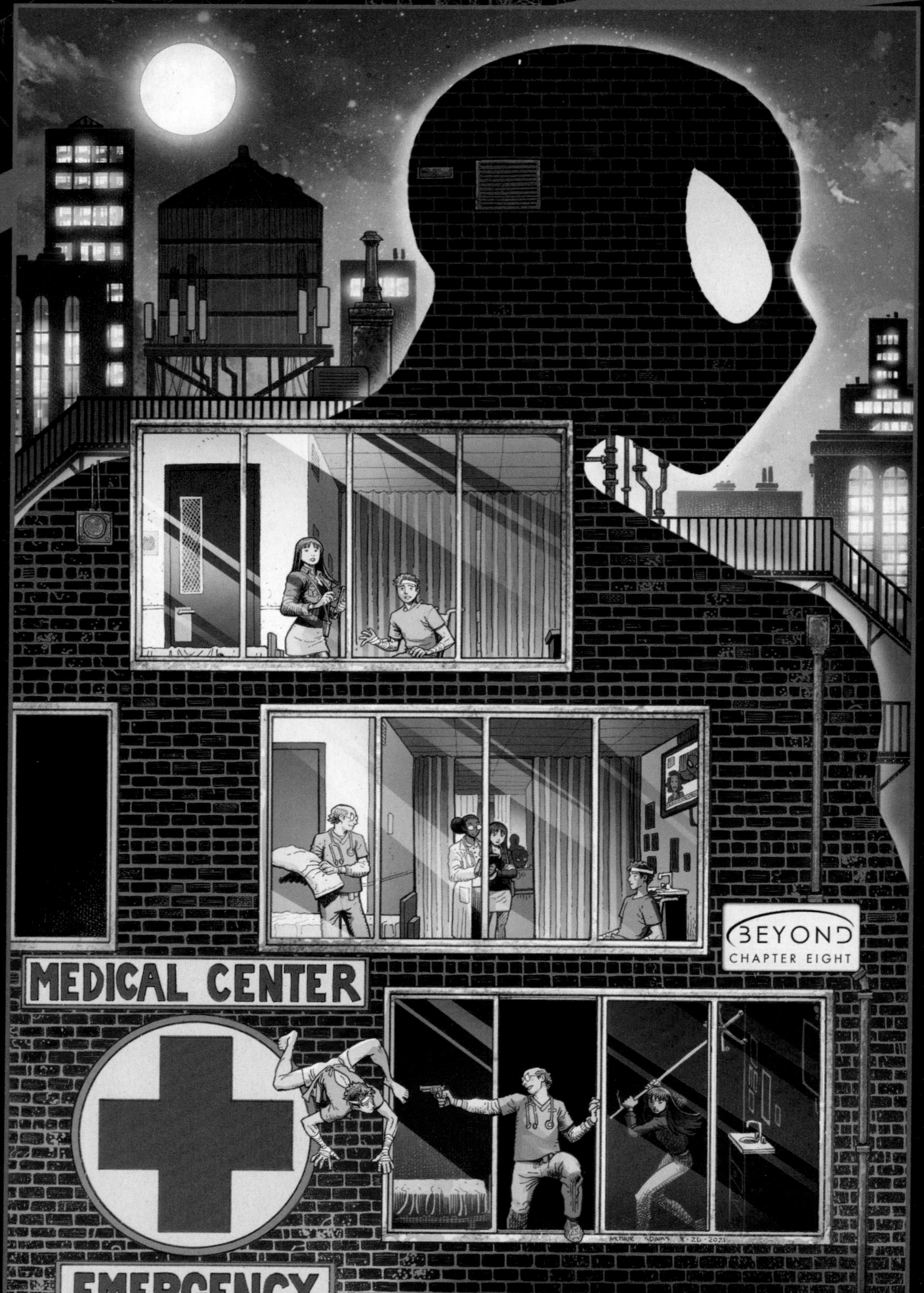

BEYOND
CHAPTER EIGHT
MEDICAL CENTER
EMERGENCY

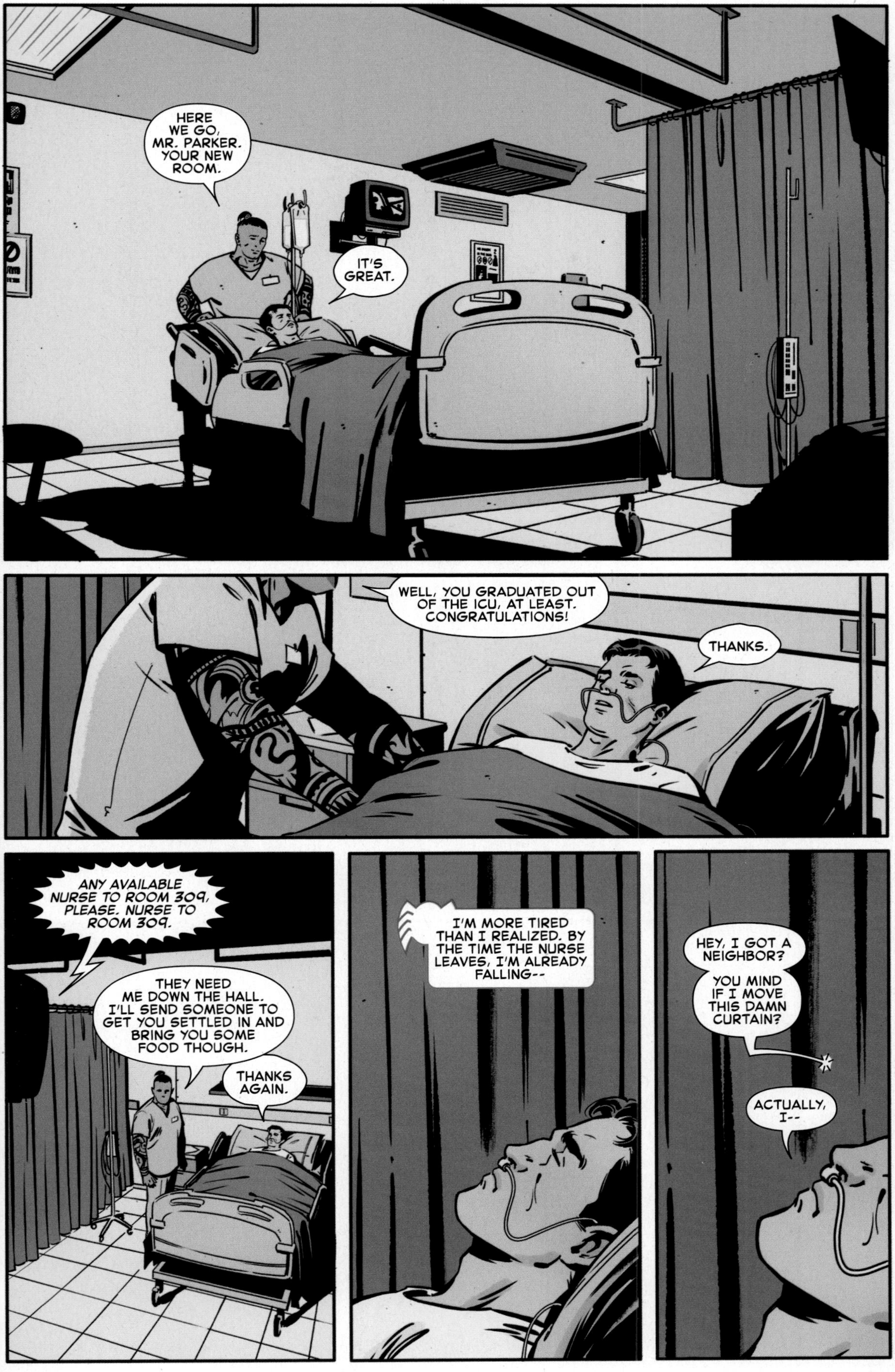
HERE WE GO, MR. PARKER. YOUR NEW ROOM.
IT'S GREAT.
WELL, YOU GRADUATED OUT OF THE ICU, AT LEAST. CONGRATULATIONS!
THANKS.
ANY AVAILABLE NURSE TO ROOM 309, PLEASE. NURSE TO ROOM 309.
THEY NEED ME DOWN THE HALL. I'LL SEND SOMEONE TO GET YOU SETTLED IN AND BRING YOU SOME FOOD THOUGH.
THANKS AGAIN.
I'M MORE TIRED THAN I REALIZED. BY THE TIME THE NURSE LEAVES, I'M ALREADY FALLING--
HEY, I GOT A NEIGHBOR?
YOU MIND IF I MOVE THIS DAMN CURTAIN?
ACTUALLY, I--

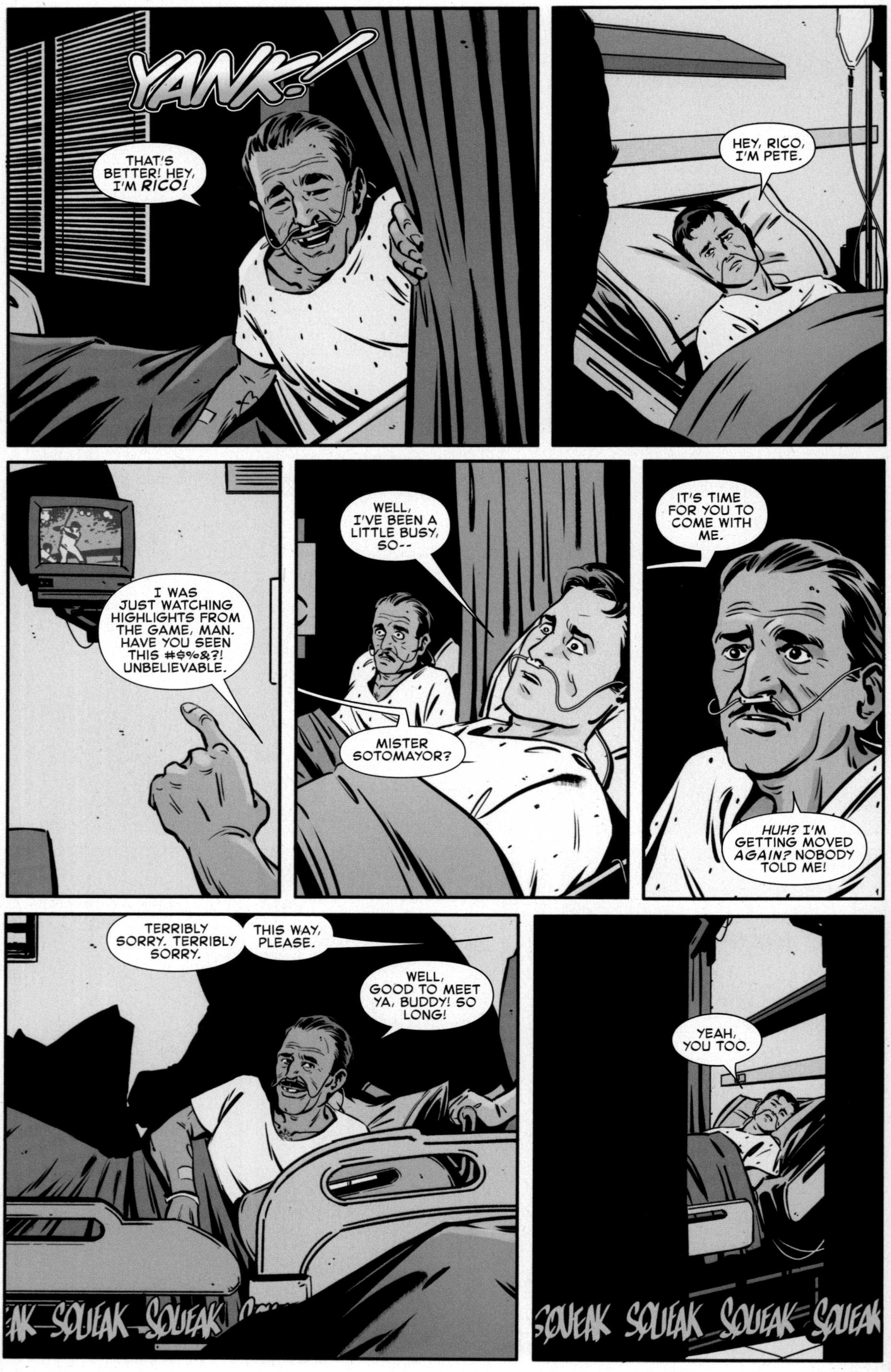
YANK!
THAT'S BETTER! HEY, I'M RICO!
HEY, RICO, I'M PETE.
I WAS JUST WATCHING HIGHLIGHTS FROM THE GAME, MAN. HAVE YOU SEEN THIS #$%&?! UNBELIEVABLE.
WELL, I'VE BEEN A LITTLE BUSY, SO--
MISTER SOTOMAYOR?
IT'S TIME FOR YOU TO COME WITH ME.
HUH? I'M GETTING MOVED AGAIN? NOBODY TOLD ME!
TERRIBLY SORRY. TERRIBLY SORRY.
THIS WAY, PLEASE.
WELL, GOOD TO MEET YA, BUDDY! SO LONG!
SQUEAK SQUEAK
YEAH, YOU TOO.
SQUEAK SQUEAK SQUEAK SQUEAK

ALONE AGAIN, I INSTANTLY START TO FALL ASL--

KNOCK KNOCK

PETER? YOU AWAKE?

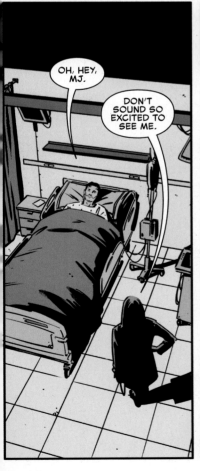

OH, HEY, MJ.

DON'T SOUND SO EXCITED TO SEE ME.

SORRY, I--

ARRRRGHHH!

PETE!

HURTS SO MUCH TO SIT UP.

SO STOP SITTING UP, GENIUS.

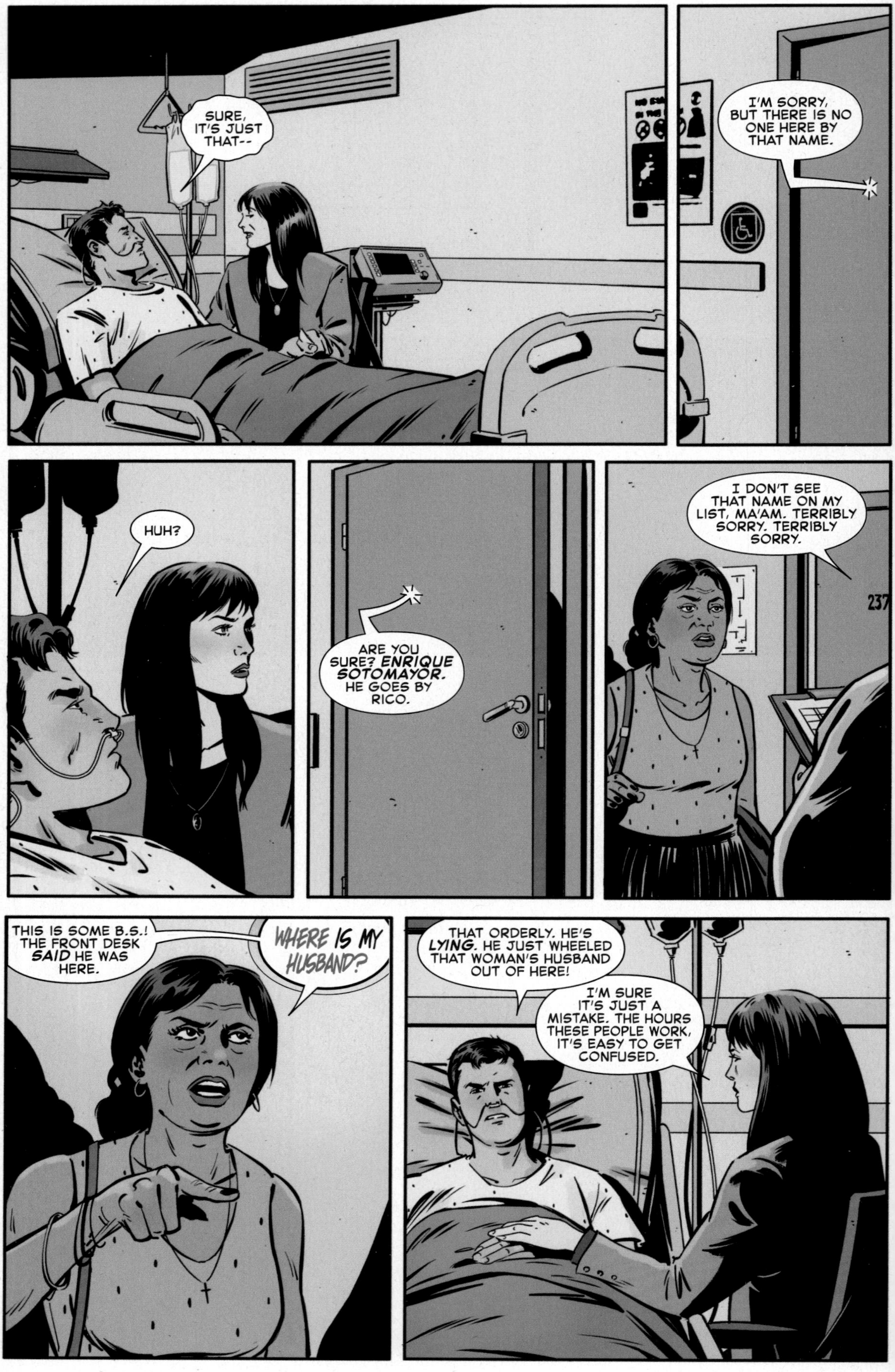
SURE, IT'S JUST THAT--
I'M SORRY, BUT THERE IS NO ONE HERE BY THAT NAME.
HUH?
ARE YOU SURE? ENRIQUE SOTOMAYOR. HE GOES BY RICO.
I DON'T SEE THAT NAME ON MY LIST, MA'AM. TERRIBLY SORRY. TERRIBLY SORRY.
237
THIS IS SOME B.S.! THE FRONT DESK SAID HE WAS HERE.
WHERE IS MY HUSBAND?
THAT ORDERLY. HE'S LYING. HE JUST WHEELED THAT WOMAN'S HUSBAND OUT OF HERE!
I'M SURE IT'S JUST A MISTAKE. THE HOURS THESE PEOPLE WORK, IT'S EASY TO GET CONFUSED.

AND YOU SOUND LIKE YOU'VE ALREADY WORN YOURSELF OUT. YOU NEED TO TAKE IT EASY, TIGER. GET SOME *ACTUAL* REST.

I DON'T NEED TO...

...DON'T NEED TO...

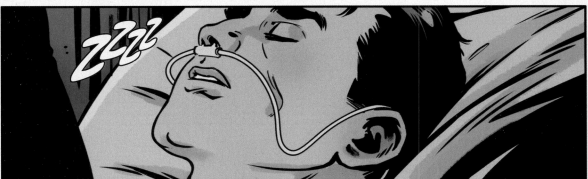

ZZZ

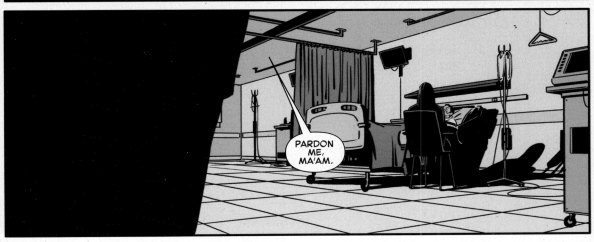

PARDON ME, MA'AM.

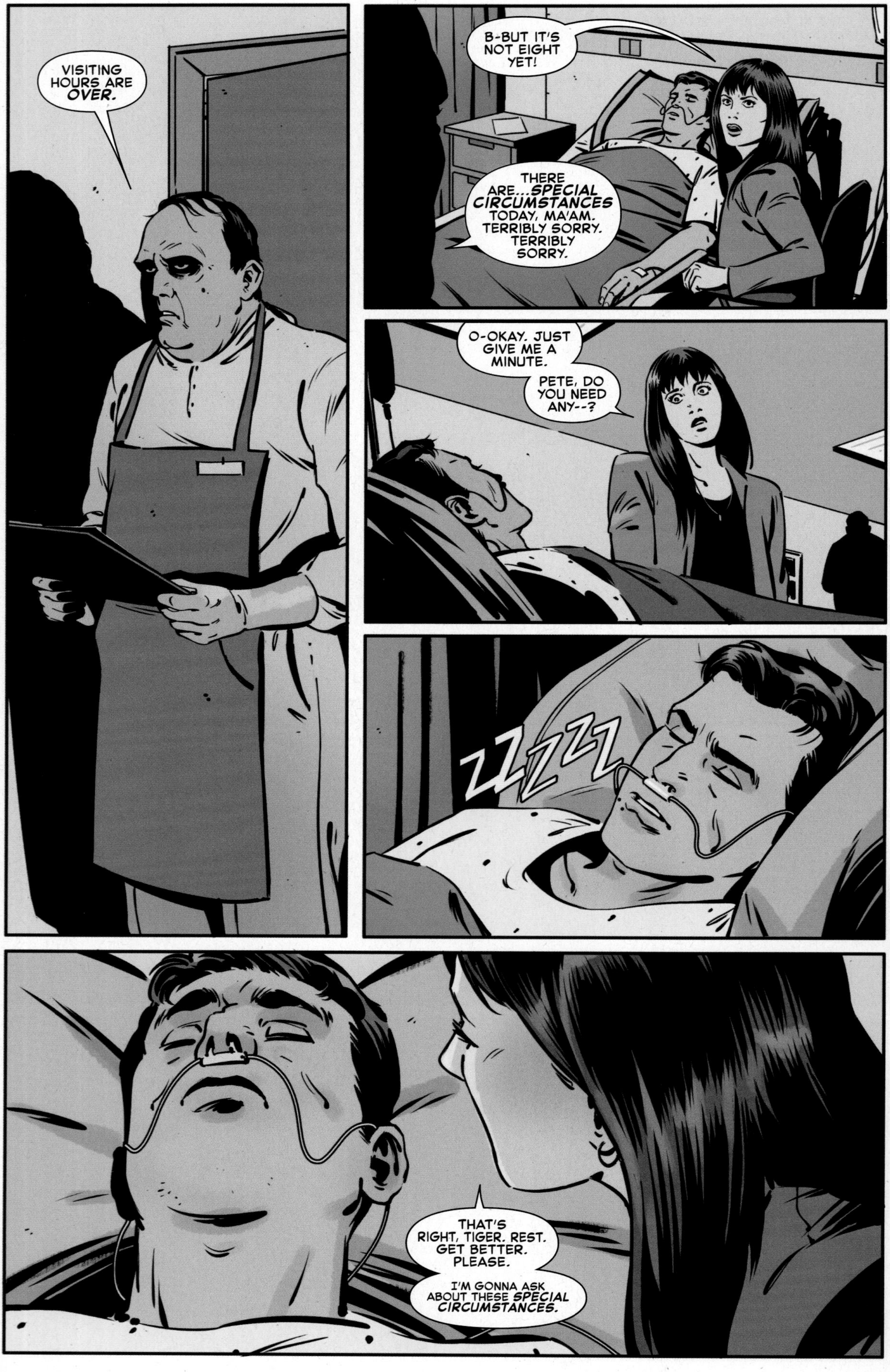
VISITING HOURS ARE OVER.
B-BUT IT'S NOT EIGHT YET!
THERE ARE...SPECIAL CIRCUMSTANCES TODAY, MA'AM. TERRIBLY SORRY. TERRIBLY SORRY.
O-OKAY. JUST GIVE ME A MINUTE.
PETE, DO YOU NEED ANY--?
ZZZZZ
THAT'S RIGHT, TIGER. REST. GET BETTER. PLEASE.
I'M GONNA ASK ABOUT THESE SPECIAL CIRCUMSTANCES.

M-MARY JANE?

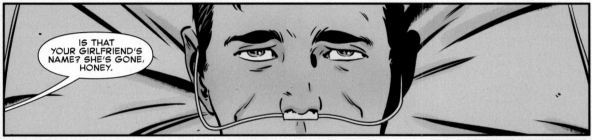

IS THAT YOUR GIRLFRIEND'S NAME? SHE'S GONE, HONEY.

THEY WERE SUPPOSED TO DISCHARGE *ME* TWO HOURS AGO! THIS PLACE IS RUN BY *BOZOS!* THEY CAN'T--

MRS. HAROIAN?

IT'S TIME FOR YOU TO COME WITH ME.

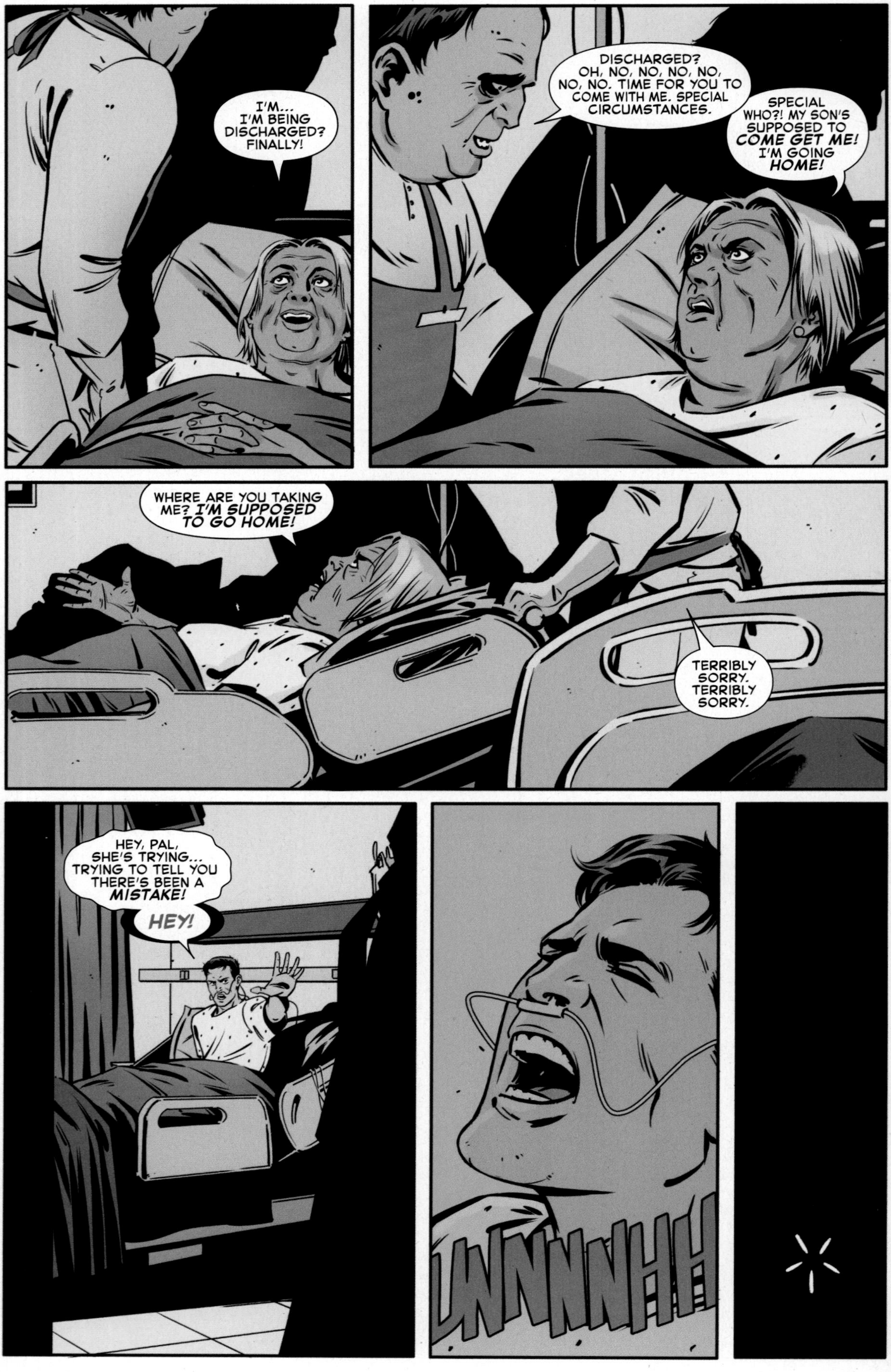
I'M... I'M BEING DISCHARGED? FINALLY!
DISCHARGED? OH, NO, NO, NO, NO, NO, NO. TIME FOR YOU TO COME WITH ME. SPECIAL CIRCUMSTANCES.
SPECIAL WHO?! MY SON'S SUPPOSED TO COME GET ME! I'M GOING HOME!
WHERE ARE YOU TAKING ME? I'M SUPPOSED TO GO HOME!
TERRIBLY SORRY. TERRIBLY SORRY.
HEY, PAL, SHE'S TRYING... TRYING TO TELL YOU THERE'S BEEN A MISTAKE!
HEY!
UNNNNHH

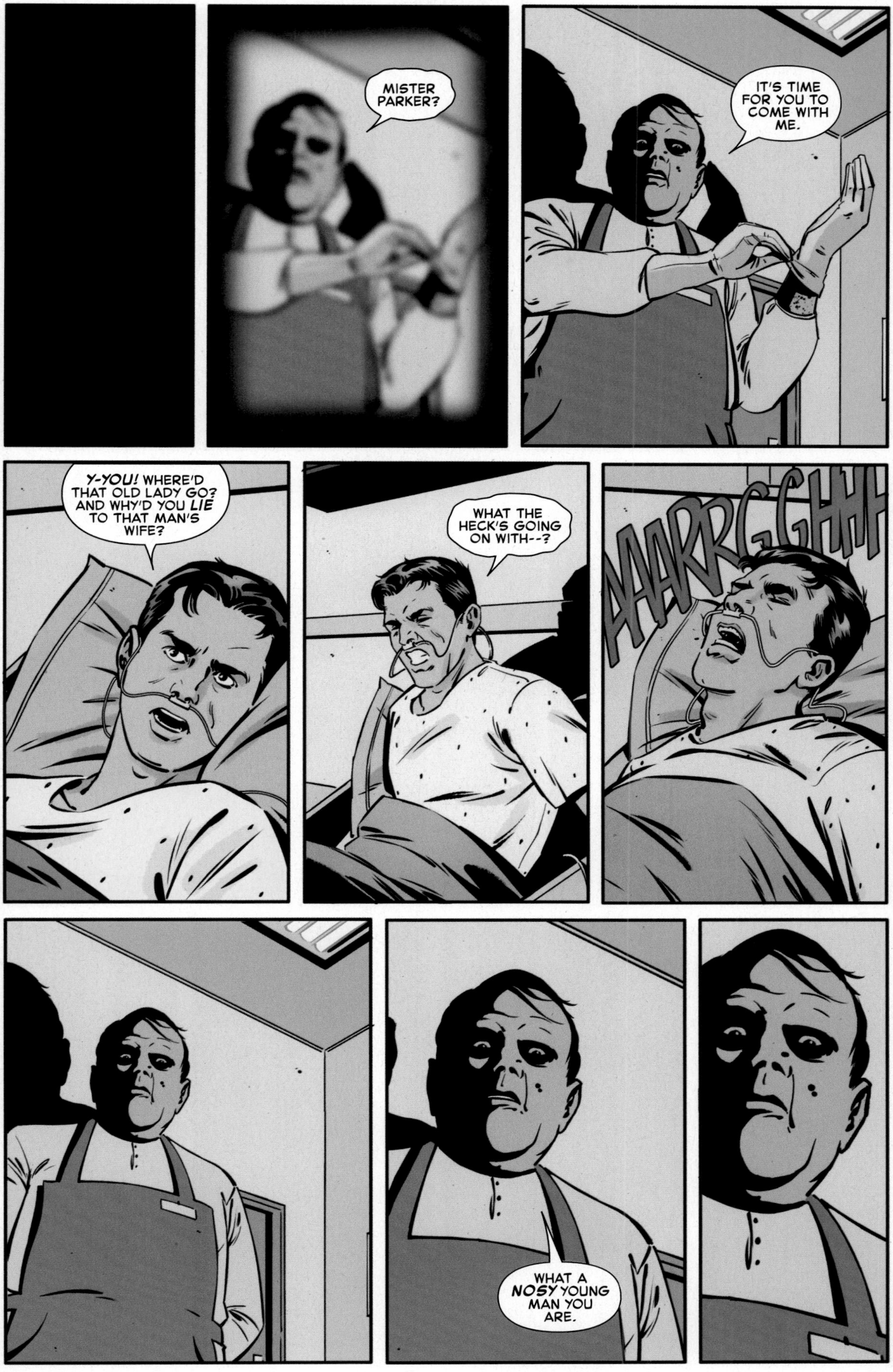
MISTER PARKER?
IT'S TIME FOR YOU TO COME WITH ME.
Y-YOU! WHERE'D THAT OLD LADY GO? AND WHY'D YOU LIE TO THAT MAN'S WIFE?
WHAT THE HECK'S GOING ON WITH--?
AAARRGGHH
WHAT A NOSY YOUNG MAN YOU ARE.

I HAD TO INCREASE YOUR DOSAGE.

TERRIBLY SORRY. TERRIBLY SORRY.

BUT IT WILL MAKE YOU MUCH LESS TROUBLESOME.

WH-WHAT?

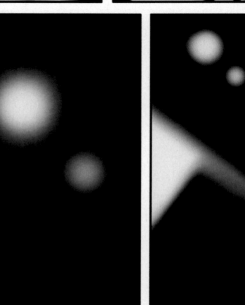

N-NO...

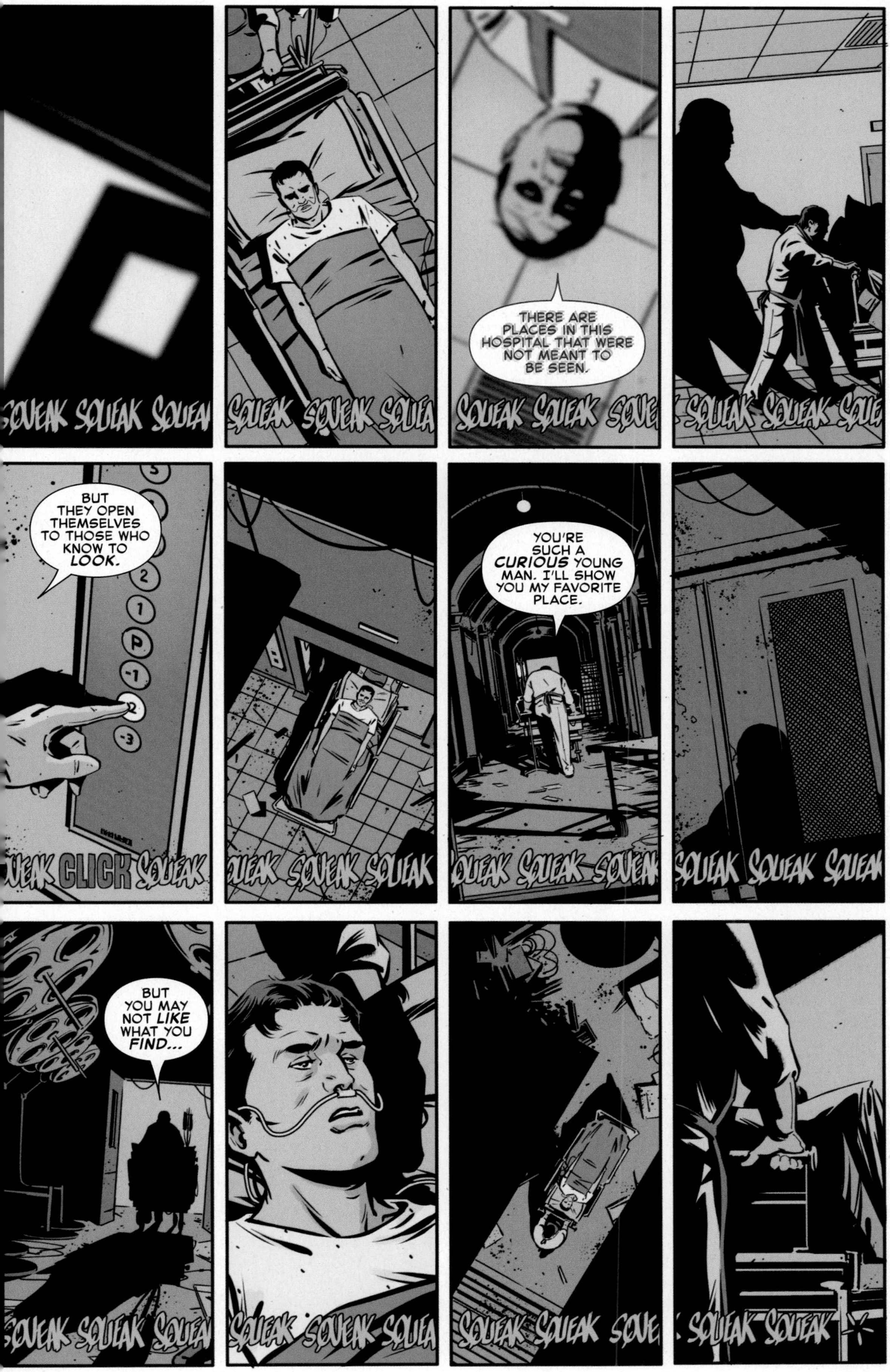
SQUEAK SQUEAK SQUEA
SQUEAK SQUEAK SQUEA
THERE ARE PLACES IN THIS HOSPITAL THAT WERE NOT MEANT TO BE SEEN.
SQUEAK SQUEAK
SQUEAK SQUEAK SQUEA
BUT THEY OPEN THEMSELVES TO THOSE WHO KNOW TO LOOK.
CLICK SQUEAK
SQUEAK SQUEAK
YOU'RE SUCH A CURIOUS YOUNG MAN. I'LL SHOW YOU MY FAVORITE PLACE.
SQUEAK SQUEAK
SQUEAK SQUEAK SQUEAK
BUT YOU MAY NOT LIKE WHAT YOU FIND...
SQUEAK SQUEAK
SQUEAK SQUEAK SQUEA
SQUEAK SQUEAK
SQUEAK SQUEAK

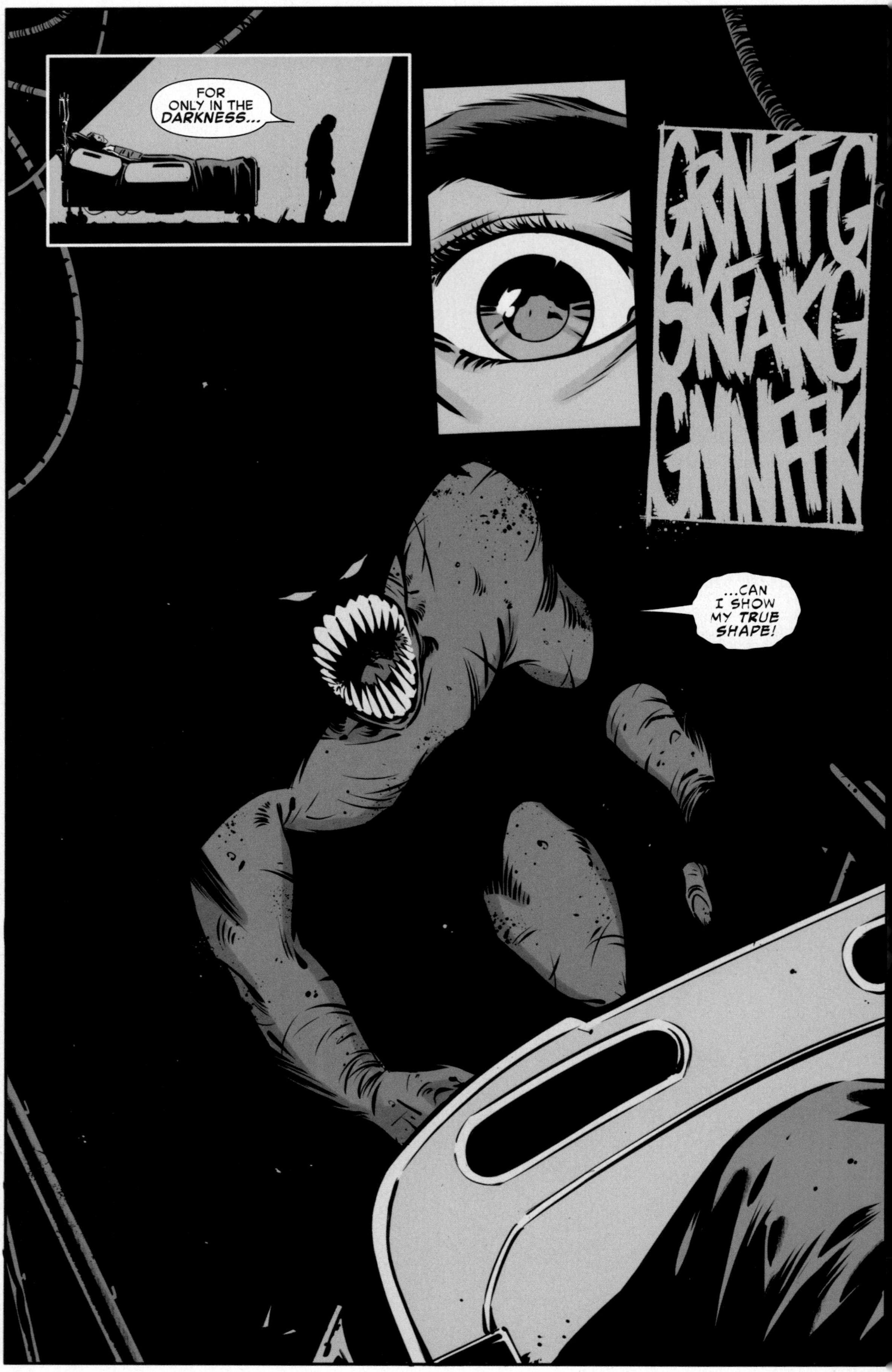
FOR ONLY IN THE DARKNESS...
GRNFFG SKFAKG GNNFFK
...CAN I SHOW MY TRUE SHAPE!

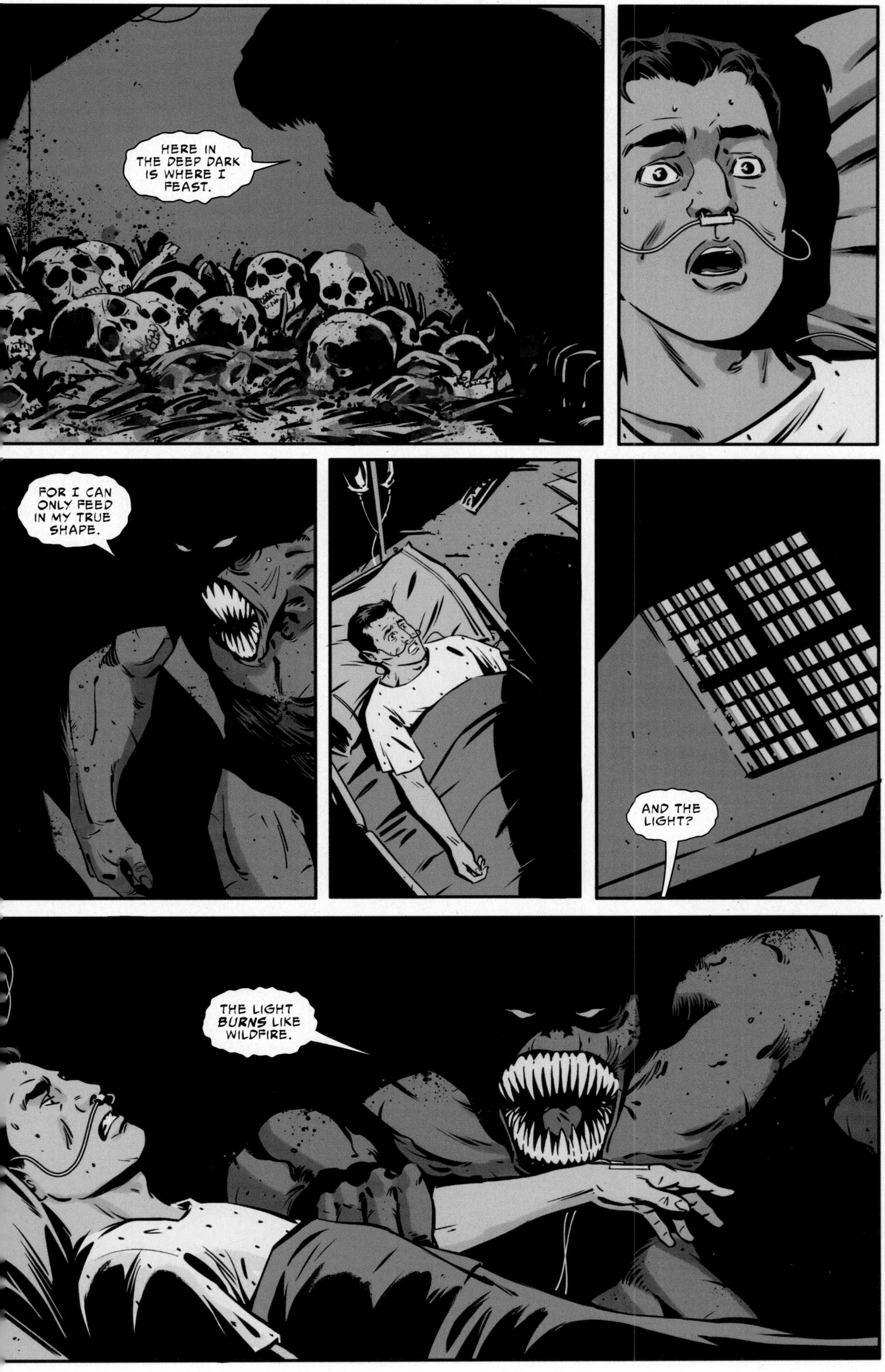
HERE IN THE DEEP DARK IS WHERE I FEAST.
FOR I CAN ONLY FEED IN MY TRUE SHAPE.
AND THE LIGHT?
THE LIGHT BURNS LIKE WILDFIRE.

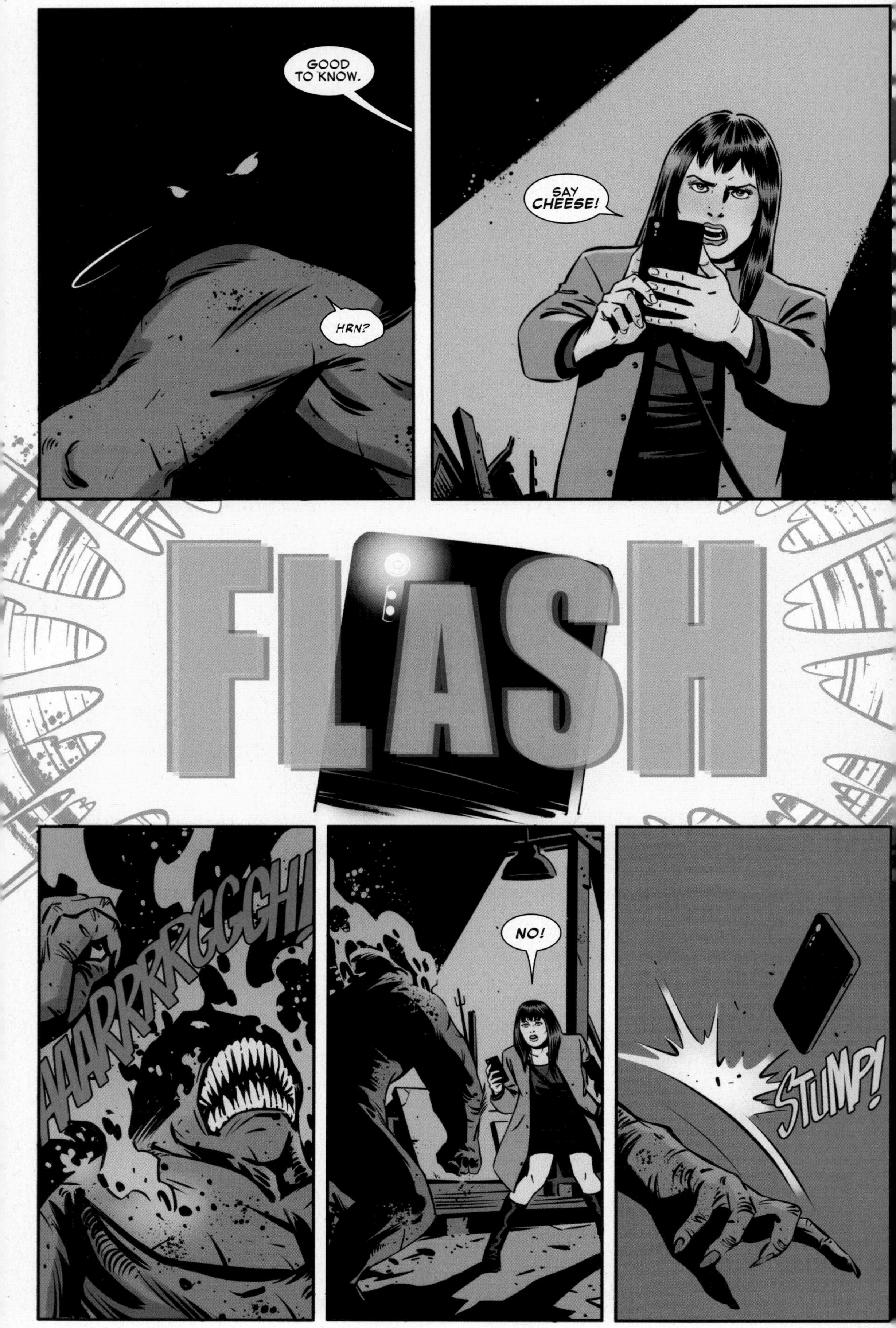
GOOD TO KNOW.
HRN?
SAY CHEESE!
FLASH
AAARRRRGGGH!
NO!
STUMP!

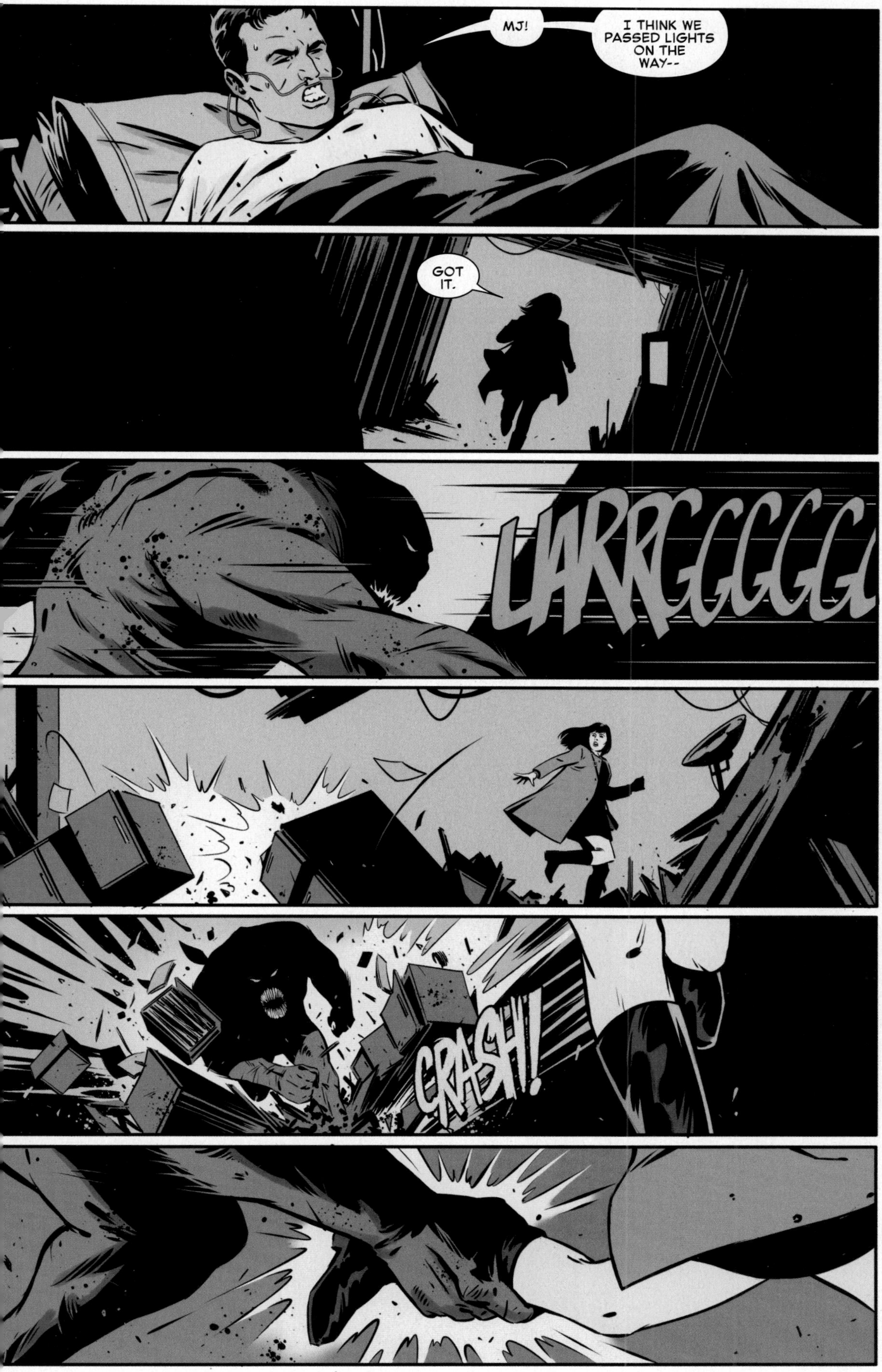
MJ!
I THINK WE PASSED LIGHTS ON THE WAY--
GOT IT.
LIARRGGGGGG
CRASH!

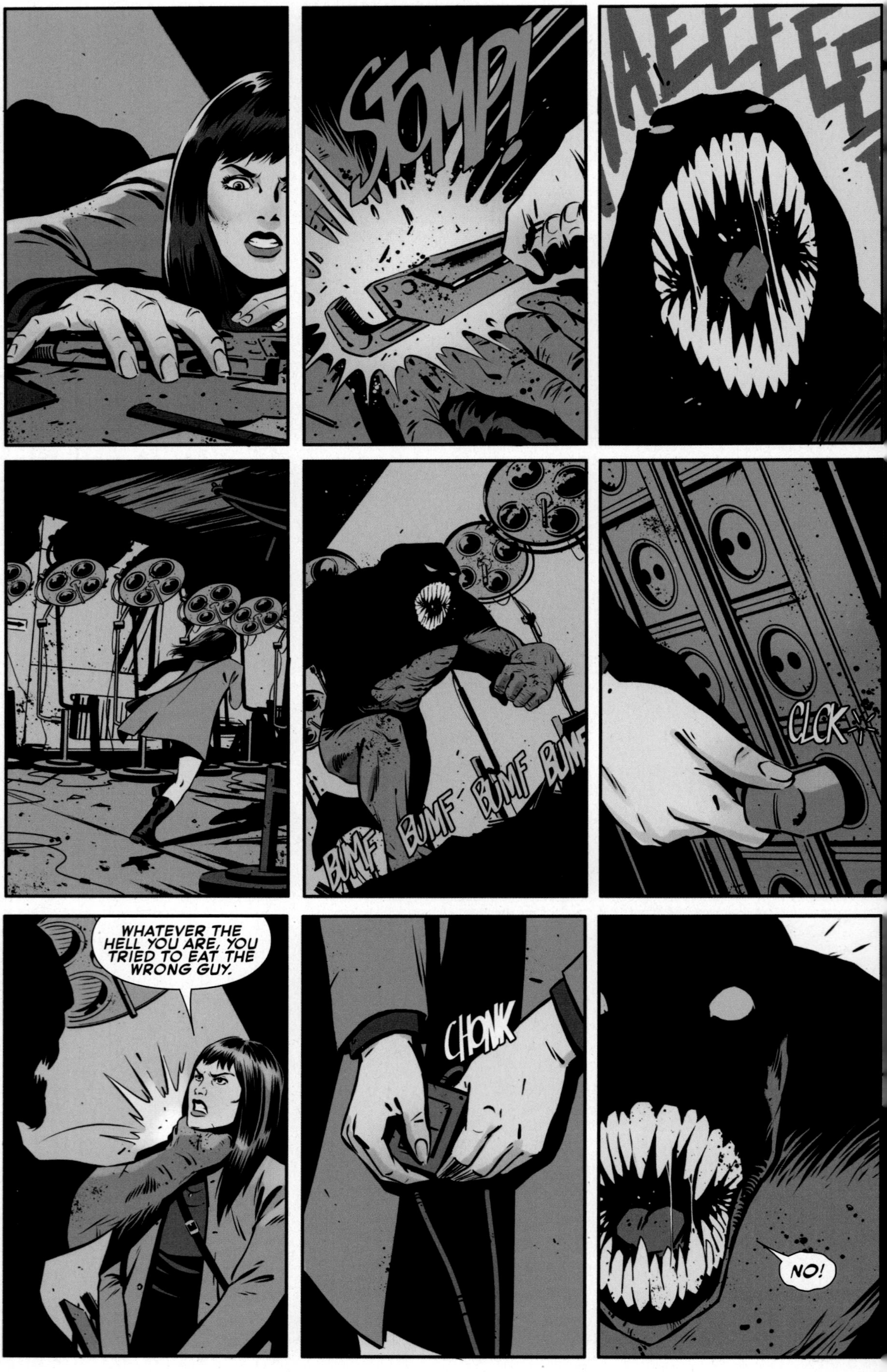
STOMP!
AEEEEE
BUMF BUMF BUMF BUMF
CLICK
WHATEVER THE HELL YOU ARE, YOU TRIED TO EAT THE WRONG GUY.
CHONK
NO!

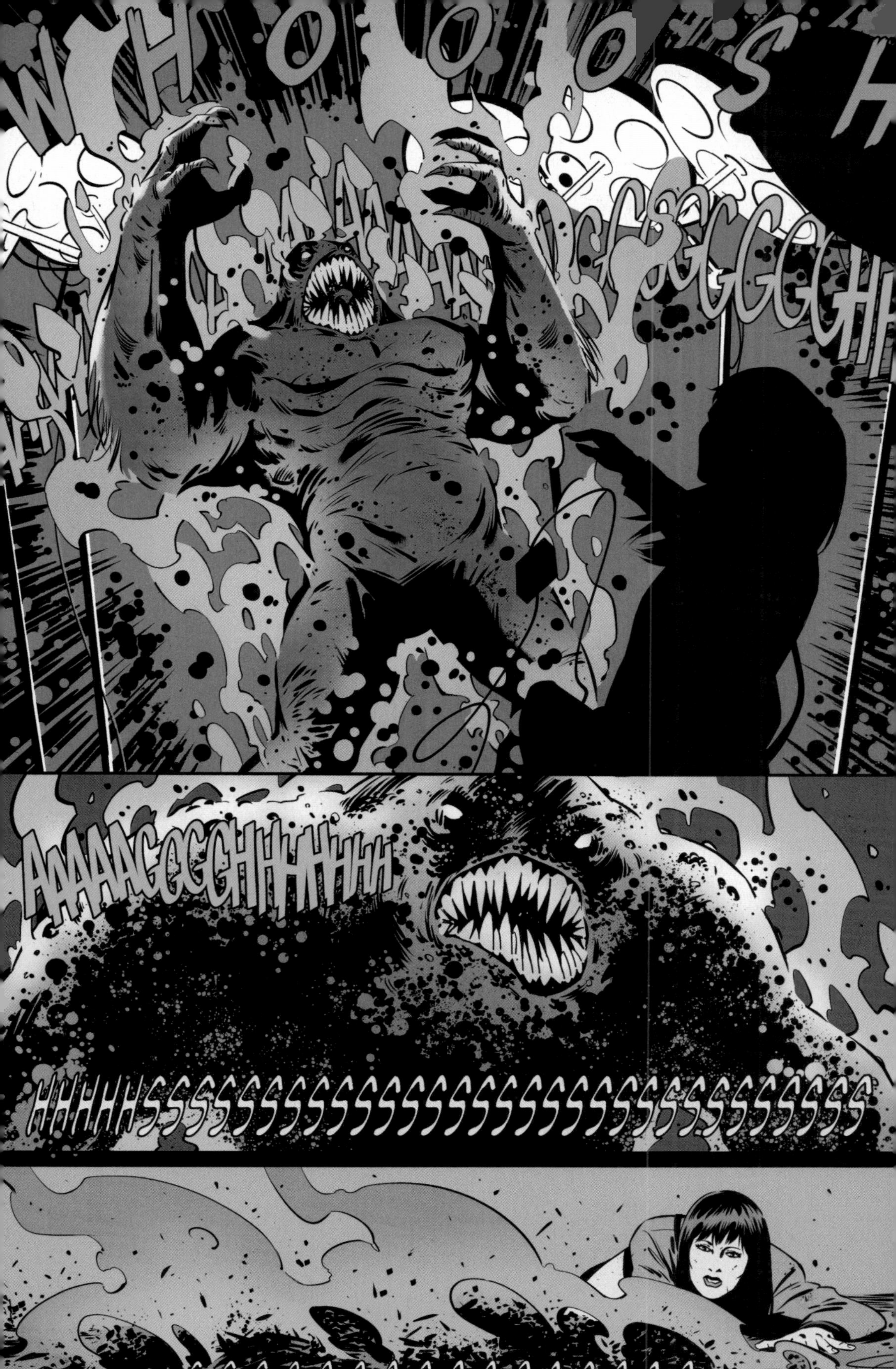
WHOOOSH
AAAAAAAAAAA
SSSGGGGGCHH
AAAAAGGGHHHHHH
HHHHHSSSSSSSSSSSSSSSSSSSSSSSSSSSSSS
SSSSSSSSSSSSSSS

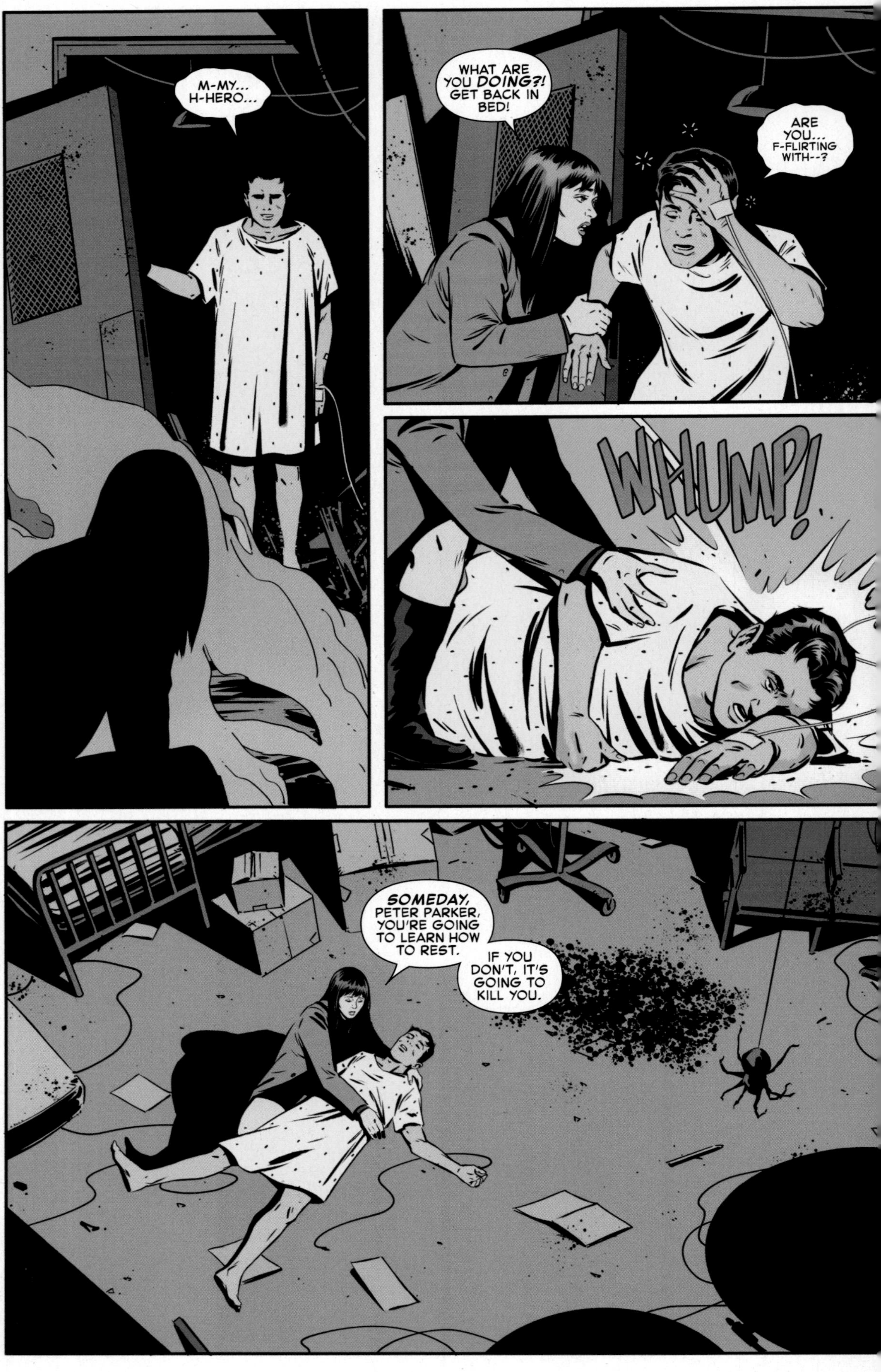
M-MY... H-HERO...
WHAT ARE YOU DOING?! GET BACK IN BED!
ARE YOU... F-FLIRTING WITH--?
WHUMP!
SOMEDAY, PETER PARKER, YOU'RE GOING TO LEARN HOW TO REST.
IF YOU DON'T, IT'S GOING TO KILL YOU.

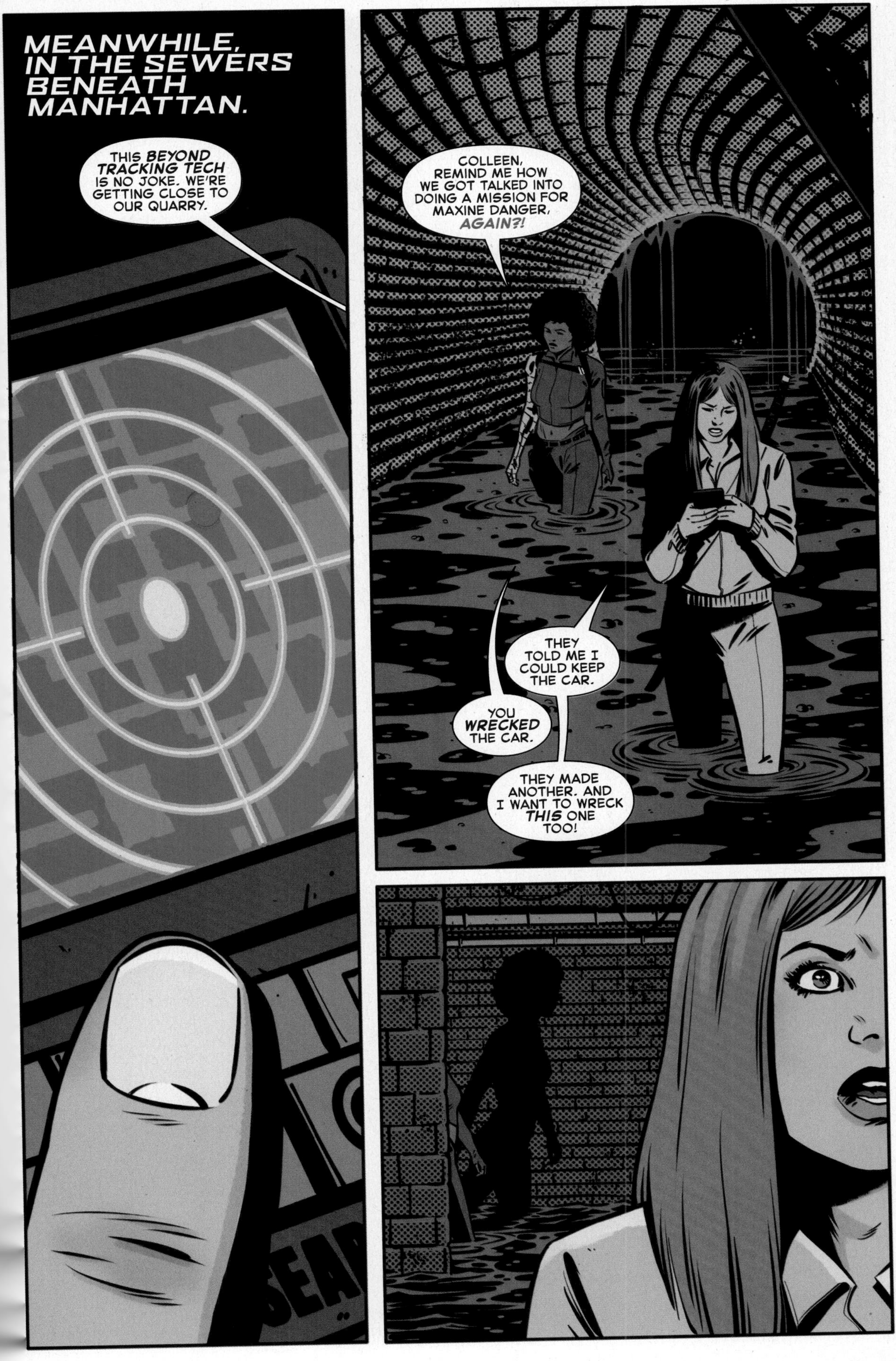
MEANWHILE, IN THE SEWERS BENEATH MANHATTAN.
THIS BEYOND TRACKING TECH IS NO JOKE. WE'RE GETTING CLOSE TO OUR QUARRY.
COLLEEN, REMIND ME HOW WE GOT TALKED INTO DOING A MISSION FOR MAXINE DANGER, AGAIN?!
THEY TOLD ME I COULD KEEP THE CAR.
YOU WRECKED THE CAR.
THEY MADE ANOTHER. AND I WANT TO WRECK THIS ONE TOO!

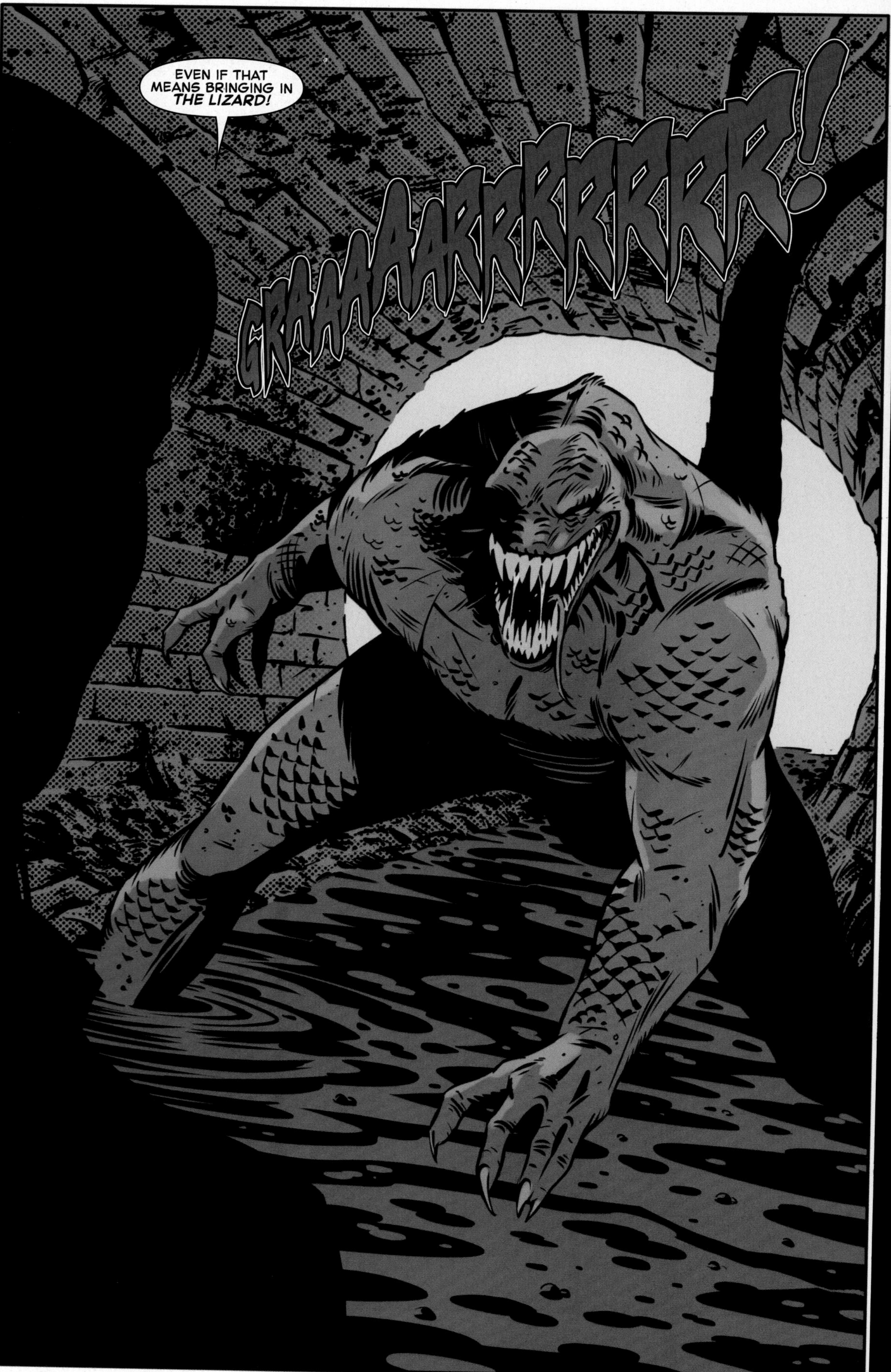
EVEN IF THAT MEANS BRINGING IN THE LIZARD!
GRAAAAARRRRRRR!

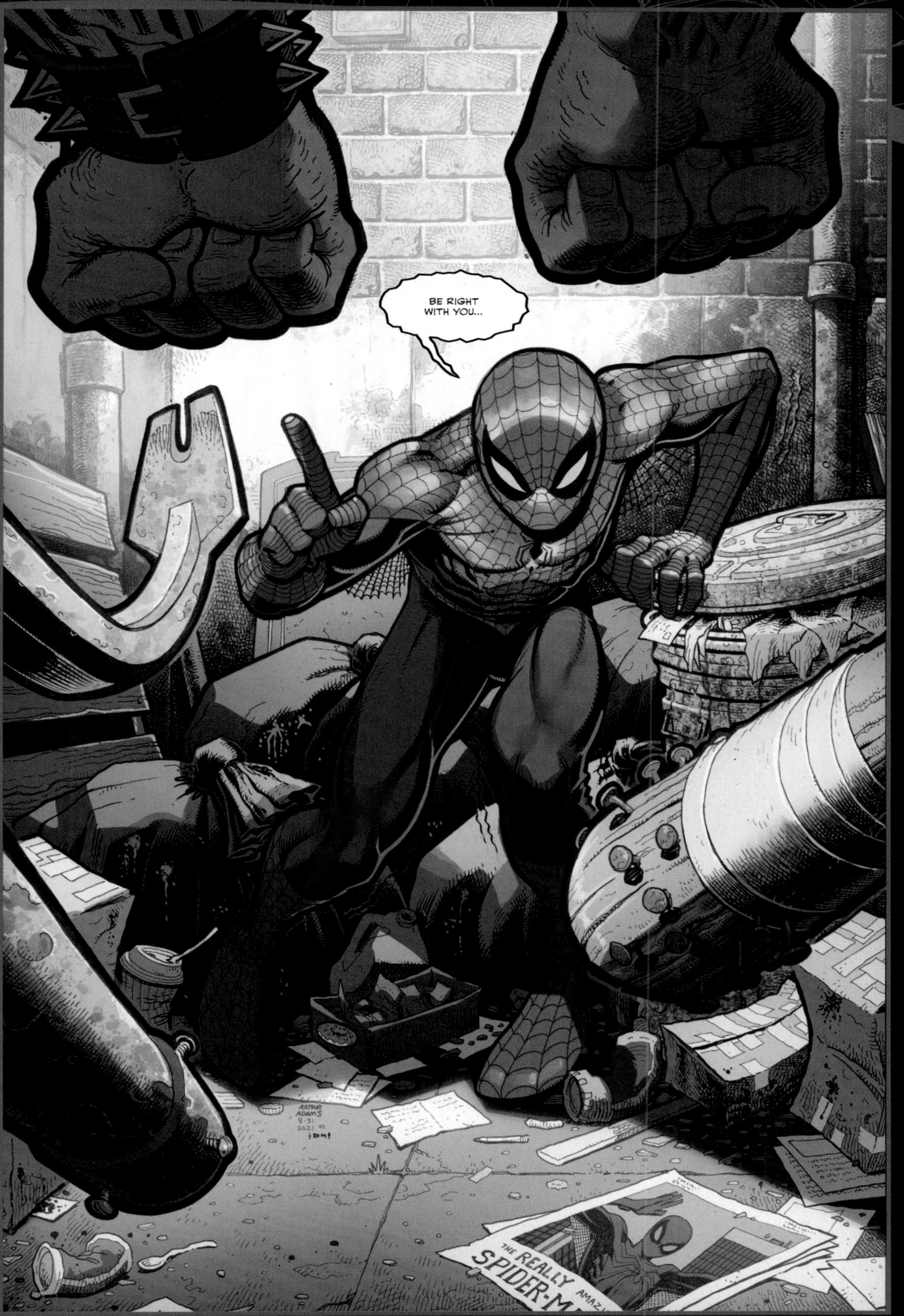
BE RIGHT WITH YOU...
THE REALLY

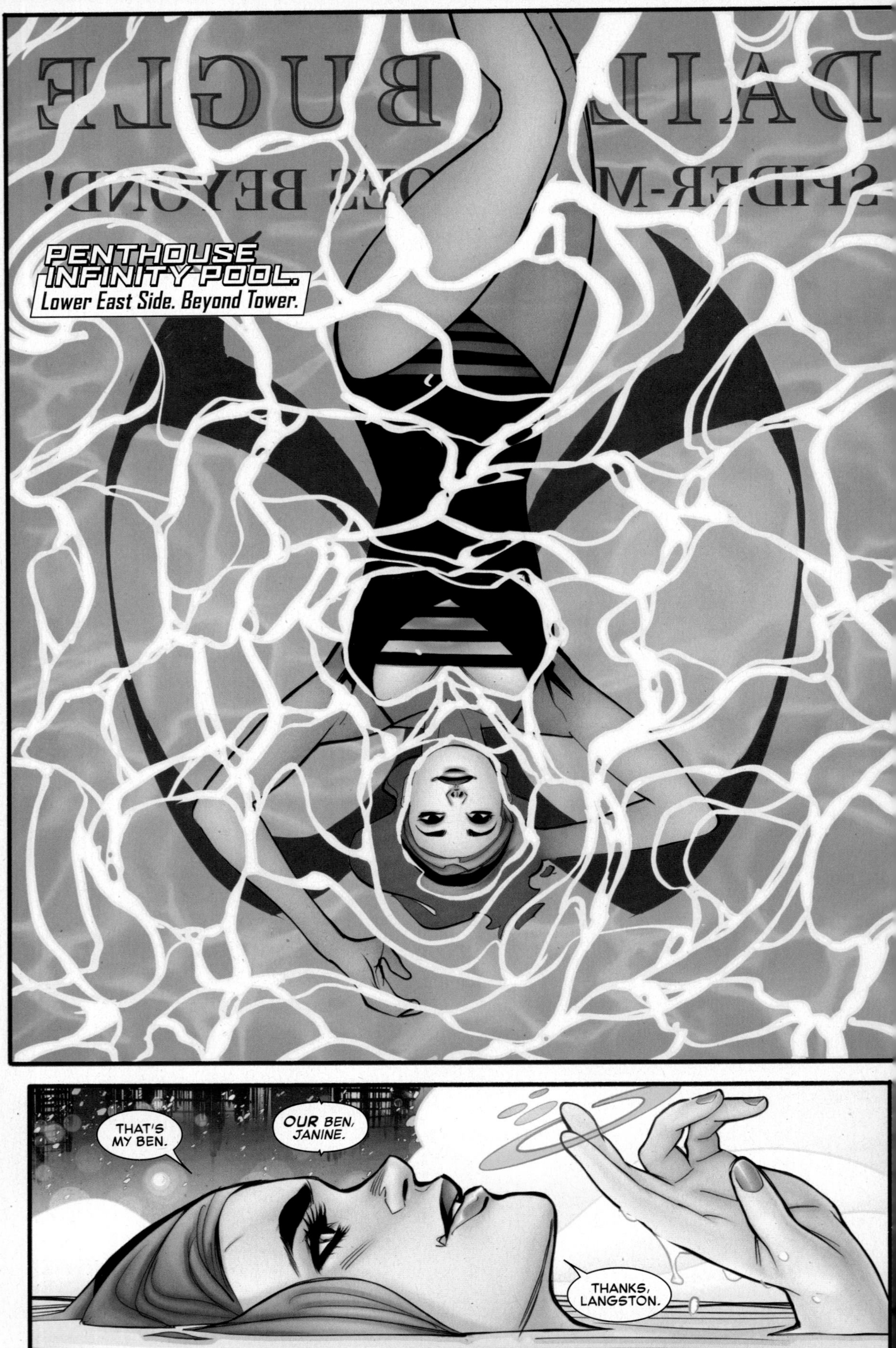
PENTHOUSE INFINITY POOL.
Lower East Side. Beyond Tower.
THAT'S MY BEN.
OUR BEN, JANINE.
THANKS, LANGSTON.

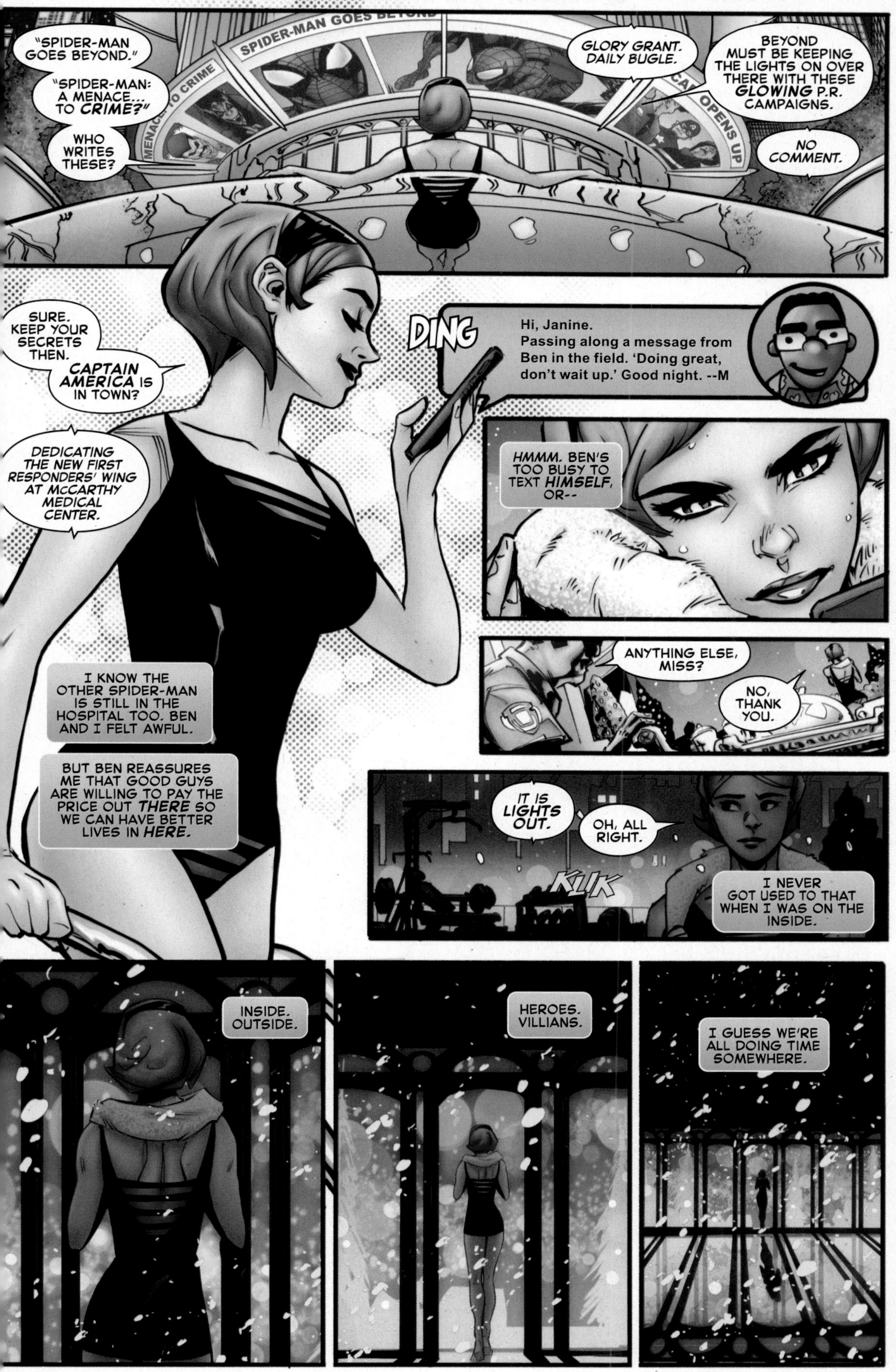

SPIDER-MAN GOES BEYOND
"SPIDER-MAN GOES BEYOND."
"SPIDER-MAN: A MENACE... TO CRIME?"
WHO WRITES THESE?
GLORY GRANT. DAILY BUGLE.
BEYOND MUST BE KEEPING THE LIGHTS ON OVER THERE WITH THESE GLOWING P.R. CAMPAIGNS.
NO COMMENT.
SURE. KEEP YOUR SECRETS THEN.
CAPTAIN AMERICA IS IN TOWN?
DEDICATING THE NEW FIRST RESPONDERS' WING AT McCARTHY MEDICAL CENTER.
DING
Hi, Janine.
Passing along a message from Ben in the field. 'Doing great, don't wait up.' Good night. --M
HMMM. BEN'S TOO BUSY TO TEXT HIMSELF, OR--
I KNOW THE OTHER SPIDER-MAN IS STILL IN THE HOSPITAL TOO. BEN AND I FELT AWFUL.
BUT BEN REASSURES ME THAT GOOD GUYS ARE WILLING TO PAY THE PRICE OUT THERE SO WE CAN HAVE BETTER LIVES IN HERE.
ANYTHING ELSE, MISS?
NO, THANK YOU.
IT IS LIGHTS OUT.
OH, ALL RIGHT.
KLIK
I NEVER GOT USED TO THAT WHEN I WAS ON THE INSIDE.
INSIDE. OUTSIDE.
HEROES. VILLIANS.
I GUESS WE'RE ALL DOING TIME SOMEWHERE.

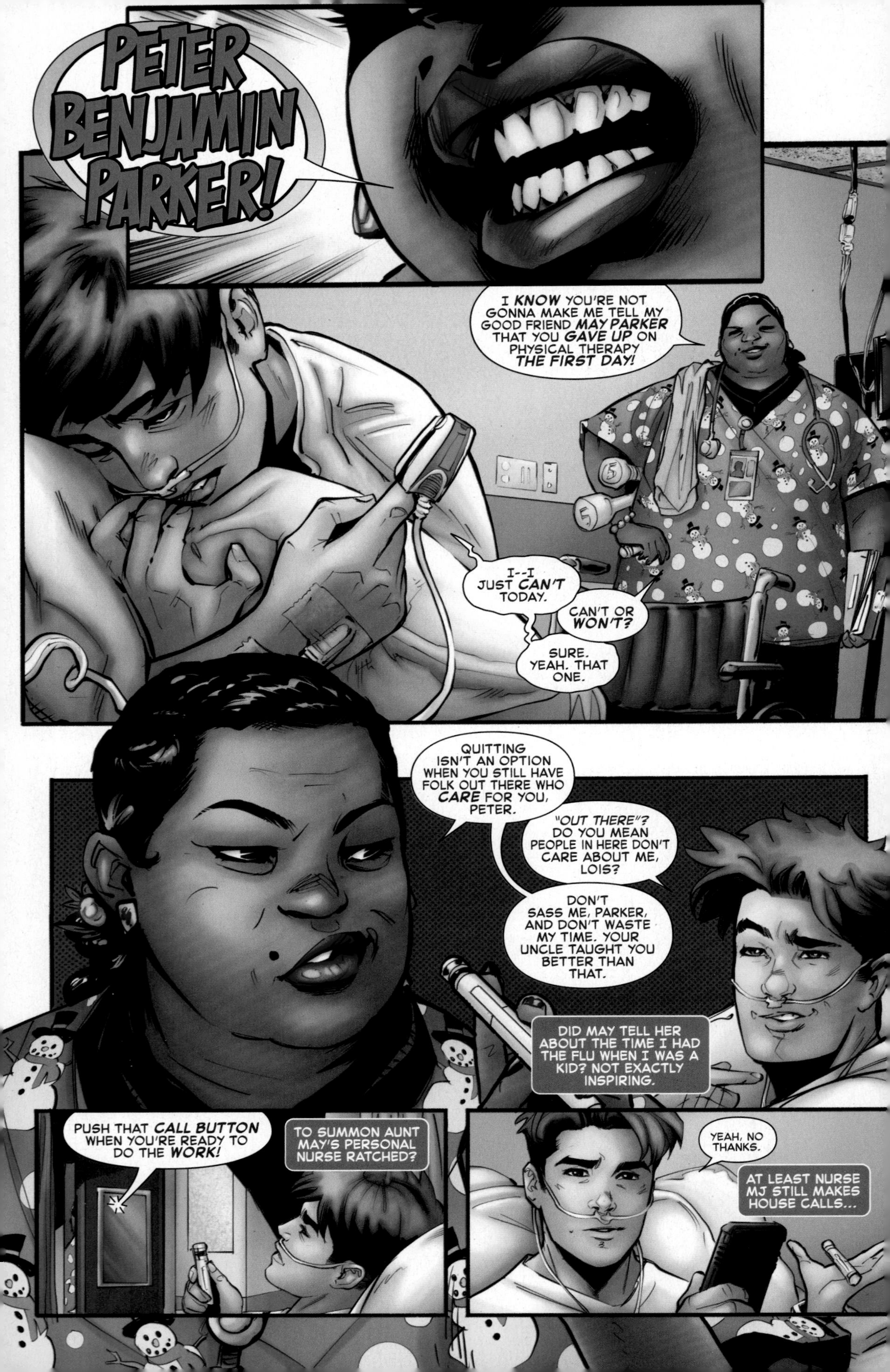
PETER BENJAMIN PARKER!
I KNOW YOU'RE NOT GONNA MAKE ME TELL MY GOOD FRIEND MAY PARKER THAT YOU GAVE UP ON PHYSICAL THERAPY THE FIRST DAY!
I--I JUST CAN'T TODAY.
CAN'T OR WON'T?
SURE. YEAH. THAT ONE.
QUITTING ISN'T AN OPTION WHEN YOU STILL HAVE FOLK OUT THERE WHO CARE FOR YOU, PETER.
"OUT THERE"? DO YOU MEAN PEOPLE IN HERE DON'T CARE ABOUT ME, LOIS?
DON'T SASS ME, PARKER, AND DON'T WASTE MY TIME. YOUR UNCLE TAUGHT YOU BETTER THAN THAT.
DID MAY TELL HER ABOUT THE TIME I HAD THE FLU WHEN I WAS A KID? NOT EXACTLY INSPIRING.
PUSH THAT CALL BUTTON WHEN YOU'RE READY TO DO THE WORK!
TO SUMMON AUNT MAY'S PERSONAL NURSE RATCHED?
YEAH, NO THANKS.
AT LEAST NURSE MJ STILL MAKES HOUSE CALLS...

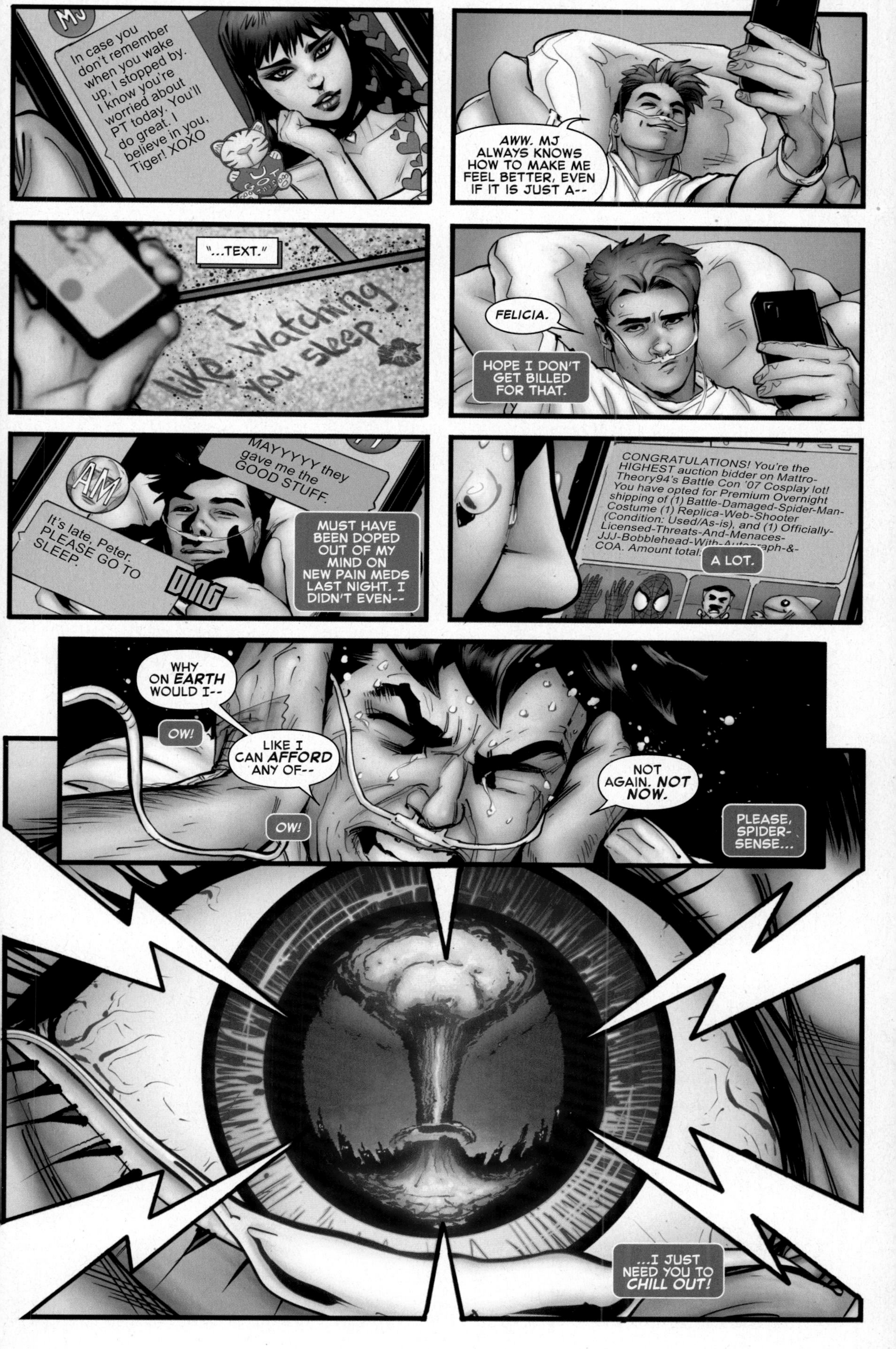
MJ
In case you don't remember when you wake up, I stopped by. I know you're worried about PT today. You'll do great. I believe in you, Tiger! XOXO
AWW. MJ ALWAYS KNOWS HOW TO MAKE ME FEEL BETTER, EVEN IF IT IS JUST A--
"...TEXT."
I like watching you sleep
FELICIA.
HOPE I DON'T GET BILLED FOR THAT.
AM
MAYYYYY they gave me the GOOD STUFF.
It's late, Peter. PLEASE GO TO SLEEP.
DING
MUST HAVE BEEN DOPED OUT OF MY MIND ON NEW PAIN MEDS LAST NIGHT. I DIDN'T EVEN--
CONGRATULATIONS! You're the HIGHEST auction bidder on Mattro-Theory94's Battle Con '07 Cosplay lot! You have opted for Premium Overnight shipping of (1) Battle-Damaged-Spider-Man-Costume (1) Replica-Web-Shooter (Condition: Used/As-is), and (1) Officially-Licensed-Threats-And-Menaces-JJJ-Bobblehead-With-Autograph-&-COA. Amount total:
A LOT.
WHY ON EARTH WOULD I--
OW!
LIKE I CAN AFFORD ANY OF--
OW!
NOT AGAIN. NOT NOW.
PLEASE, SPIDER-SENSE...
...I JUST NEED YOU TO CHILL OUT!

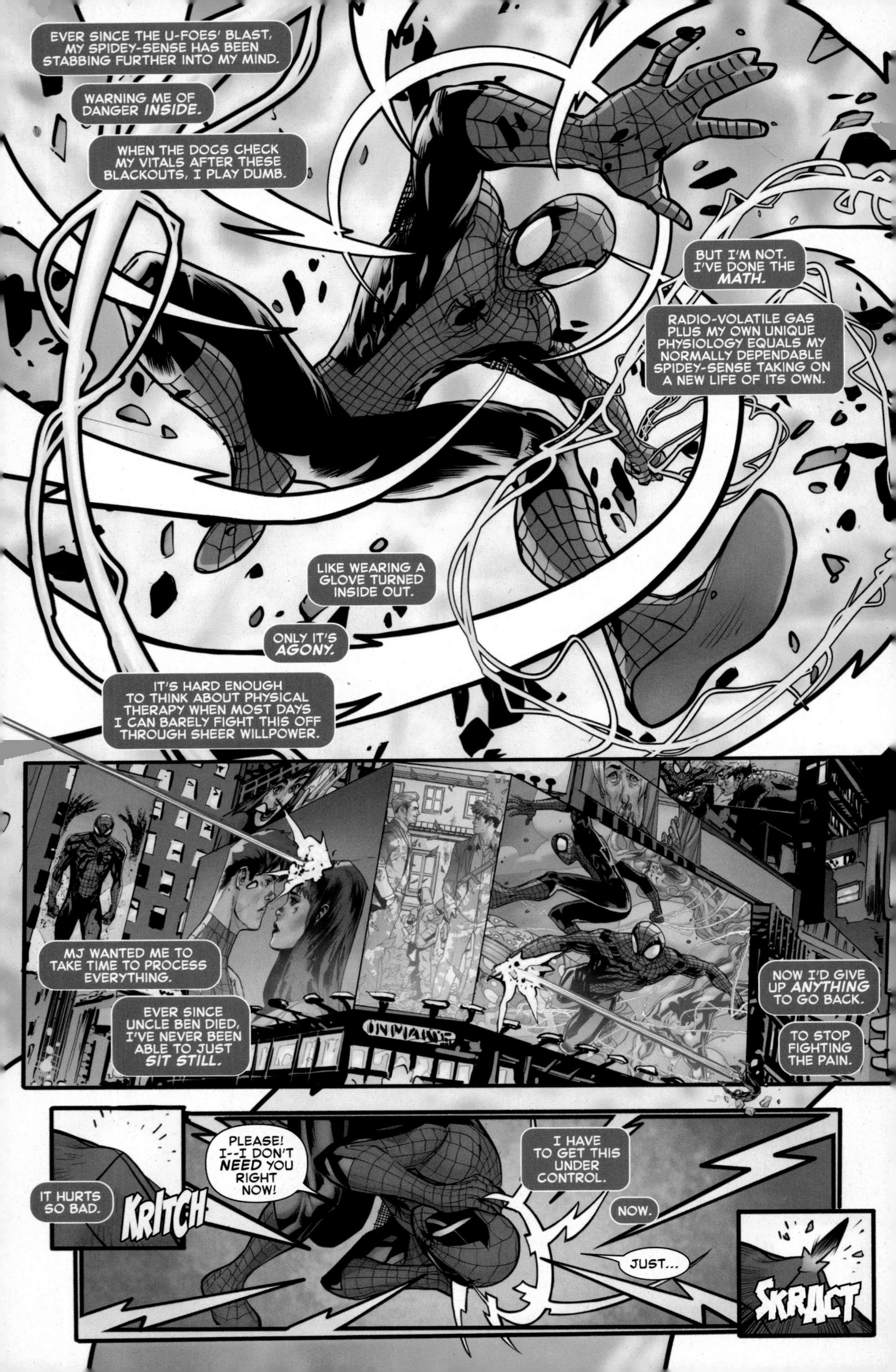

EVER SINCE THE U-FOES' BLAST, MY SPIDEY-SENSE HAS BEEN STABBING FURTHER INTO MY MIND.
WARNING ME OF DANGER *INSIDE.*
WHEN THE DOCS CHECK MY VITALS AFTER THESE BLACKOUTS, I PLAY DUMB.
BUT I'M NOT. I'VE DONE THE *MATH.*
RADIO-VOLATILE GAS PLUS MY OWN UNIQUE PHYSIOLOGY EQUALS MY NORMALLY DEPENDABLE SPIDEY-SENSE TAKING ON A NEW LIFE OF ITS OWN.
LIKE WEARING A GLOVE TURNED INSIDE OUT.
ONLY IT'S *AGONY.*
IT'S HARD ENOUGH TO THINK ABOUT PHYSICAL THERAPY WHEN MOST DAYS I CAN BARELY FIGHT THIS OFF THROUGH SHEER WILLPOWER.
MJ WANTED ME TO TAKE TIME TO PROCESS EVERYTHING.
EVER SINCE UNCLE BEN DIED, I'VE NEVER BEEN ABLE TO JUST *SIT STILL.*
NOW I'D GIVE UP *ANYTHING* TO GO BACK.
TO STOP FIGHTING THE PAIN.
IT HURTS SO BAD.
KRITCH
PLEASE! I--I DON'T *NEED* YOU RIGHT NOW!
I HAVE TO GET THIS UNDER CONTROL.
NOW.
JUST...
SKRACT

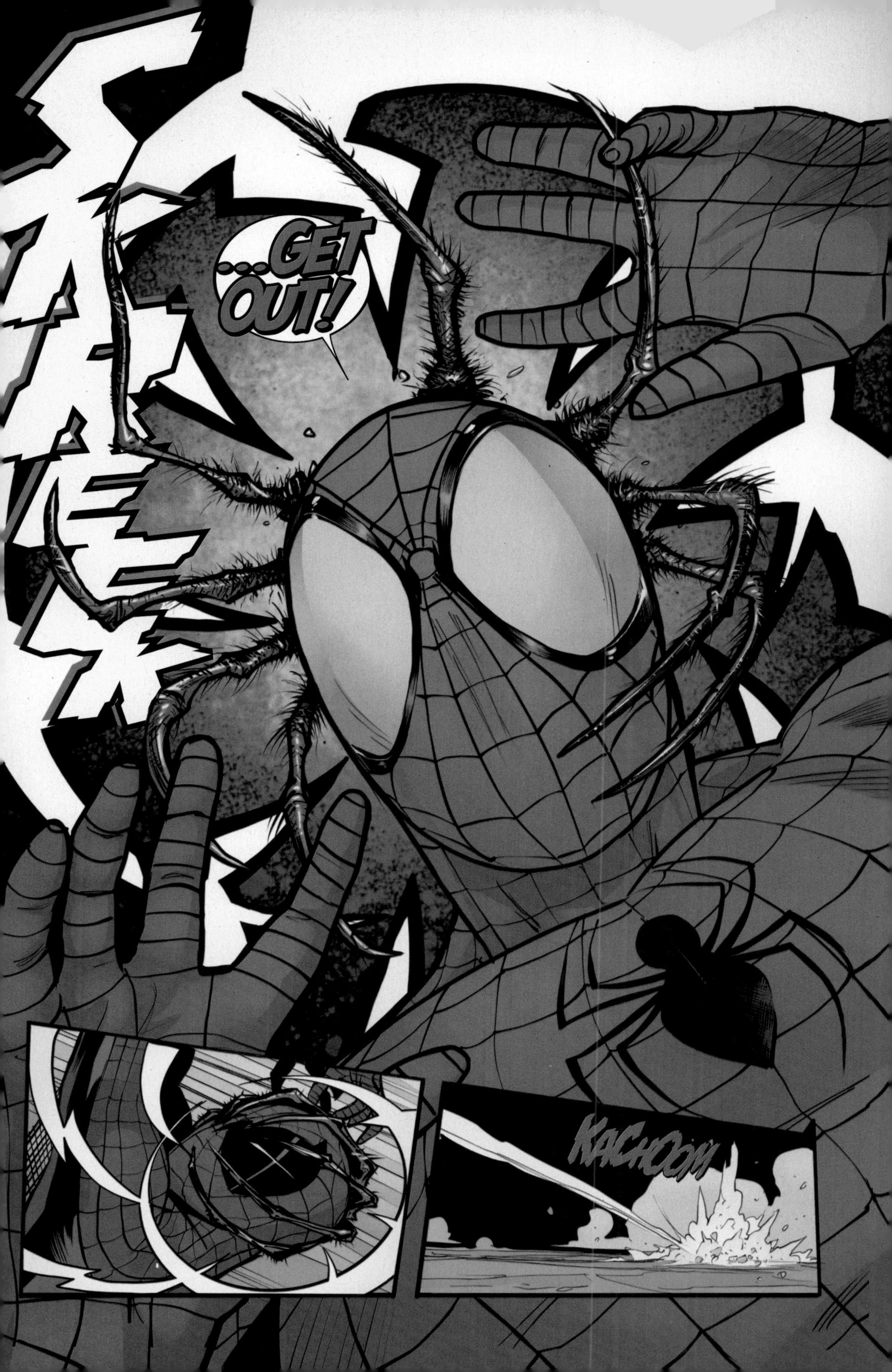
...GET OUT!
KACHOOM

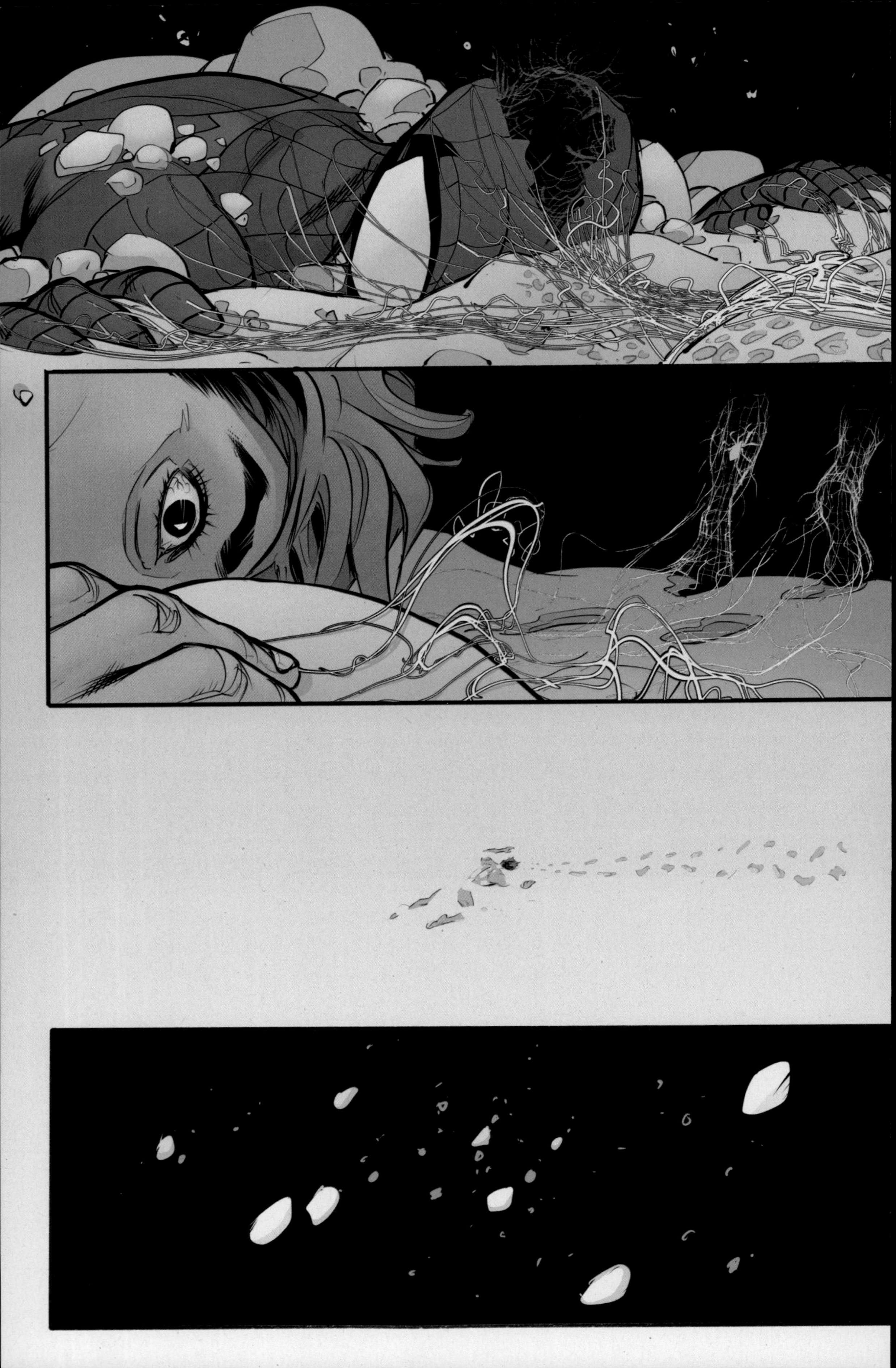

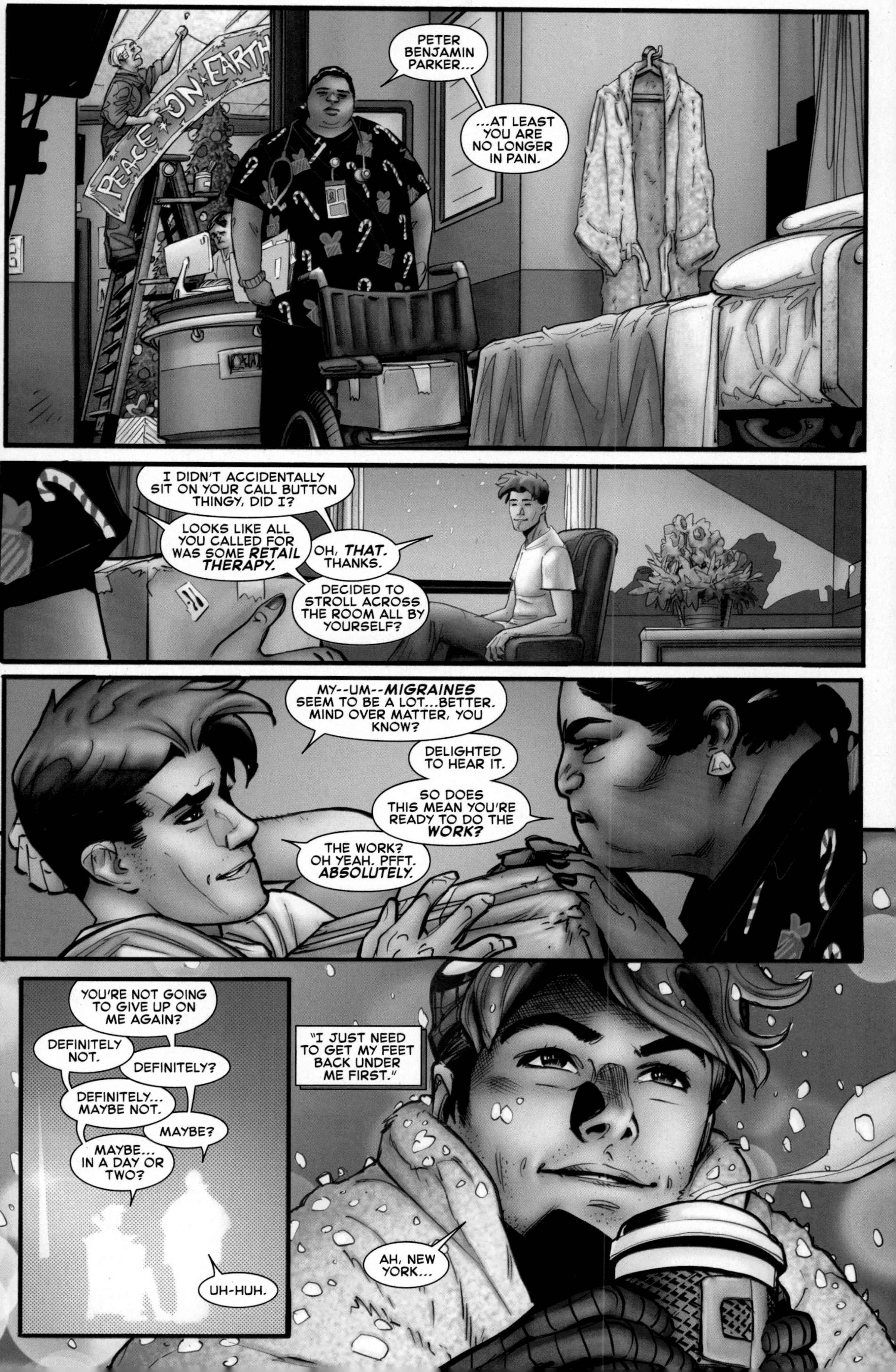

PEACE ON EARTH
PETER BENJAMIN PARKER...
...AT LEAST YOU ARE NO LONGER IN PAIN.
I DIDN'T ACCIDENTALLY SIT ON YOUR CALL BUTTON THINGY, DID I?
LOOKS LIKE ALL YOU CALLED FOR WAS SOME RETAIL THERAPY.
OH, THAT. THANKS.
DECIDED TO STROLL ACROSS THE ROOM ALL BY YOURSELF?
MY--UM--MIGRAINES SEEM TO BE A LOT...BETTER. MIND OVER MATTER, YOU KNOW?
DELIGHTED TO HEAR IT.
SO DOES THIS MEAN YOU'RE READY TO DO THE WORK?
THE WORK? OH YEAH. PFFT. ABSOLUTELY.
YOU'RE NOT GOING TO GIVE UP ON ME AGAIN?
DEFINITELY NOT.
DEFINITELY?
DEFINITELY... MAYBE NOT.
MAYBE?
MAYBE... IN A DAY OR TWO?
UH-HUH.
"I JUST NEED TO GET MY FEET BACK UNDER ME FIRST."
AH, NEW YORK...

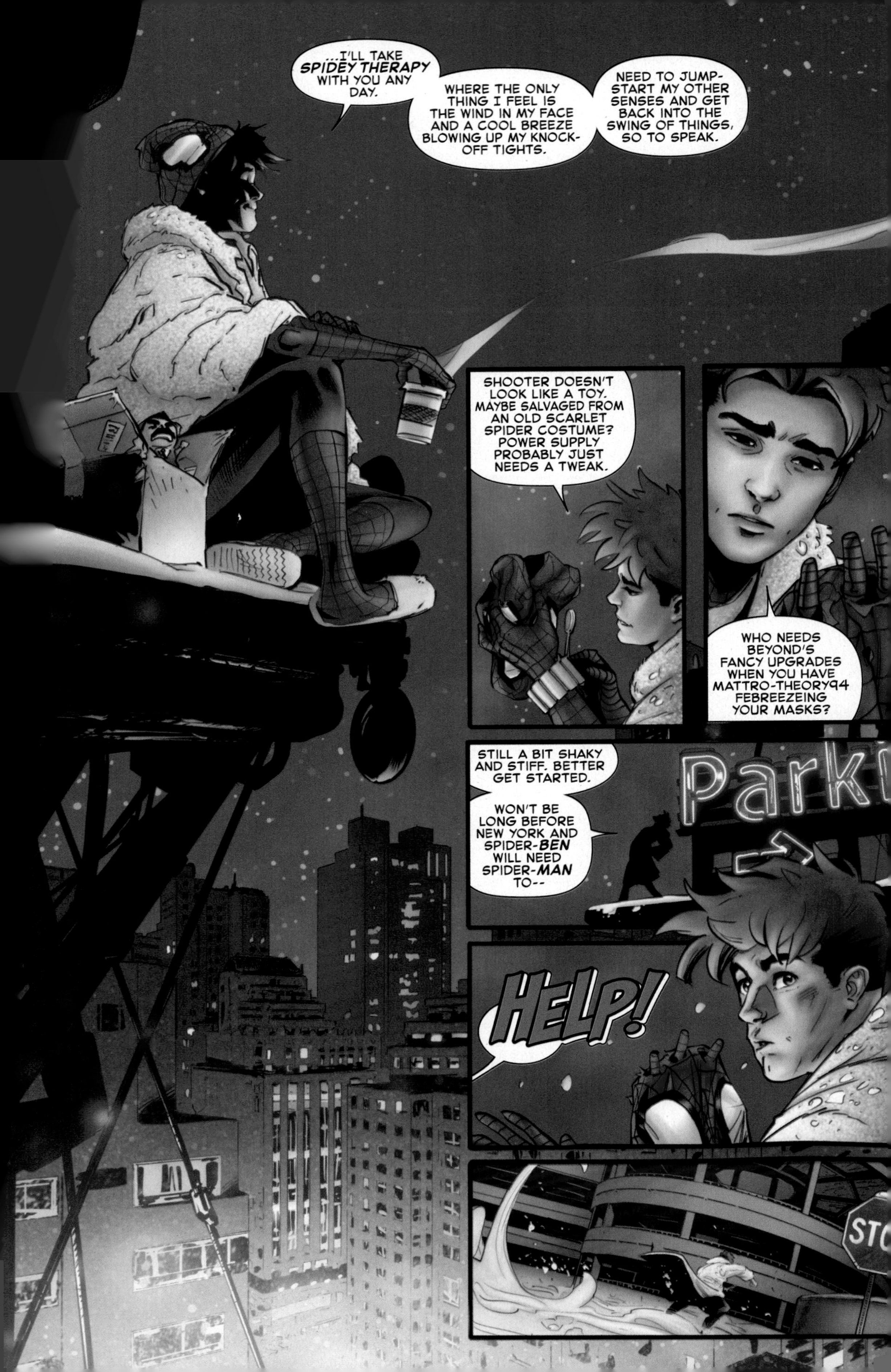
...I'LL TAKE SPIDEY THERAPY WITH YOU ANY DAY.
WHERE THE ONLY THING I FEEL IS THE WIND IN MY FACE AND A COOL BREEZE BLOWING UP MY KNOCK-OFF TIGHTS.
NEED TO JUMP-START MY OTHER SENSES AND GET BACK INTO THE SWING OF THINGS, SO TO SPEAK.
SHOOTER DOESN'T LOOK LIKE A TOY. MAYBE SALVAGED FROM AN OLD SCARLET SPIDER COSTUME? POWER SUPPLY PROBABLY JUST NEEDS A TWEAK.
WHO NEEDS BEYOND'S FANCY UPGRADES WHEN YOU HAVE MATTRO-THEORY94 FEBREEZEING YOUR MASKS?
STILL A BIT SHAKY AND STIFF. BETTER GET STARTED.
WON'T BE LONG BEFORE NEW YORK AND SPIDER-BEN WILL NEED SPIDER-MAN TO--
Park
HELP!
STO

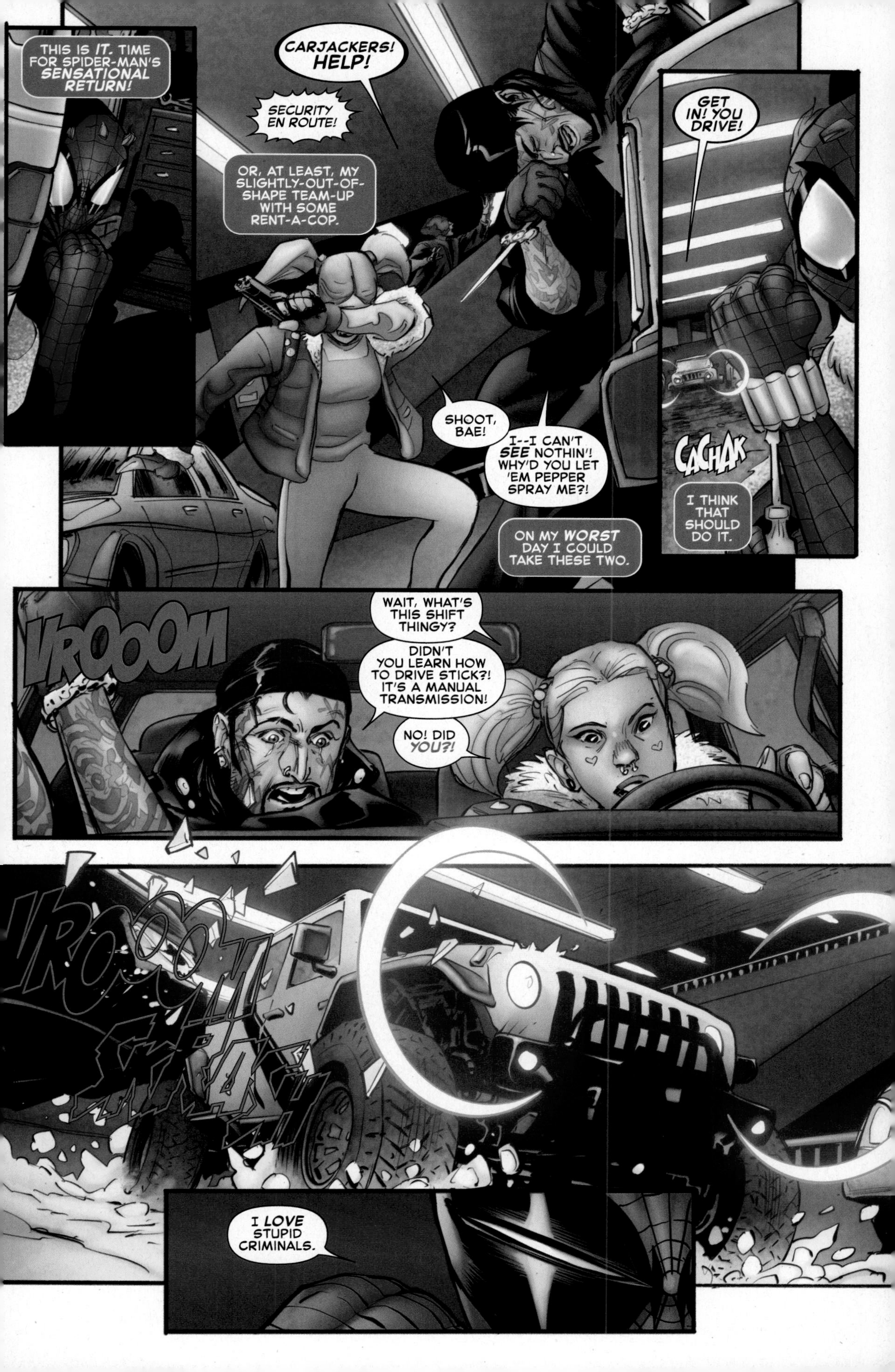
THIS IS IT. TIME FOR SPIDER-MAN'S SENSATIONAL RETURN!
CARJACKERS! HELP!
SECURITY EN ROUTE!
OR, AT LEAST, MY SLIGHTLY-OUT-OF-SHAPE TEAM-UP WITH SOME RENT-A-COP.
SHOOT, BAE!
I--I CAN'T SEE NOTHIN'! WHY'D YOU LET 'EM PEPPER SPRAY ME?!
ON MY WORST DAY I COULD TAKE THESE TWO.
GET IN! YOU DRIVE!
CACHAK
I THINK THAT SHOULD DO IT.
VROOOM
WAIT, WHAT'S THIS SHIFT THINGY?
DIDN'T YOU LEARN HOW TO DRIVE STICK?! IT'S A MANUAL TRANSMISSION!
NO! DID YOU?!
I LOVE STUPID CRIMINALS.

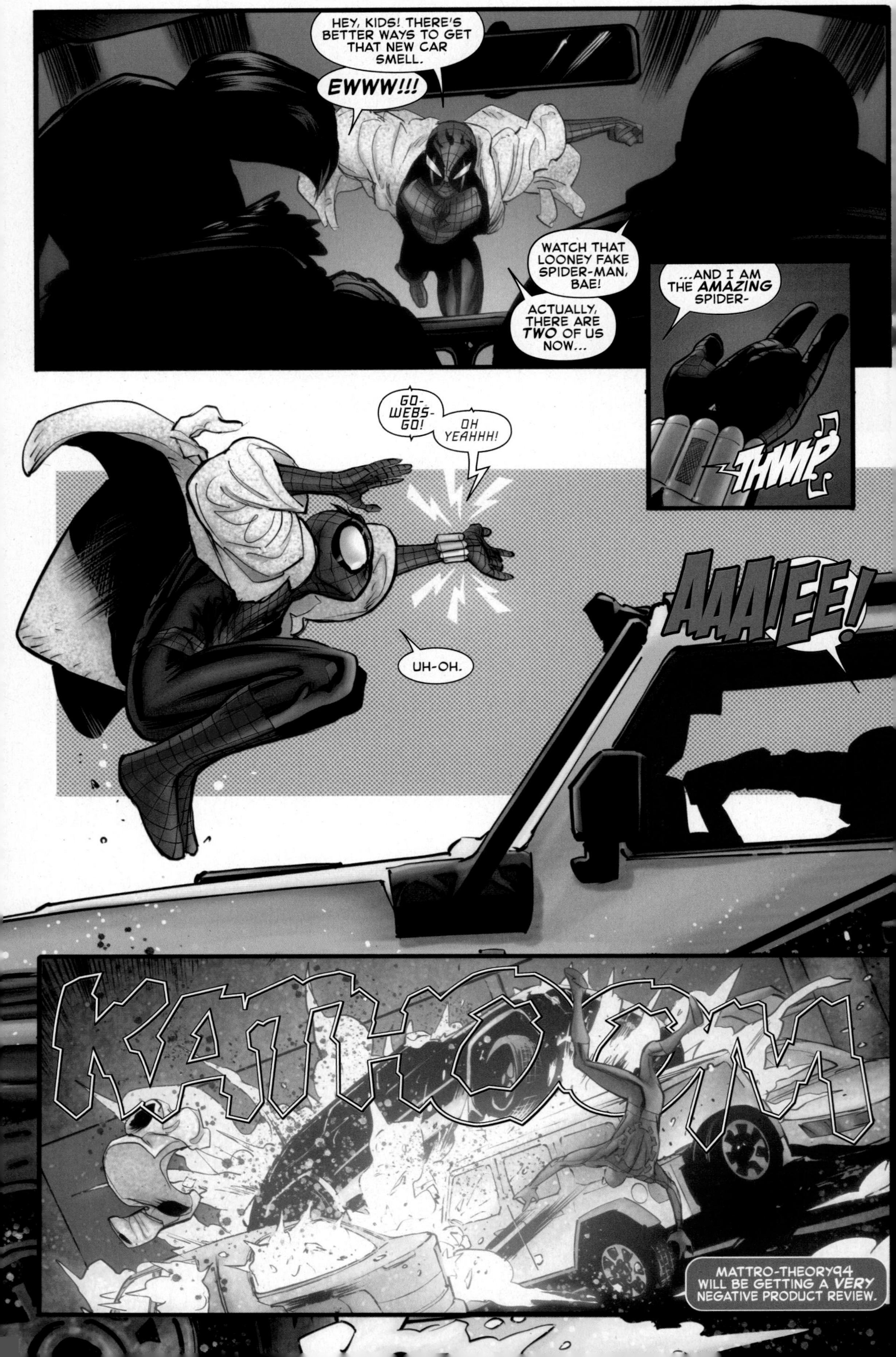
HEY, KIDS! THERE'S BETTER WAYS TO GET THAT NEW CAR SMELL.
EWWW!!!
WATCH THAT LOONEY FAKE SPIDER-MAN, BAE!
ACTUALLY, THERE ARE TWO OF US NOW...
...AND I AM THE AMAZING SPIDER-
THWIP
GO-WEBS-GO!
OH YEAHHH!
AAAIEE!
UH-OH.
KATHOOM
MATTRO-THEORY94 WILL BE GETTING A VERY NEGATIVE PRODUCT REVIEW.

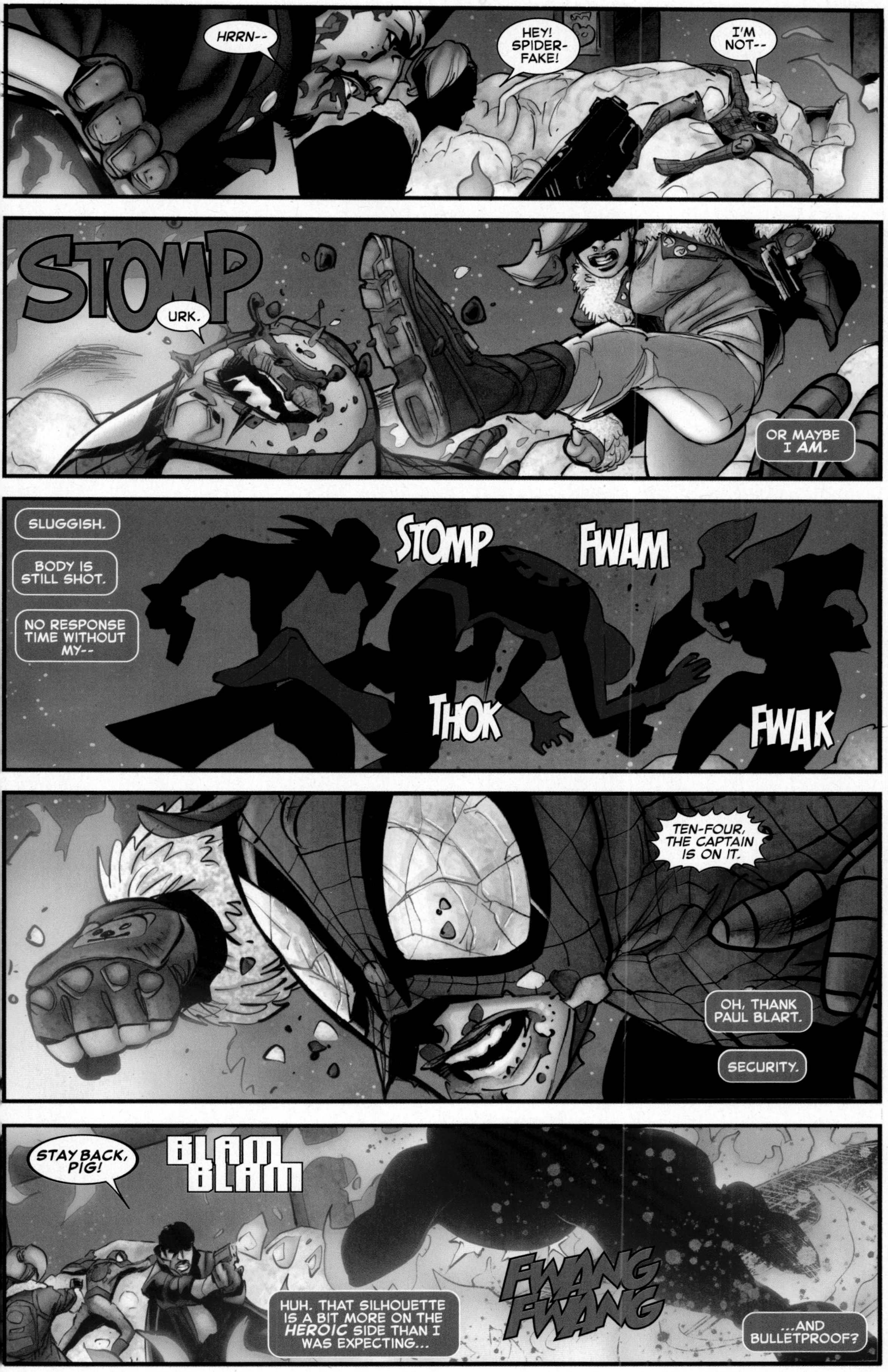
HRRN--
HEY! SPIDER-FAKE!
I'M NOT--
STOMP
URK.
OR MAYBE I *AM*.
SLUGGISH.
BODY IS STILL SHOT.
NO RESPONSE TIME WITHOUT MY--
STOMP
FWAM
THOK
FWAK
TEN-FOUR, THE CAPTAIN IS ON IT.
OH, THANK PAUL BLART.
SECURITY.
STAY BACK, PIG!
BLAM BLAM
HUH. THAT SILHOUETTE IS A BIT MORE ON THE *HEROIC* SIDE THAN I WAS EXPECTING...
FWANG FWANG
...AND BULLETPROOF?

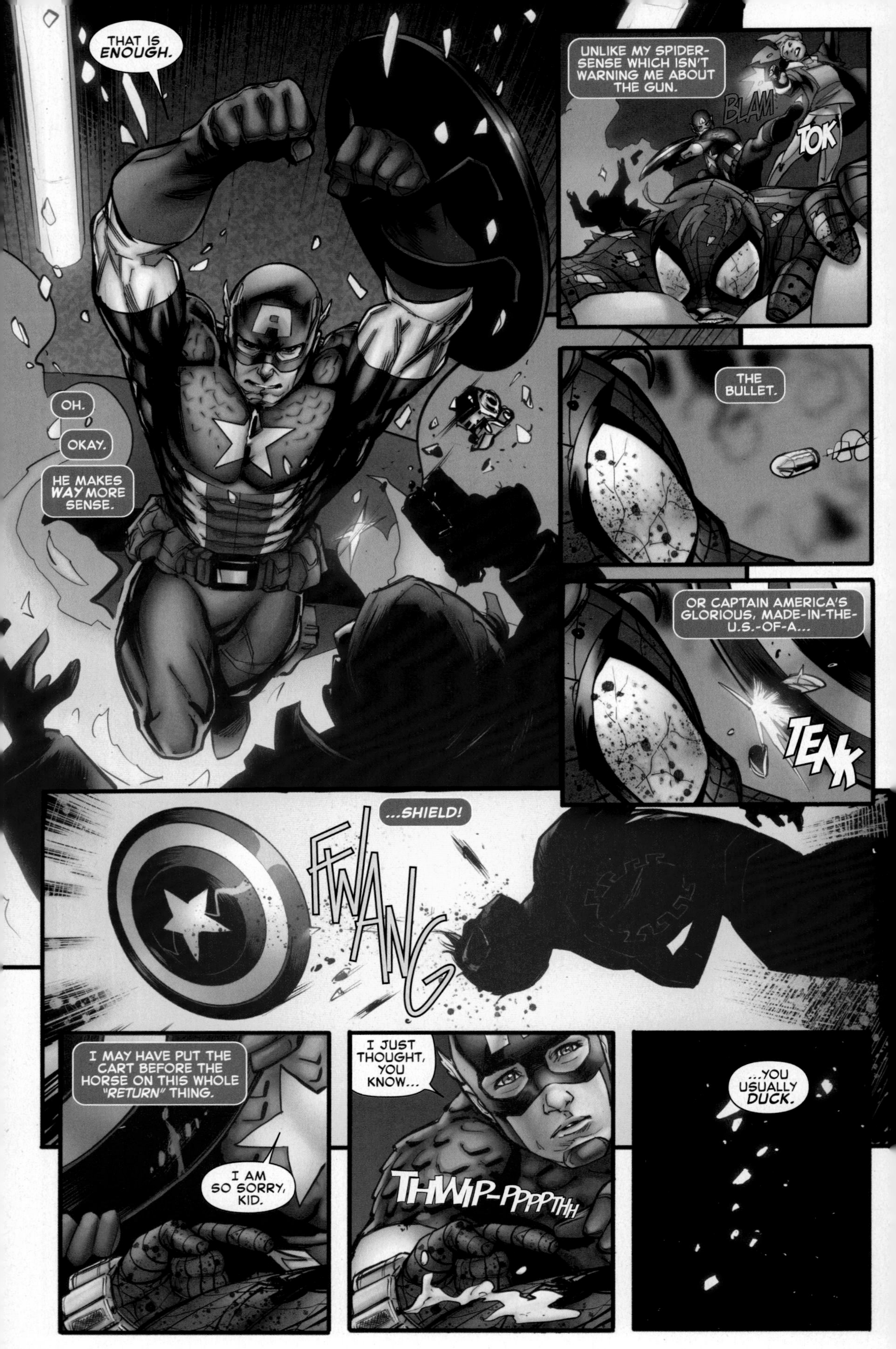
THAT IS ENOUGH.
OH.
OKAY.
HE MAKES WAY MORE SENSE.
UNLIKE MY SPIDER-SENSE WHICH ISN'T WARNING ME ABOUT THE GUN.
BLAM
TOK
THE BULLET.
OR CAPTAIN AMERICA'S GLORIOUS, MADE-IN-THE-U.S.-OF-A...
TENK
...SHIELD!
FFWANG
I MAY HAVE PUT THE CART BEFORE THE HORSE ON THIS WHOLE "RETURN" THING.
I AM SO SORRY, KID.
I JUST THOUGHT, YOU KNOW...
THWIP-PPPPTHH
...YOU USUALLY DUCK.

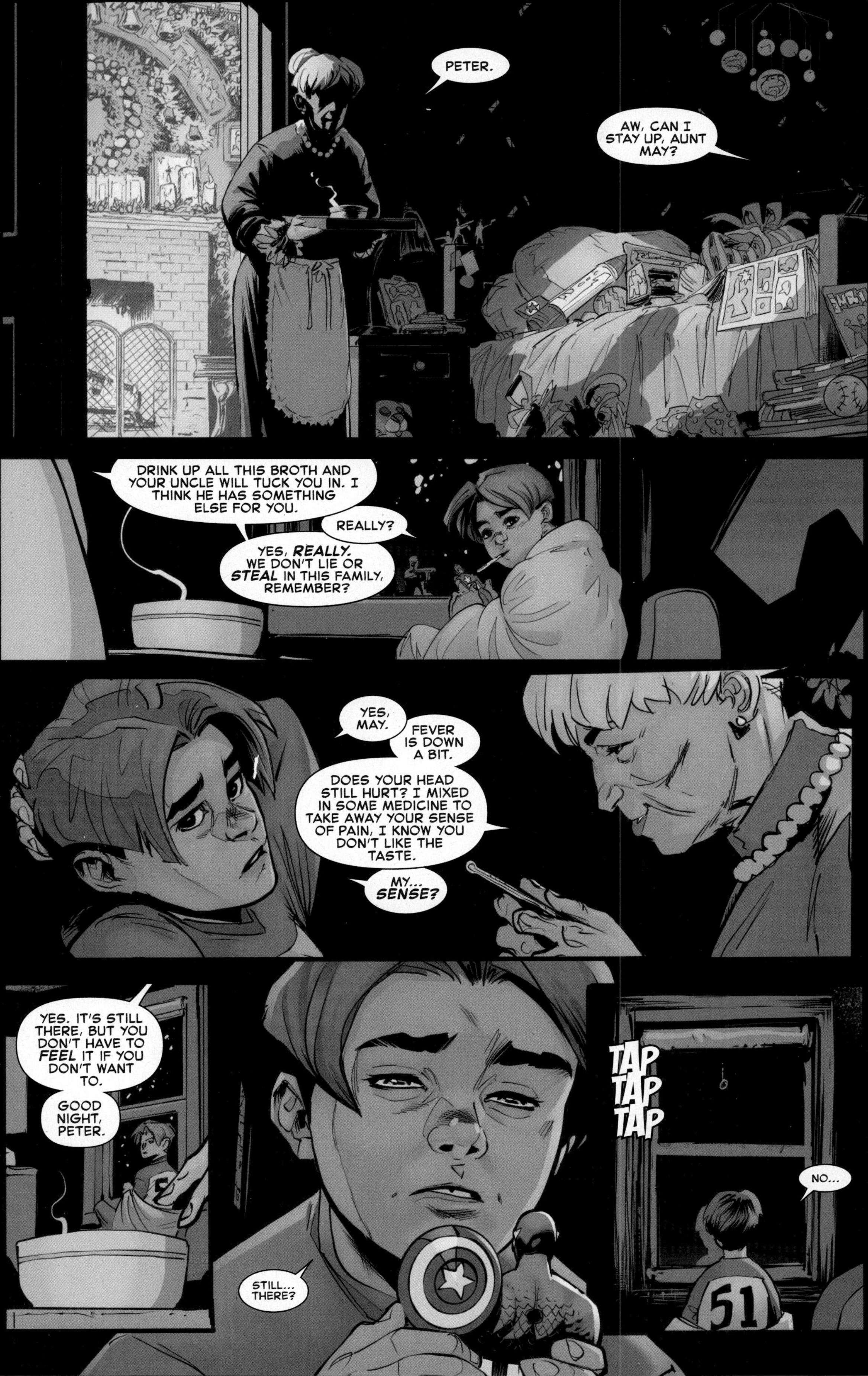
PETER.
AW, CAN I STAY UP, AUNT MAY?
DRINK UP ALL THIS BROTH AND YOUR UNCLE WILL TUCK YOU IN. I THINK HE HAS SOMETHING ELSE FOR YOU.
REALLY?
YES, REALLY. WE DON'T LIE OR STEAL IN THIS FAMILY, REMEMBER?
YES, MAY.
FEVER IS DOWN A BIT.
DOES YOUR HEAD STILL HURT? I MIXED IN SOME MEDICINE TO TAKE AWAY YOUR SENSE OF PAIN, I KNOW YOU DON'T LIKE THE TASTE.
MY... SENSE?
YES. IT'S STILL THERE, BUT YOU DON'T HAVE TO FEEL IT IF YOU DON'T WANT TO.
GOOD NIGHT, PETER.
STILL... THERE?
TAP TAP TAP
NO...
51

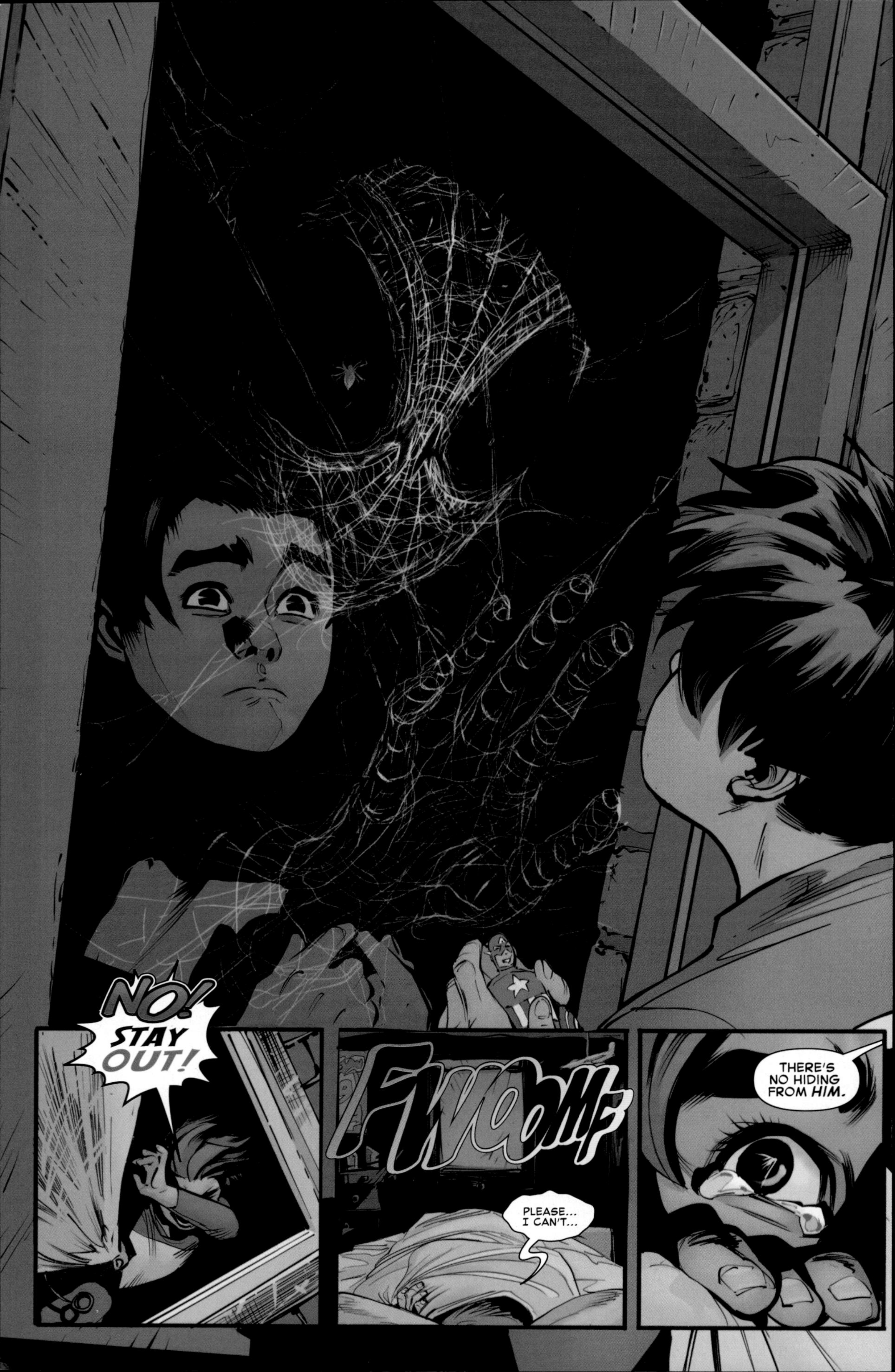
NO! STAY OUT!
FWOOMF
PLEASE... I CAN'T...
THERE'S NO HIDING FROM HIM.

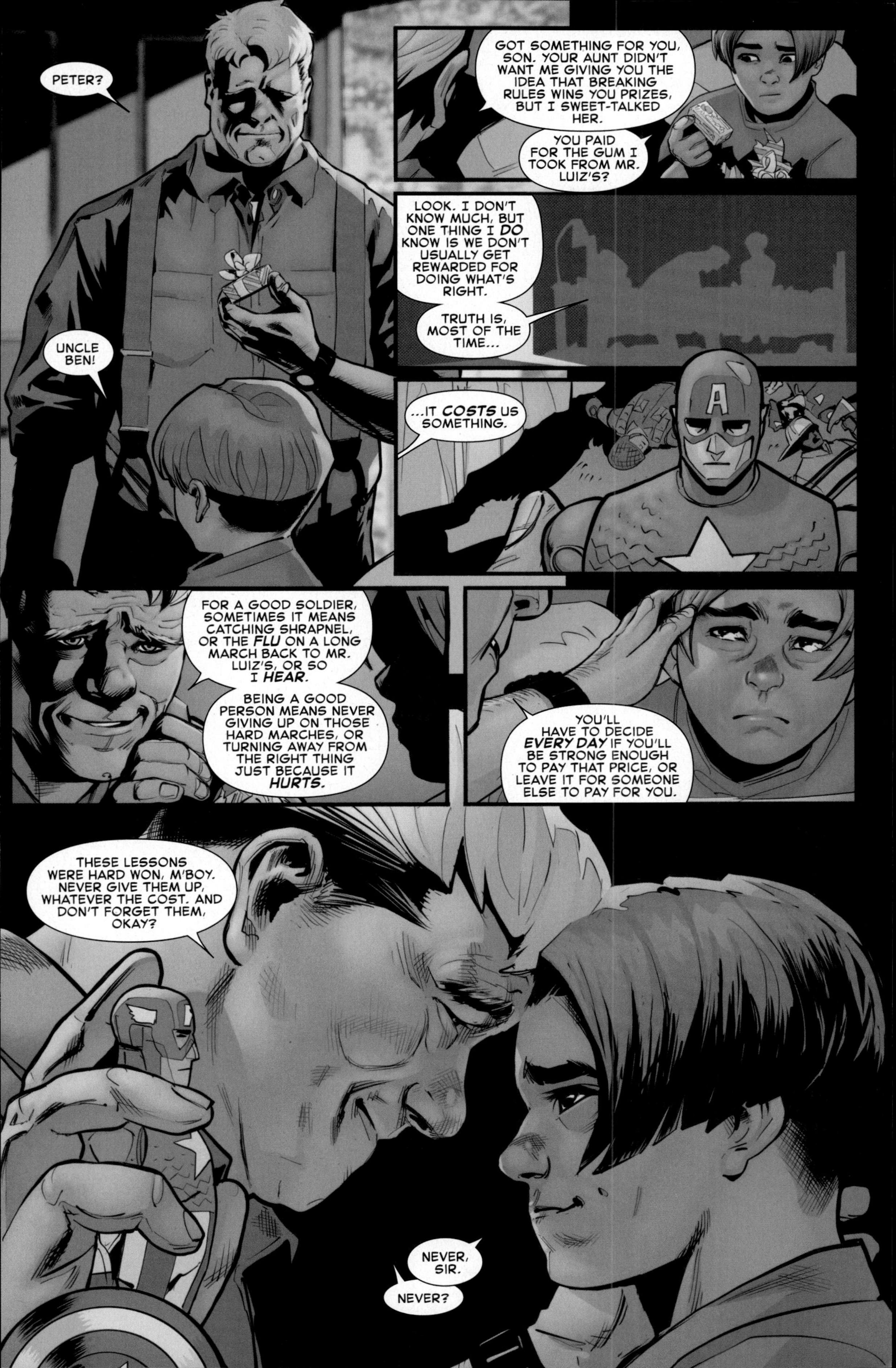
PETER?
GOT SOMETHING FOR YOU, SON. YOUR AUNT DIDN'T WANT ME GIVING YOU THE IDEA THAT BREAKING RULES WINS YOU PRIZES, BUT I SWEET-TALKED HER.
YOU PAID FOR THE GUM I TOOK FROM MR. LUIZ'S?
LOOK. I DON'T KNOW MUCH, BUT ONE THING I *DO* KNOW IS WE DON'T USUALLY GET REWARDED FOR DOING WHAT'S RIGHT.
TRUTH IS, MOST OF THE TIME...
UNCLE BEN!
...IT *COSTS* US SOMETHING.
FOR A GOOD SOLDIER, SOMETIMES IT MEANS CATCHING SHRAPNEL, OR THE *FLU* ON A LONG MARCH BACK TO MR. LUIZ'S, OR SO I *HEAR*.
BEING A GOOD PERSON MEANS NEVER GIVING UP ON THOSE HARD MARCHES, OR TURNING AWAY FROM THE RIGHT THING JUST BECAUSE IT *HURTS*.
YOU'LL HAVE TO DECIDE *EVERY DAY* IF YOU'LL BE STRONG ENOUGH TO PAY THAT PRICE, OR LEAVE IT FOR SOMEONE ELSE TO PAY FOR YOU.
THESE LESSONS WERE HARD WON, M'BOY. NEVER GIVE THEM UP, WHATEVER THE COST. AND DON'T FORGET THEM, OKAY?
NEVER, SIR.
NEVER?

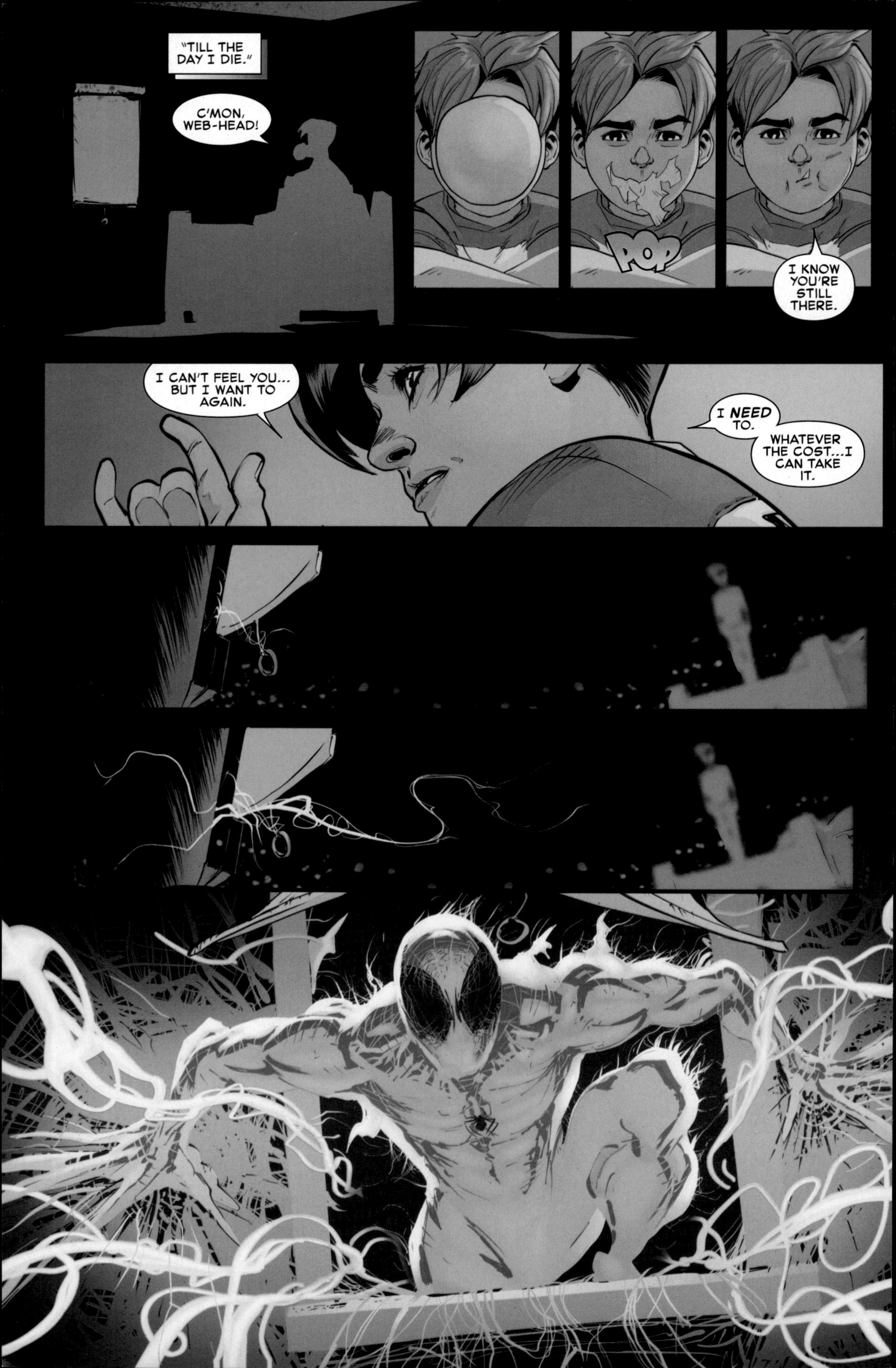
"TILL THE DAY I DIE."
C'MON, WEB-HEAD!
POP
I KNOW YOU'RE STILL THERE.
I CAN'T FEEL YOU... BUT I WANT TO AGAIN.
I NEED TO.
WHATEVER THE COST...I CAN TAKE IT.

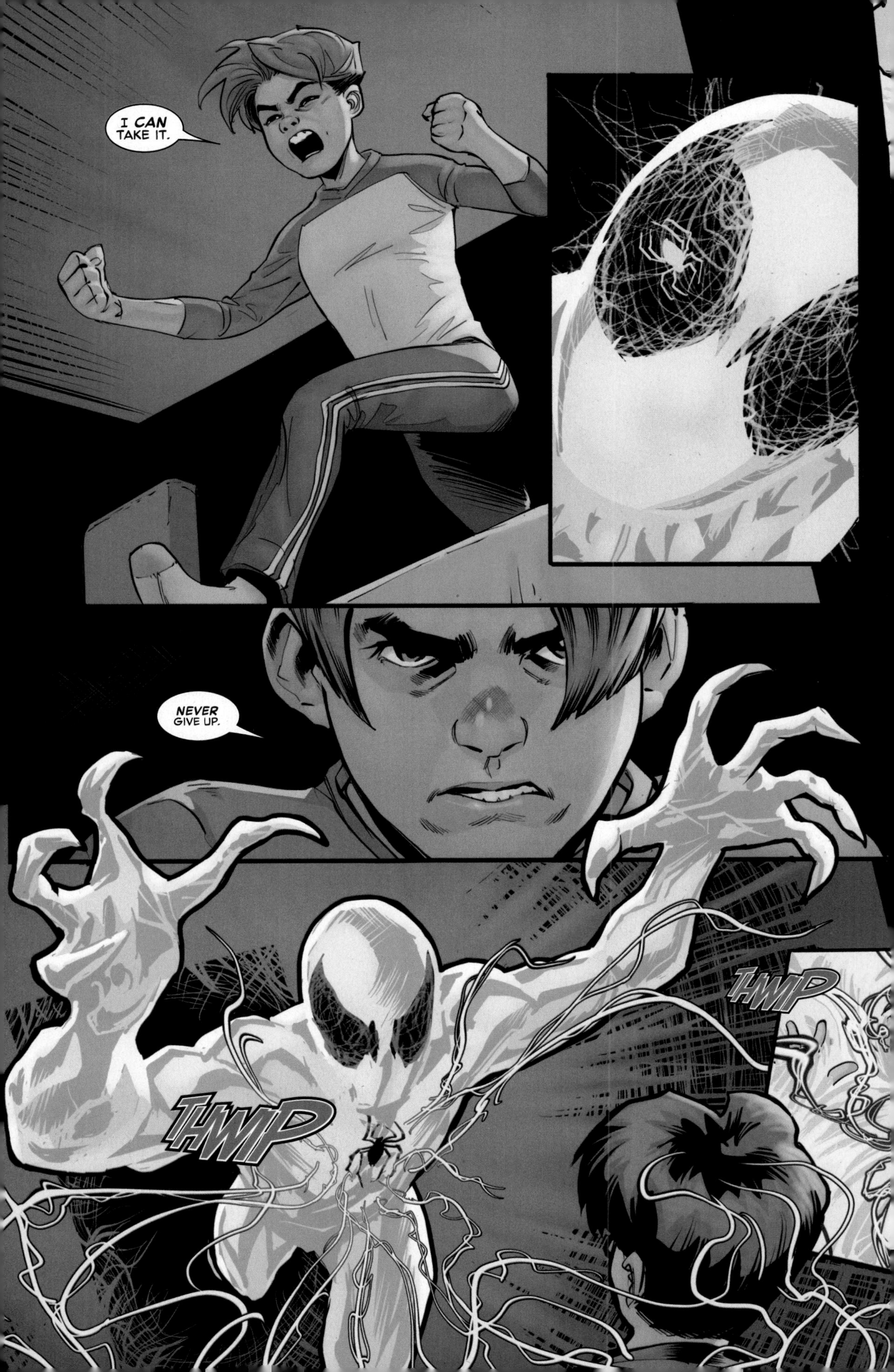
I CAN TAKE IT.
NEVER GIVE UP.
THMP
THMP

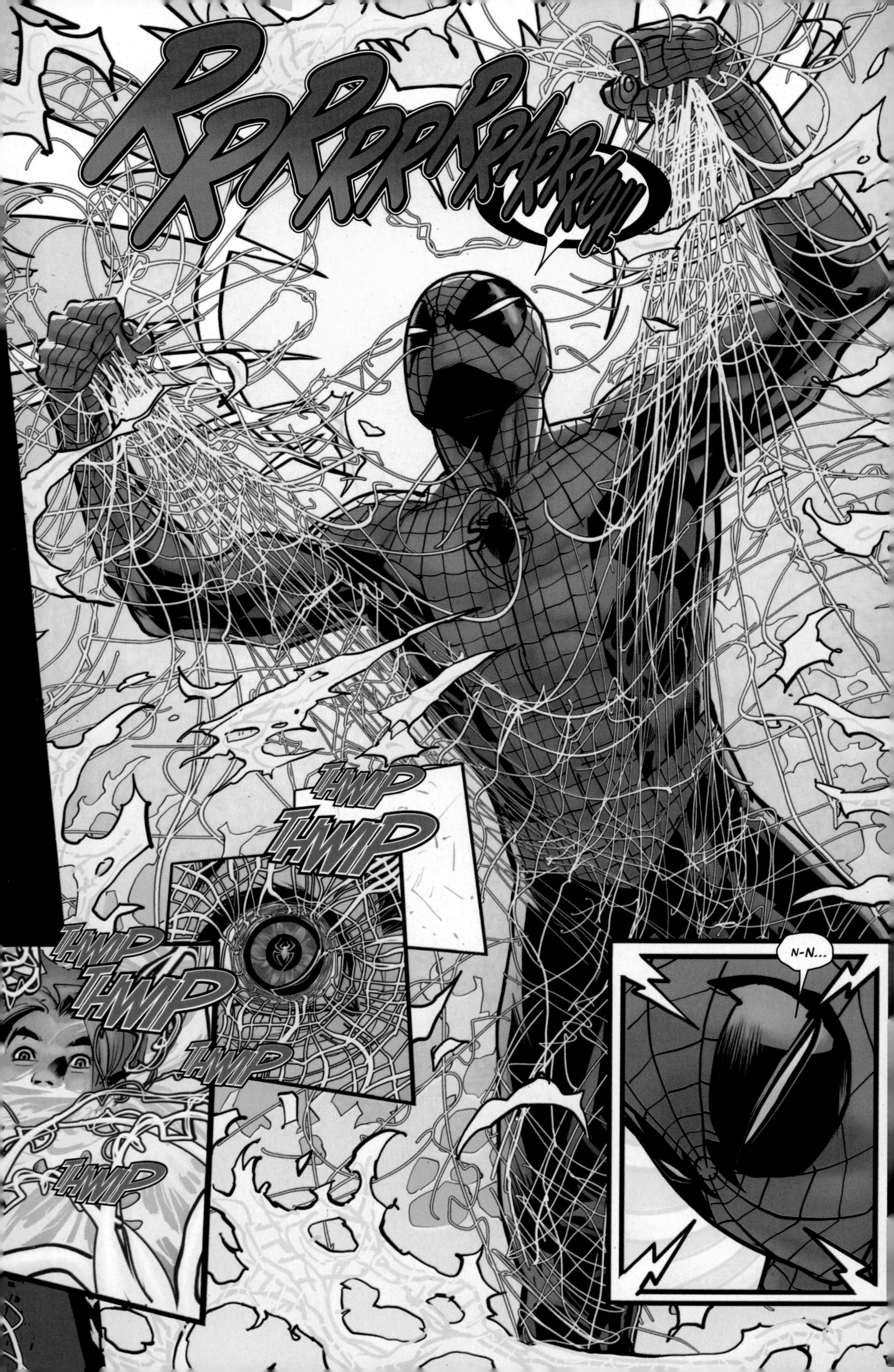
RRRRRRRRRAARRGH!!
THWIP
THWIP
THWIP
THWIP
THWIP
THWIP
N-N...

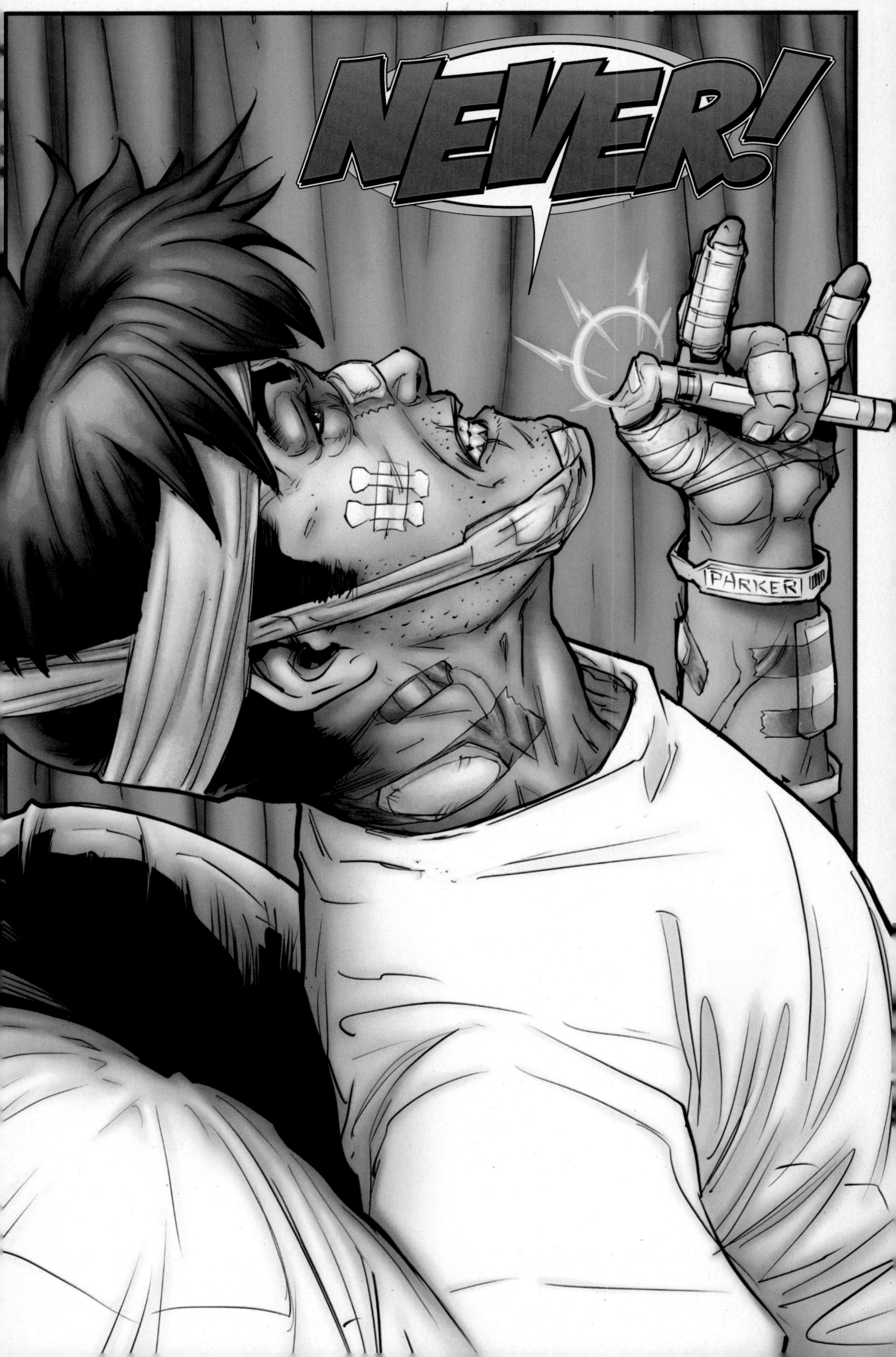
NEVER!
PARKER

BEYOND CORPORATION #84

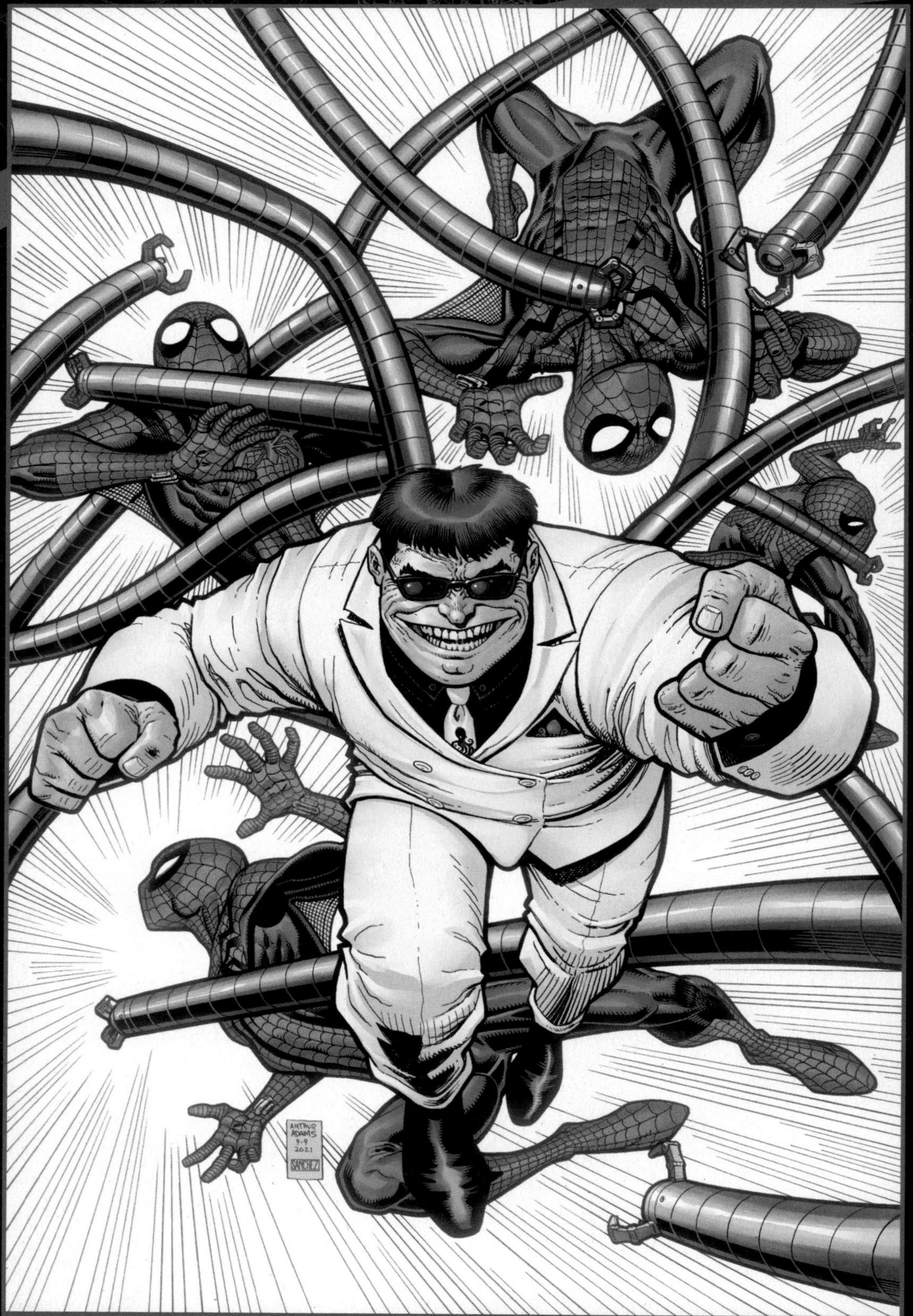
ARTHUR ADAMS 9-9 2021
SANCHEZ

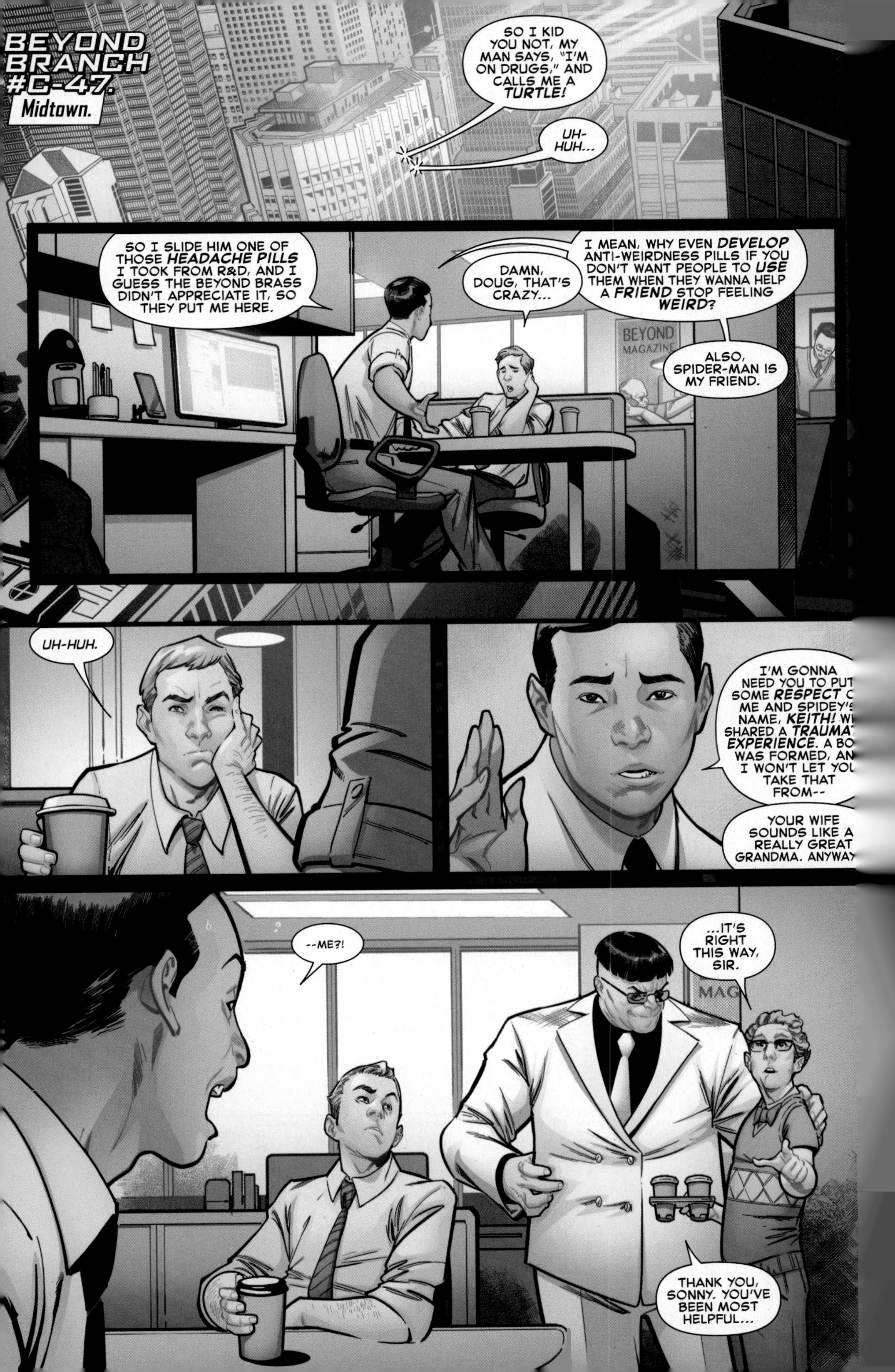
BEYOND BRANCH #C-47.
Midtown.
SO I KID YOU NOT, MY MAN SAYS, "I'M ON DRUGS," AND CALLS ME A TURTLE!
UH-HUH...
SO I SLIDE HIM ONE OF THOSE HEADACHE PILLS I TOOK FROM R&D, AND I GUESS THE BEYOND BRASS DIDN'T APPRECIATE IT, SO THEY PUT ME HERE.
DAMN, DOUG, THAT'S CRAZY...
I MEAN, WHY EVEN DEVELOP ANTI-WEIRDNESS PILLS IF YOU DON'T WANT PEOPLE TO USE THEM WHEN THEY WANNA HELP A FRIEND STOP FEELING WEIRD?
ALSO, SPIDER-MAN IS MY FRIEND.
BEYOND MAGAZINE
UH-HUH.
I'M GONNA NEED YOU TO PUT SOME RESPECT ON ME AND SPIDEY'S NAME, KEITH! WE SHARED A TRAUMATIC EXPERIENCE. A BOND WAS FORMED, AND I WON'T LET YOU TAKE THAT FROM--
YOUR WIFE SOUNDS LIKE A REALLY GREAT GRANDMA. ANYWAY
--ME?!
...IT'S RIGHT THIS WAY, SIR.
THANK YOU, SONNY. YOU'VE BEEN MOST HELPFUL...

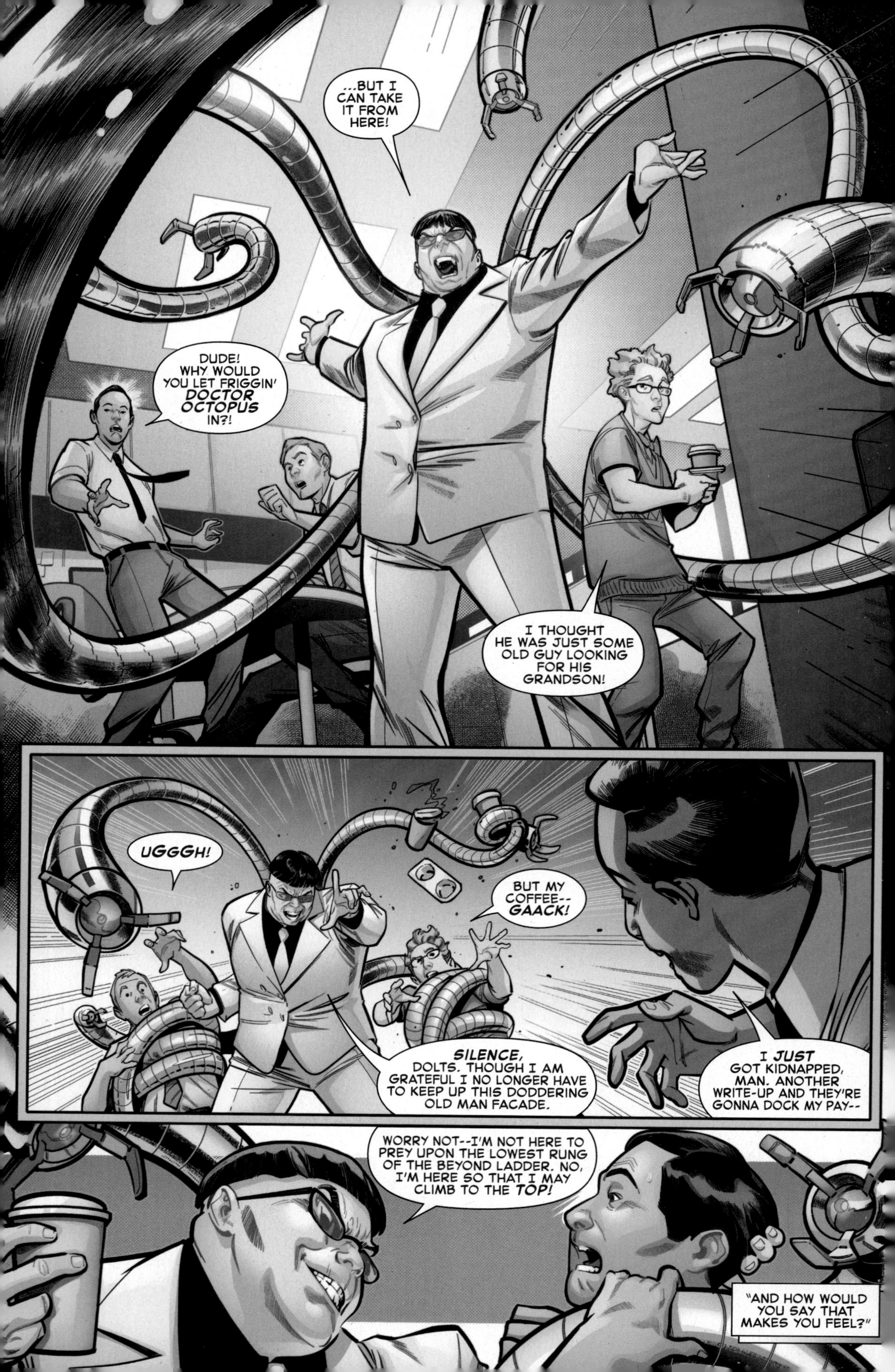
...BUT I CAN TAKE IT FROM HERE!
DUDE! WHY WOULD YOU LET FRIGGIN' DOCTOR OCTOPUS IN?!
I THOUGHT HE WAS JUST SOME OLD GUY LOOKING FOR HIS GRANDSON!
UGGGH!
BUT MY COFFEE-- GAACK!
SILENCE, DOLTS. THOUGH I AM GRATEFUL I NO LONGER HAVE TO KEEP UP THIS DODDERING OLD MAN FACADE.
I JUST GOT KIDNAPPED, MAN. ANOTHER WRITE-UP AND THEY'RE GONNA DOCK MY PAY--
WORRY NOT--I'M NOT HERE TO PREY UPON THE LOWEST RUNG OF THE BEYOND LADDER. NO, I'M HERE SO THAT I MAY CLIMB TO THE TOP!
"AND HOW WOULD YOU SAY THAT MAKES YOU FEEL?"

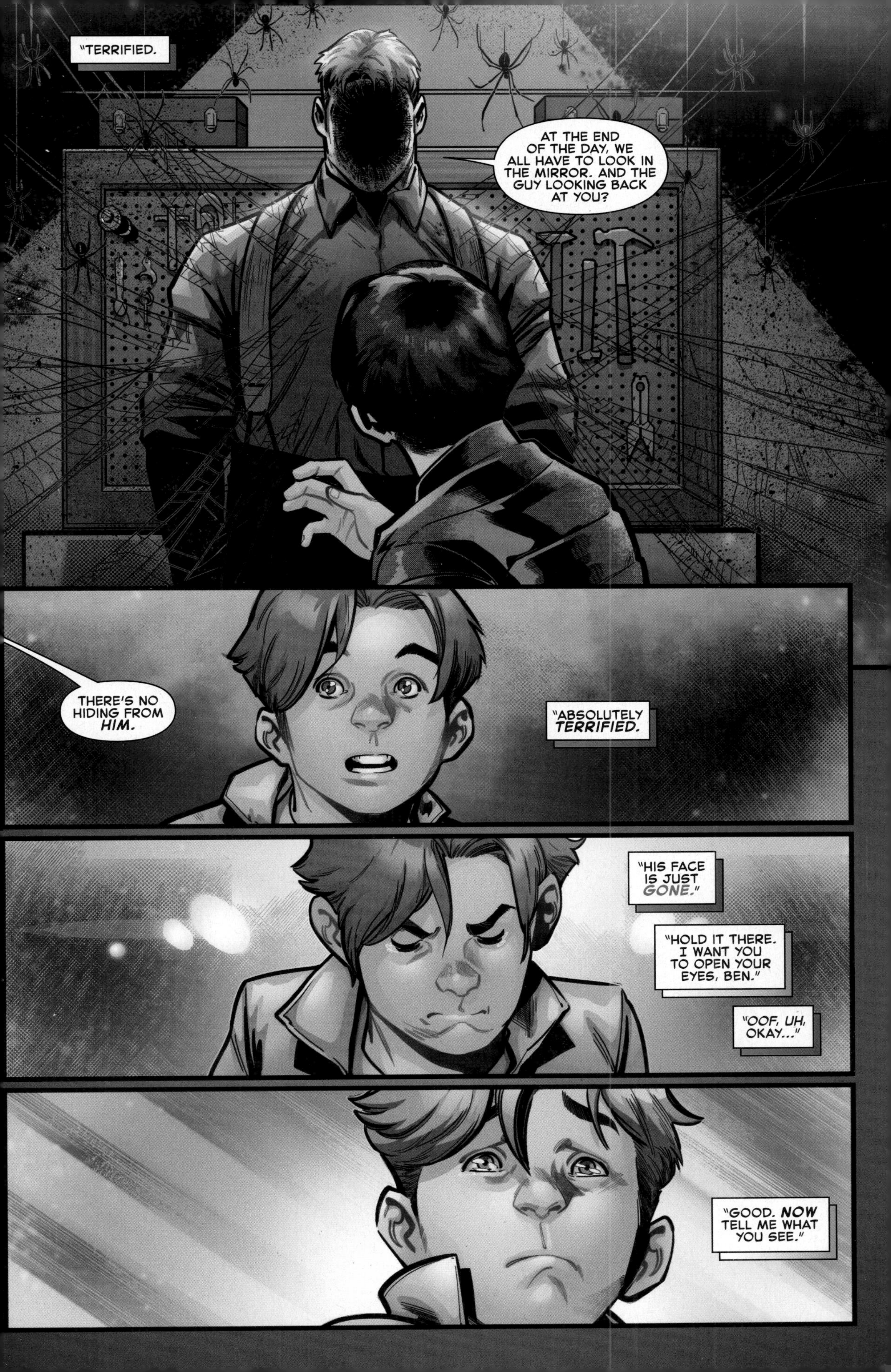
"TERRIFIED.
AT THE END OF THE DAY, WE ALL HAVE TO LOOK IN THE MIRROR. AND THE GUY LOOKING BACK AT YOU?
THERE'S NO HIDING FROM *HIM.*
"ABSOLUTELY *TERRIFIED.*
"HIS FACE IS JUST *GONE.*"
"HOLD IT THERE. I WANT YOU TO OPEN YOUR EYES, BEN."
"OOF, UH, OKAY..."
"GOOD. **NOW** TELL ME WHAT YOU SEE."

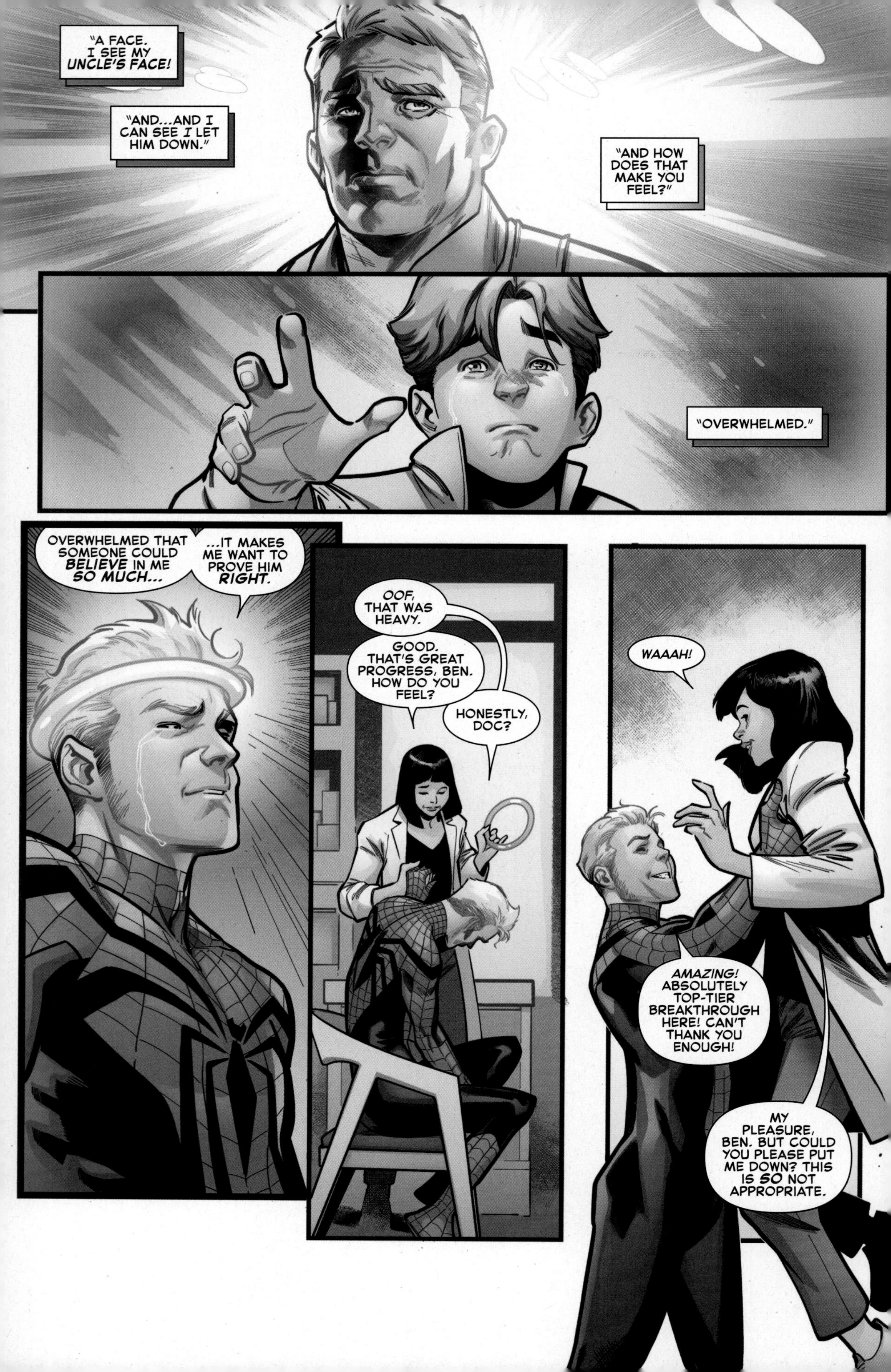
"A FACE. I SEE MY UNCLE'S FACE!
"AND...AND I CAN SEE I LET HIM DOWN."
"AND HOW DOES THAT MAKE YOU FEEL?"
"OVERWHELMED."
OVERWHELMED THAT SOMEONE COULD BELIEVE IN ME SO MUCH...
...IT MAKES ME WANT TO PROVE HIM RIGHT.
OOF, THAT WAS HEAVY.
GOOD. THAT'S GREAT PROGRESS, BEN. HOW DO YOU FEEL?
HONESTLY, DOC?
WAAAH!
AMAZING! ABSOLUTELY TOP-TIER BREAKTHROUGH HERE! CAN'T THANK YOU ENOUGH!
MY PLEASURE, BEN. BUT COULD YOU PLEASE PUT ME DOWN? THIS IS SO NOT APPROPRIATE.

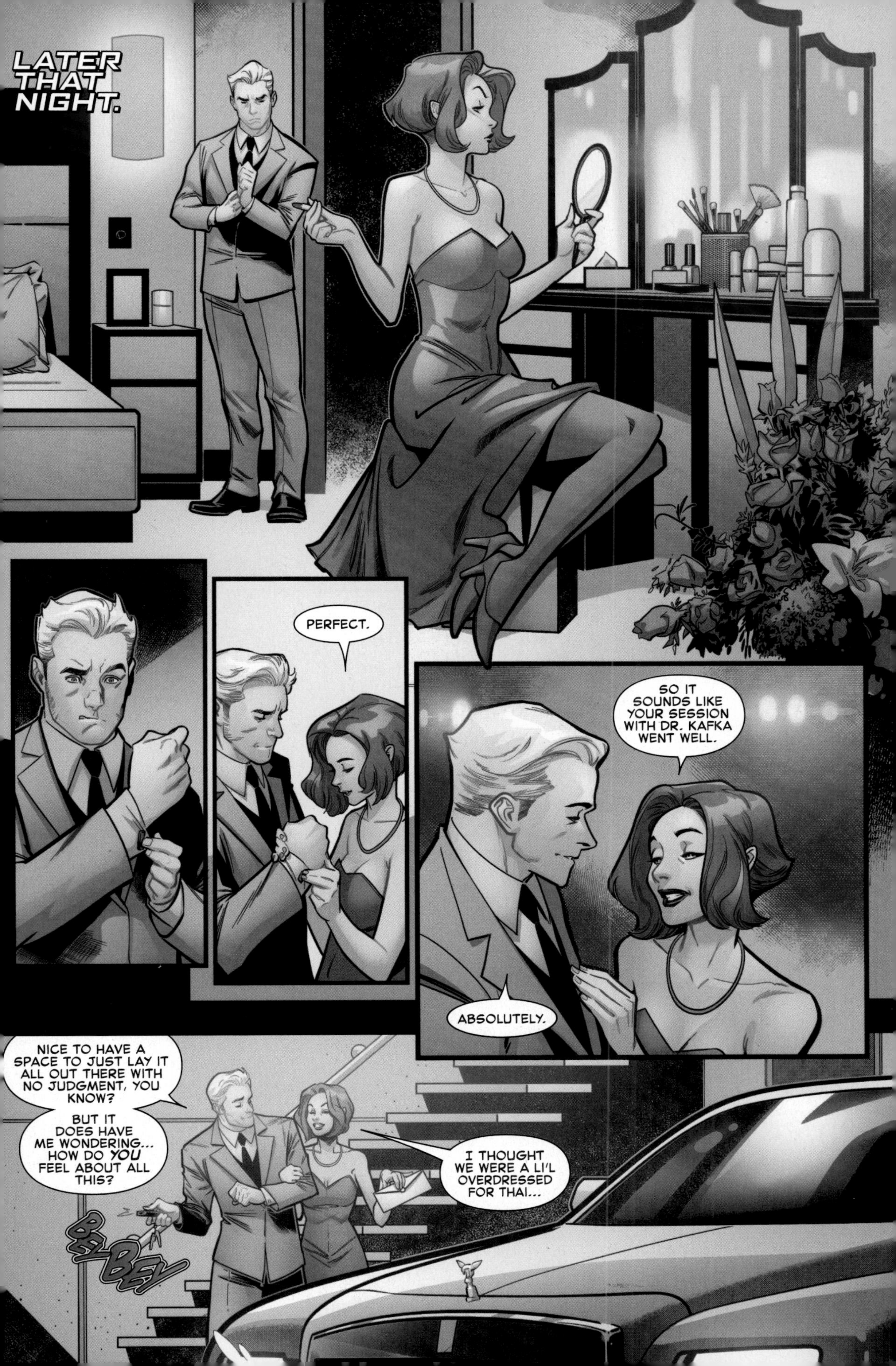
LATER THAT NIGHT.
PERFECT.
SO IT SOUNDS LIKE YOUR SESSION WITH DR. KAFKA WENT WELL.
ABSOLUTELY.
NICE TO HAVE A SPACE TO JUST LAY IT ALL OUT THERE WITH NO JUDGMENT, YOU KNOW?
BUT IT DOES HAVE ME WONDERING... HOW DO YOU FEEL ABOUT ALL THIS?
I THOUGHT WE WERE A LI'L OVERDRESSED FOR THAI...
BEEBEEP

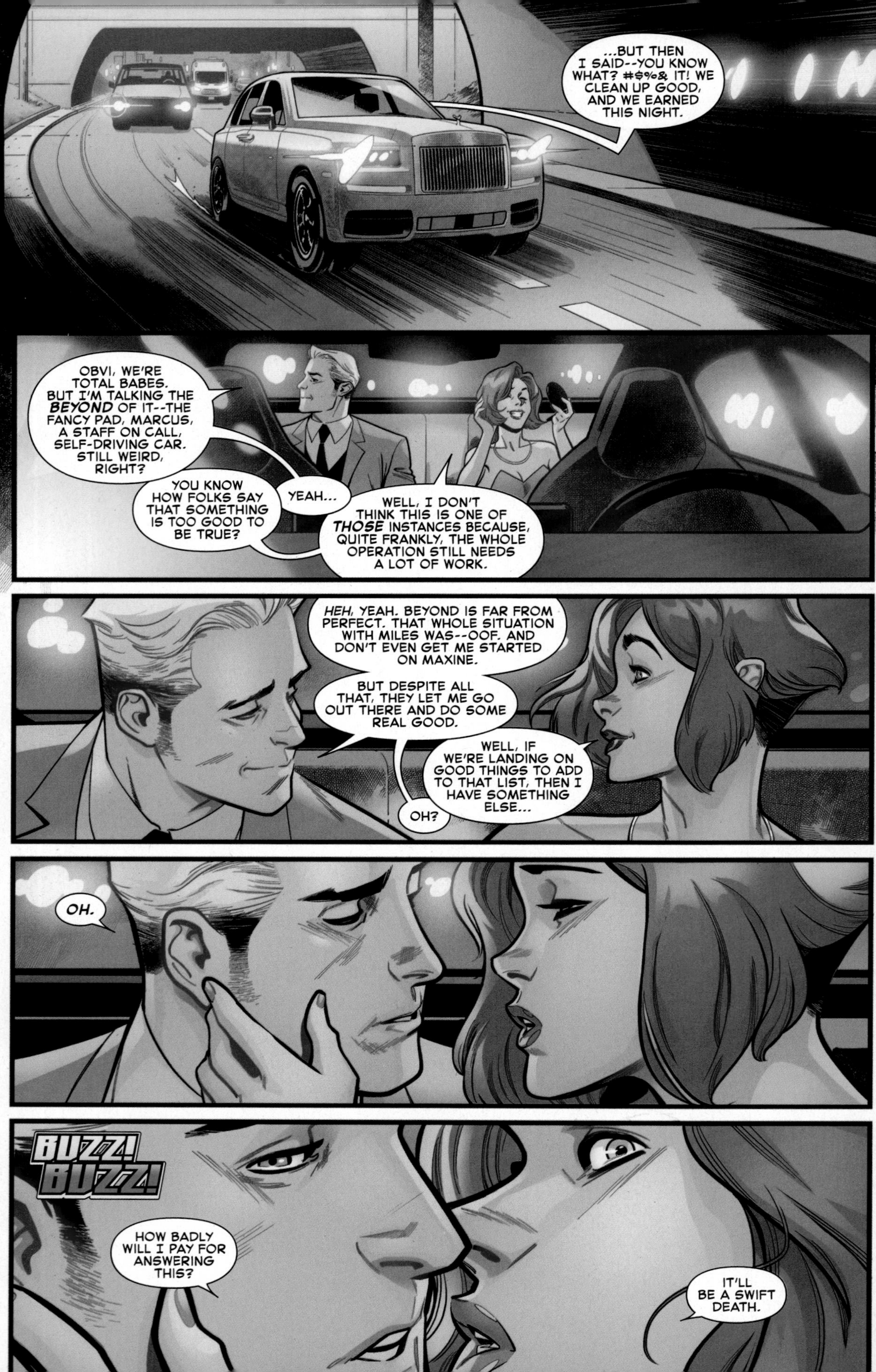

...BUT THEN I SAID--YOU KNOW WHAT? #$%& IT! WE CLEAN UP GOOD, AND WE EARNED THIS NIGHT.
OBVI, WE'RE TOTAL BABES. BUT I'M TALKING THE BEYOND OF IT--THE FANCY PAD, MARCUS, A STAFF ON CALL, SELF-DRIVING CAR. STILL WEIRD, RIGHT?
YEAH...
YOU KNOW HOW FOLKS SAY THAT SOMETHING IS TOO GOOD TO BE TRUE?
WELL, I DON'T THINK THIS IS ONE OF THOSE INSTANCES BECAUSE, QUITE FRANKLY, THE WHOLE OPERATION STILL NEEDS A LOT OF WORK.
HEH, YEAH. BEYOND IS FAR FROM PERFECT. THAT WHOLE SITUATION WITH MILES WAS--OOF. AND DON'T EVEN GET ME STARTED ON MAXINE.
BUT DESPITE ALL THAT, THEY LET ME GO OUT THERE AND DO SOME REAL GOOD.
WELL, IF WE'RE LANDING ON GOOD THINGS TO ADD TO THAT LIST, THEN I HAVE SOMETHING ELSE...
OH?
OH.
BUZZ! BUZZ!
HOW BADLY WILL I PAY FOR ANSWERING THIS?
IT'LL BE A SWIFT DEATH.

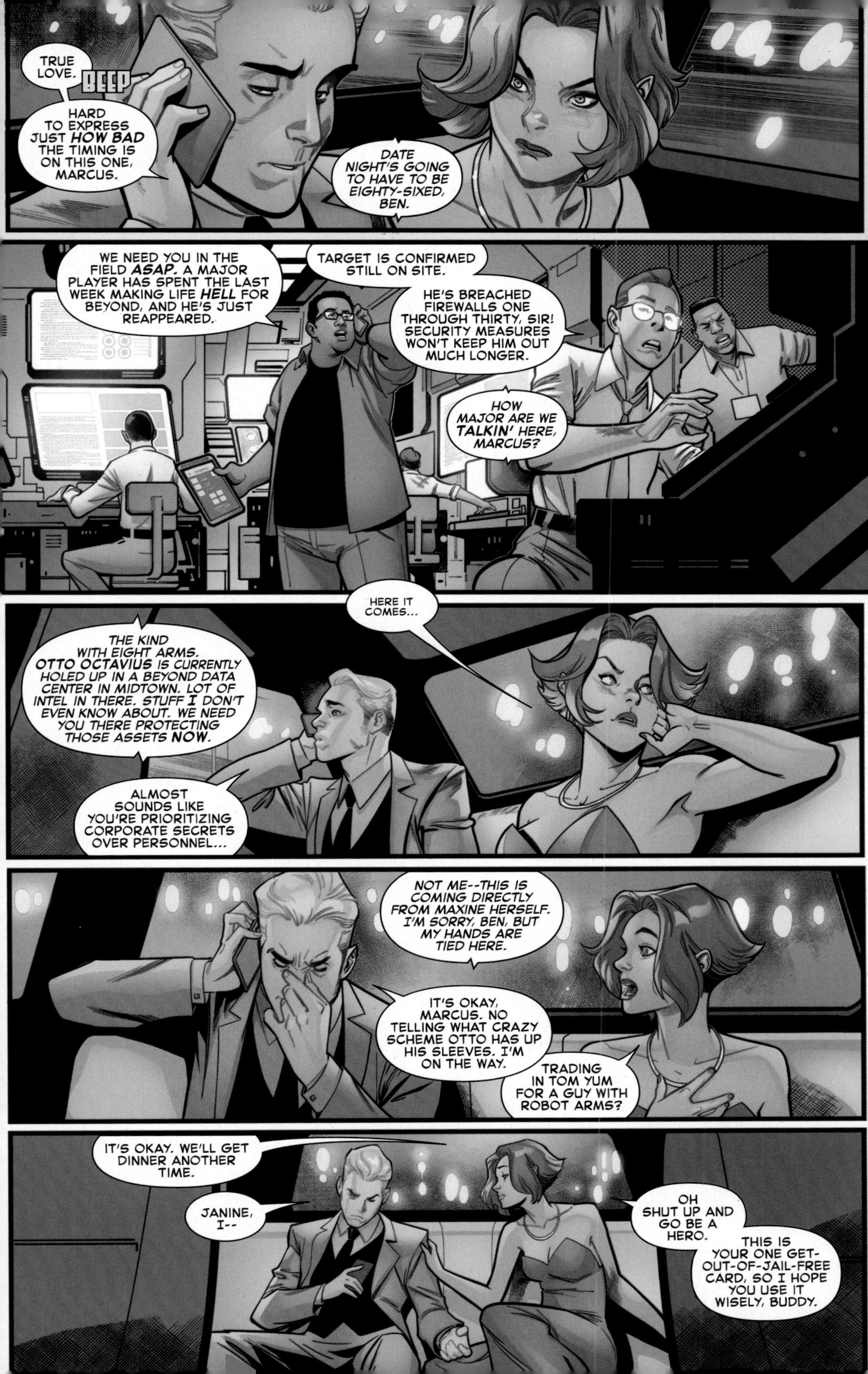
TRUE LOVE.
BEEP
HARD TO EXPRESS JUST HOW BAD THE TIMING IS ON THIS ONE, MARCUS.
DATE NIGHT'S GOING TO HAVE TO BE EIGHTY-SIXED, BEN.
WE NEED YOU IN THE FIELD ASAP. A MAJOR PLAYER HAS SPENT THE LAST WEEK MAKING LIFE HELL FOR BEYOND, AND HE'S JUST REAPPEARED.
TARGET IS CONFIRMED STILL ON SITE.
HE'S BREACHED FIREWALLS ONE THROUGH THIRTY, SIR! SECURITY MEASURES WON'T KEEP HIM OUT MUCH LONGER.
HOW MAJOR ARE WE TALKIN' HERE, MARCUS?
HERE IT COMES...
THE KIND WITH EIGHT ARMS. OTTO OCTAVIUS IS CURRENTLY HOLED UP IN A BEYOND DATA CENTER IN MIDTOWN. LOT OF INTEL IN THERE. STUFF I DON'T EVEN KNOW ABOUT. WE NEED YOU THERE PROTECTING THOSE ASSETS NOW.
ALMOST SOUNDS LIKE YOU'RE PRIORITIZING CORPORATE SECRETS OVER PERSONNEL...
NOT ME--THIS IS COMING DIRECTLY FROM MAXINE HERSELF. I'M SORRY, BEN, BUT MY HANDS ARE TIED HERE.
IT'S OKAY, MARCUS. NO TELLING WHAT CRAZY SCHEME OTTO HAS UP HIS SLEEVES. I'M ON THE WAY.
TRADING IN TOM YUM FOR A GUY WITH ROBOT ARMS?
IT'S OKAY. WE'LL GET DINNER ANOTHER TIME.
JANINE, I--
OH SHUT UP AND GO BE A HERO.
THIS IS YOUR ONE GET-OUT-OF-JAIL-FREE CARD, SO I HOPE YOU USE IT WISELY, BUDDY.

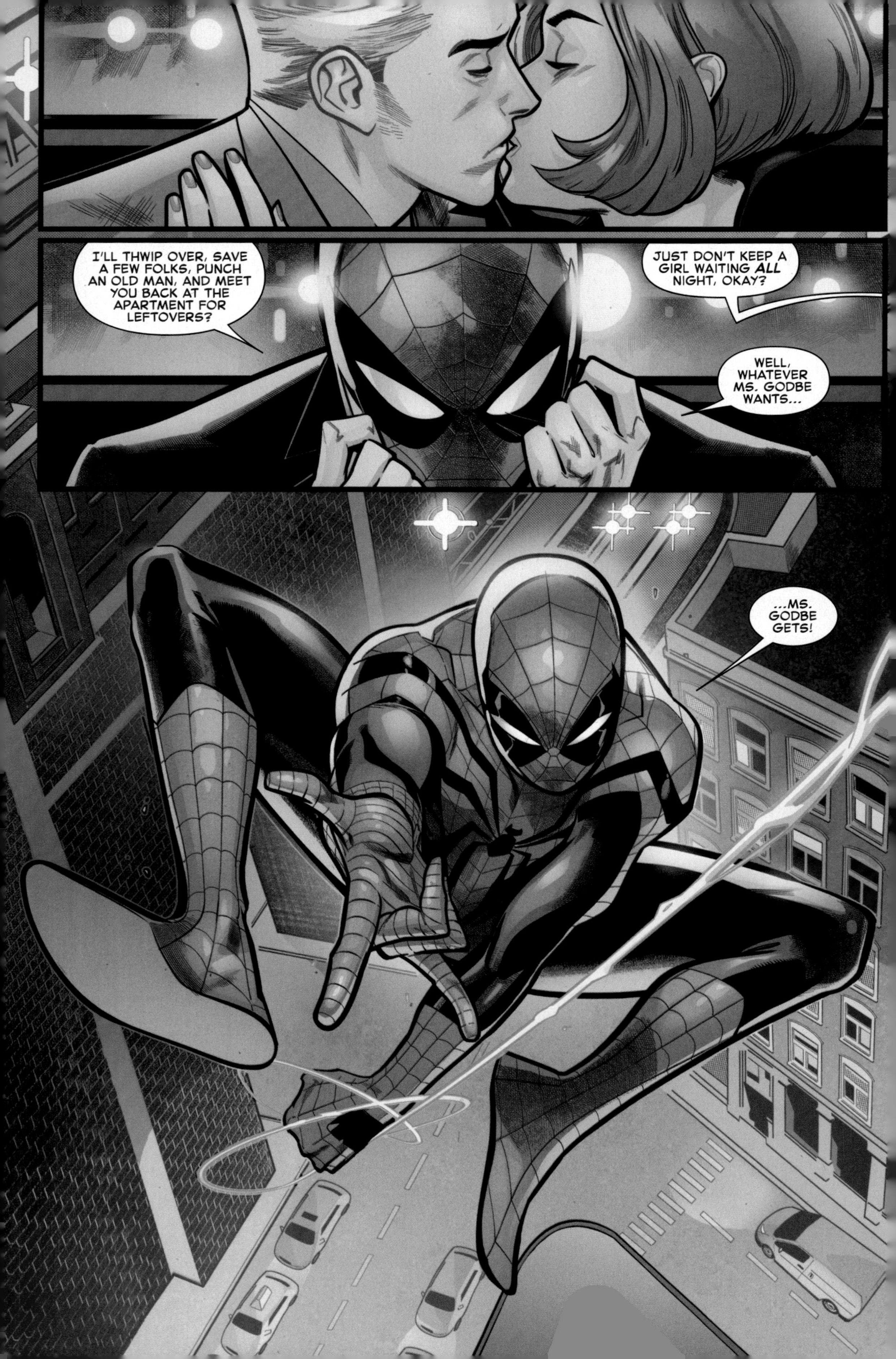
I'LL THWIP OVER, SAVE A FEW FOLKS, PUNCH AN OLD MAN, AND MEET YOU BACK AT THE APARTMENT FOR LEFTOVERS?
JUST DON'T KEEP A GIRL WAITING ALL NIGHT, OKAY?
WELL, WHATEVER MS. GODBE WANTS...
...MS. GODBE GETS!

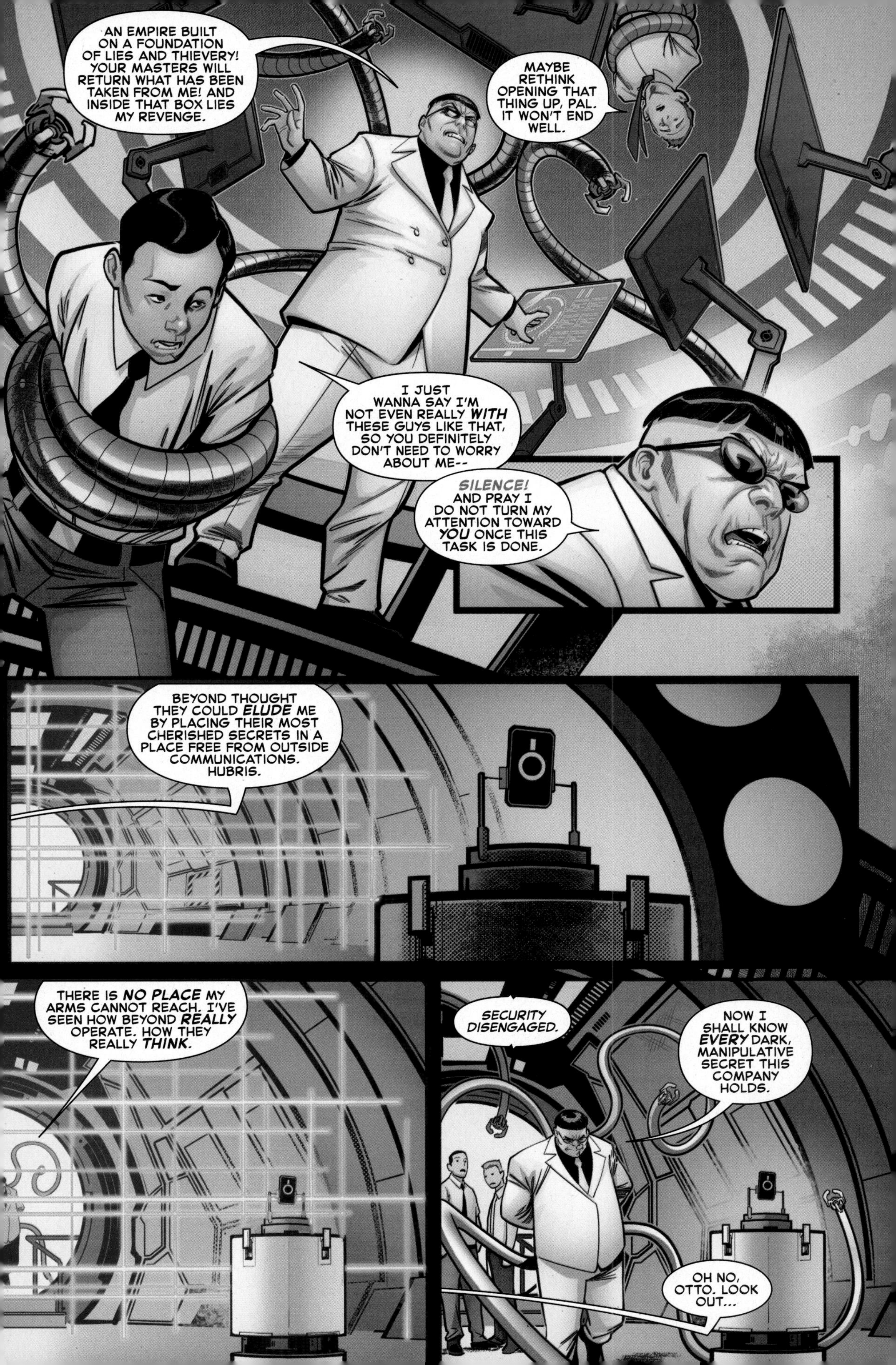
AN EMPIRE BUILT ON A FOUNDATION OF LIES AND THIEVERY! YOUR MASTERS WILL RETURN WHAT HAS BEEN TAKEN FROM ME! AND INSIDE THAT BOX LIES MY REVENGE.
MAYBE RETHINK OPENING THAT THING UP, PAL. IT WON'T END WELL.
I JUST WANNA SAY I'M NOT EVEN REALLY *WITH* THESE GUYS LIKE THAT, SO YOU DEFINITELY DON'T NEED TO WORRY ABOUT ME--
SILENCE! AND PRAY I DO NOT TURN MY ATTENTION TOWARD *YOU* ONCE THIS TASK IS DONE.
BEYOND THOUGHT THEY COULD *ELUDE* ME BY PLACING THEIR MOST CHERISHED SECRETS IN A PLACE FREE FROM OUTSIDE COMMUNICATIONS. HUBRIS.
THERE IS *NO PLACE* MY ARMS CANNOT REACH. I'VE SEEN HOW BEYOND *REALLY* OPERATE. HOW THEY REALLY *THINK*.
SECURITY DISENGAGED.
NOW I SHALL KNOW *EVERY* DARK, MANIPULATIVE SECRET THIS COMPANY HOLDS.
OH NO, OTTO. LOOK OUT...

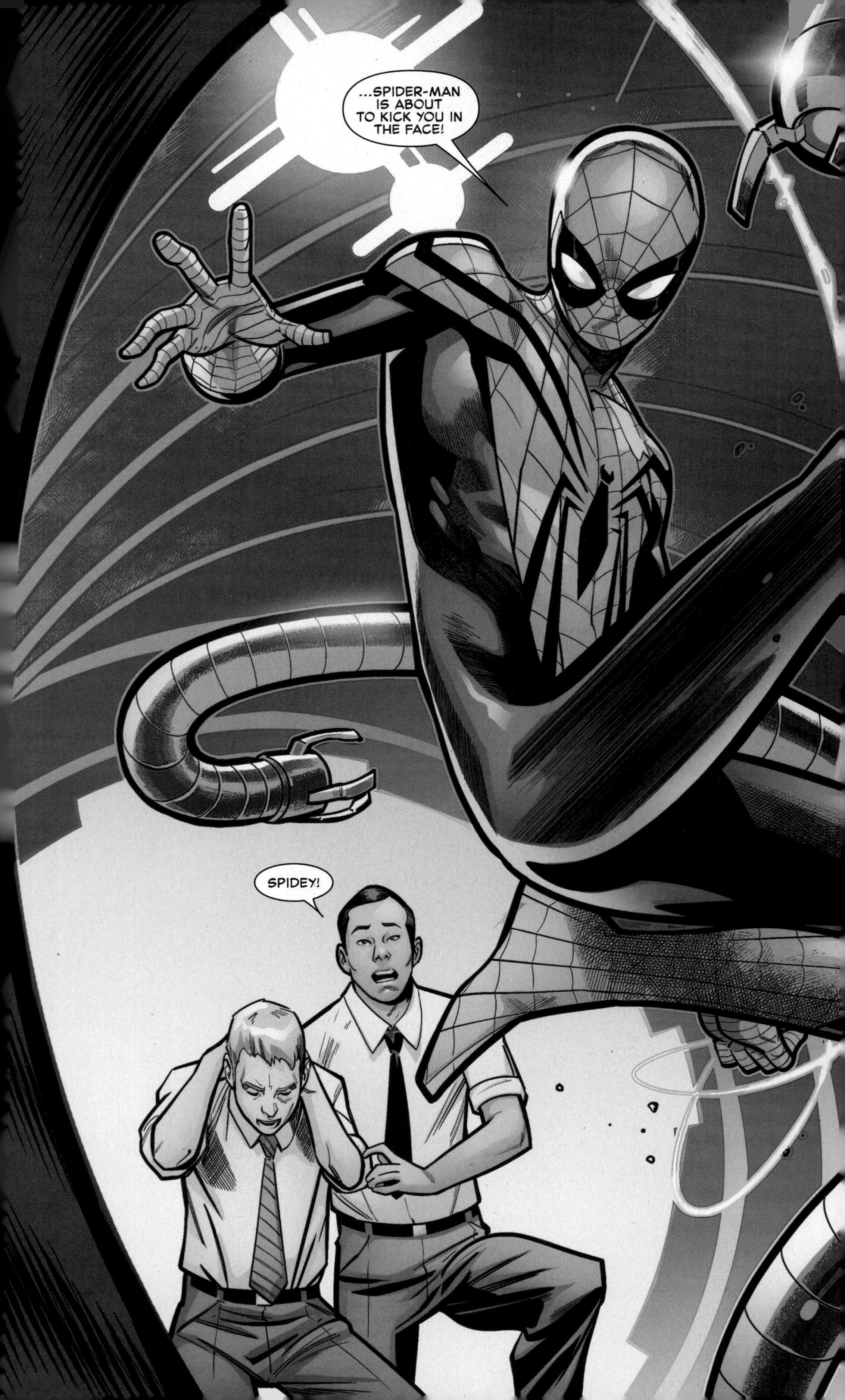
...SPIDER-MAN IS ABOUT TO KICK YOU IN THE FACE!
SPIDEY!

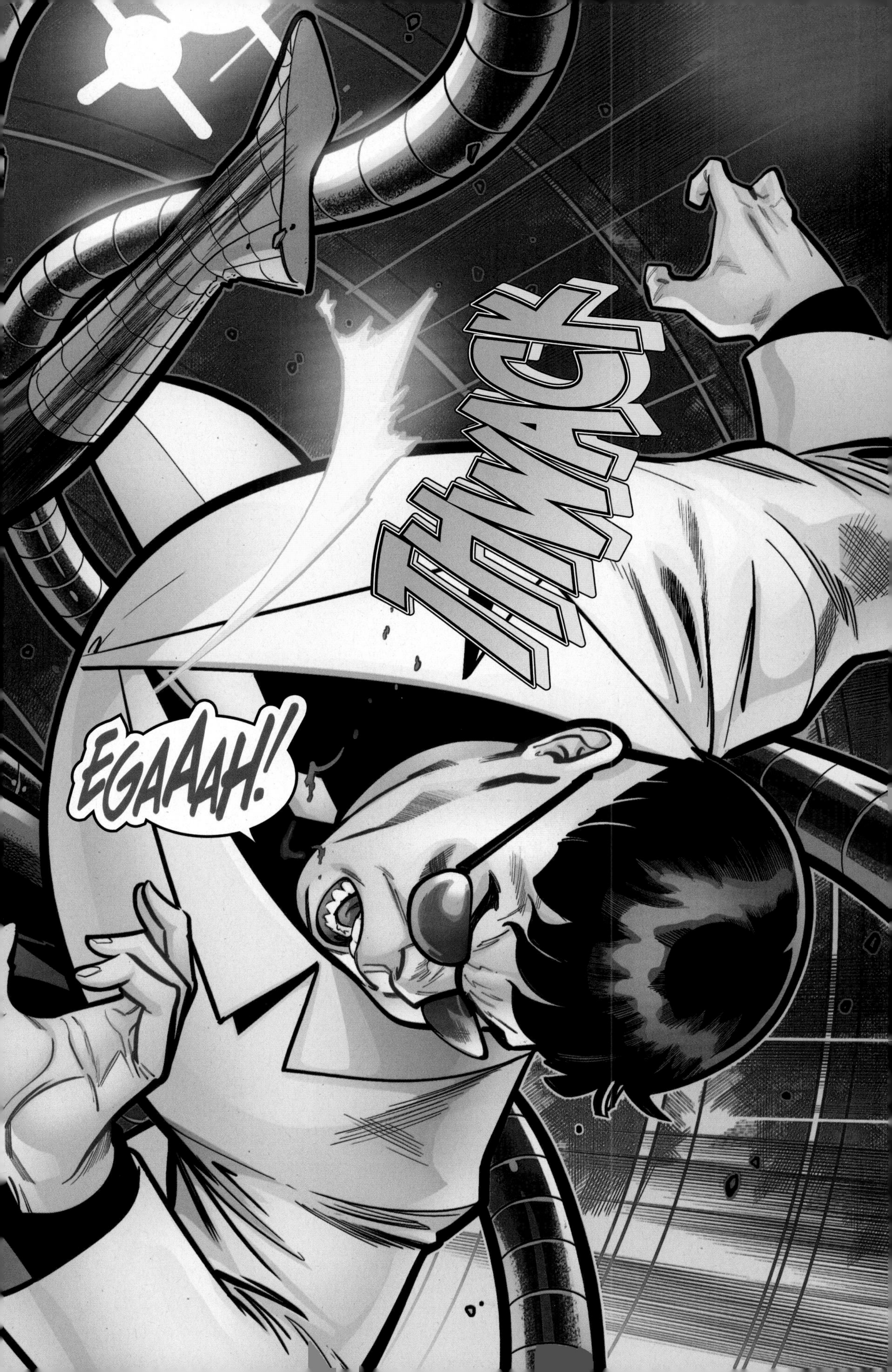
THWACK
EGAAAH!

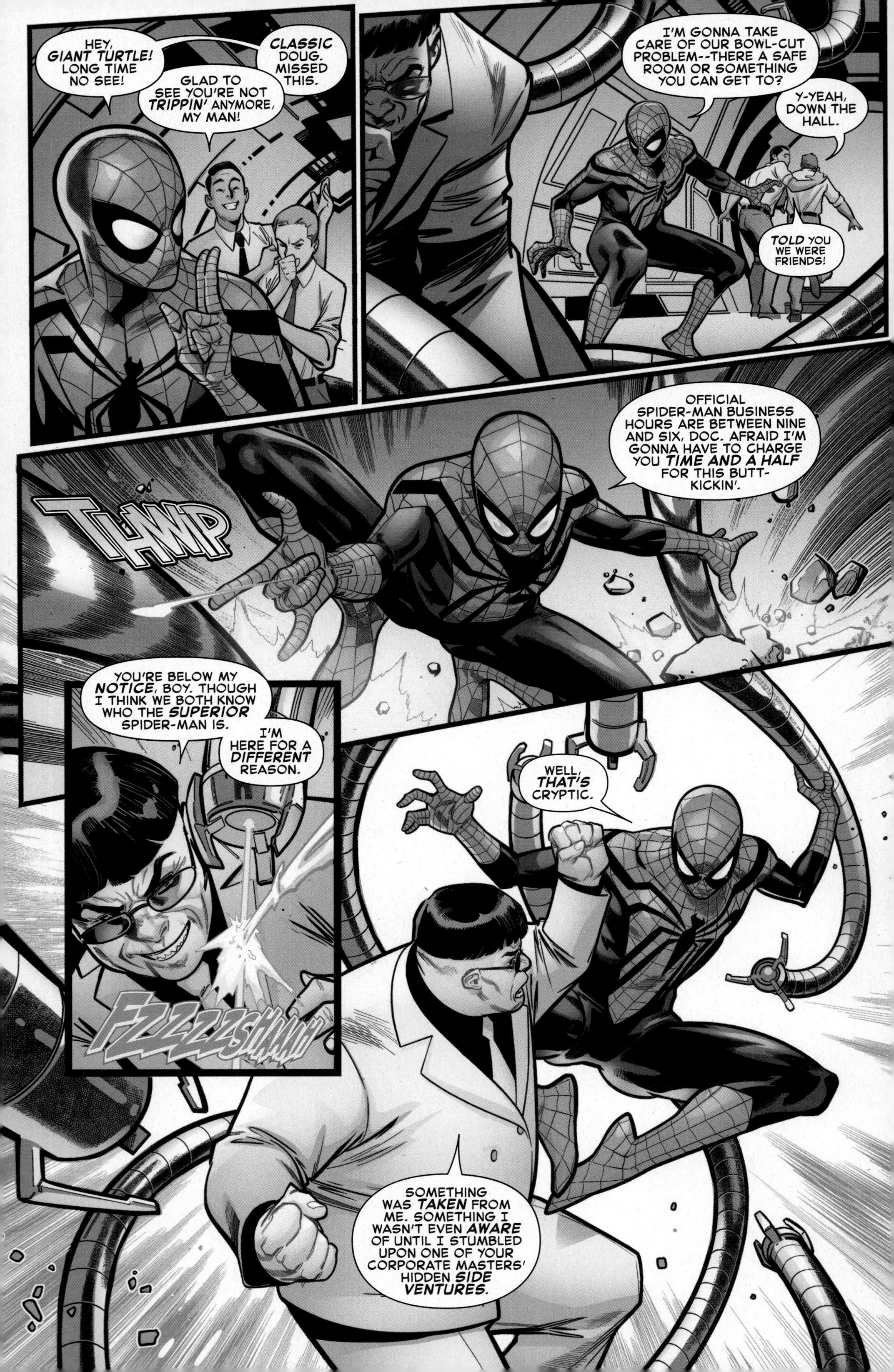
HEY, GIANT TURTLE! LONG TIME NO SEE!
CLASSIC DOUG. MISSED THIS.
GLAD TO SEE YOU'RE NOT TRIPPIN' ANYMORE, MY MAN!
I'M GONNA TAKE CARE OF OUR BOWL-CUT PROBLEM--THERE A SAFE ROOM OR SOMETHING YOU CAN GET TO?
Y-YEAH, DOWN THE HALL.
TOLD YOU WE WERE FRIENDS!
OFFICIAL SPIDER-MAN BUSINESS HOURS ARE BETWEEN NINE AND SIX, DOC. AFRAID I'M GONNA HAVE TO CHARGE YOU TIME AND A HALF FOR THIS BUTT-KICKIN'.
THWIP
YOU'RE BELOW MY NOTICE, BOY. THOUGH I THINK WE BOTH KNOW WHO THE SUPERIOR SPIDER-MAN IS.
I'M HERE FOR A DIFFERENT REASON.
FZZZZZSHAAAH
WELL, THAT'S CRYPTIC.
SOMETHING WAS TAKEN FROM ME. SOMETHING I WASN'T EVEN AWARE OF UNTIL I STUMBLED UPON ONE OF YOUR CORPORATE MASTERS' HIDDEN SIDE VENTURES.

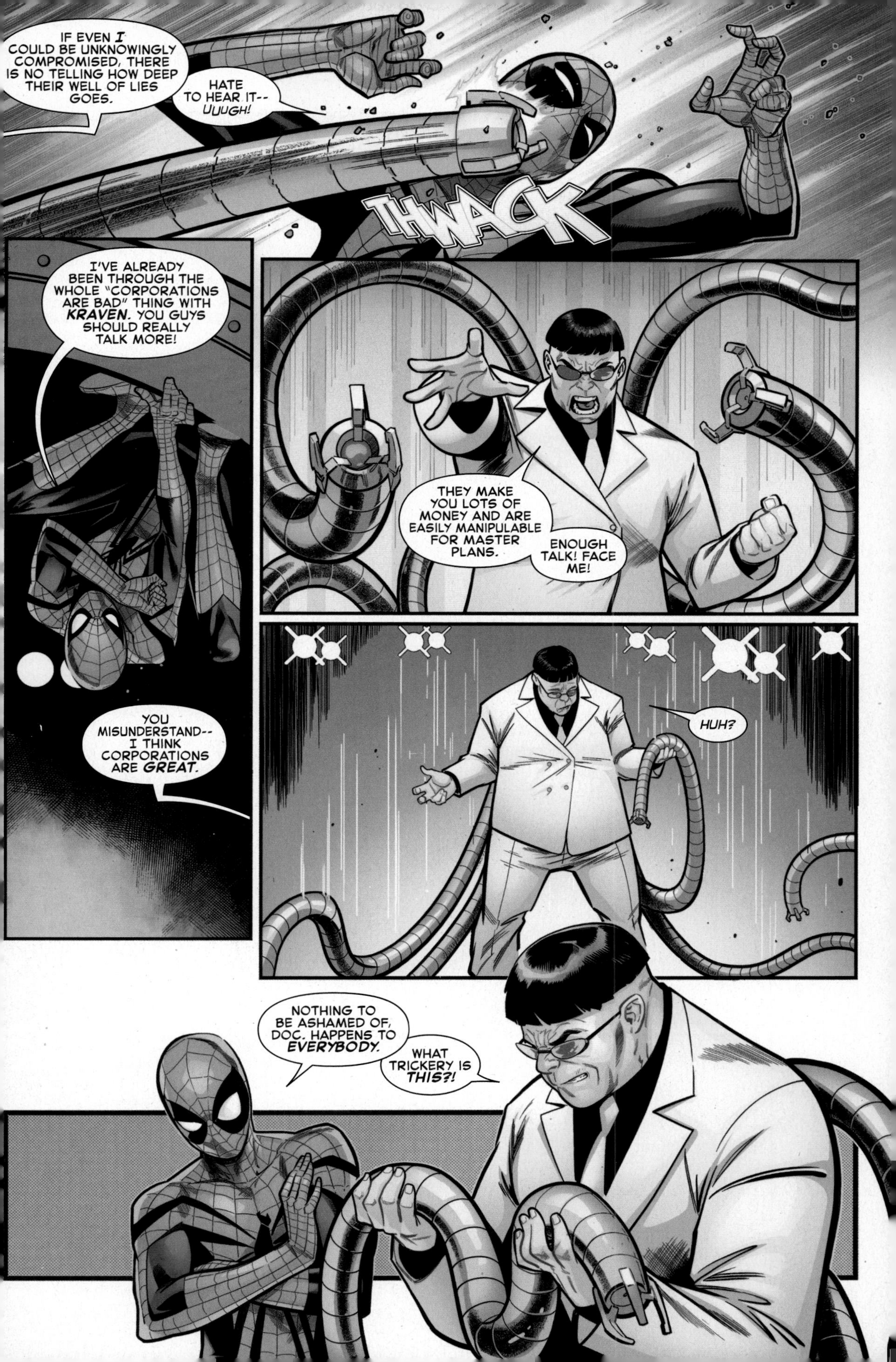
IF EVEN I COULD BE UNKNOWINGLY COMPROMISED, THERE IS NO TELLING HOW DEEP THEIR WELL OF LIES GOES.
HATE TO HEAR IT-- UUUGH!
THWACK
I'VE ALREADY BEEN THROUGH THE WHOLE "CORPORATIONS ARE BAD" THING WITH KRAVEN. YOU GUYS SHOULD REALLY TALK MORE!
YOU MISUNDERSTAND-- I THINK CORPORATIONS ARE GREAT.
THEY MAKE YOU LOTS OF MONEY AND ARE EASILY MANIPULABLE FOR MASTER PLANS.
ENOUGH TALK! FACE ME!
HUH?
NOTHING TO BE ASHAMED OF, DOC. HAPPENS TO EVERYBODY.
WHAT TRICKERY IS THIS?!

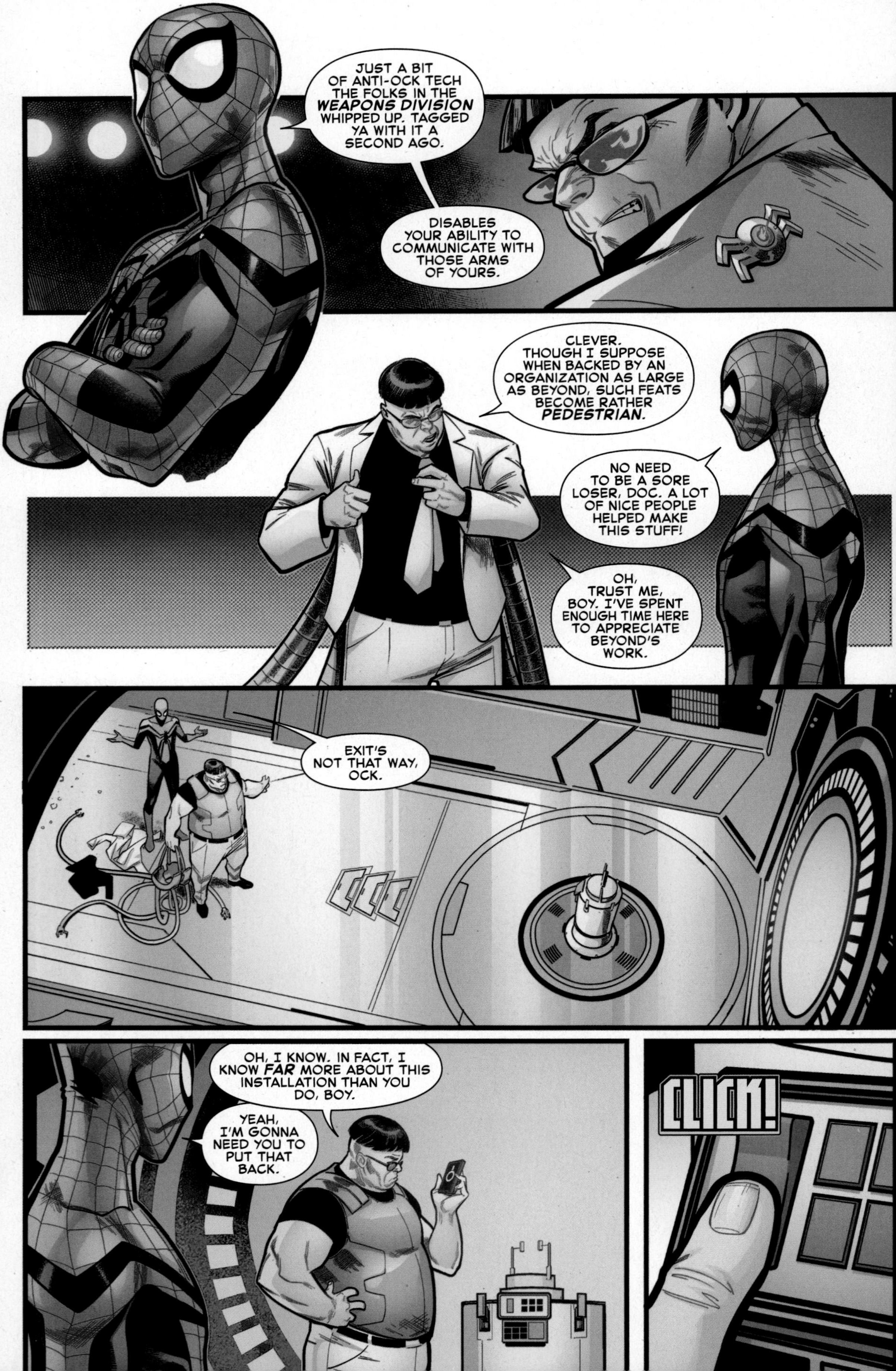

JUST A BIT OF ANTI-OCK TECH THE FOLKS IN THE WEAPONS DIVISION WHIPPED UP. TAGGED YA WITH IT A SECOND AGO.
DISABLES YOUR ABILITY TO COMMUNICATE WITH THOSE ARMS OF YOURS.
CLEVER. THOUGH I SUPPOSE WHEN BACKED BY AN ORGANIZATION AS LARGE AS BEYOND, SUCH FEATS BECOME RATHER PEDESTRIAN.
NO NEED TO BE A SORE LOSER, DOC. A LOT OF NICE PEOPLE HELPED MAKE THIS STUFF!
OH, TRUST ME, BOY. I'VE SPENT ENOUGH TIME HERE TO APPRECIATE BEYOND'S WORK.
EXIT'S NOT THAT WAY, OCK.
OH, I KNOW. IN FACT, I KNOW FAR MORE ABOUT THIS INSTALLATION THAN YOU DO, BOY.
YEAH, I'M GONNA NEED YOU TO PUT THAT BACK.
CLICK!

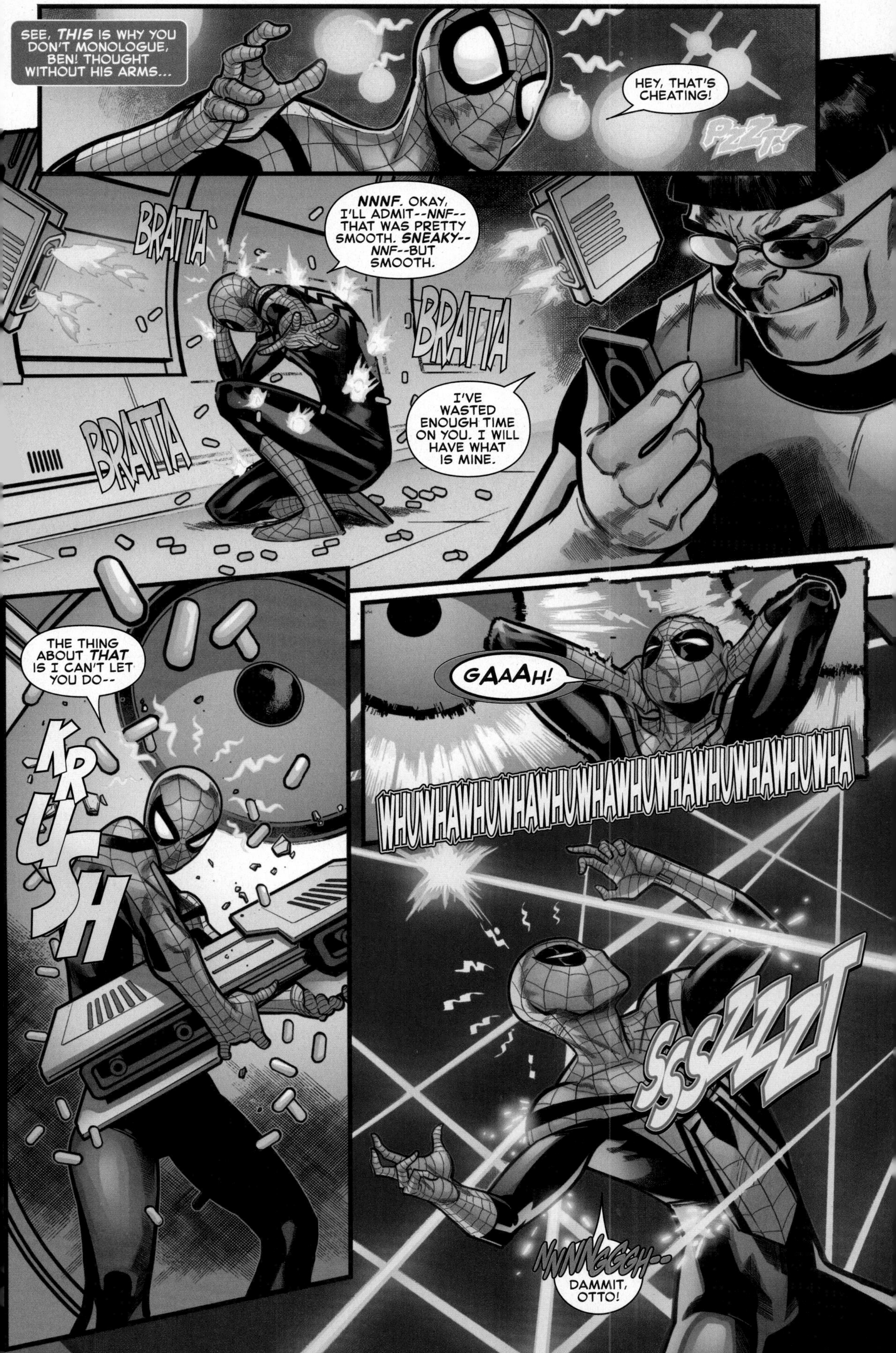
SEE, *THIS* IS WHY YOU DON'T MONOLOGUE, BEN! THOUGHT WITHOUT HIS ARMS...
HEY, THAT'S CHEATING!
PZZZT!
BRATTA
NNNF. OKAY, I'LL ADMIT--NNF--THAT WAS PRETTY SMOOTH. SNEAKY--NNF--BUT SMOOTH.
BRATTA
BRATTA
I'VE WASTED ENOUGH TIME ON YOU. I WILL HAVE WHAT IS MINE.
THE THING ABOUT *THAT* IS I CAN'T LET YOU DO--
KRUSH
GAAAH!
WHUWHAWHUWHAWHUWHAWHUWHAWHUWHAWHUWHA
SSSZZZT
NNNNGGGH--
DAMMIT, OTTO!

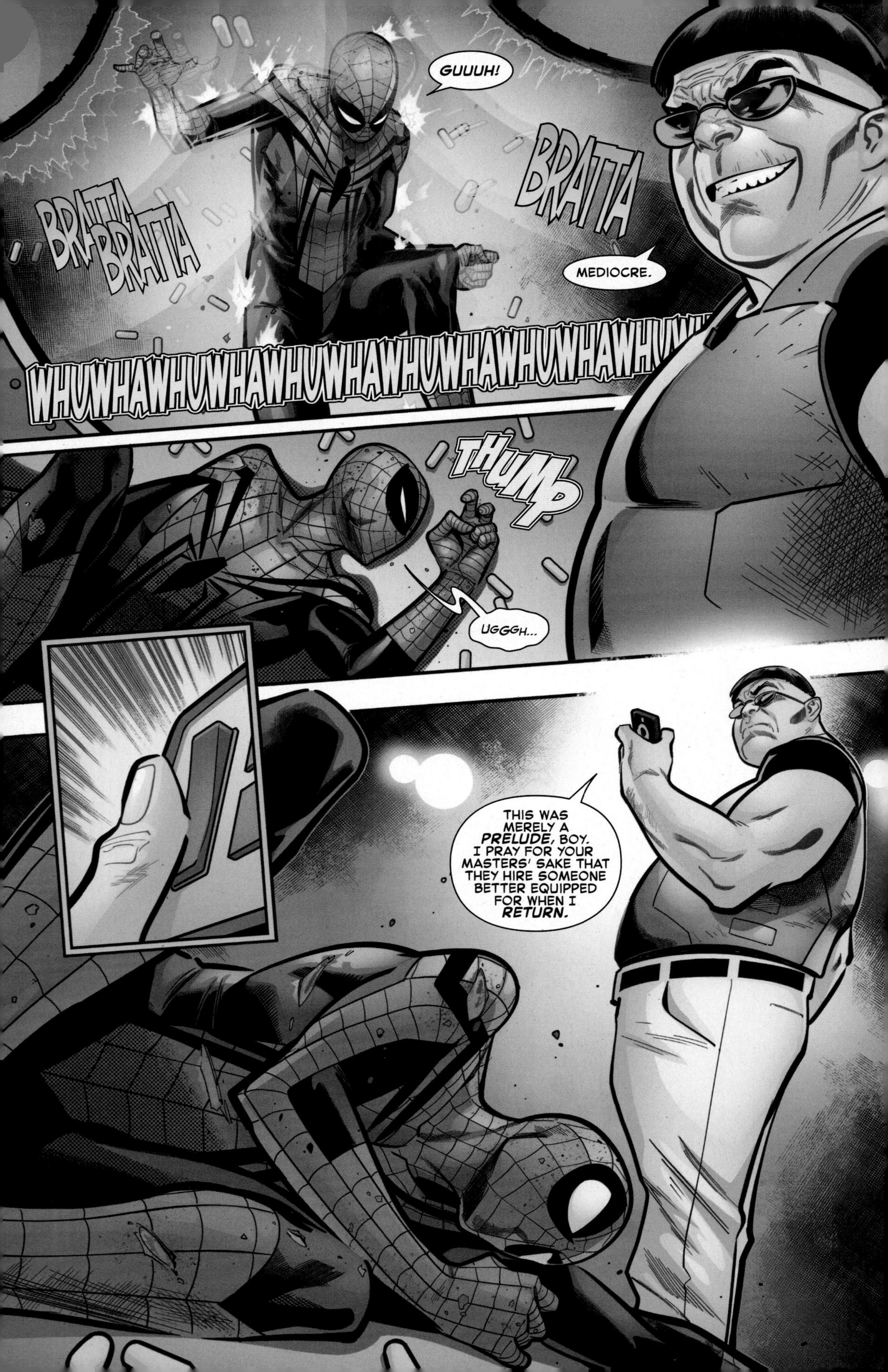
GUUUH!
BRATTA BRATTA
BRATTA
MEDIOCRE.
WHUWHAWHUWHAWHUWHAWHUWHAWHUWHAWHU
THUMP
UGGGH...
THIS WAS MERELY A PRELUDE, BOY. I PRAY FOR YOUR MASTERS' SAKE THAT THEY HIRE SOMEONE BETTER EQUIPPED FOR WHEN I RETURN.

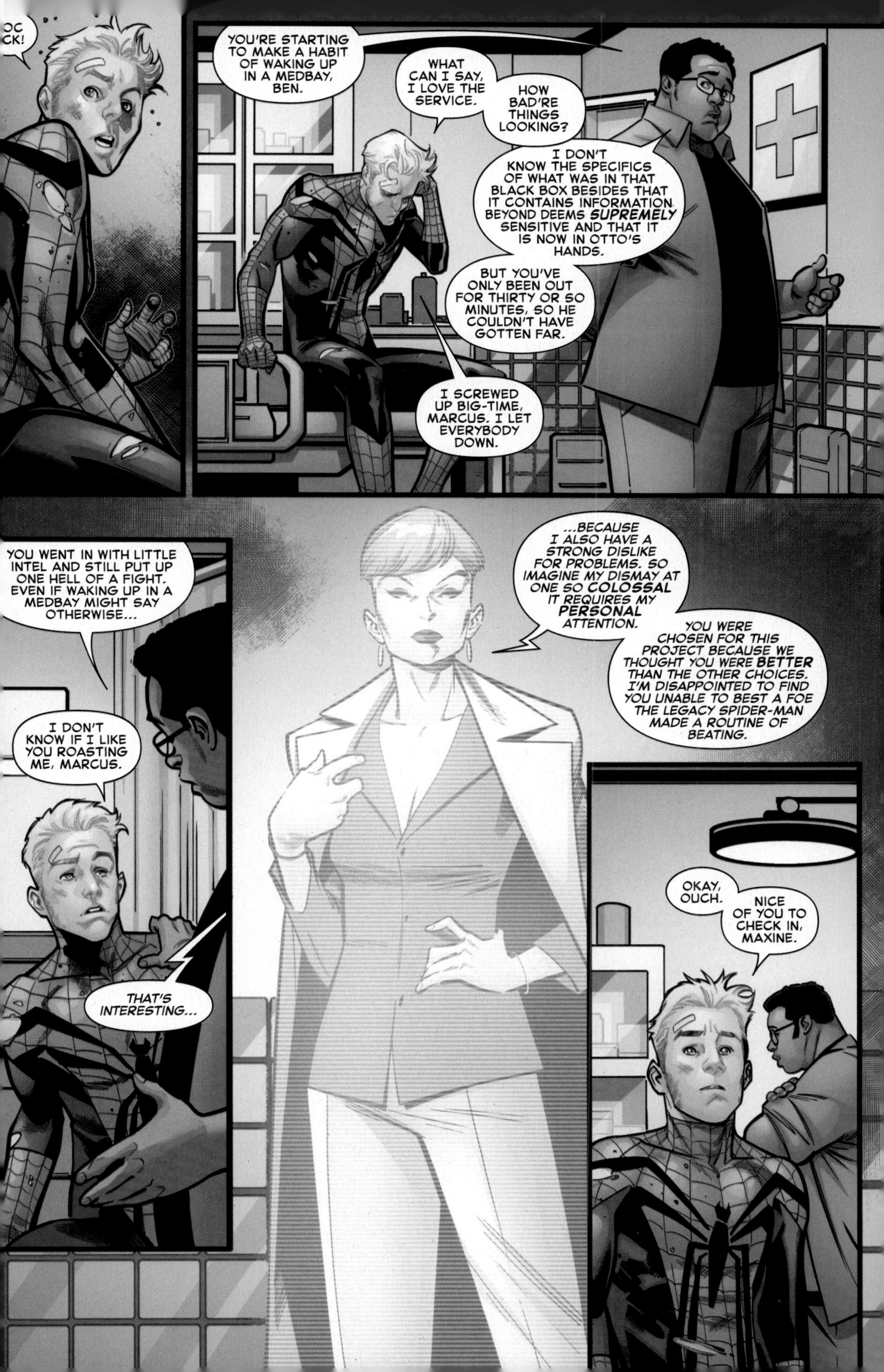
OC
CK!
YOU'RE STARTING TO MAKE A HABIT OF WAKING UP IN A MEDBAY, BEN.
WHAT CAN I SAY, I LOVE THE SERVICE.
HOW BAD'RE THINGS LOOKING?
I DON'T KNOW THE SPECIFICS OF WHAT WAS IN THAT BLACK BOX BESIDES THAT IT CONTAINS INFORMATION BEYOND DEEMS SUPREMELY SENSITIVE AND THAT IT IS NOW IN OTTO'S HANDS.
BUT YOU'VE ONLY BEEN OUT FOR THIRTY OR SO MINUTES, SO HE COULDN'T HAVE GOTTEN FAR.
I SCREWED UP BIG-TIME, MARCUS. I LET EVERYBODY DOWN.
YOU WENT IN WITH LITTLE INTEL AND STILL PUT UP ONE HELL OF A FIGHT. EVEN IF WAKING UP IN A MEDBAY MIGHT SAY OTHERWISE...
I DON'T KNOW IF I LIKE YOU ROASTING ME, MARCUS.
THAT'S INTERESTING...
...BECAUSE I ALSO HAVE A STRONG DISLIKE FOR PROBLEMS. SO IMAGINE MY DISMAY AT ONE SO COLOSSAL IT REQUIRES MY PERSONAL ATTENTION.
YOU WERE CHOSEN FOR THIS PROJECT BECAUSE WE THOUGHT YOU WERE BETTER THAN THE OTHER CHOICES. I'M DISAPPOINTED TO FIND YOU UNABLE TO BEST A FOE THE LEGACY SPIDER-MAN MADE A ROUTINE OF BEATING.
OKAY, OUCH.
NICE OF YOU TO CHECK IN, MAXINE.

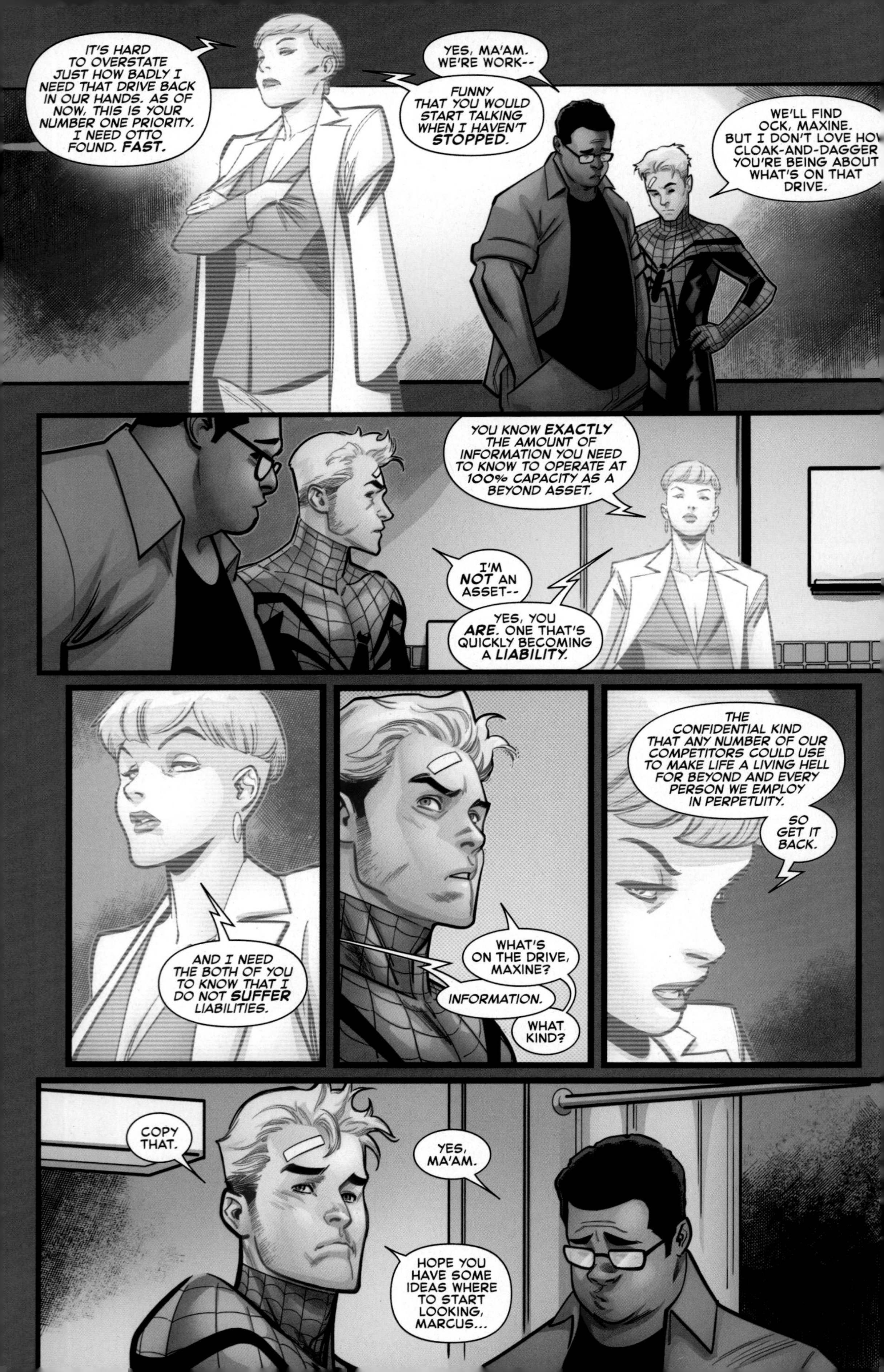
IT'S HARD TO OVERSTATE JUST HOW BADLY I NEED THAT DRIVE BACK IN OUR HANDS. AS OF NOW, THIS IS YOUR NUMBER ONE PRIORITY. I NEED OTTO FOUND. FAST.
YES, MA'AM. WE'RE WORK--
FUNNY THAT YOU WOULD START TALKING WHEN I HAVEN'T STOPPED.
WE'LL FIND OCK, MAXINE. BUT I DON'T LOVE HOW CLOAK-AND-DAGGER YOU'RE BEING ABOUT WHAT'S ON THAT DRIVE.
YOU KNOW EXACTLY THE AMOUNT OF INFORMATION YOU NEED TO KNOW TO OPERATE AT 100% CAPACITY AS A BEYOND ASSET.
I'M NOT AN ASSET--
YES, YOU ARE. ONE THAT'S QUICKLY BECOMING A LIABILITY.
AND I NEED THE BOTH OF YOU TO KNOW THAT I DO NOT SUFFER LIABILITIES.
WHAT'S ON THE DRIVE, MAXINE?
INFORMATION.
WHAT KIND?
THE CONFIDENTIAL KIND THAT ANY NUMBER OF OUR COMPETITORS COULD USE TO MAKE LIFE A LIVING HELL FOR BEYOND AND EVERY PERSON WE EMPLOY IN PERPETUITY.
SO GET IT BACK.
COPY THAT.
YES, MA'AM.
HOPE YOU HAVE SOME IDEAS WHERE TO START LOOKING, MARCUS...

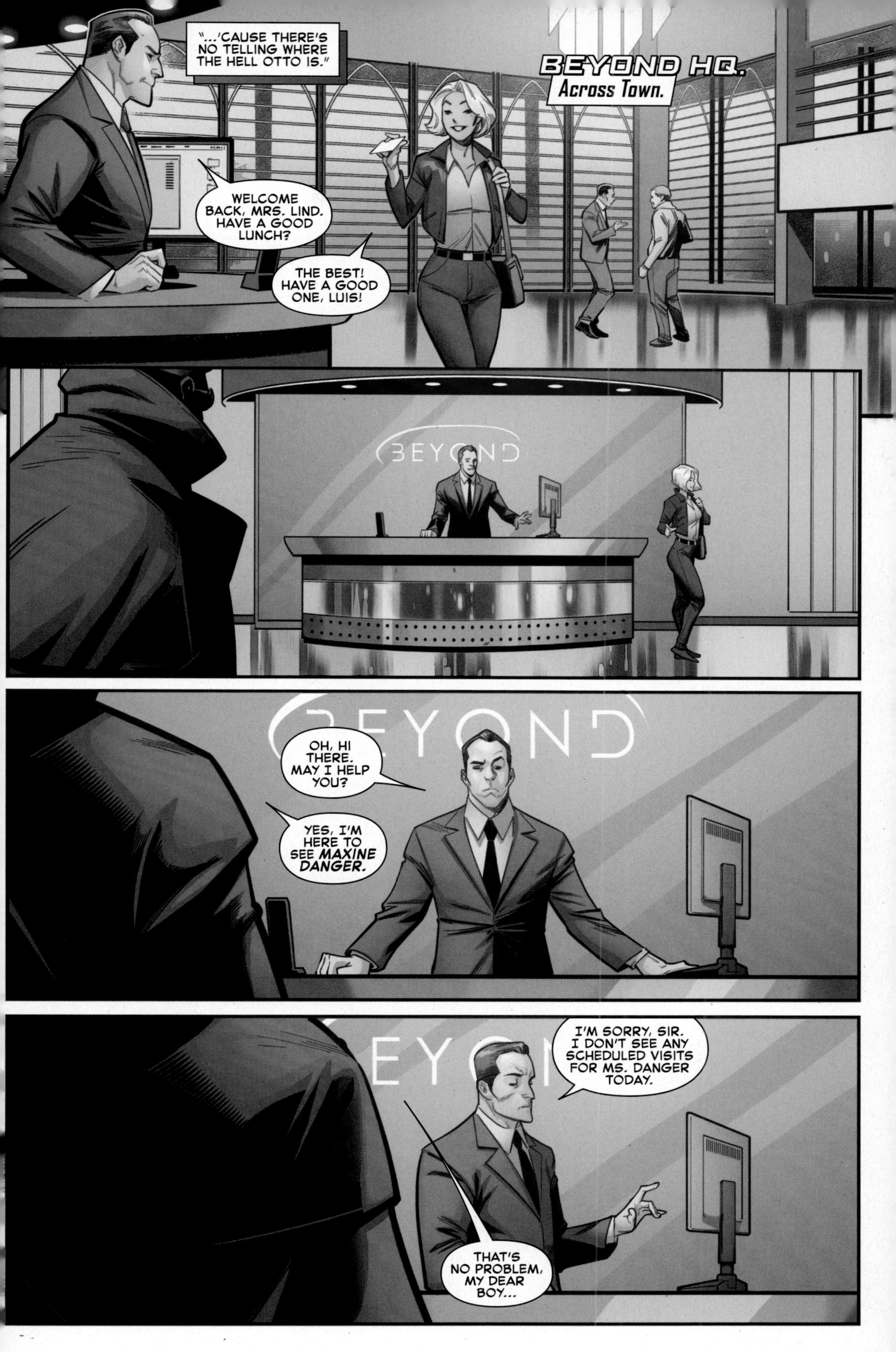
"...'CAUSE THERE'S NO TELLING WHERE THE HELL OTTO IS."
BEYOND HQ.
Across Town.
WELCOME BACK, MRS. LIND. HAVE A GOOD LUNCH?
THE BEST! HAVE A GOOD ONE, LUIS!
BEYOND
BEYOND
OH, HI THERE. MAY I HELP YOU?
YES, I'M HERE TO SEE MAXINE DANGER.
I'M SORRY, SIR. I DON'T SEE ANY SCHEDULED VISITS FOR MS. DANGER TODAY.
THAT'S NO PROBLEM, MY DEAR BOY...

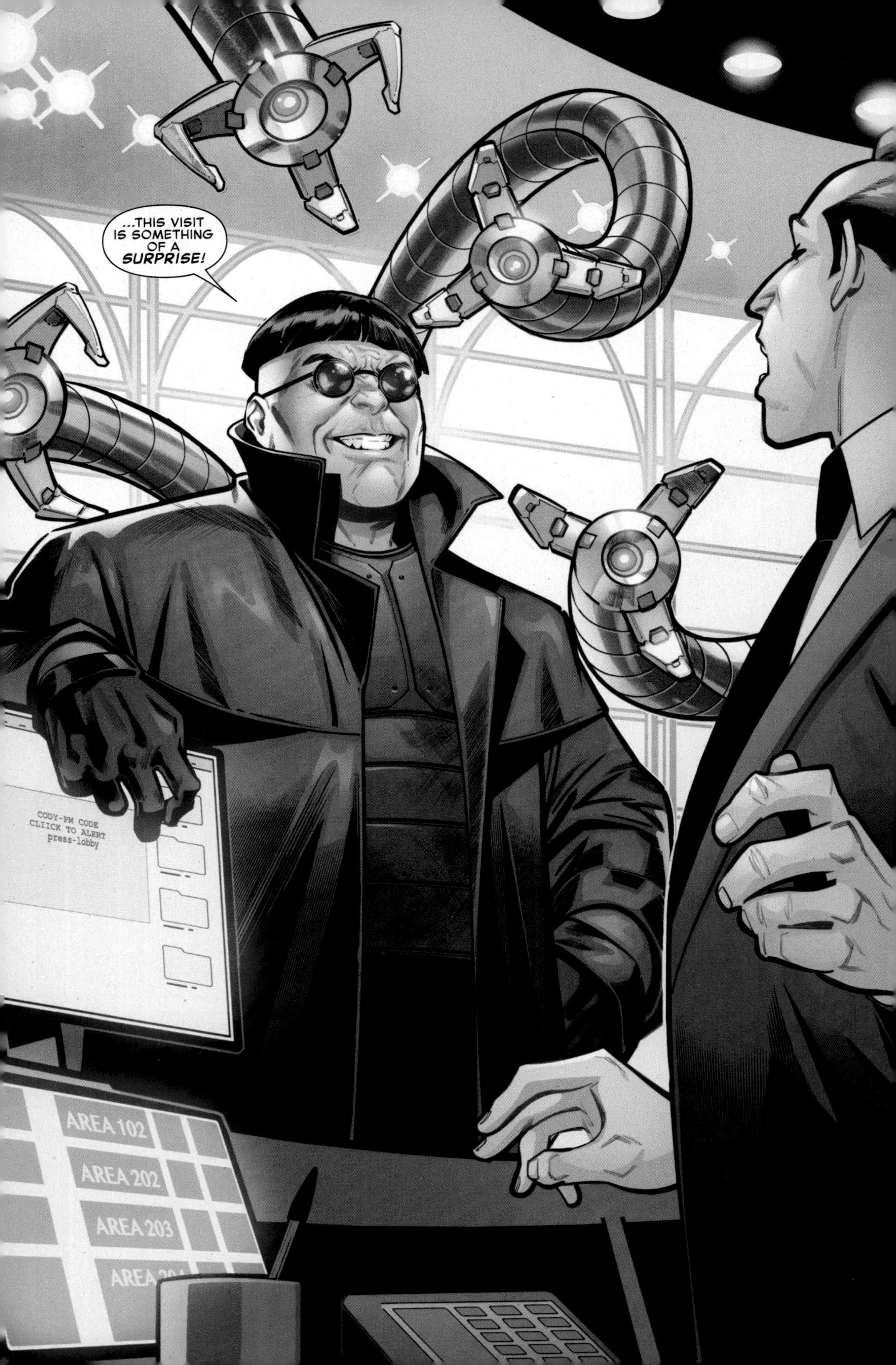
...THIS VISIT IS SOMETHING OF A SURPRISE!
CODY-PM CODE
CLIICK TO ALERT
press-lobby
AREA 102
AREA 202
AREA 203

#85 BEYOND CORPORATION

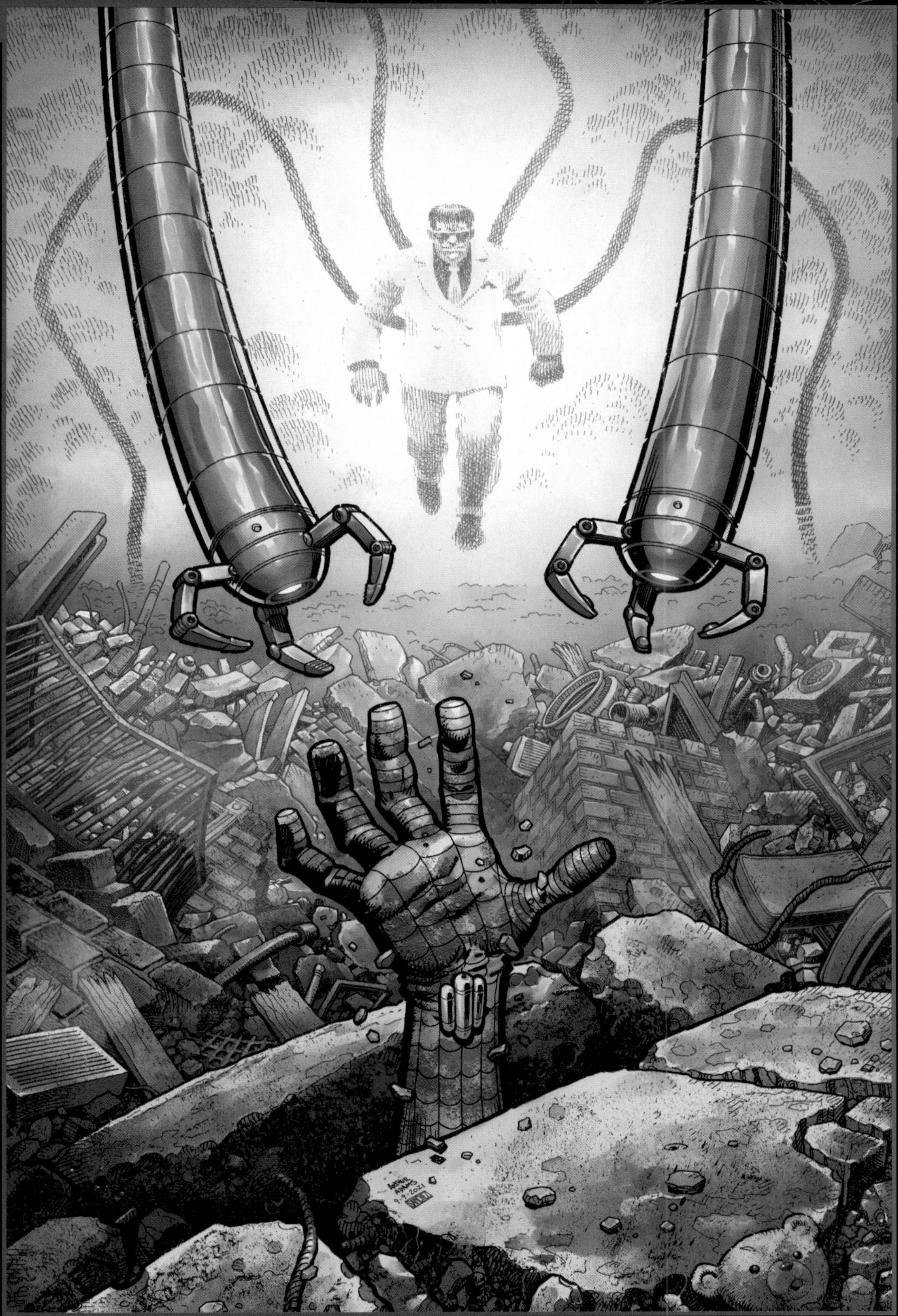

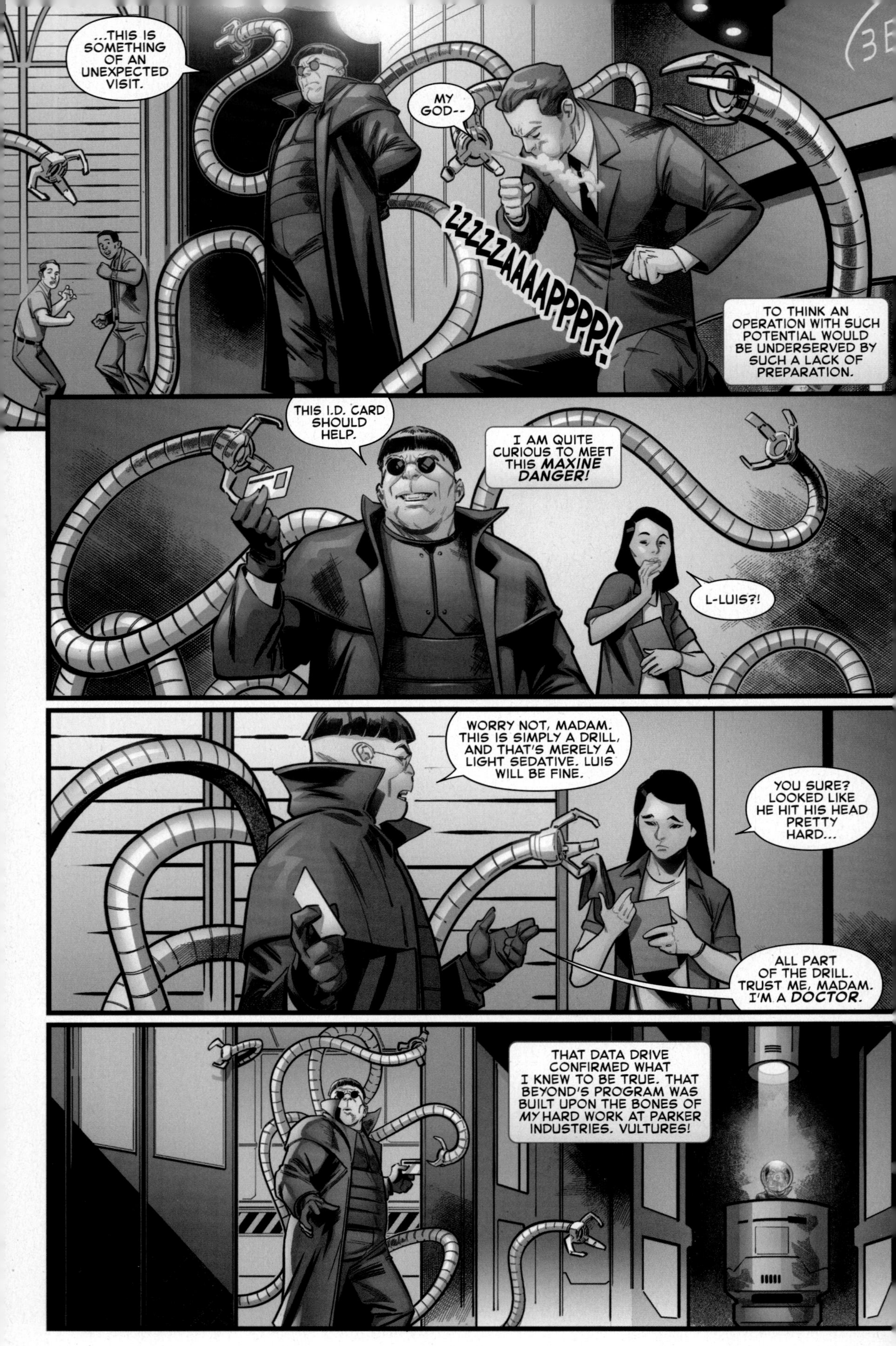
...THIS IS SOMETHING OF AN UNEXPECTED VISIT.
MY GOD--
ZZZZZAAAAPPPPP!
TO THINK AN OPERATION WITH SUCH POTENTIAL WOULD BE UNDERSERVED BY SUCH A LACK OF PREPARATION.
THIS I.D. CARD SHOULD HELP.
I AM QUITE CURIOUS TO MEET THIS MAXINE DANGER!
L-LUIS?!
WORRY NOT, MADAM. THIS IS SIMPLY A DRILL, AND THAT'S MERELY A LIGHT SEDATIVE. LUIS WILL BE FINE.
YOU SURE? LOOKED LIKE HE HIT HIS HEAD PRETTY HARD...
ALL PART OF THE DRILL. TRUST ME, MADAM. I'M A DOCTOR.
THAT DATA DRIVE CONFIRMED WHAT I KNEW TO BE TRUE. THAT BEYOND'S PROGRAM WAS BUILT UPON THE BONES OF MY HARD WORK AT PARKER INDUSTRIES. VULTURES!

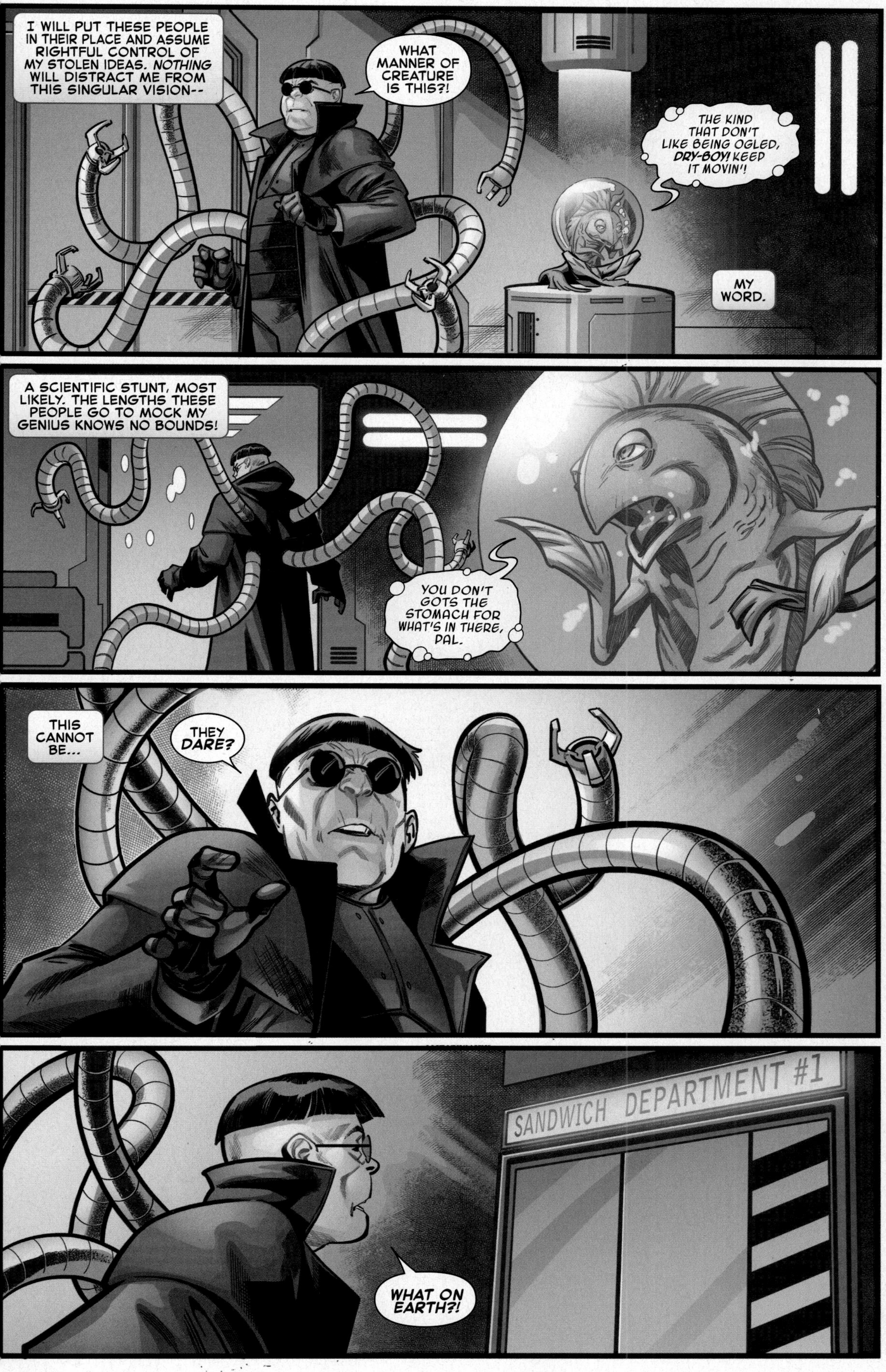
I WILL PUT THESE PEOPLE IN THEIR PLACE AND ASSUME RIGHTFUL CONTROL OF MY STOLEN IDEAS. NOTHING WILL DISTRACT ME FROM THIS SINGULAR VISION--
WHAT MANNER OF CREATURE IS THIS?!
THE KIND THAT DON'T LIKE BEING OGLED, DRY-BOY! KEEP IT MOVIN'!
MY WORD.
A SCIENTIFIC STUNT, MOST LIKELY. THE LENGTHS THESE PEOPLE GO TO MOCK MY GENIUS KNOWS NO BOUNDS!
YOU DON'T GOTS THE STOMACH FOR WHAT'S IN THERE, PAL.
THIS CANNOT BE...
THEY DARE?
SANDWICH DEPARTMENT #1
WHAT ON EARTH?!

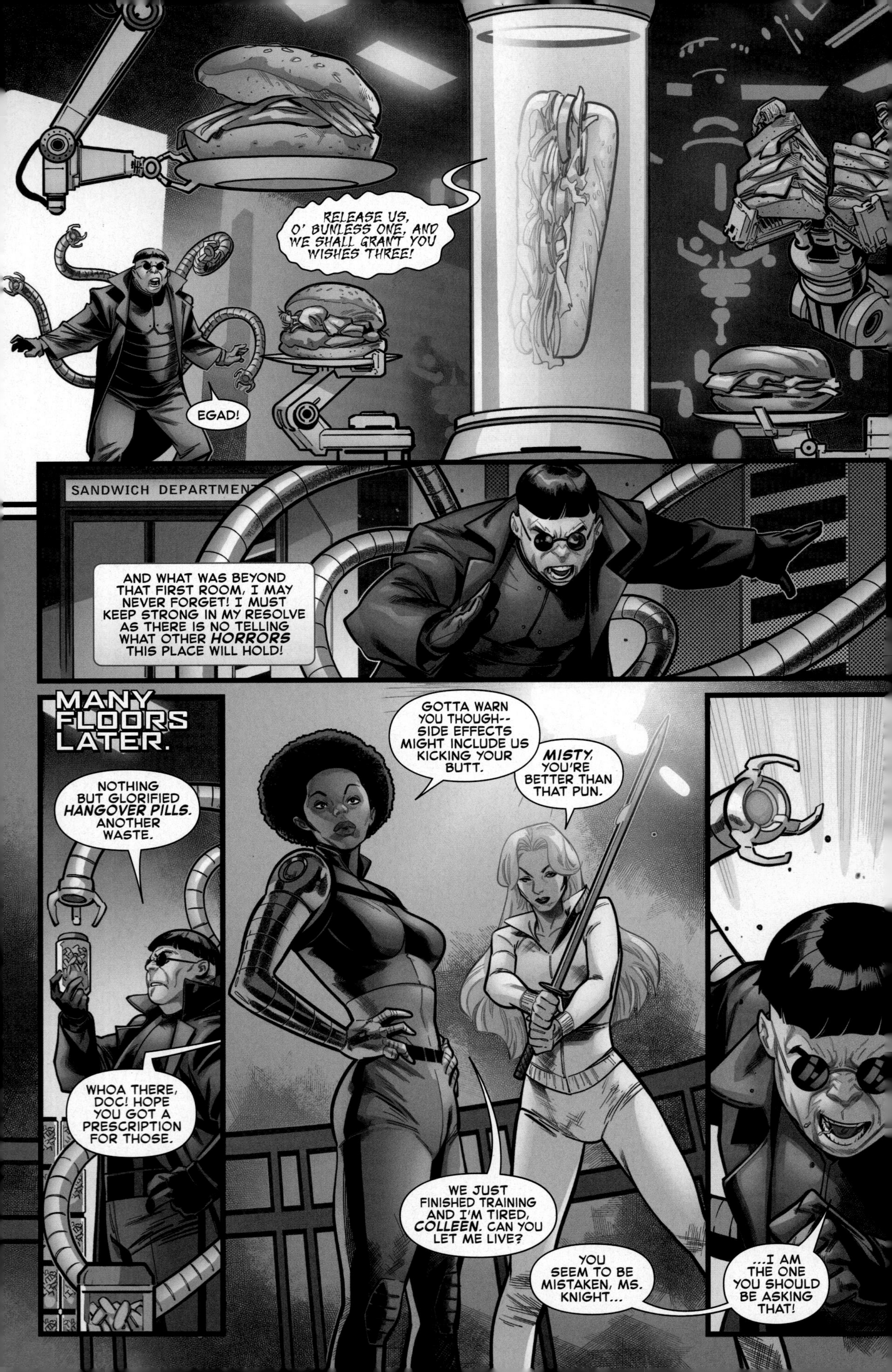
RELEASE US, O' BUNLESS ONE, AND WE SHALL GRANT YOU WISHES THREE!
EGAD!
SANDWICH DEPARTMENT
AND WHAT WAS BEYOND THAT FIRST ROOM, I MAY NEVER FORGET! I MUST KEEP STRONG IN MY RESOLVE AS THERE IS NO TELLING WHAT OTHER HORRORS THIS PLACE WILL HOLD!
MANY FLOORS LATER.
NOTHING BUT GLORIFIED HANGOVER PILLS. ANOTHER WASTE.
WHOA THERE, DOC! HOPE YOU GOT A PRESCRIPTION FOR THOSE.
GOTTA WARN YOU THOUGH-- SIDE EFFECTS MIGHT INCLUDE US KICKING YOUR BUTT.
MISTY, YOU'RE BETTER THAN THAT PUN.
WE JUST FINISHED TRAINING AND I'M TIRED, COLLEEN. CAN YOU LET ME LIVE?
YOU SEEM TO BE MISTAKEN, MS. KNIGHT...
...I AM THE ONE YOU SHOULD BE ASKING THAT!

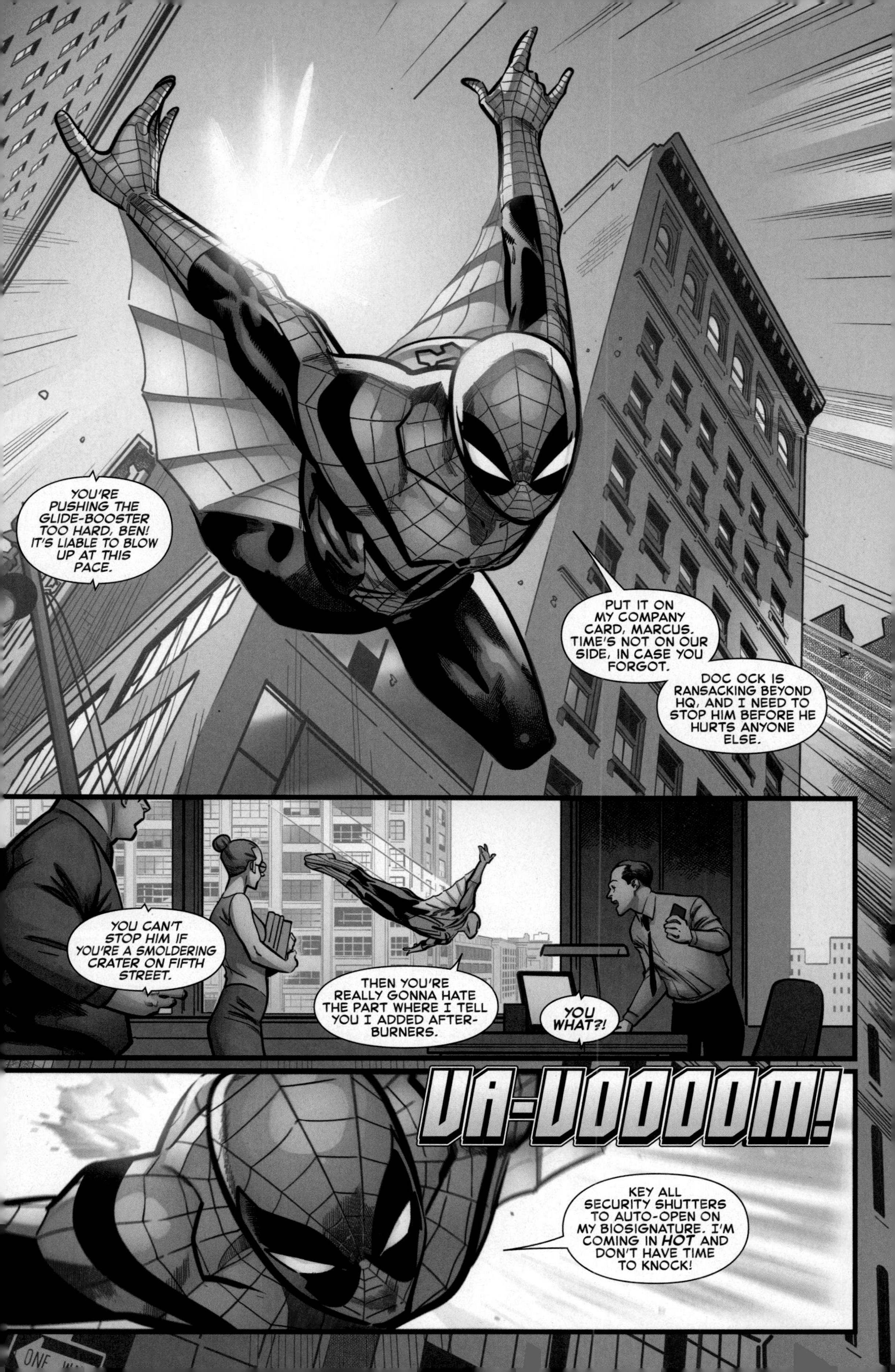
YOU'RE PUSHING THE GLIDE-BOOSTER TOO HARD, BEN! IT'S LIABLE TO BLOW UP AT THIS PACE.
PUT IT ON MY COMPANY CARD, MARCUS. TIME'S NOT ON OUR SIDE, IN CASE YOU FORGOT.
DOC OCK IS RANSACKING BEYOND HQ, AND I NEED TO STOP HIM BEFORE HE HURTS ANYONE ELSE.
YOU CAN'T STOP HIM IF YOU'RE A SMOLDERING CRATER ON FIFTH STREET.
THEN YOU'RE REALLY GONNA HATE THE PART WHERE I TELL YOU I ADDED AFTER-BURNERS.
YOU WHAT?!
VA-VOOOOM!
KEY ALL SECURITY SHUTTERS TO AUTO-OPEN ON MY BIOSIGNATURE. I'M COMING IN HOT AND DON'T HAVE TIME TO KNOCK!

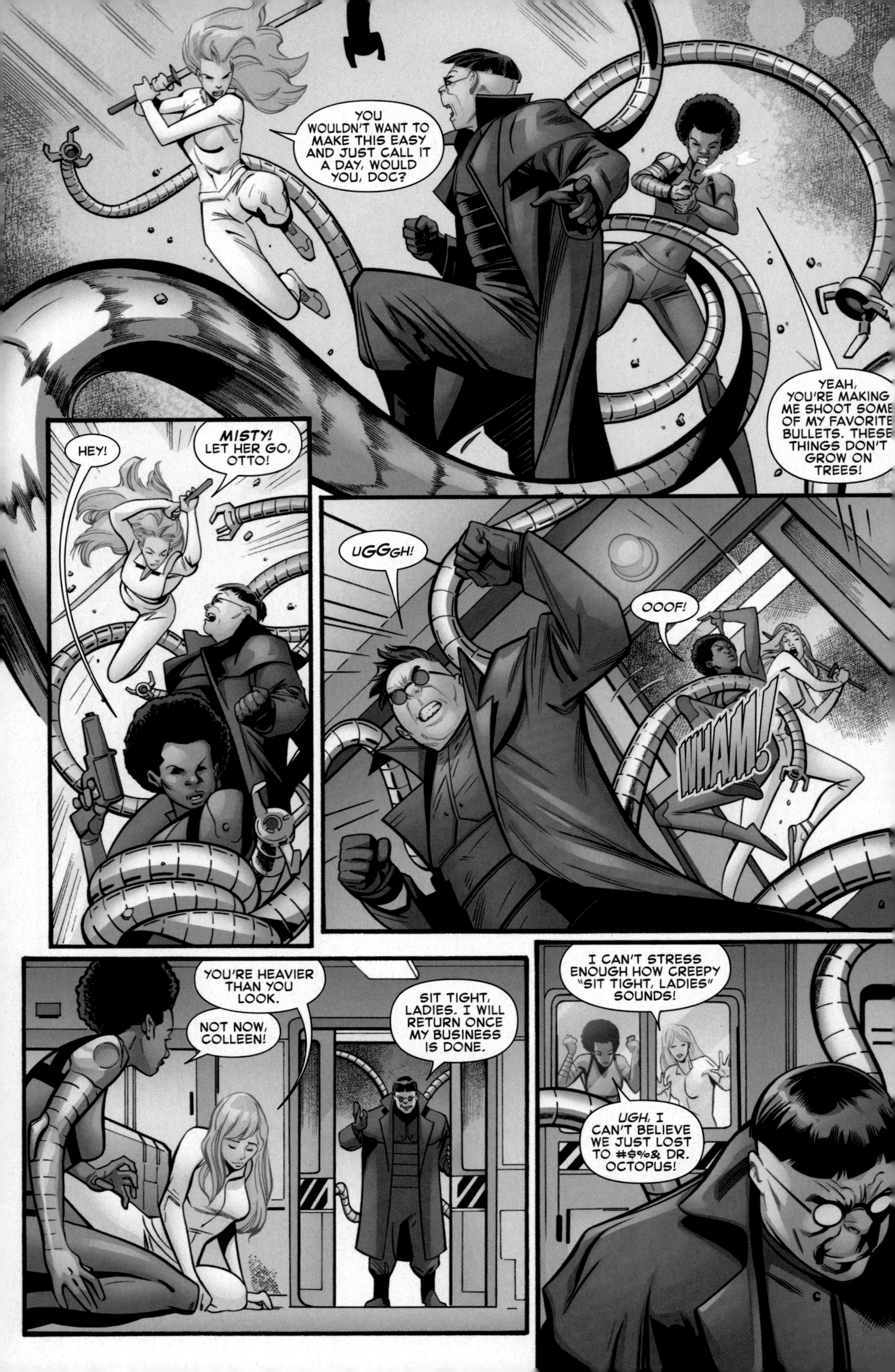
YOU WOULDN'T WANT TO MAKE THIS EASY AND JUST CALL IT A DAY, WOULD YOU, DOC?
YEAH, YOU'RE MAKING ME SHOOT SOME OF MY FAVORITE BULLETS. THESE THINGS DON'T GROW ON TREES!
HEY!
MISTY! LET HER GO, OTTO!
UGGGH!
OOOF!
WHAM!!
YOU'RE HEAVIER THAN YOU LOOK.
NOT NOW, COLLEEN!
SIT TIGHT, LADIES. I WILL RETURN ONCE MY BUSINESS IS DONE.
I CAN'T STRESS ENOUGH HOW CREEPY "SIT TIGHT, LADIES" SOUNDS!
UGH, I CAN'T BELIEVE WE JUST LOST TO #$%& DR. OCTOPUS!

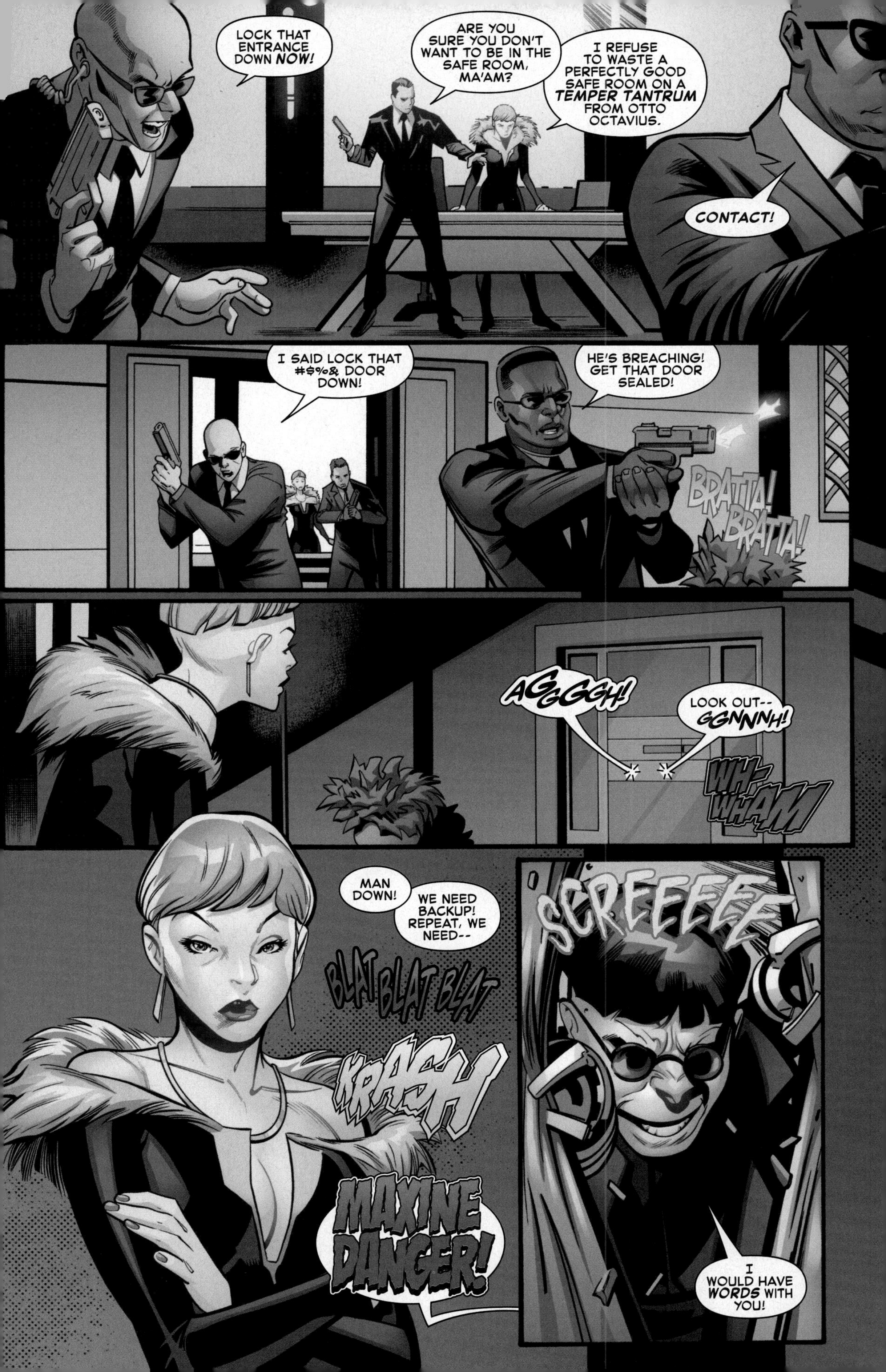
LOCK THAT ENTRANCE DOWN NOW!
ARE YOU SURE YOU DON'T WANT TO BE IN THE SAFE ROOM, MA'AM?
I REFUSE TO WASTE A PERFECTLY GOOD SAFE ROOM ON A TEMPER TANTRUM FROM OTTO OCTAVIUS.
CONTACT!
I SAID LOCK THAT #$%& DOOR DOWN!
HE'S BREACHING! GET THAT DOOR SEALED!
BRATTA! BRATTA!
AGGGGH!
LOOK OUT-- GGNNNH!
WH-WHAM
MAN DOWN!
WE NEED BACKUP! REPEAT, WE NEED--
BLAT BLAT BLAT
KRASH
MAXINE DANGER!
SCREEEEE
I WOULD HAVE WORDS WITH YOU!

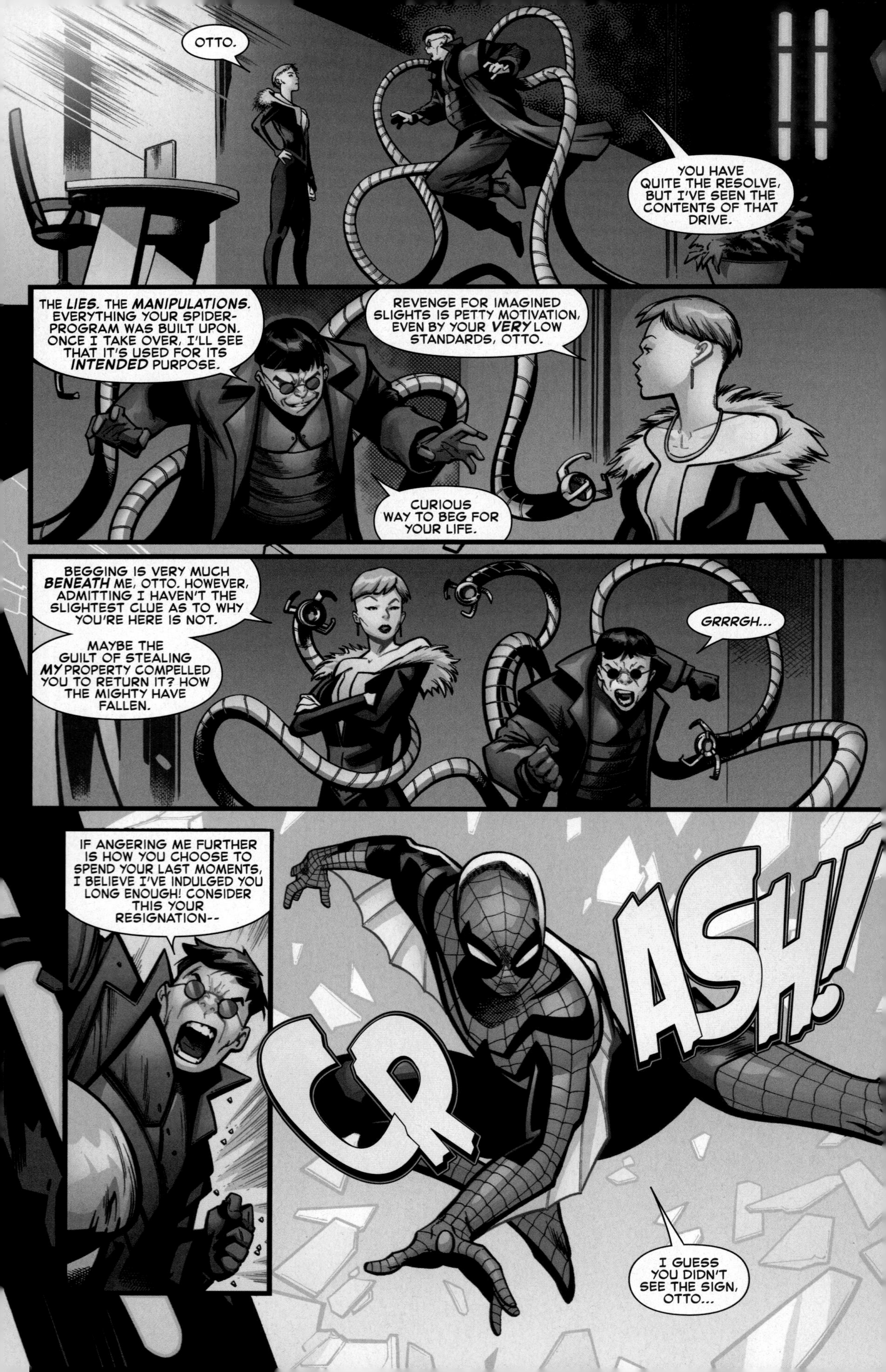
OTTO.
YOU HAVE QUITE THE RESOLVE, BUT I'VE SEEN THE CONTENTS OF THAT DRIVE.
THE LIES. THE MANIPULATIONS. EVERYTHING YOUR SPIDER-PROGRAM WAS BUILT UPON. ONCE I TAKE OVER, I'LL SEE THAT IT'S USED FOR ITS INTENDED PURPOSE.
REVENGE FOR IMAGINED SLIGHTS IS PETTY MOTIVATION, EVEN BY YOUR VERY LOW STANDARDS, OTTO.
CURIOUS WAY TO BEG FOR YOUR LIFE.
BEGGING IS VERY MUCH BENEATH ME, OTTO. HOWEVER, ADMITTING I HAVEN'T THE SLIGHTEST CLUE AS TO WHY YOU'RE HERE IS NOT.
MAYBE THE GUILT OF STEALING MY PROPERTY COMPELLED YOU TO RETURN IT? HOW THE MIGHTY HAVE FALLEN.
GRRRGH...
IF ANGERING ME FURTHER IS HOW YOU CHOOSE TO SPEND YOUR LAST MOMENTS, I BELIEVE I'VE INDULGED YOU LONG ENOUGH! CONSIDER THIS YOUR RESIGNATION--
CRASH!
I GUESS YOU DIDN'T SEE THE SIGN, OTTO...

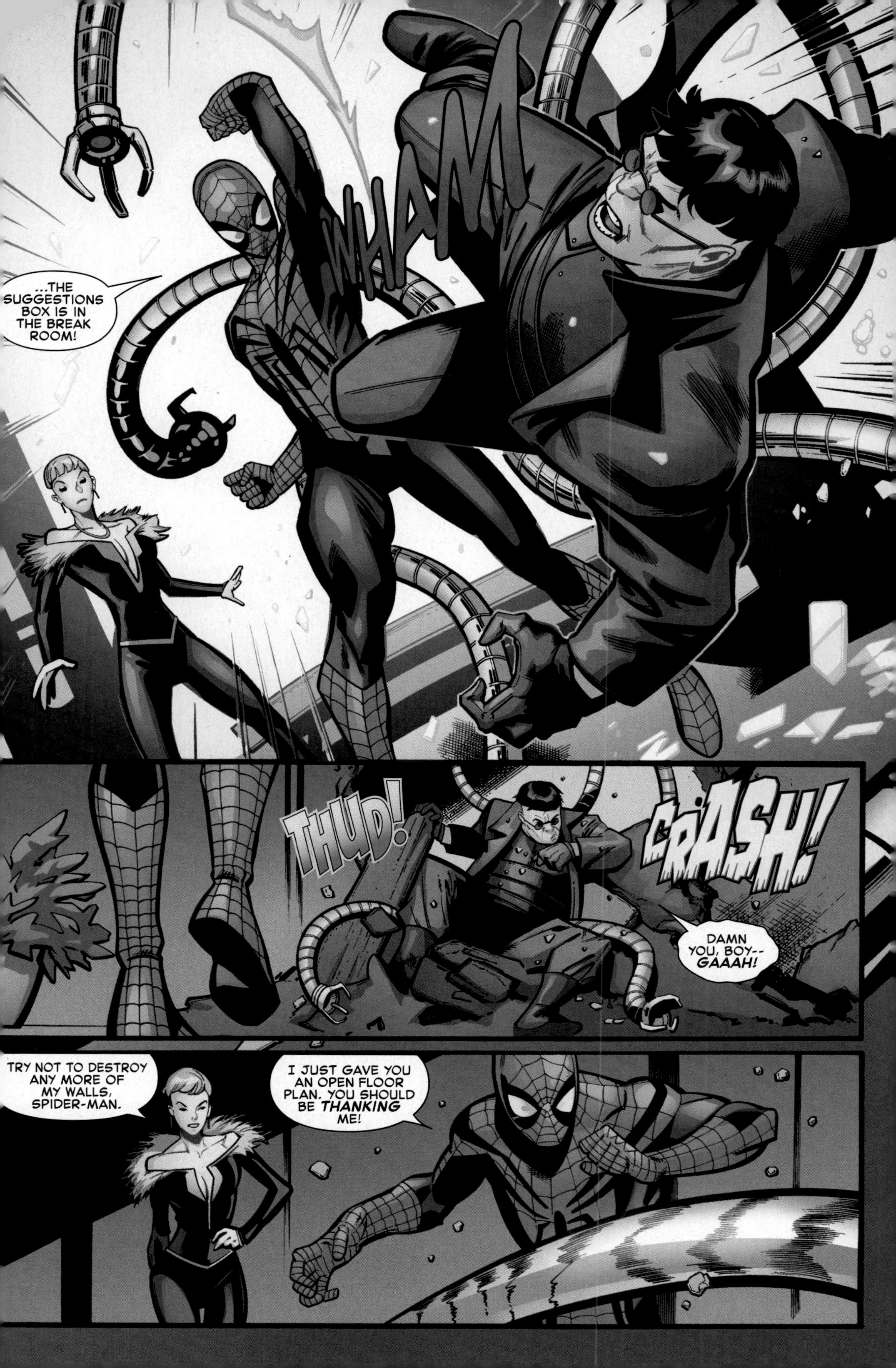
WHAM
...THE SUGGESTIONS BOX IS IN THE BREAK ROOM!
THUD!
CRASH!
DAMN YOU, BOY-- GAAAH!
TRY NOT TO DESTROY ANY MORE OF MY WALLS, SPIDER-MAN.
I JUST GAVE YOU AN OPEN FLOOR PLAN. YOU SHOULD BE *THANKING* ME!

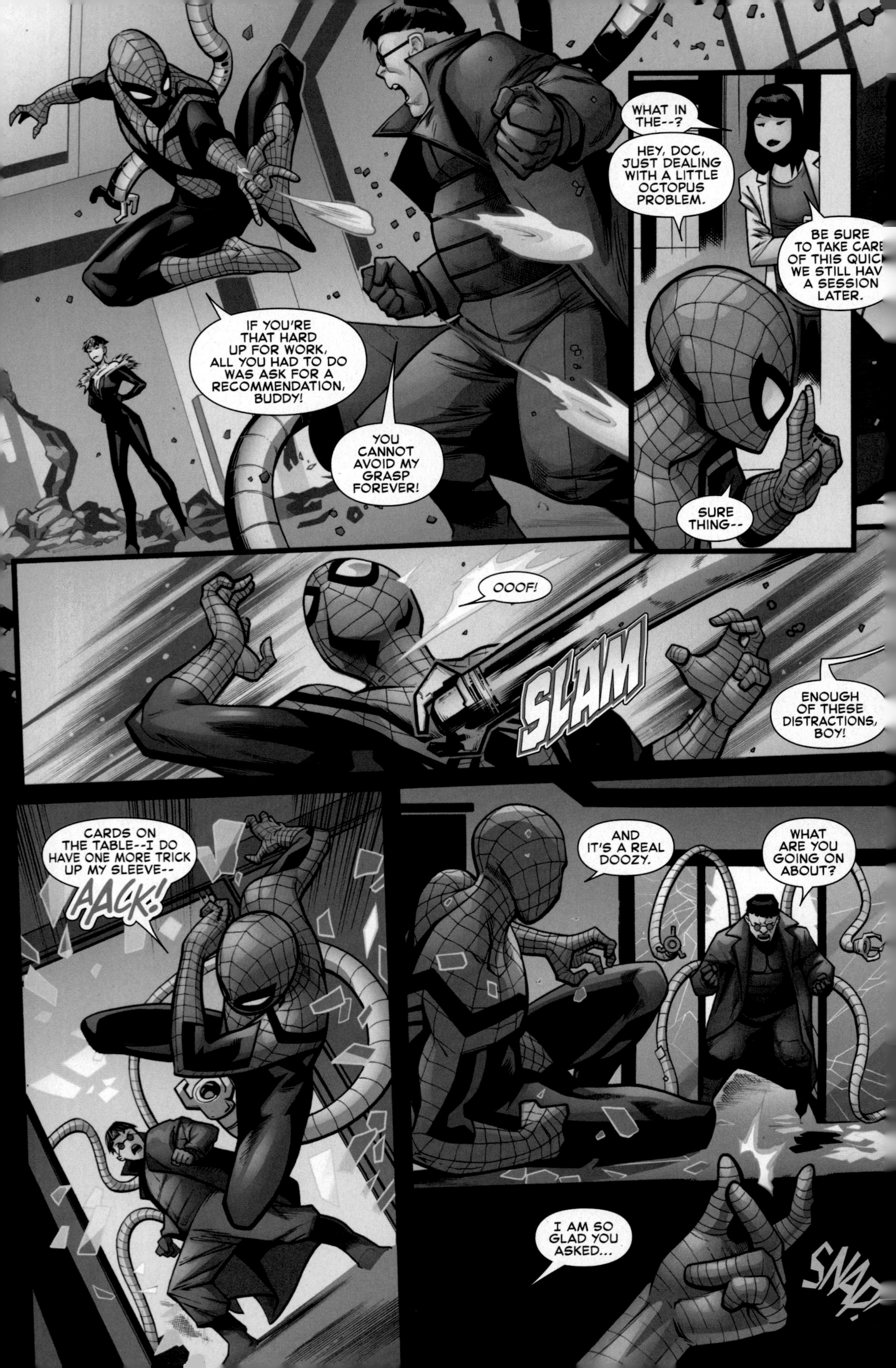

IF YOU'RE THAT HARD UP FOR WORK, ALL YOU HAD TO DO WAS ASK FOR A RECOMMENDATION, BUDDY!
YOU CANNOT AVOID MY GRASP FOREVER!
WHAT IN THE--?
HEY, DOC, JUST DEALING WITH A LITTLE OCTOPUS PROBLEM.
BE SURE TO TAKE CARE OF THIS QUICK WE STILL HAV A SESSION LATER.
SURE THING--
OOOF!
SLAM
ENOUGH OF THESE DISTRACTIONS, BOY!
CARDS ON THE TABLE--I DO HAVE ONE MORE TRICK UP MY SLEEVE--
AACK!
AND IT'S A REAL DOOZY.
WHAT ARE YOU GOING ON ABOUT?
I AM SO GLAD YOU ASKED...
SNAP!

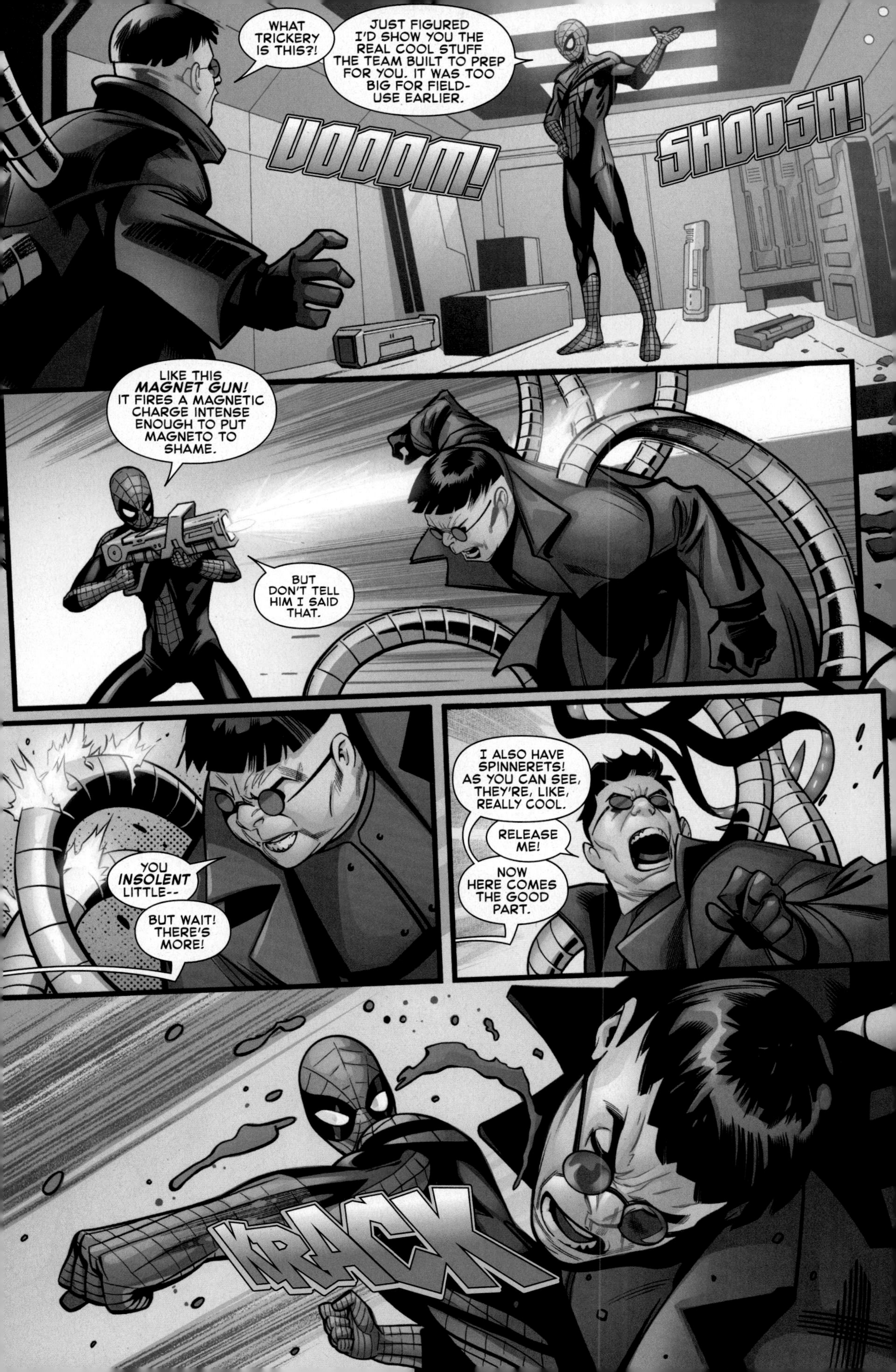
WHAT TRICKERY IS THIS?!
JUST FIGURED I'D SHOW YOU THE REAL COOL STUFF THE TEAM BUILT TO PREP FOR YOU. IT WAS TOO BIG FOR FIELD-USE EARLIER.
VOOOM!
SHOOSH!
LIKE THIS MAGNET GUN! IT FIRES A MAGNETIC CHARGE INTENSE ENOUGH TO PUT MAGNETO TO SHAME.
BUT DON'T TELL HIM I SAID THAT.
YOU INSOLENT LITTLE--
BUT WAIT! THERE'S MORE!
I ALSO HAVE SPINNERETS! AS YOU CAN SEE, THEY'RE, LIKE, REALLY COOL.
RELEASE ME!
NOW HERE COMES THE GOOD PART.
KRACK

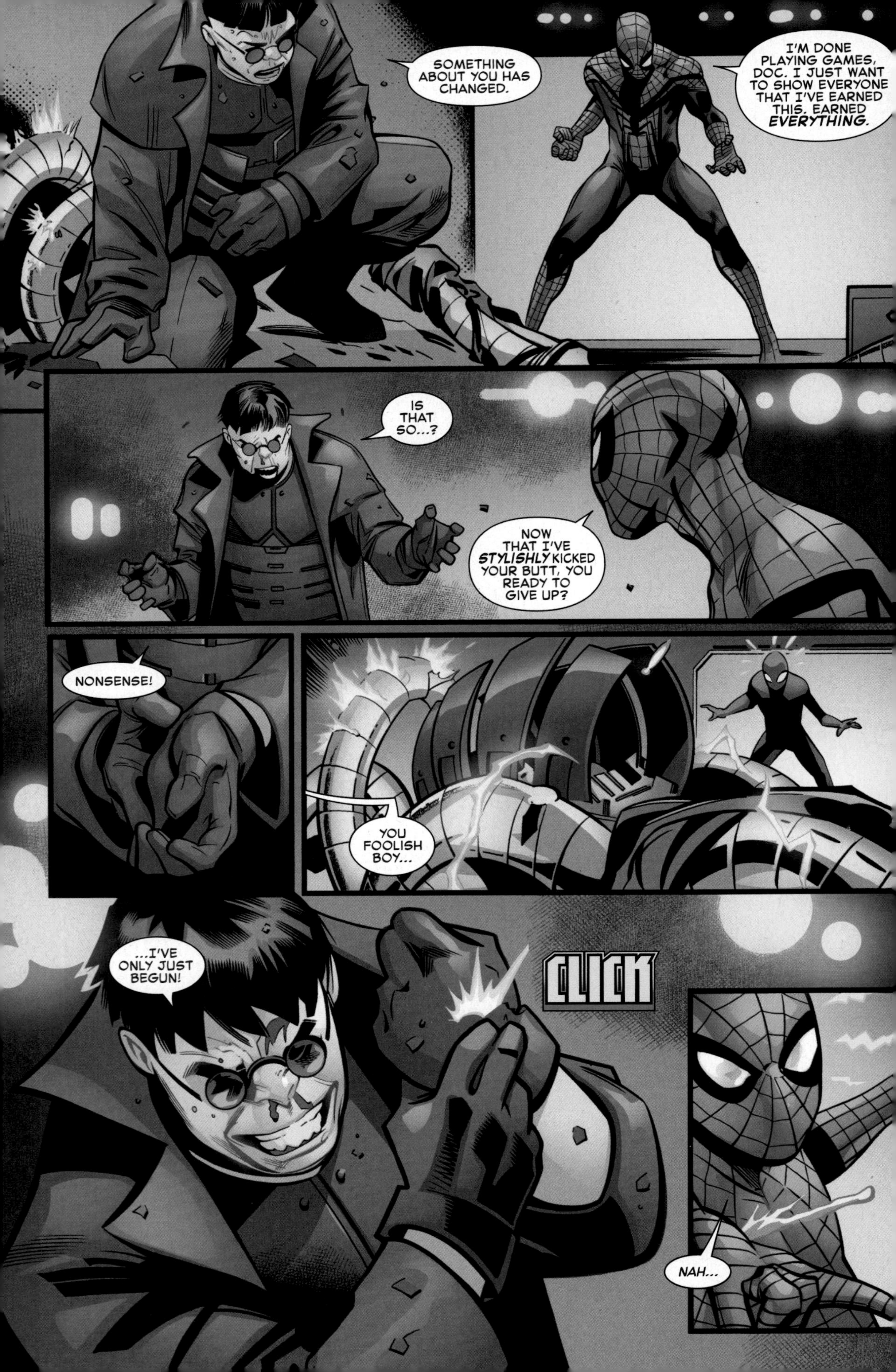
SOMETHING ABOUT YOU HAS CHANGED.
I'M DONE PLAYING GAMES, DOC. I JUST WANT TO SHOW EVERYONE THAT I'VE EARNED THIS. EARNED EVERYTHING.
IS THAT SO...?
NOW THAT I'VE STYLISHLY KICKED YOUR BUTT, YOU READY TO GIVE UP?
NONSENSE!
YOU FOOLISH BOY...
...I'VE ONLY JUST BEGUN!
CLICK
NAH...

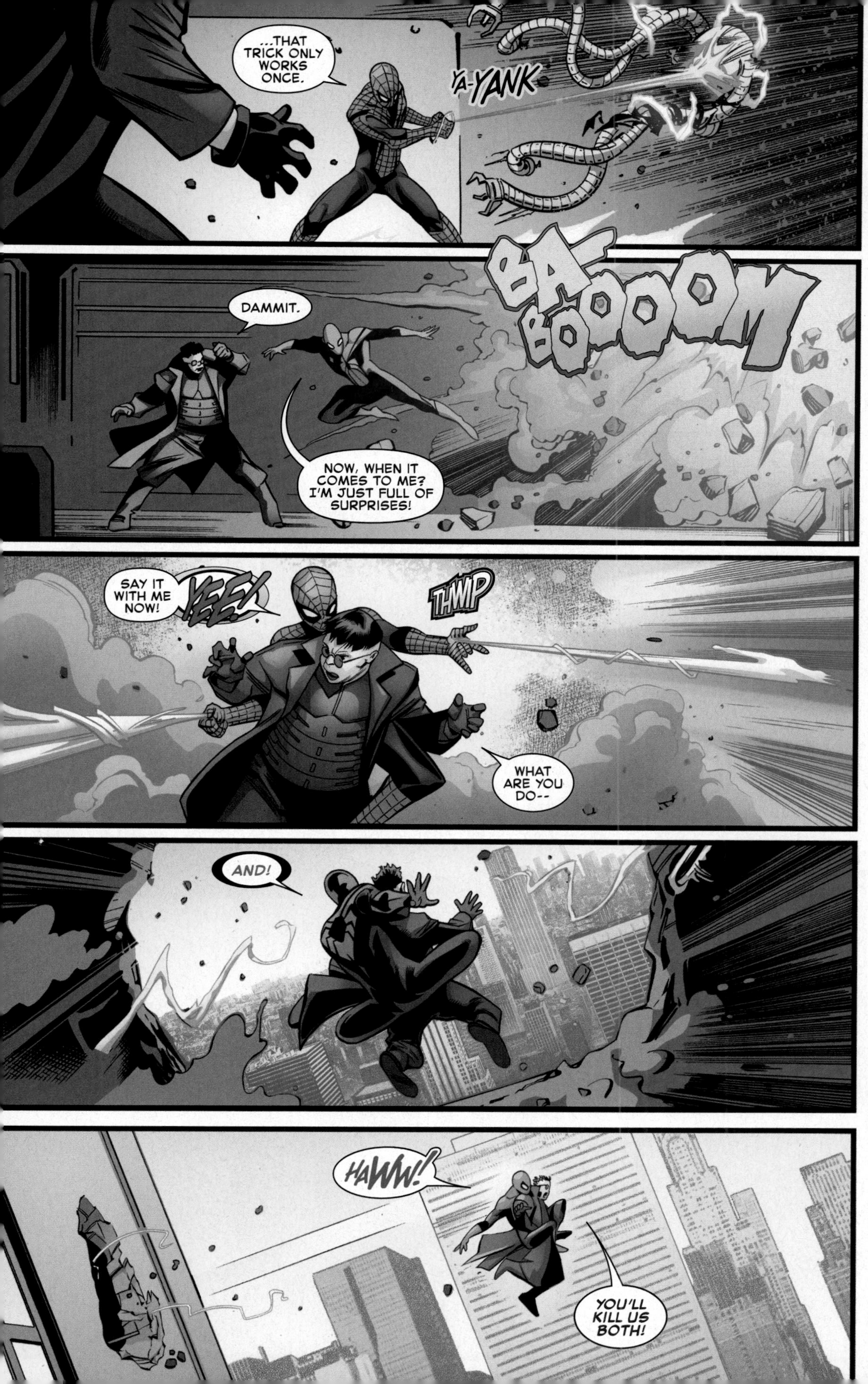

...THAT TRICK ONLY WORKS ONCE.
YA-YANK
BA-BOOOOOM
DAMMIT.
NOW, WHEN IT COMES TO ME? I'M JUST FULL OF SURPRISES!
SAY IT WITH ME NOW!
YEE!
THWIP
WHAT ARE YOU DO--
AND!
HAWW!
YOU'LL KILL US BOTH!

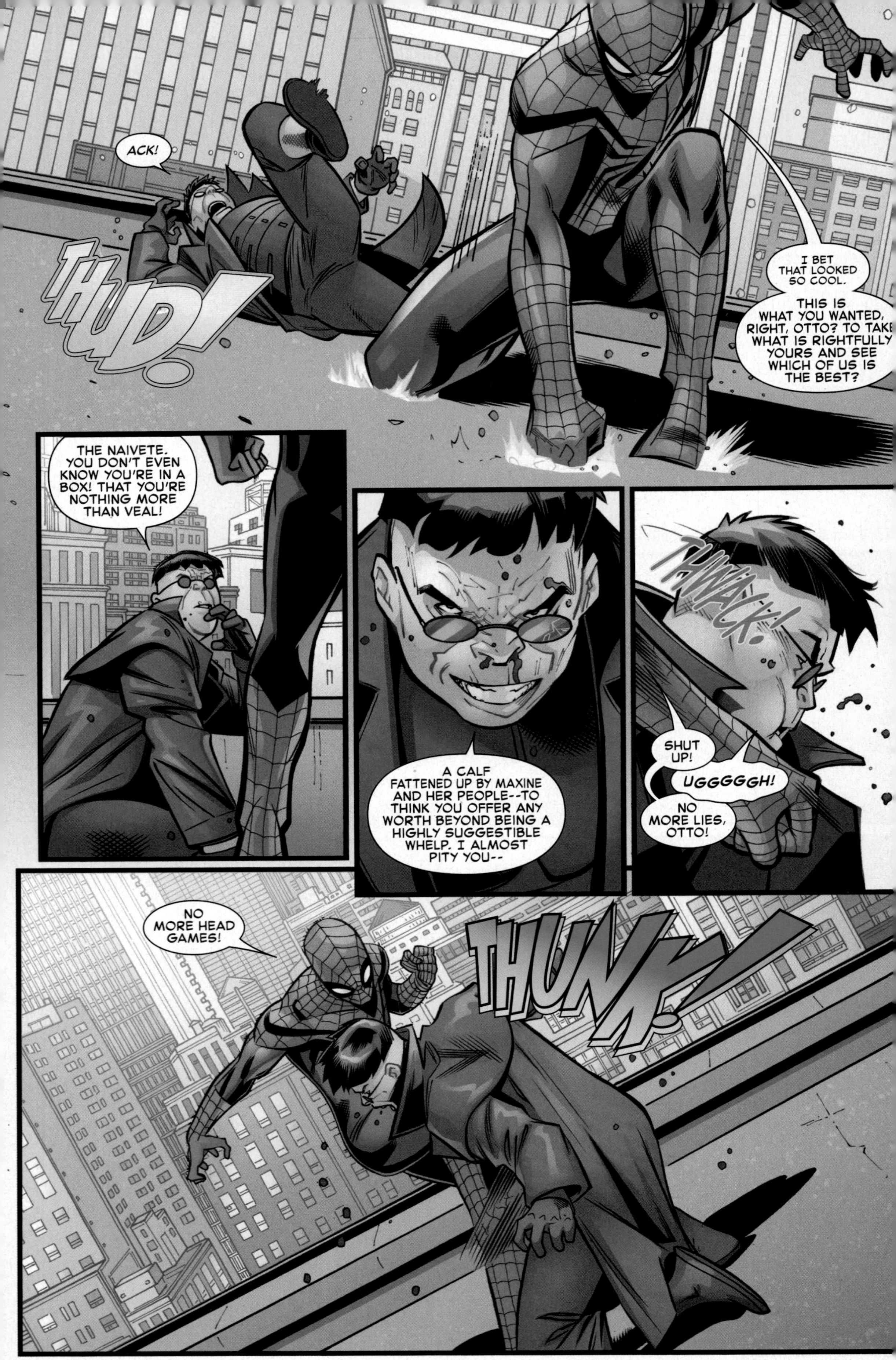
ACK!
THUD!
I BET THAT LOOKED SO COOL.
THIS IS WHAT YOU WANTED, RIGHT, OTTO? TO TAKE WHAT IS RIGHTFULLY YOURS AND SEE WHICH OF US IS THE BEST?
THE NAIVETE. YOU DON'T EVEN KNOW YOU'RE IN A BOX! THAT YOU'RE NOTHING MORE THAN VEAL!
A CALF FATTENED UP BY MAXINE AND HER PEOPLE--TO THINK YOU OFFER ANY WORTH BEYOND BEING A HIGHLY SUGGESTIBLE WHELP. I ALMOST PITY YOU--
THWACK!
SHUT UP!
UGGGGGH!
NO MORE LIES, OTTO!
NO MORE HEAD GAMES!
THUNK!

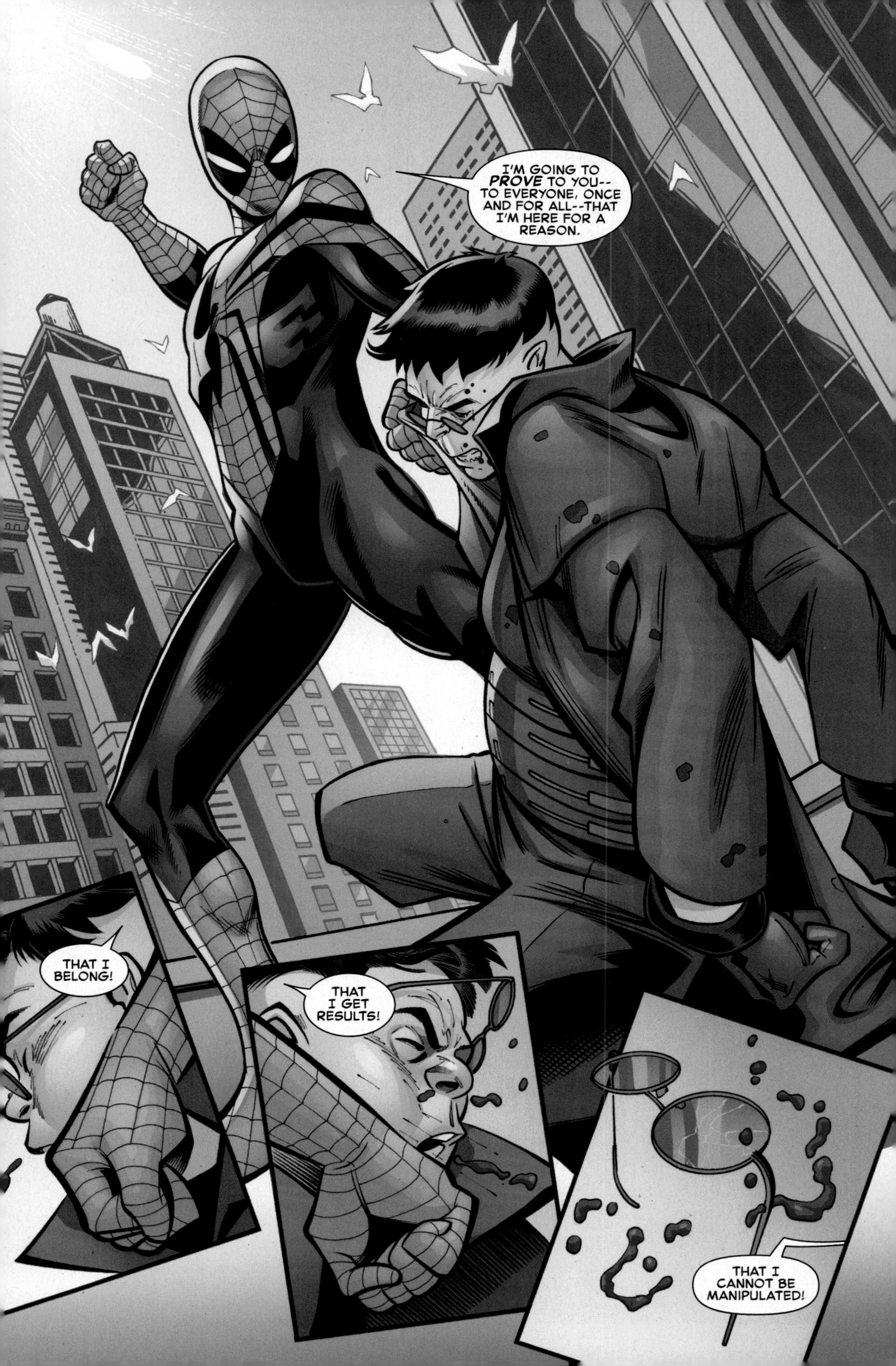
I'M GOING TO PROVE TO YOU-- TO EVERYONE, ONCE AND FOR ALL--THAT I'M HERE FOR A REASON.
THAT I BELONG!
THAT I GET RESULTS!
THAT I CANNOT BE MANIPULATED!

A FOOL.

WHAT WAS THAT?

I SAID YOU'RE A DAMNED FOOL, BOY! BEYOND DIDN'T CHOOSE YOU FOR YOUR "STRONG WILL" BUT BECAUSE YOU'RE PSYCHOLOGICALLY COMPROMISED! BECAUSE YOU ARE WEAK!

AN EASILY CONTROLLED LAPDOG PRONE TO EMOTIONAL OUTBURSTS AND DISTRACTIONS WHOSE LEASH ENDS IN BEYOND'S HANDS.

SOMEONE THEY COULD BEND TO DO WHATEVER THEY BID-- SO LONG AS THEY JUST APPLY THE RIGHT PRESSURE.

DON'T BELIEVE ME, BOY? I HAVE THE PROOF HERE.

A DATA DRIVE OF ALL OF MAXINE AND BEYOND'S TERRIBLE LITTLE SECRETS. I BARELY SCRATCHED THE SURFACE.

I'VE DISABLED THE SECURITY PROTOCOLS. NO ONE WILL KNOW IT'S BEEN OPENED. ITS CONTENTS WILL BE KNOWN TO YOU AND YOU ALONE.

I'M NOT SEEING THE ENDGAME FOR THIS CON, OTTO...

THIS IS NO RUSE, BOY.

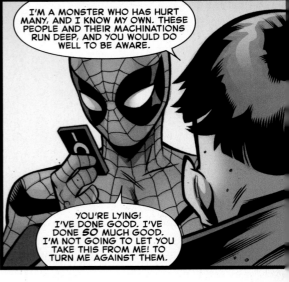

I'M A MONSTER WHO HAS HURT MANY, AND I KNOW MY OWN. THESE PEOPLE AND THEIR MACHINATIONS RUN DEEP, AND YOU WOULD DO WELL TO BE AWARE.

YOU'RE LYING! I'VE DONE GOOD. I'VE DONE SO MUCH GOOD. I'M NOT GOING TO LET YOU TAKE THIS FROM ME! TO TURN ME AGAINST THEM.

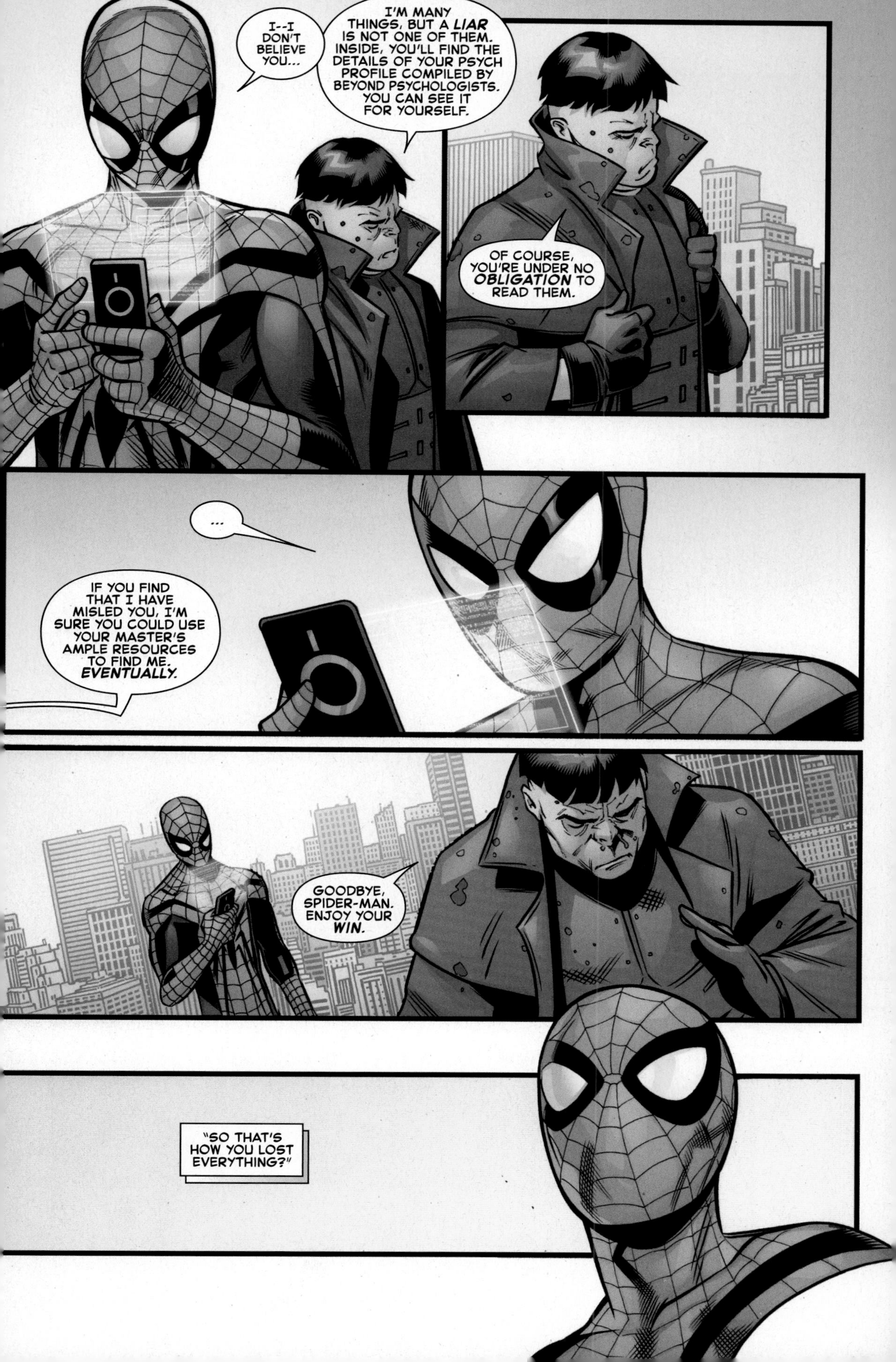
I--I DON'T BELIEVE YOU...
I'M MANY THINGS, BUT A LIAR IS NOT ONE OF THEM. INSIDE, YOU'LL FIND THE DETAILS OF YOUR PSYCH PROFILE COMPILED BY BEYOND PSYCHOLOGISTS. YOU CAN SEE IT FOR YOURSELF.
OF COURSE, YOU'RE UNDER NO OBLIGATION TO READ THEM.
...
IF YOU FIND THAT I HAVE MISLED YOU, I'M SURE YOU COULD USE YOUR MASTER'S AMPLE RESOURCES TO FIND ME. EVENTUALLY.
GOODBYE, SPIDER-MAN. ENJOY YOUR WIN.
"SO THAT'S HOW YOU LOST EVERYTHING?"

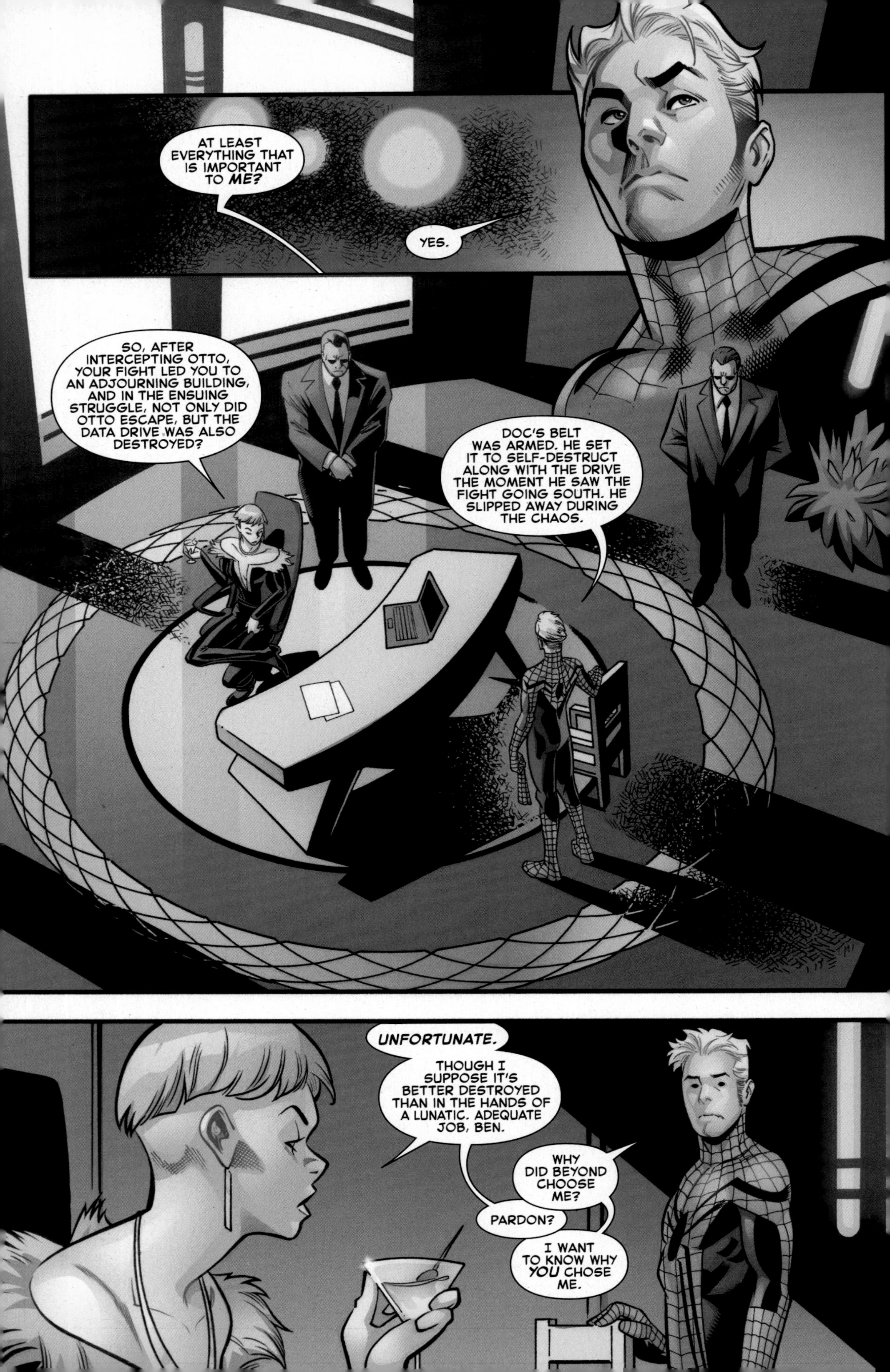
AT LEAST EVERYTHING THAT IS IMPORTANT TO ME?
YES.
SO, AFTER INTERCEPTING OTTO, YOUR FIGHT LED YOU TO AN ADJOURNING BUILDING, AND IN THE ENSUING STRUGGLE, NOT ONLY DID OTTO ESCAPE, BUT THE DATA DRIVE WAS ALSO DESTROYED?
DOC'S BELT WAS ARMED. HE SET IT TO SELF-DESTRUCT ALONG WITH THE DRIVE THE MOMENT HE SAW THE FIGHT GOING SOUTH. HE SLIPPED AWAY DURING THE CHAOS.
UNFORTUNATE.
THOUGH I SUPPOSE IT'S BETTER DESTROYED THAN IN THE HANDS OF A LUNATIC. ADEQUATE JOB, BEN.
WHY DID BEYOND CHOOSE ME?
PARDON?
I WANT TO KNOW WHY YOU CHOSE ME.

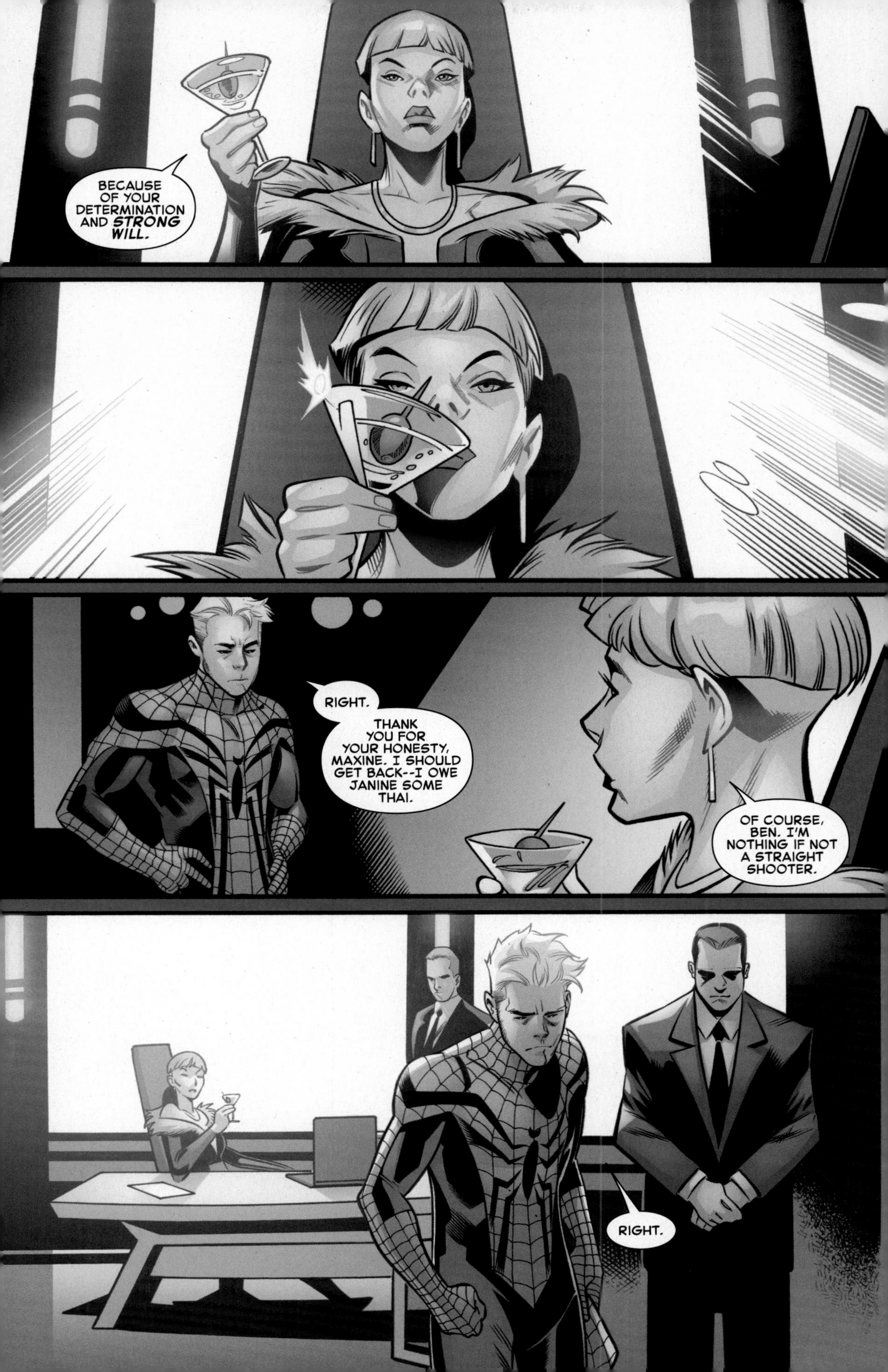
BECAUSE OF YOUR DETERMINATION AND STRONG WILL.
RIGHT.
THANK YOU FOR YOUR HONESTY, MAXINE. I SHOULD GET BACK--I OWE JANINE SOME THAI.
OF COURSE, BEN. I'M NOTHING IF NOT A STRAIGHT SHOOTER.
RIGHT.

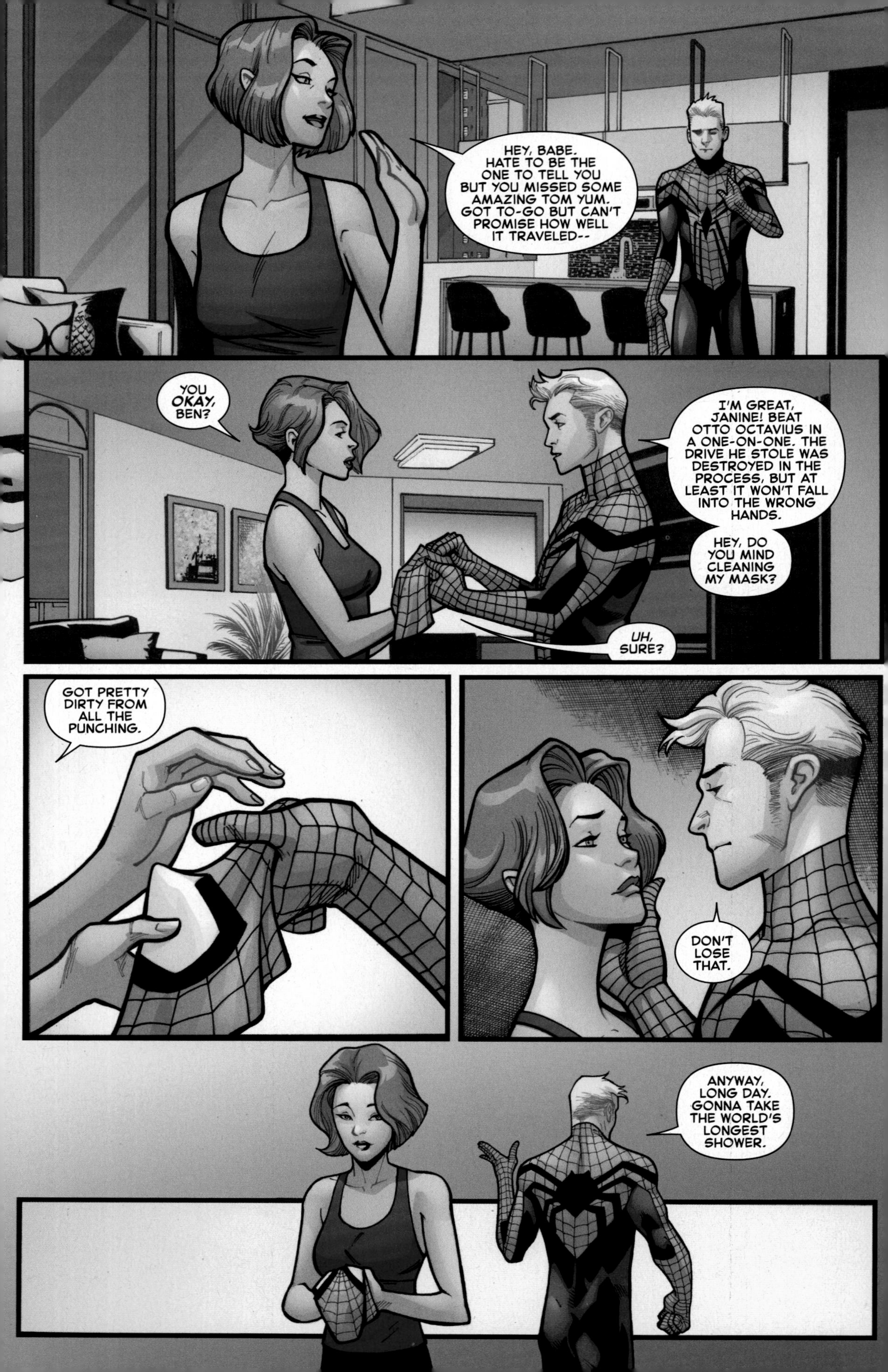

HEY, BABE. HATE TO BE THE ONE TO TELL YOU BUT YOU MISSED SOME AMAZING TOM YUM. GOT TO-GO BUT CAN'T PROMISE HOW WELL IT TRAVELED--
YOU OKAY, BEN?
I'M GREAT, JANINE! BEAT OTTO OCTAVIUS IN A ONE-ON-ONE. THE DRIVE HE STOLE WAS DESTROYED IN THE PROCESS, BUT AT LEAST IT WON'T FALL INTO THE WRONG HANDS.
HEY, DO YOU MIND CLEANING MY MASK?
UH, SURE?
GOT PRETTY DIRTY FROM ALL THE PUNCHING.
DON'T LOSE THAT.
ANYWAY, LONG DAY. GONNA TAKE THE WORLD'S LONGEST SHOWER.

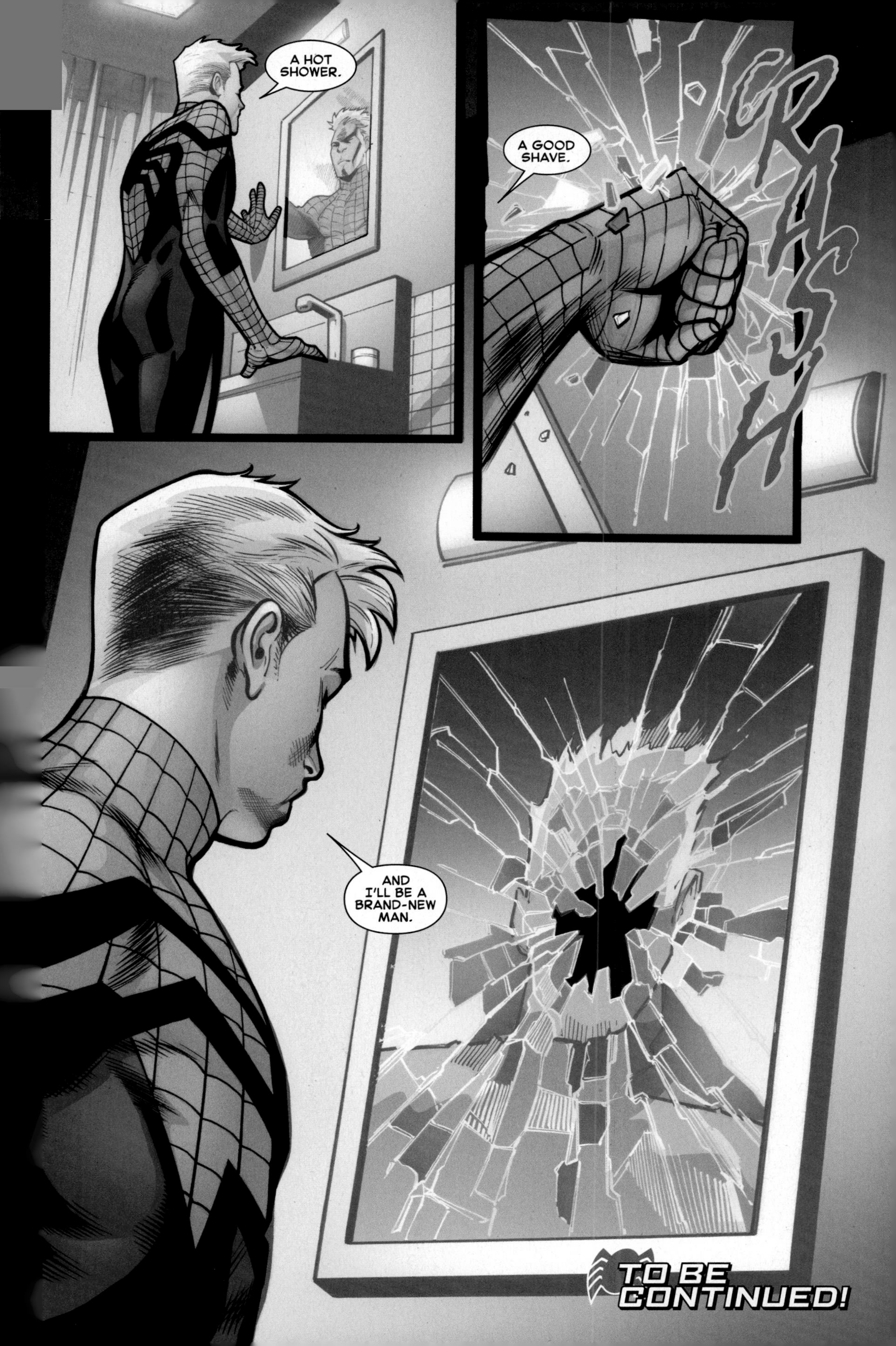
A HOT SHOWER.
A GOOD SHAVE.
CRASSH
AND I'LL BE A BRAND-NEW MAN.
TO BE CONTINUED!

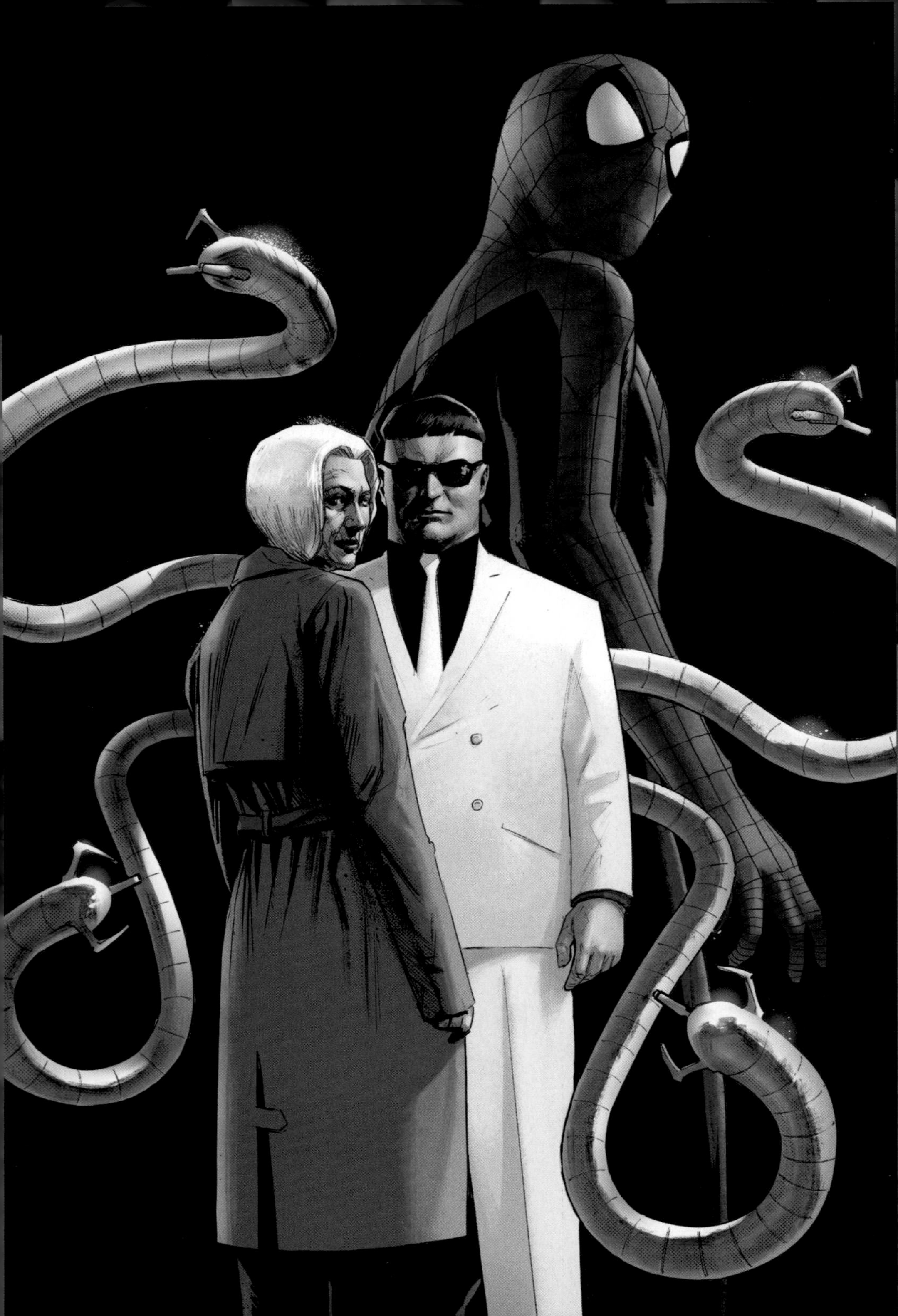

#81 DEVIL'S REIGN VARIANT BY
MAHMUD ASRAR & **MATTHEW WILSON**

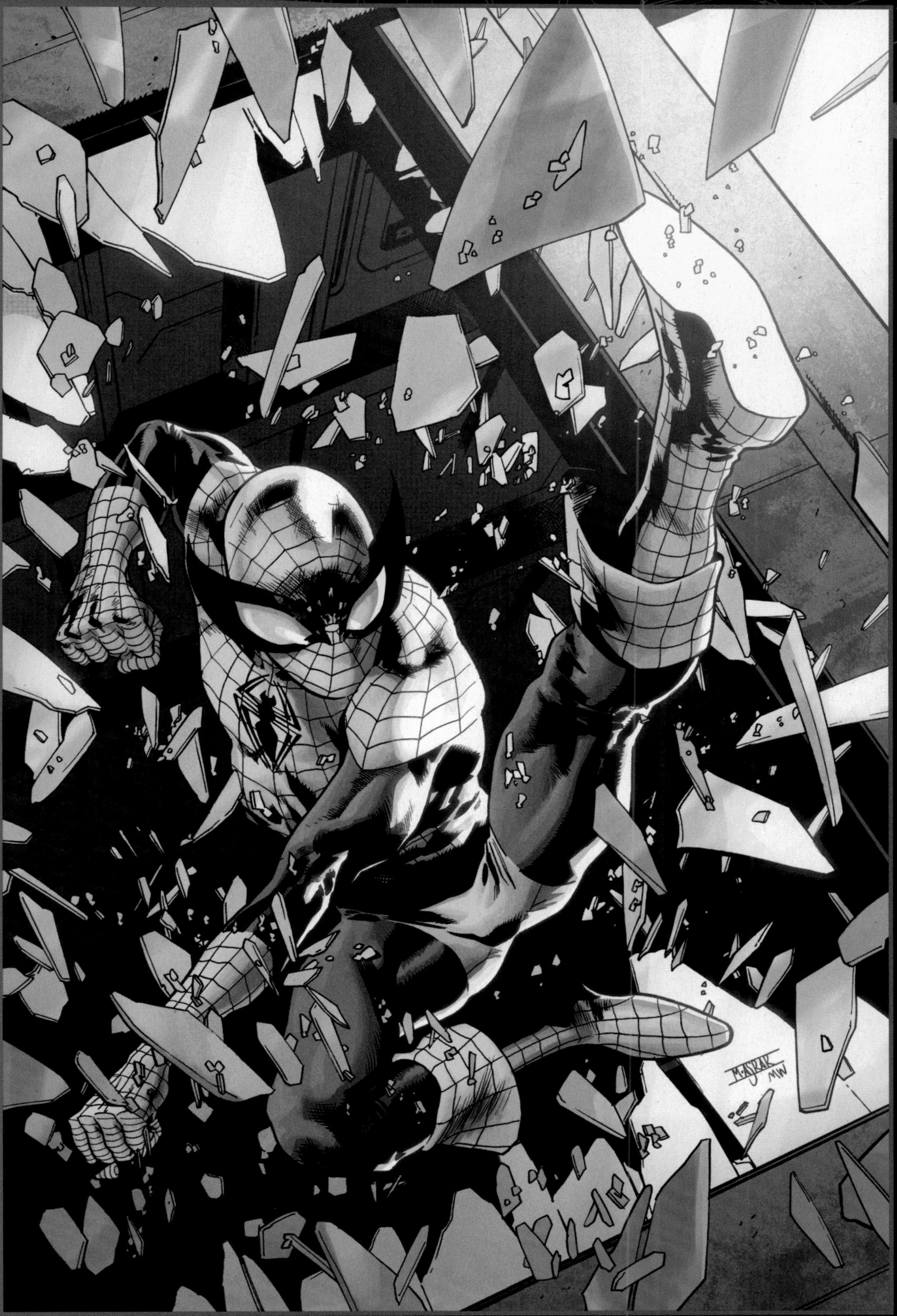
M. ASRAR
MW

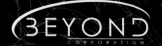

BEYOND CORPORATION

#81 VARIANT BY
ARIST DEYN

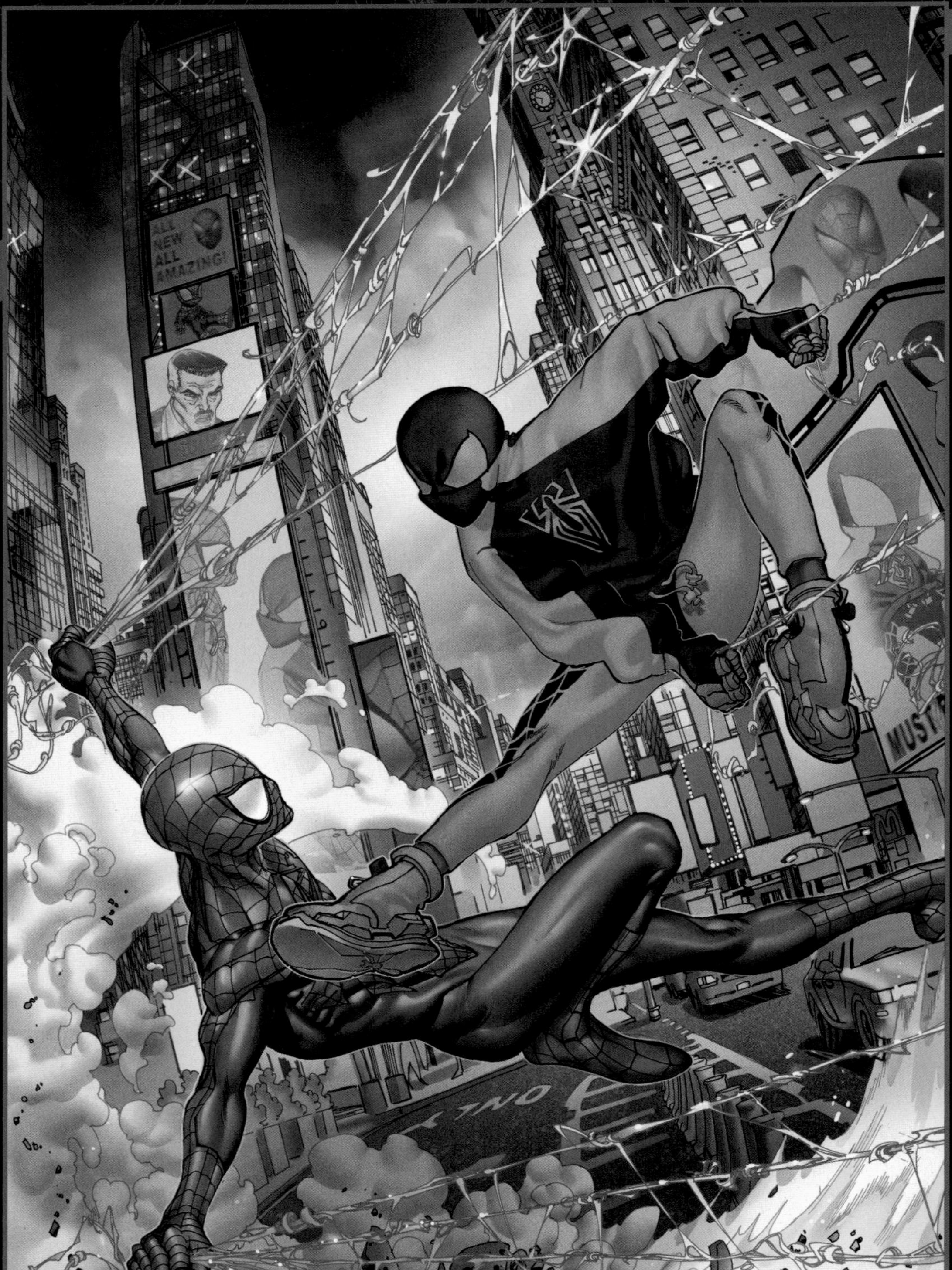
ALL NEW ALL AMAZING!
ONLY
MUSTR

#82 DEVIL'S REIGN VARIANT BY
JOSHUA "SWAY" SWABY

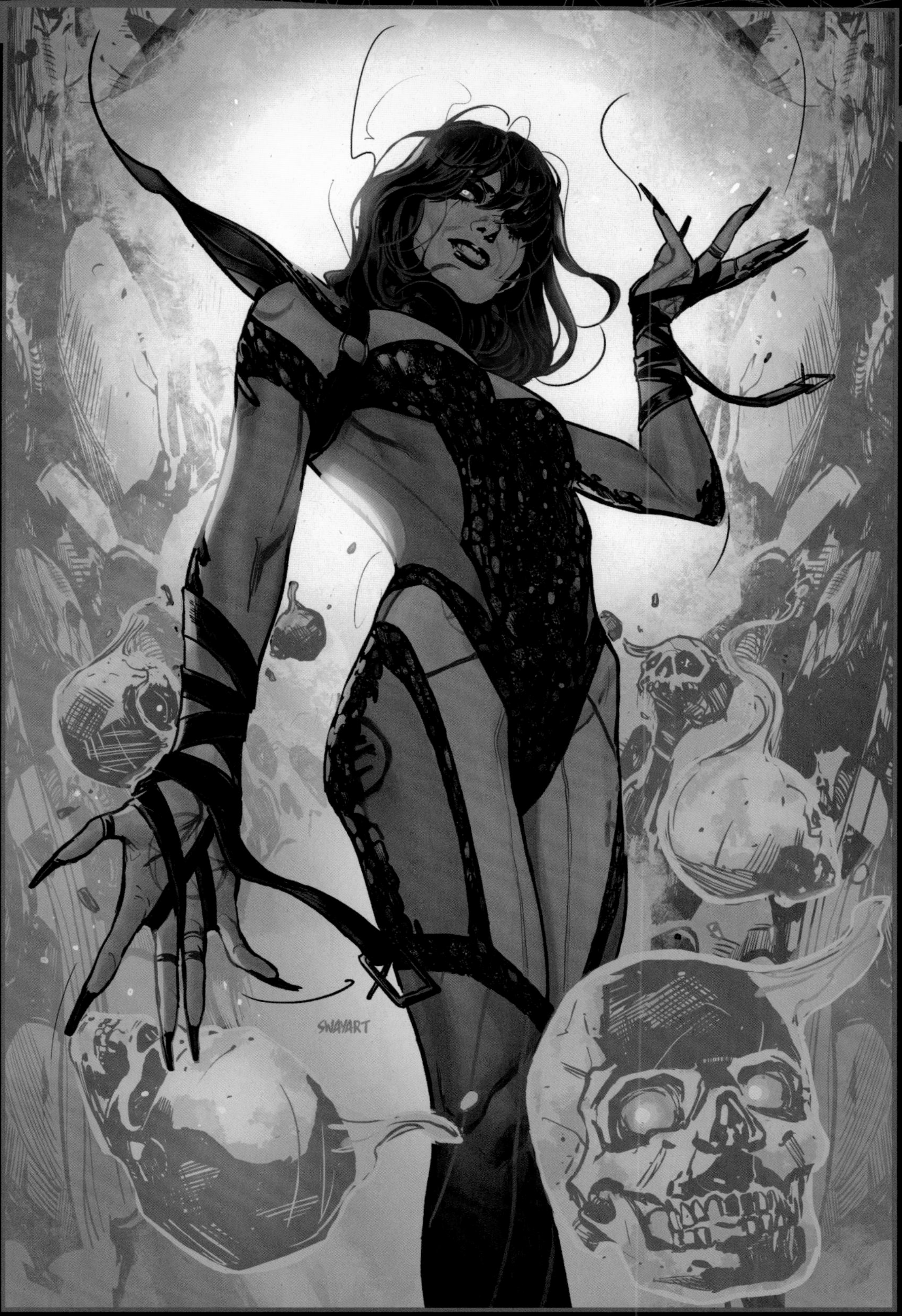
SWAYART

#82 VARIANT BY
JORGE FORNÉS

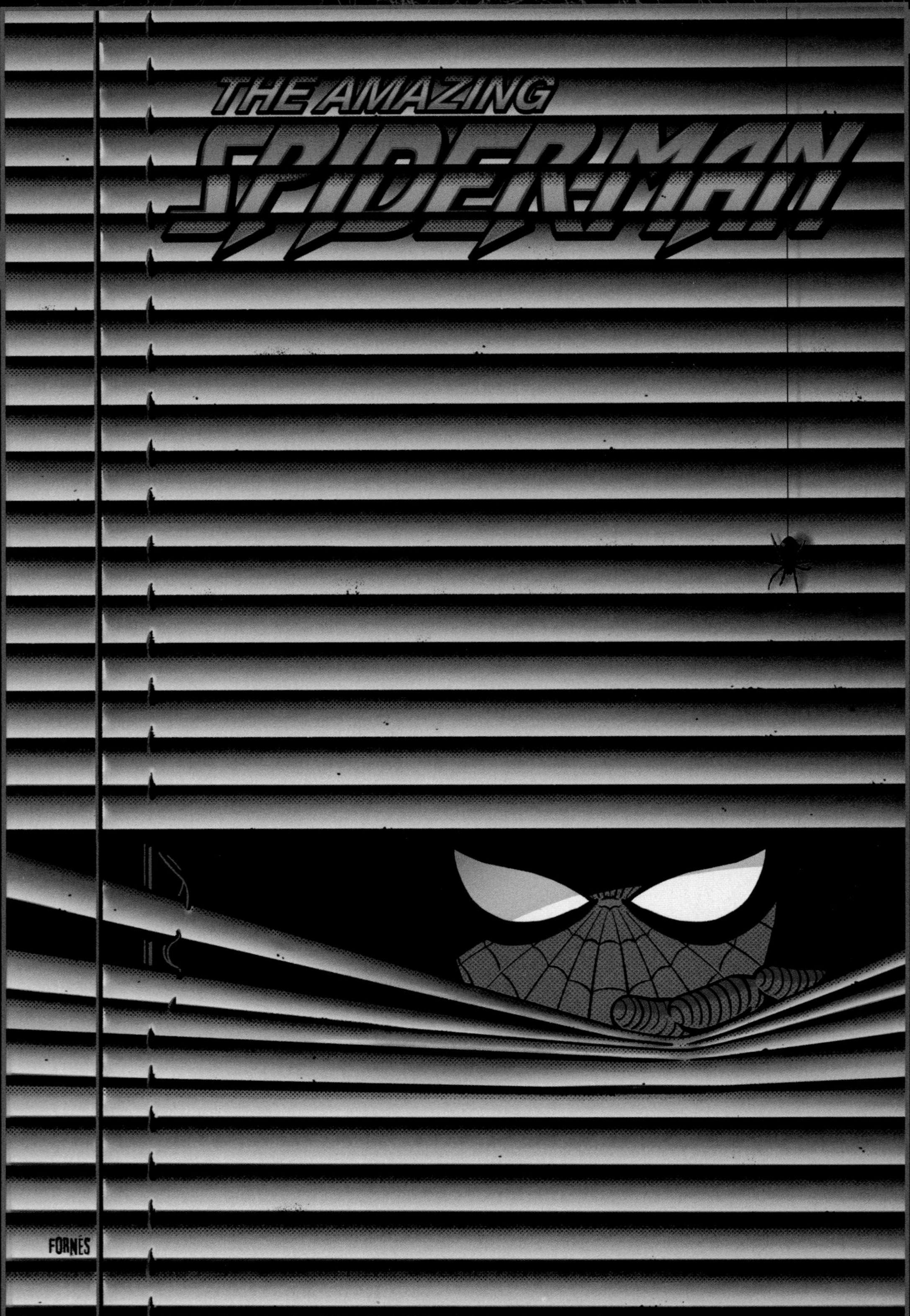
THE AMAZING
SPIDER-MAN
FORNÉS

#83 DEVIL'S REIGN VARIANT BY
DAVID BALDEÓN & **ISRAEL SILVA**

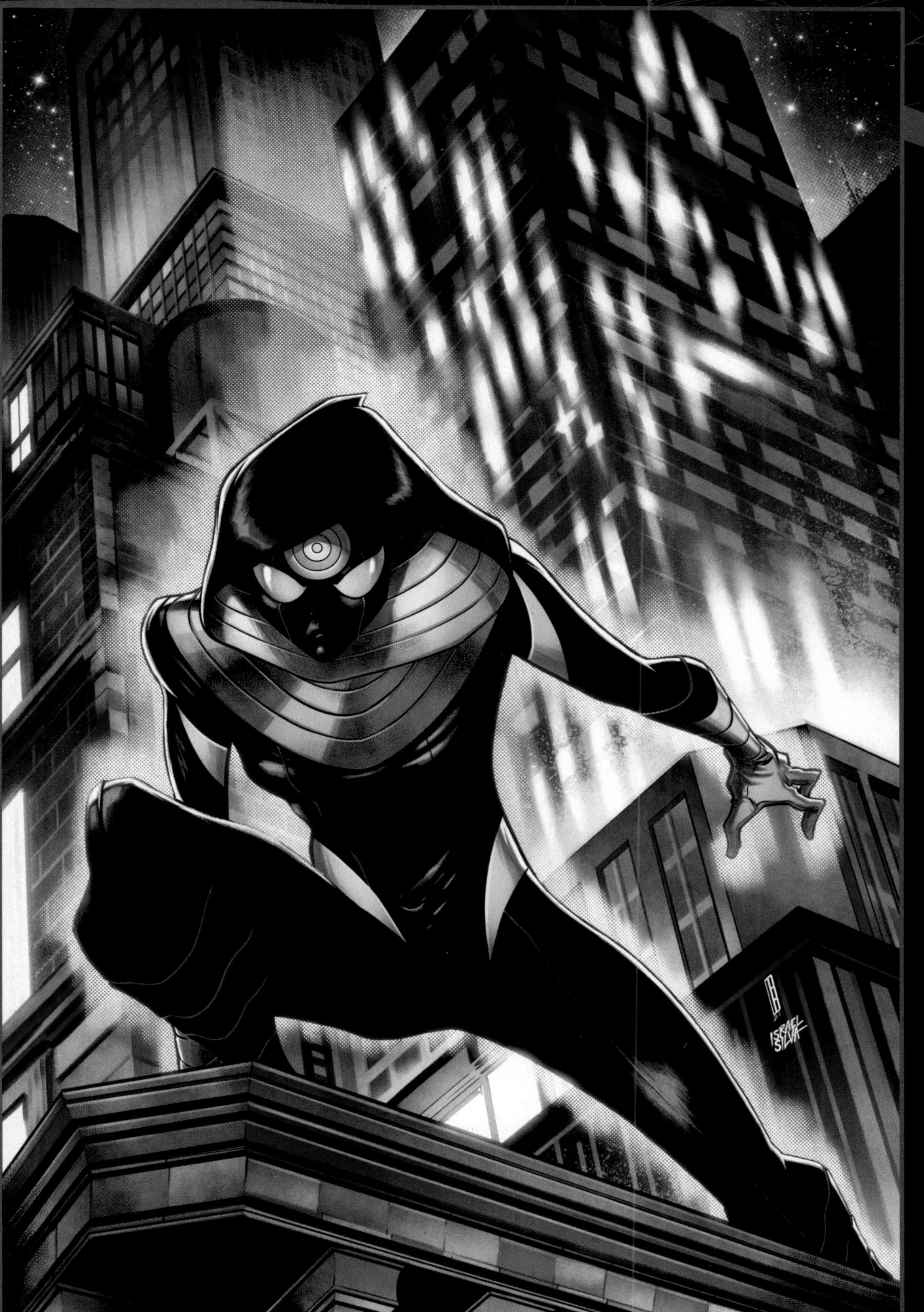
ISRAEL SILVA

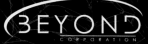

#83 VARIANT BY
PATRICK GLEASON

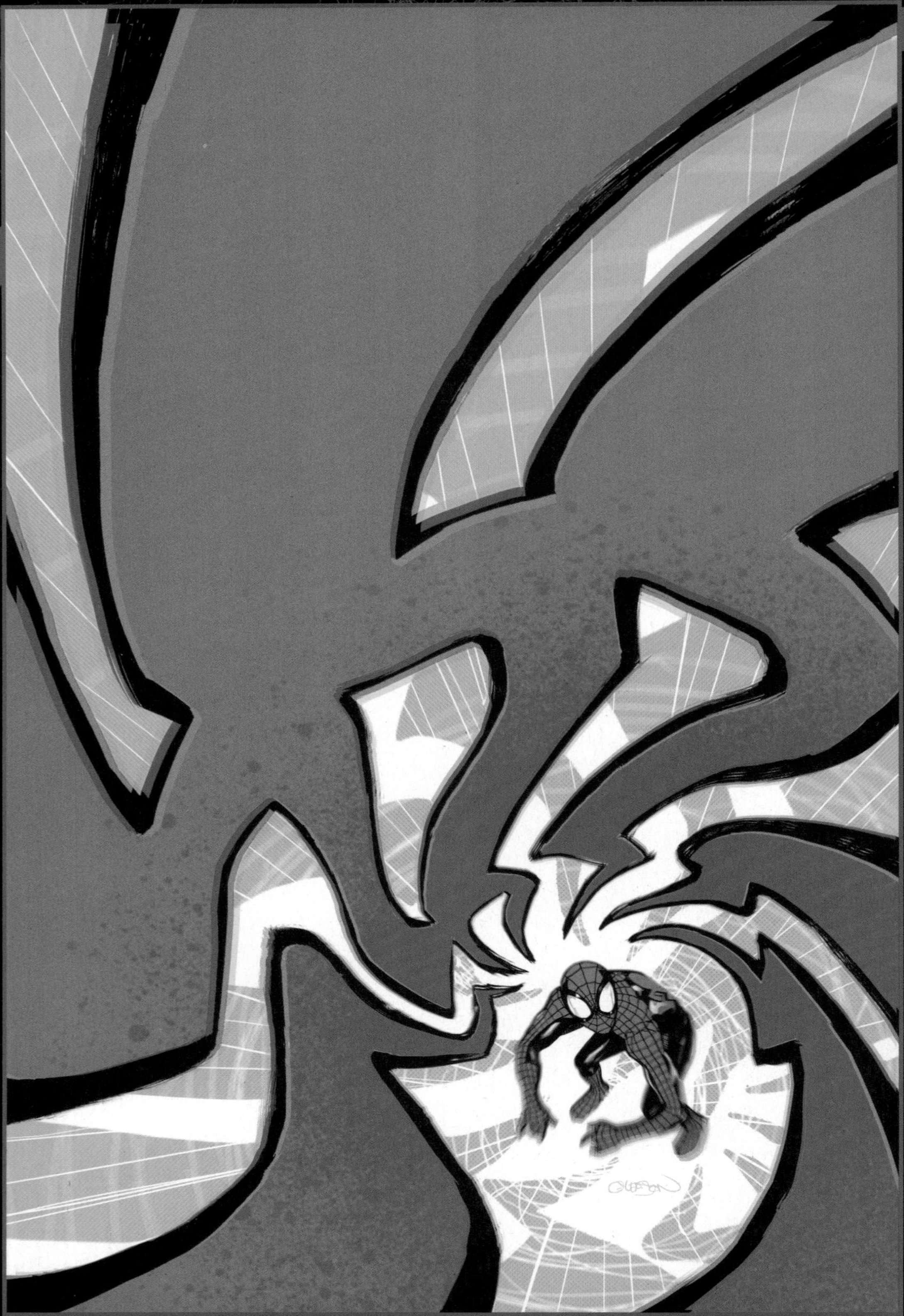

GLEASON

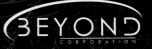

#84 DEVIL'S REIGN VARIANT BY
DAVID LAFUENTE & RACHELLE ROSENBERG

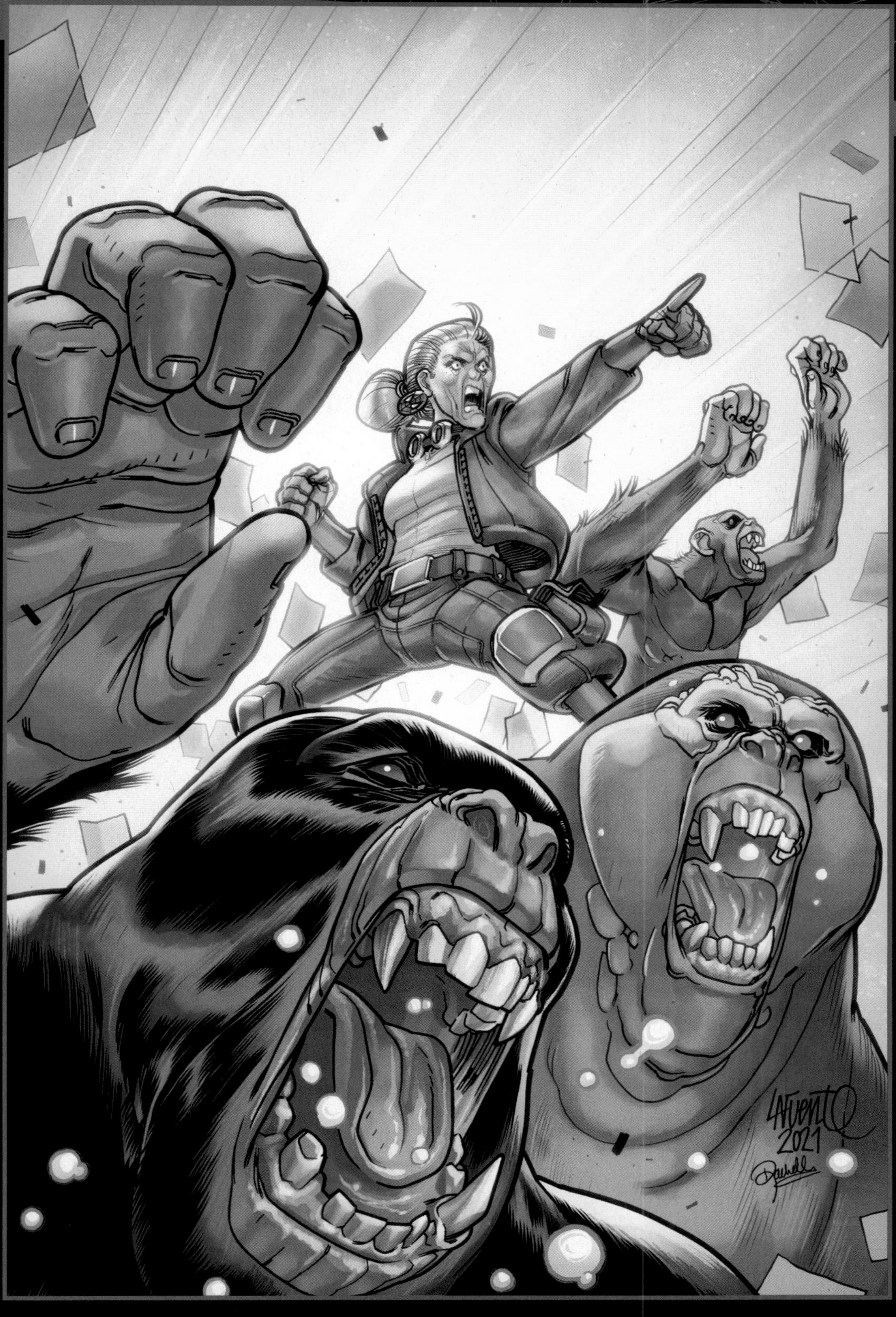
LAFUENTE
2021

BEYOND CORPORATION

#84 VARIANT BY
CORY SMITH & **MORRY HOLLOWELL**

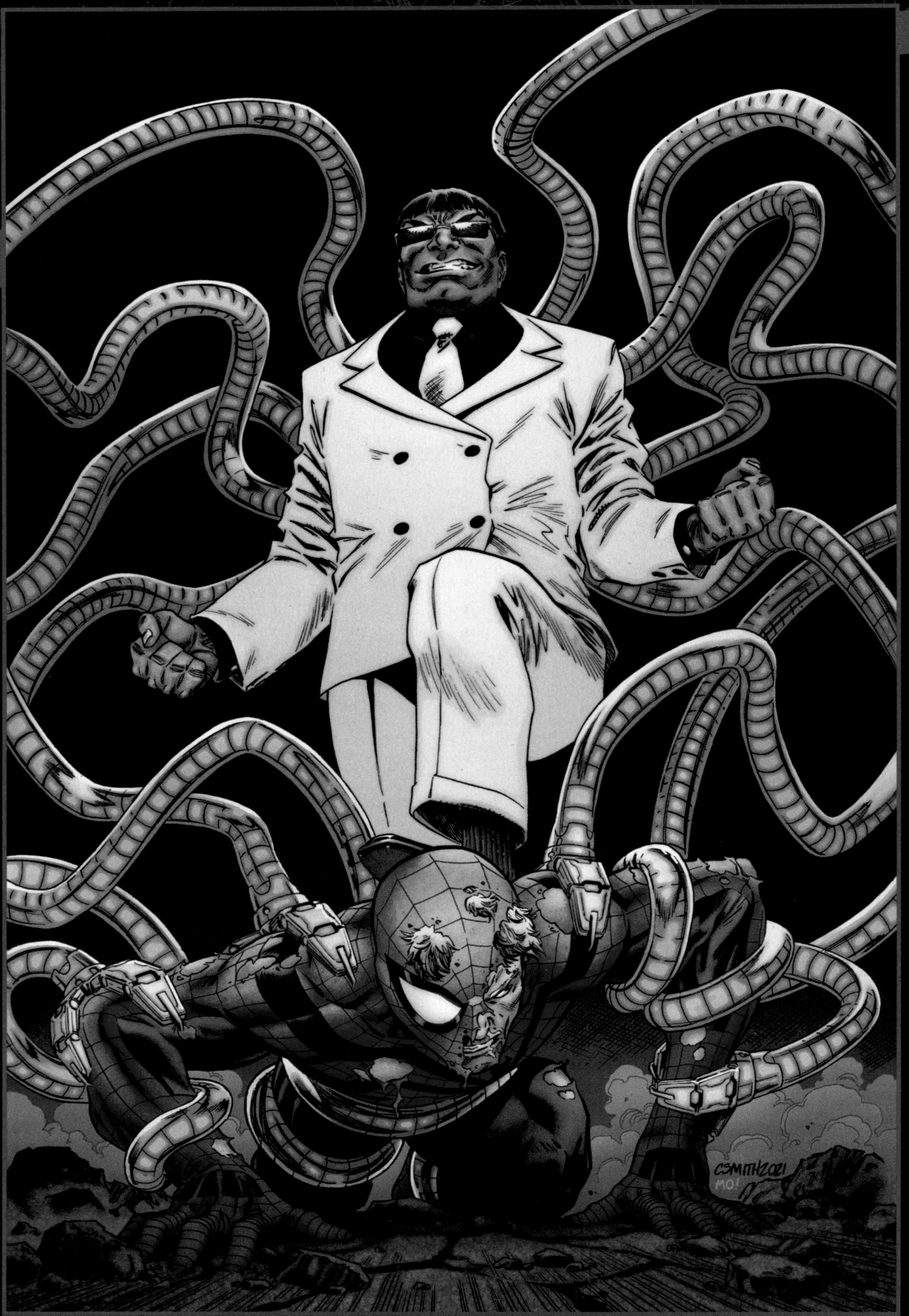
CSMITH2021
MO!

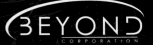

#85 CLASSIC HOMAGE VARIANT BY
PEACH MOMOKO

BEYOND
CORPORATION

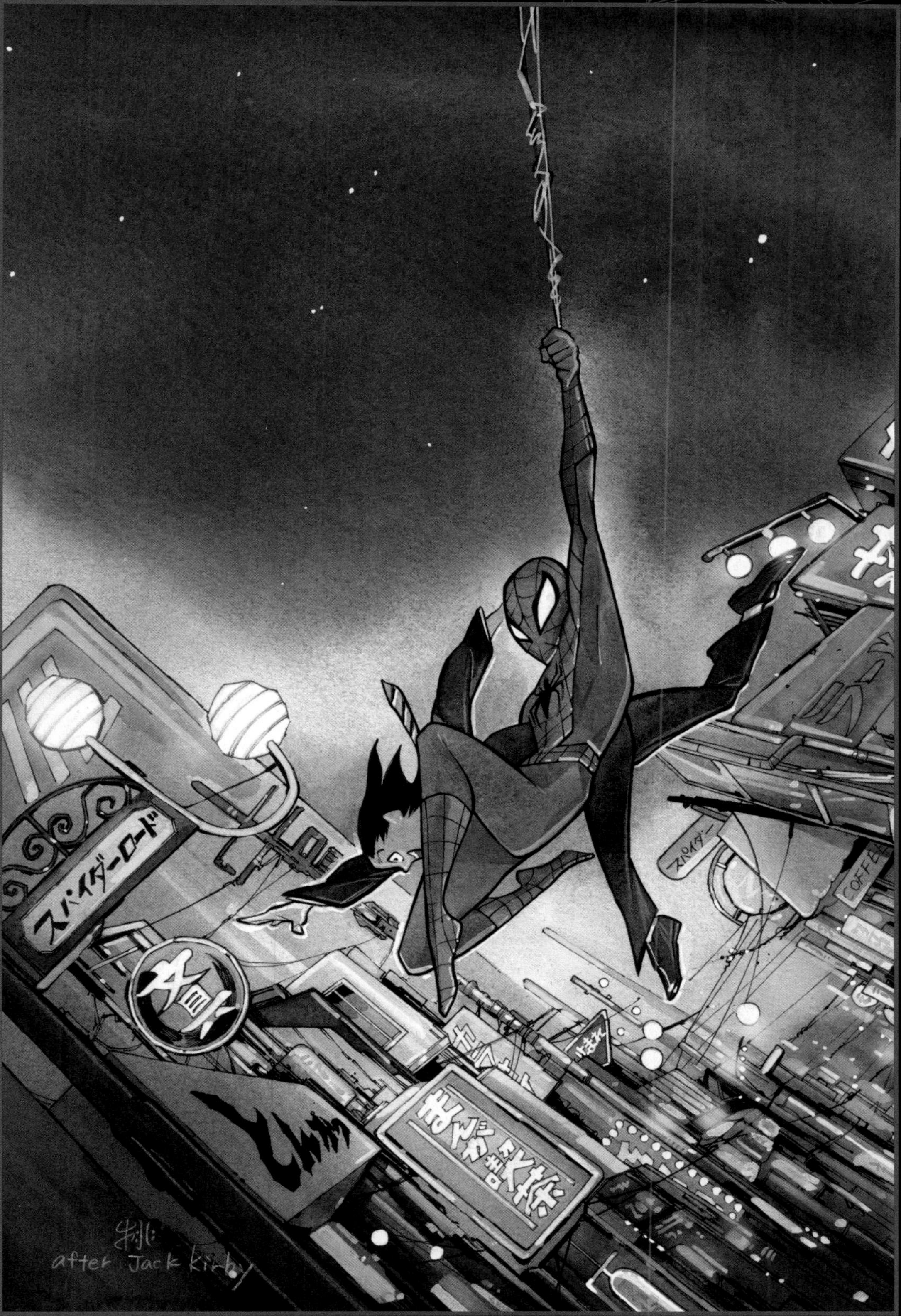

スパイダーロード
スパイダー
after Jack Kirby

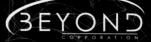

BEYOND
CORPORATION

#85 VARIANT BY
LEINIL FRANCIS YU & **SUNNY GHO**

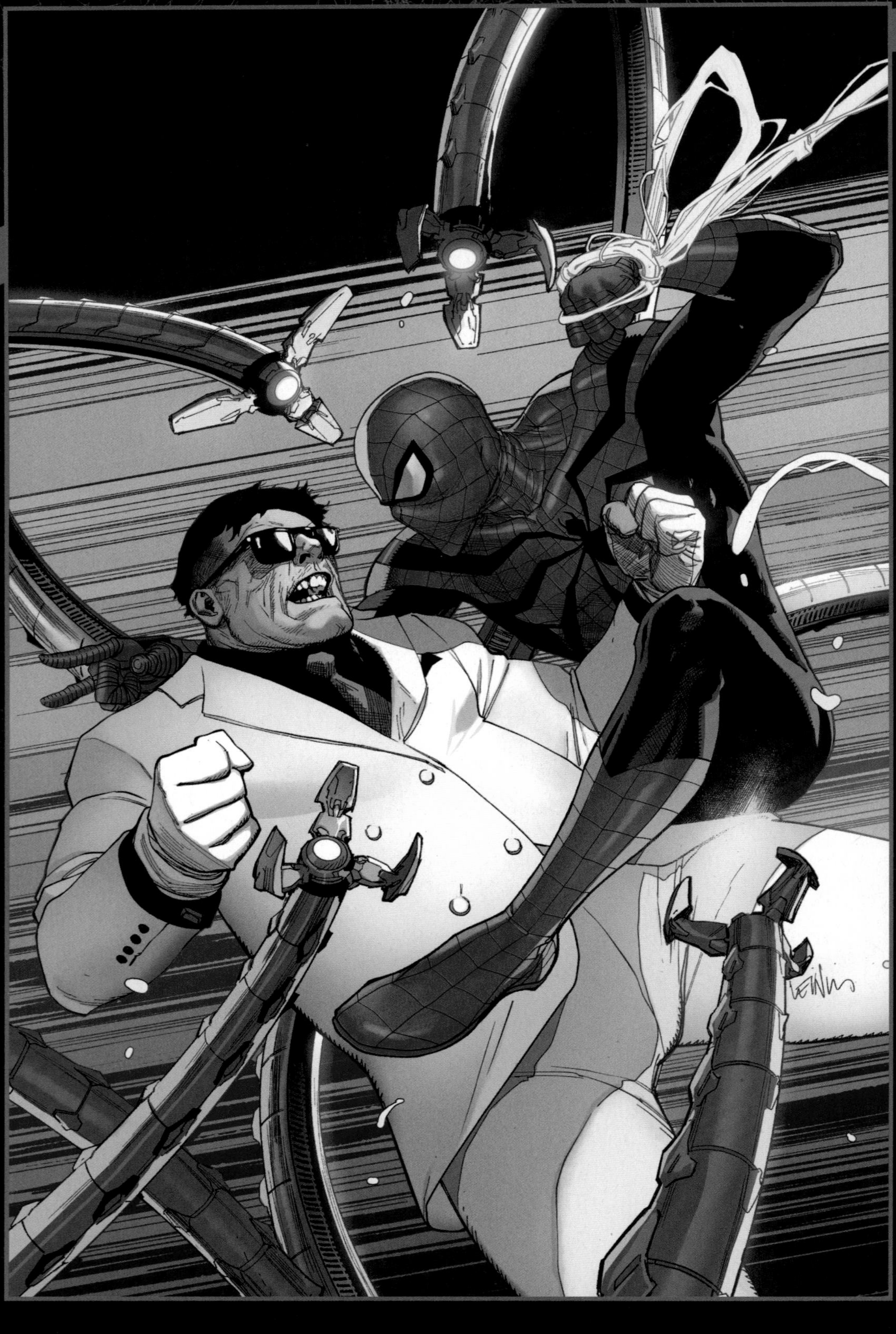

#81 PAGES 3-6 ART BY
CARLOS GÓMEZ

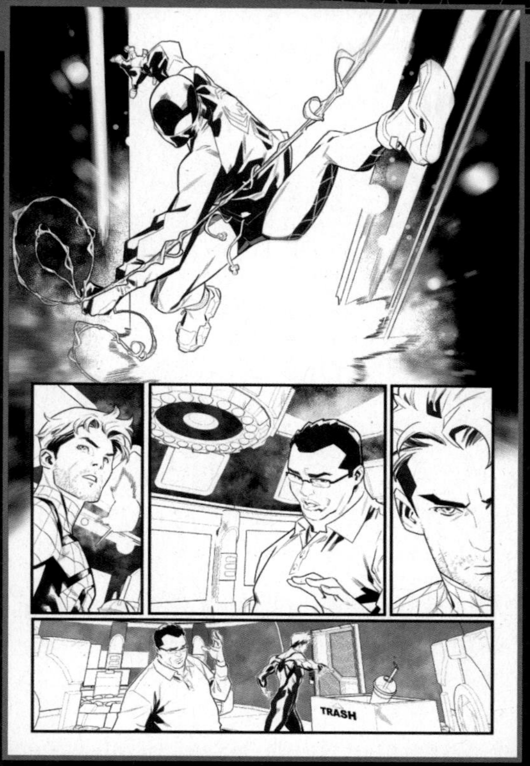
TRASH

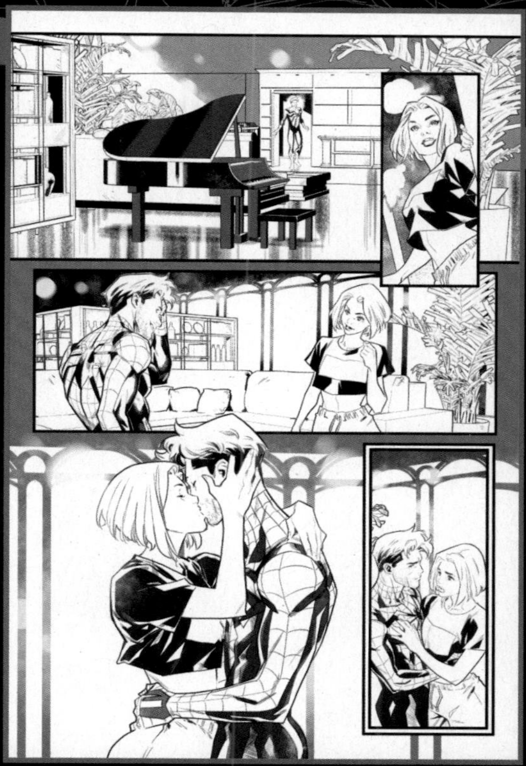

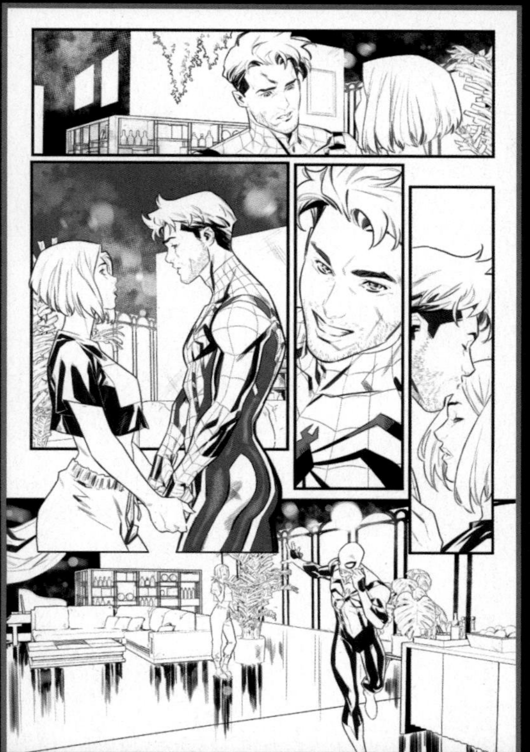

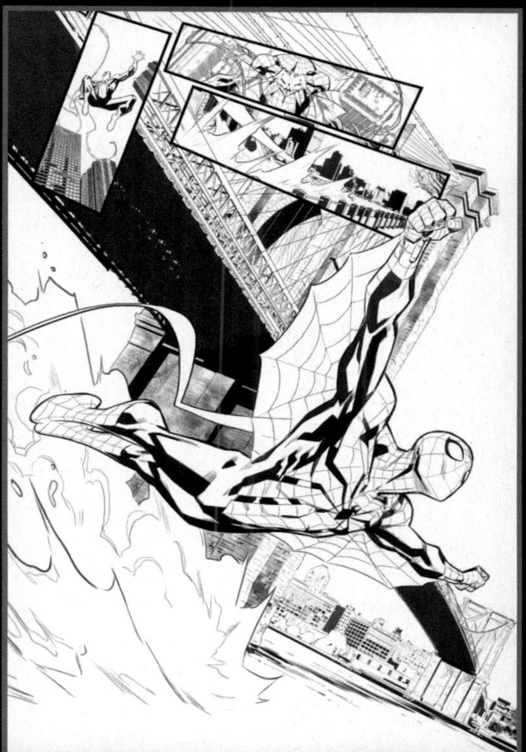

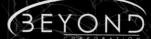

#82 PAGES 15-18 ART BY
JORGE FORNÉS

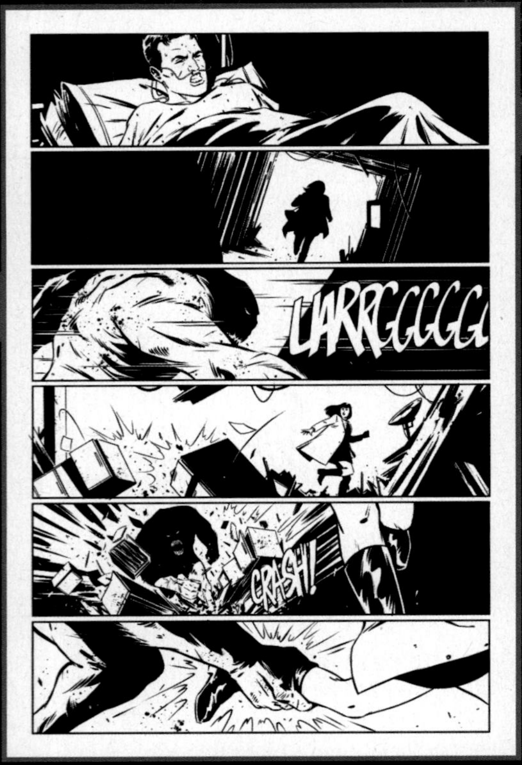
UARRGGGGG
CRASH!

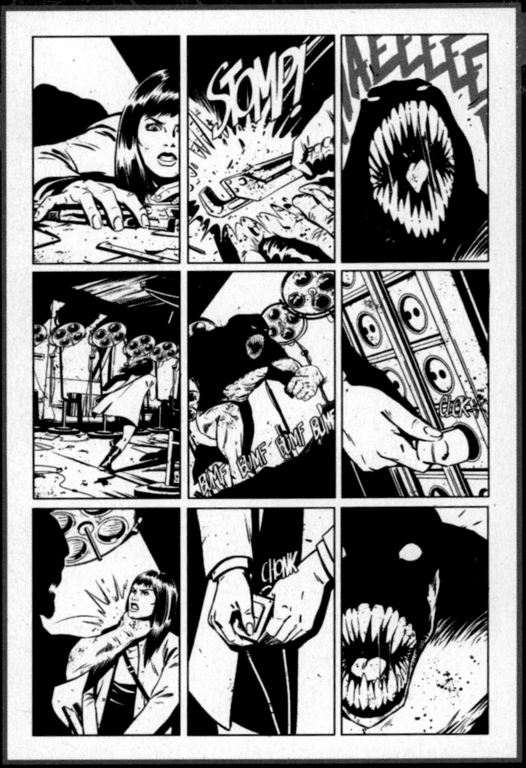
STOMP!
BUMF BUMF BUMF BUMF
CHONK

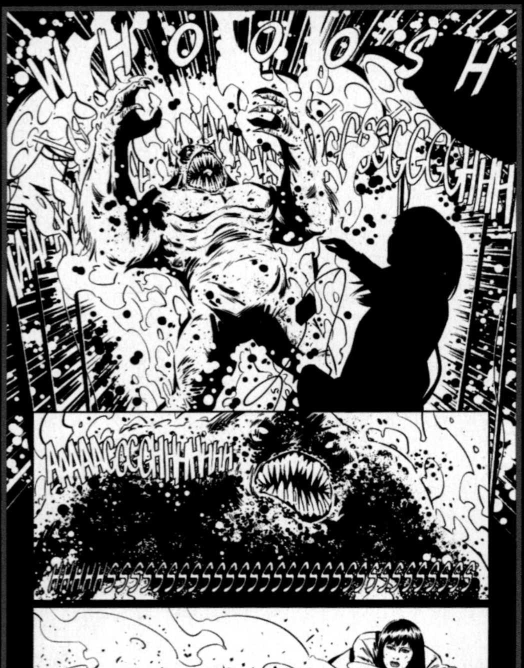
WHOOOSH
AAAAGGGHHHHHH
HHHHISSSSSSSSSSSSSSSSSSSSSSSSSSSSSS

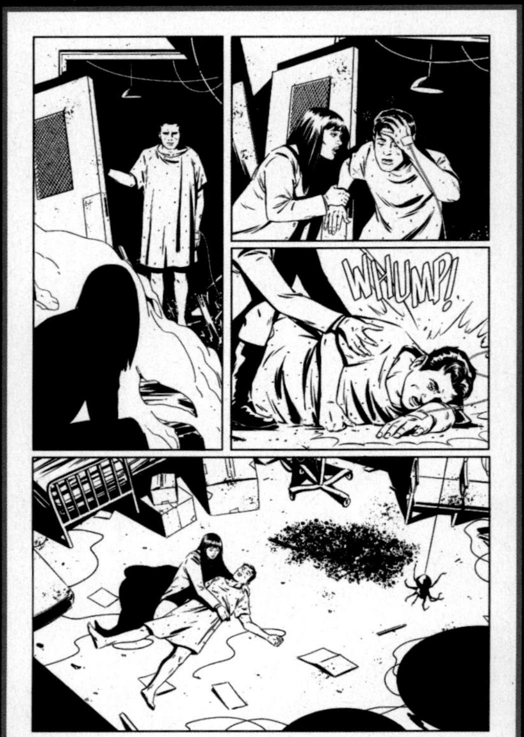
WHUMP!

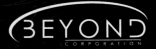